D0082985

Organizing
ASIAN AMERICAN
LABOR

In the series

Asian American History and Culture,
edited by Sucheng Chan

Organizing
ASIAN AMERICAN
LABOR

The Pacific Coast
Canned-Salmon Industry,
1870–1942

Chris Friday

 TEMPLE UNIVERSITY PRESS
Philadelphia

Temple University Press, Philadelphia 19122
Copyright © 1994 by Temple University. All rights reserved
Published 1994
Printed in the United States of America

The paper used in this publication meets the minimum requirements of American
National Standard for Information Sciences—Permanence of Paper for Printed
Library Materials,
ANSI Z39.48-1984 ⊗

Library of Congress Cataloging-in-Publication Data
Friday, Chris, 1959–
    Organizing Asian American labor : the Pacific Coast canned-salmon
industry, 1870–1942 / Chris Friday.
        p.   cm.—(Asian American history and culture series)
    Includes bibliographical references and index.
    ISBN 1-56639-139-3 (alk. paper)
    1. Trade-unions—Cannery workers—Pacific Coast (U.S.)   2. Salmon
canning industry—Pacific Coast (U.S.)—Employees.   3. Asian
Americans—Employment—Pacific Coast (U.S.)   I. Title.   II. Series.
HD6515.C27F75   1994
331.6'25079—dc20   93-29471

The poem quoted on p. 193 is from *Songs of Gold Mountain: Cantonese Rhymes from
San Francisco Chinatown*, by Marlon K. Hom. Copyright © 1987 The Regents of the
University of California. Reprinted by kind permission of the publisher, University of
California Press, Berkeley.

CONTENTS

ACKNOWLEDGMENTS

A PROJECT of this scope would have been impossible without the assistance of many others. I owe a great deal to the corps of people who interviewed the subjects of this book. Among the most important interviews are those done by the Demonstration Project for Asian Americans in Seattle, Washington, some of which are included in the Washington State Oral/Aural History Project. Many local librarians, museum directors, and park officials allowed me free rein in collections they oversaw. They, along with archivists and librarians at universities, government agencies, and historical societies, proved invaluable in helping me locate the rich records that made this study possible. Yuji Ichioka, Him Mark Lai, and Steven G. Doi also generously shared important documents from their private collections and offered critical advice and insights.

My colleagues Ellen Slatkin, Susan Neel, Brian Hayashi, Margi Lee, James Riding-In, Cynthia Orozco, Robin Kelley, Neil Greenwood, Doug Lowell, Sherry Katz, and Barbara Berstein have contributed many hours of conversation and much needed instruction over the years. Fred Notehlfer and Alexander Saxton also offered consistent encouragement and support throughout this project. Paul Ong asked tough questions at various stages and was most helpful. Valerie Matsumoto played an inestimable part as a critic and role model. Tom Gariepy, Andre Goddu, and John Cashman offered assistance, commentary, and friendship at an important time near the completion of this study. Above all others, Norris Hundley deserves much credit for his quiet guidance and sharp pencil. Without him, this work might well have foundered on its own verbiage. To that end, Sucheng Chan and Janet Francendese also figure large. Their quick and thoughtful responses to my writings and queries as this study emerged as a book were most helpful. I am indebted to my family, to whom I apologize for my obsessive and morose behavior during this project. I fear that the many hours in archives and libraries by myself has done little to enhance my personality.

A special commendation goes to Stephen Dow Beckham. This study originated with a naive question posed to him in my undergraduate studies. "How," I asked, "can I combine my personal interests in Pacific Northwest history and my Chinese-language studies?" He pointed me toward the mouth of the Columbia River and to the manuscript records of the federal population census. From that nudge came a senior thesis, which when completed I mistakenly believed represented all that might be known about the Chinese in the Columbia River canneries before 1900. I was wrong.

Finally, my greatest debt is to the men and women who labored in the canneries. Their stories provided me with an opportunity to puzzle over the meaning of history. If I have failed to capture the richness of their lives or to portray their actions appropriately, the responsibility is mine, not theirs or those who have influenced my thinking since I began this study.

Organizing
ASIAN AMERICAN
LABOR

Introduction

THIS BOOK seeks to demonstrate that the working lives of Asian immigrants and their children in the canned-salmon industry are at the center of the history of the Pacific Northwest and the American West.[1] Along with a growing number of historical studies that reassess entrenched ideas about nonwhite ethnic peoples as peripheral to this nation's history, it challenges the notions of nineteenth- and twentieth-century immigration as solely a trans-Atlantic phenomenon and of the era's industrial developments as confined to the belt stretching from Boston and New York to Chicago. *Organizing Asian American Labor* focuses on the roles that people of Chinese, Japanese, and Filipino ancestry played in shaping the canned-salmon industry and extracting a resource that was almost as significant to the West's development as timber, minerals, or agriculture. The story of these Asian and Asian American workers shows how labor, resources, and capital are allocated within a world system for the ultimate benefit of those with the greatest political and economic power—a fact that defines the "Western" experience for many.[2] Yet this history also reveals that immigrants were by no means cogs in the wheel of some larger machinery that ground human lives into insignificant dust.

While European Americans and Native Americans in the canneries, on the boats, and on the traps were important elements in the industry's history and deserve careful study, I have focused on Asian immigrants and Asian Americans because their long-standing participation in the industry best illustrates how people consistently negotiated to empower themselves and make their lives more tolerable within large and rather harsh structural constraints. Those limitations included a national U.S. culture that was largely hostile to them; labor in a seasonal, extractive industry; and the relatively weak position of the immigrants' ancestral homelands in the global political economy.

Between the 1870s and World War II, Asian immigrants and Asian Americans formed the predominant body of workers in the salmon canneries that ran along the narrow coastal zone between the Cascades and the Pacific Ocean from Alaska to central California.[3] Although

1

established in 1864, the industry employed no Asians until 1870 when a single Columbia River plant hired thirteen Chinese. After that date, Asian immigrants entered the labor market with incredible rapidity; by 1880, they numbered nearly three thousand in several dozen canneries on the river.[4] For the rest of the nineteenth century and well into the twentieth, salmon-cannery jobs remained a significant source of Asian employment.[5]

Although the number of laborers the industry required was no match for the huge contingent of laborers in California's commercial agriculture, which in 1880 had 28,546 farm workers,[6] or the Hawaiian sugar industry, which in 1882 employed 10,243 plantation workers,[7] the number of Chinese in the Columbia River salmon canneries rivaled the number in San Francisco's various industries. In 1880 some 2,148 Chinese worked as laundry operatives, 2,724 as cigar makers, and 2,443 as servants in the city;[8] approximately the same number in each of these occupations worked in the salmon canneries. The economic opportunities for Chinese in San Francisco were more varied, however, and the city's jobs formed the economic backbone of the Chinese immigrant community not only in San Francisco but along the entire Pacific Coast. Still, the large number of Chinese working so distant from the major American Chinatown reveals just how important an employer the canning industry was.[9]

The canned-salmon industry also played a central role in the economic development of the far western states and territories. Canned salmon produced in Alaska between 1880 and 1937 had a greater value than the total value of minerals mined in the territory in the same period.[10] In Oregon and Washington before World War II, canned salmon ranked third behind timber and wheat in value.[11]

By 1900, the industry's demand for labor far surpassed the availability of Chinese immigrants; their numbers had declined because of exclusionary legislation that prevented their immigration and return migration from China.[12] Although Chinese employment in the canneries continued, many Japanese and Filipinos, along with Mexicans and Mexican Americans, Native Americans, and European Americans, including women and children, also entered the labor market over the first four decades of the twentieth century. Asian immigrants and Asian Americans, though, continued to make up the bulk of the workers. In 1909 the Columbia River, Puget Sound, and Alaska canneries employed 7,167 Chinese and Japanese out of a total of 12,934 shoreworkers.[13] (Asian American cannery workers had available to them a very narrow range of tasks in the industry, limited mostly to "line" jobs inside the plant. The only data available are for shoreworkers, which includes transporters. They do not accurately reflect the level of Asian immigrant and Asian American involvement in the canning process.) The number of Chinese and Japanese was equal to more than half of the 12,994 Chinese and Japanese who labored on California's farms the following year.[14] Through the 1920s and into the early 1930s, the Asian presence in the canned-salmon industry remained at roughly the same level, although their activities came to be focused increasingly on work in Alaska. In 1920 Chinese, Japanese, and Filipinos in Alaska canneries constituted 5,348 of the 15,376 shoreworkers; in 1930 they made up 6,172 of 22,324 shoreworkers.[15] In 1936, on the eve of the recognition of local unions established by the Congress of Industrial Organizations, 652 Chinese, 1,179 Japanese, and 3,730 Filipino workers out of 15,023 shoreworkers toiled in Alaska canneries.[16] On the Columbia, however, fewer than forty Asians—mostly Chinese and a few Japanese—found employment.[17]

From the late 1870s to the mid-1930s, an elite group of Asian labor contractors recruited and managed the Asian and Asian American cannery crews. The system provided minimal benefits for workers, though contractors and canners gained much more. In the early 1930s, some Filipino laborers in the Northwest began to push for unionization in the Alaska canneries in order to place labor recruitment and management in the hands of workers, rather than contractors. In a parallel development, Asian Americans and other waterfront workers in San Francisco formed their own local. By 1937, the two regional locals had joined forces, pushed aside contractors, and begun to represent the broad coalition of Asian and Asian American workers' interests in negotiations with the companies.[18] After that initial success, shifts in company headquarters, the start of the Pacific war, and the consequent internment of Japanese and Japanese Americans limited union activity largely to Filipino workers. With the loss of many Chinese and all Japanese workers, the multiethnic and racial alliance encouraged by the union crumbled.[19]

Shifts in the ethnic makeup of cannery labor and the causes and consequences of these changes provide the themes for this study. Chapters 1 through 4 discuss how Chinese, between 1870 and 1900, entered the cannery labor market and participated in the building of the labor contracting system; how they responded to the seasonal canning process by establishing a set of formal and informal rules of behavior; and how they coped with life at the plants through the creation of various workers' communities. During that era, the canned-salmon industry provided a site where the capitalist transformation of the American West interacted with international labor migrations. The process also illustrates how workers, particularly Asian immigrants and Asian Americans, learned to better their lives despite the many constraints on their efforts.

Many authors have discussed this early period of the industry and have mentioned cannery laborers in their studies, but few have examined them in depth.[20] Among the latter, Robert A. Nash, in his pioneering article "The 'China Gangs' in the Alaska Packers Association Canneries, 1892–1935," reveals the exploitative nature of labor contracting.[21] His focus on the contractors brings to the fore much valuable information, but he did not examine how Asian and Asian American workers negotiated with the seemingly omnipotent contractors for better working and living conditions or the relationships that developed among owners, contractors, and workers in regions outside Alaska.

Jack Masson and Donald Guimary, in "Asian Labor Contractors in the Alaskan Canned Salmon Industry, 1880–1937" and "Pilipinos and the Unionization of the Alaskan Canned Salmon Industry," expand on Nash's study.[22] They suggest that until the late 1920s, ethnic antagonisms deeply divided workers, allowing contractors and owners to exploit them ruthlessly. Their studies provide a thorough analysis of Filipino activities in the industry, but, like Nash, they replicate the argument regarding contracting set forth by the economist Lloyd Fisher in *The Harvest Labor Market*. Fisher notes that in California agriculture the Chinese initiated labor contracting and that it was "one of the few organizing influences in a disorganized market. It . . . provided an element of stability and regularity in a chaotic market."[23] Fisher points out that Chinese contracting was "a primitive form of organization compared with that achieved by the Japanese," and later by the Filipinos, who had cultural tendencies toward a " 'club' organization."[24] Fisher's analysis rests on work done by the Federal Writers Project during 1938,[25] which took observations from the 1930s and read Chinese activities of the twentieth century back into the nineteenth, as do Masson and Guimary. Moreover, those studies neglect to analyze ties—kinship, emigrant district associations, and friendship—that linked workers and contractors.[26] We need to examine in detail the evolution of labor contracting among the Chinese from its beginnings and to trace changes in its form as Japanese and Filipinos moved into the labor market. The canned-salmon industry provides a case study for such an investigation.

Chapters 5 and 6 analyze how Chinese workers dealt with restrictive immigration legislation and the canners' push to harvest salmon that led to the implementation of new canning technology and increased ethnic divisions in the labor market; how a few Japanese began subcontracting and then emerged as contractors; how Issei[27] men and women and their Nisei[28] children created spheres of influence within the industry; and how Filipinos attempted, but largely failed, to follow the path laid down by the Chinese and Japanese. Chapter 6 ends with Filipino immigrants searching for alternatives to the contracting system.

The role and aspirations of Filipino workers in the twentieth century, especially in Hawaii's sugar plantations, has been studied.[29] The labor history of other Asian immigrant and Asian American groups has received little attention. The relations among Chinese, Japanese, and Filipinos have received even less treatment.[30] This book provides a balanced assessment of each group's role as well as how the groups interacted.

Masson's and Guimary's study of Filipinos and unionization is the only available work on the topic. It ends with the important "big event" of union recognition in 1937 and portrays the contract system as grinding to a sudden halt with unionization.[31] What happened after the achievement of union recognition and how certain features of the contract system continued in new forms within the new union Masson and Guimary leave unexplored. To fill this gap, Chapters 7 and 8 delineate the creation, triumph, maintenance, short-lived expansion, and final destruction of a broad union program led by many Asian immigrants and Asian Americans. These chapters reveal how the contract work culture evolved into a union work culture, and how class, ethnic, and political affiliations affected workers' actions. They also demonstrate how government intervention influenced the course of events.

Industrialization, or the capitalist transformation of the American West,[32] and international labor migrations[33] provide the contexts for this book. Before World War II, the conjunction of money from local, regional, and national investors, labor from outside the United States, and the area's natural resources made the region a player, albeit a peripheral one, in the global economy.[34] European Americans saw in the West opportunities to extract natural resources.[35] Concentrations of wealth and power, dependency on outside political support, recruitment of workers, and racial and ethnic antagonisms attended the removal of that wealth. Such an approach to exploiting the economy and ecology was made possible by an oligarchic control of finances and the exercise of political power. The canned-salmon industry epitomized the extractive process so common to the American West—the provision, through the transformation of nature's bounty into commercial products, of wealth for a relative few and toil for the comparatively many.[36]

Resource rich though it was, the American West before World War II lacked sufficient indigenous labor to carry out that extraction. Owners of the region's enterprises had to rely on voluntary and coerced migration from labor-rich areas within and outside the continent to fill their crews.[37] International political developments, the commercialization of agriculture, and the expansion of capitalism thus tied the region into a global economic system that pushed and pulled people around the world. Immigrants and seasonal migrant workers nevertheless did not simply become mere commodities of an international trade in labor. As Ewa Morawska has explained in "The Sociology and Historiography of Immigration," "immigrants and their families creatively coped with the structural limitations by maneuvering within them and playing against constraints in an effort to bring their environment into closer conformity with their purposes." In short, they were "playing within structures."[38] As I show in this book, Asian immigrants and Asian Americans participated in the creation of work cultures—sets of formal and informal rules of behavior and action that softened the harsh conditions they faced.[39] While they tacitly accepted the boundaries set by economic, political, and social forces beyond their control, in their immediate surroundings they sought to function as actors, not mere subjects. To study the West as a place and a process, as "an evolving human ecology," in Donald Worster's words, one must consider the ethnic histories of the residents, migrants, and immigrants involved in the extraction of the region's great natural wealth.[40]

In many ways, salmon fishing was akin to buffalo hunting.[41] Both were semirenewable resources. The millions of animals in the herds, separated and slaughtered, foreshadowed the near-decimation of Pacific salmon by industrial fisheries and the collateral damage done to waterways and spawning grounds.[42]

Salmon canning was a quintessentially western industry. Its employment of wage laborers, segmented by ethnic differences, marked it as a child of the West. As Patricia Nelson Limerick has reminded readers, the region's cultural diversity "could make the turn-of-the-century Northeastern urban confrontation between European immigrants and American nativists look like a family reunion. Similarly, in the diversity of languages, religions, and cultures, it far surpassed the South."[43] The West thus "put a strain on the simpler varieties of racism" prevalent in the larger United States.[44] Its upper echelons of European American owners, managers, fishermen, and machinists, often embroiled in antagonistic relations, and its well-divided crews of Asian and Asian

American, Mexican and Mexican American, and African American male workers, as well as Native American and European American women workers, indeed manifested the diversity of the West.

The use of sources also sets this book apart from existing treatments of the topic. Local newspapers and popular magazine accounts, published government reports, manuscript population census records, as well as some valuable, if limited, business records illustrate nineteenth-century Chinese activities in the industry. Twentieth-century materials are much richer, for they include substantial records of canning companies, government agencies, and union locals. Asian American newspapers, life histories compiled by contemporary social scientists,[45] oral history collections,[46] and my own interviews with cannery workers and union officials complete the roster.

Despite the rather sweeping geographic, chronological, and ethnic scope of this book, it still only scratches the surface of nineteenth- and twentieth-century social relations in the canneries. I have chosen to limit the study, for the most part, to Asians and Asian Americans. I have focused on them because of their long involvement and central position in the industry. More than that, their activities demonstrate that Asian workers were not mere coolies or slaves but active participants in the shaping of their work environment.[47]

1

The Spawning Grounds

ANKLE DEEP in the fish gurry, his hands, arms, and front smeared red by the blood and viscera of salmon, twenty-year-old Ah Shing stood on the canning "line," perhaps before a waist-high filling table stuffing salmon into one- and two-pound tins for ten, twelve, sixteen, and more hours at a stretch. In 1870 such a sight was unusual; Ah Shing and fourteen of his countrymen were the first Chinese to work in a salmon cannery. George Hume had hired a dozen Chinese for positions in the canning line, plus two as tinsmiths and one as a cook, to supplant a supposedly contentious "riff-raff and criminal element" of non-Chinese workers. According to an early canneryman, these first Chinese "soon learned the work and liked it, and they were dependable."[1]

Hume's move provided an important precedent in the industry, for shortly thereafter, Chinese made up the vast majority of salmon-cannery workers along the Pacific Coast. It also allowed Hume and other owners to avoid heavy investments in mechanization because they had at their disposal a flexible supply of labor. Labor, together with natural resources, capital (i.e., goods used to produce more goods), and entrepreneurship, are, according to economists, the fundamental factors of production.[2] During the 1860s, vast salmon runs provided the resource. Money pooled by family members and their friends purchased the minimal capital used to produce the goods, and those same people took the risks typical of entrepreneurs.[3] Canning on the Pacific Coast during the 1860s was on such a small scale that the labor, resource, and capital proved sufficient for the few tins of salmon then produced. By the end of the 1860s and into the early 1870s, however, cannery owners' efforts to expand production were blocked at various times by the availability of the resource and the lack of sufficient labor.

Early canners solved the problem of finding enough quality salmon by moving their operations, in 1866, from the Sacramento River to the Columbia River.[4] Finding labor was more difficult. In fits and starts the canners experimented with ethnically diverse workers from nearby towns and cities, ultimately tapping Chinese labor. Overseas markets and international migrants, both essential to the continued growth of the industry, tied the industry and the region into the burgeoning global economy and aided in the capitalist transformation of the American West.[5]

The choice of Chinese cannery labor was neither easy nor inescapable. Cannery owners and industry observers alike oversimplified explanations of the Chinese "displacement" of "white" workers and their numerical domination in processing by 1880 as the preference for an indispensable and cheap labor force. Such notions of Asian immigrants as docile and dependable persisted for nearly a century,[6] and indeed, the presence of Asian immigrant labor in the American West is generally discussed in those terms.[7] Before the Chinese entered the canneries, owners maintained tight control of every aspect of the industry. By expanding their enterprises, canners recruited workers outside their original circle of families and friends and eventually delegated their authority in the canneries to others. In a widening gap between owners and workers, Chinese found employment and worked well enough to satisfy their employers. In time they created a semiautonomous sphere of action. In small ways, Ah Shing and the others in that first Chinese crew helped set precedents that persisted for the next seven decades.

A "Haphazard Business"

From the construction of the earliest salmon cannery on the Sacramento River in 1864 through its transplantion to the Columbia River in 1866, one family-run partnership constituted the entire "industry." Its owners had little reason or desire to hire Chinese. The original partners believed the most desirable route to success lay in their direct participation and supervision of the work process and their employment of those who shared similar values. The Hume brothers, William, John, George, and Robert (joined later by Joseph), together with Andrew Hapgood, formed the partnership that launched the first two canneries.[8]

No absentee owners, the partners participated directly in all aspects of the work, adding their skills to the task and shaping the direction and mission of the firm. Andrew Hapgood, more than a Hume family friend, had previously worked as a tinsmith and even canned lobsters in Maine. He set up and supervised the canning operations. William Hume, the eldest brother, managed operations at the cannery when he was not out fishing. George kept the books and worked in the cannery. John and Robert fished, and Robert served double duty as cook in the cannery for a time. Joseph joined his brothers and Hapgood after the Civil War and served as general factotum. The Humes and Hapgood had duties that pulled them into direct contact with the other workers. The Humes and Hapgood constituted nearly 40 percent of the thirteen or fourteen workers in the Sacramento River cannery and heavily influenced employer–worker relations in the small-shop setting.[9]

Additional workers hired for the enterprise tended to be like their employers. The new men, often tinsmiths, received relatively high wages and performed the critical function of manufacturing the airtight cans on which the whole operation depended. The partners looked on the tinsmiths as fellow workers, rather than mere employees, as men of a common ilk. The new boys, employed to wipe cans clean, were little different from the younger Hume brothers, who earned less than the skilled workers but probably saw their jobs as an apprenticeship in the fledgling industry. Workers and owners had common stakes in the success of the enterprise. The Humes and Hapgood plants served as the training ground for many future cannery managers.[10]

Built on an old scow, the first plant used small-shop production methods; its size and its finances further reinforced close relations. The Humes and Hapgood used rather crude machinery and methods in canning the salmon so that workers, not machines, dominated the workplace. Since the partners had little capital, their shoestring operations required them to become directly involved in the work and strengthened owner–worker unity.[11]

The results of the first year did not encourage the partners to seek any sizable additions to their labor force. Their minimal capital, untried canning methods, and limited facility and crew allowed them to produce only two thousand cases of canned salmon. Other problems plagued the enterprise. Salmon decomposed in the hot California summer weather faster than the Maine-raised partners had anticipated, and when they at times packed spoiled fish, they rendered their product useless. The tins posed additional problems. Andrew Hapgood and his crew of experienced tinsmiths proved unable to make containers that consistently remained airtight throughout the cooking process; one of the partners claimed that faulty seams in tins caused "at least fifty percent" of the pack to spoil. The remainder was not well received in local markets, where consumers were skeptical about the quality of canned meats, especially fish, and fresh meat was available in abundance.[12]

The partners at first took an active role in marketing their product. Unable to find an immediate buyer, William Hume and Andrew Hapgood for a time unsuccessfully attempted to peddle their goods from door to door in Sacramento. Luckily for them, a San Francisco merchant agreed to buy and market their canned salmon in Australia, New Zealand, and Latin America. Major markets did not emerge until 1871 when merchants in Great Britain began to sell canned salmon to industrial workers as a cheap source of protein; even then, canners had to wait for nearly two more decades for the development of substantial domestic markets for canned salmon. Still, the promise of at least a limited market encouraged the partners to continue.[13]

Their second year was a disappointment. When the scow on which the Humes and Hapgood had built the first cannery sank, they were able to salvage the machinery and stores, but the loss of the vessel foreshadowed their immediate fate on the Sacramento. Silt from hydraulic mining, pollution from increased human population, and several years of drought gave Sacramento River salmon a "peculiar flavor" that not only hurt sales but also adversely affected future salmon runs in the area. In its second year, the cannery produced only two thousand cases of questionable-quality salmon.[14]

Frustrated by this "haphazard business," Robert Hume estimated that "a few hundred dollars would have purchased all their interests in the business." In an attempt to salvage their investment the partners scouted for a new location and in 1866 settled on the Columbia River with its huge salmon runs, which during the 1860s reached record highs—in part a result of the decimation of local Native American groups. Ravaged by diseases in the first half of the century, the Native American population of the Pacific Northwest had significantly decreased, particularly along the lower Columbia River, and consequently, they harvested less salmon. European American activities had not yet caused substantial disruptions in the number of Columbia River salmon or in the quality of the spawning beds.[15]

At the outset of the Columbia River operations the partners sought to re-create the work culture of their Sacramento River cannery, including a common owner–worker identification and their direct involvement in the canning process. They transplanted men and machines from the original cannery and continued their established methods. Just as he had on the Sacramento River, Andrew Hapgood did all the cooking in order to keep the process secret and prevent competition. He shut himself in a small, windowless room with a large cast-iron kettle for boiling the packed salmon cans. He passed the cans in and out through a slot in the wall to prevent casual observers from discovering the "secret process," which amounted to little more than the cooking time and the amount of salt added to the brine solution in which the partners boiled the salmon. The higher boiling point of the brine solution cooked the salmon more thoroughly and softened the bones in less time than pure water yet remained at a low enough temperature so as not to melt the solder that held the cans together. When production increased, Hapgood hired only one assistant. Refusing to pass on any information, he allowed his assistant to help only with heavy lifting. The other partners, just as secretive, posted a *No Admittance* sign to keep observers from "stealing" their methods. Their secrecy served to limit production and the size of the crew and kept the proprietors directly involved in the canning process.[16]

Robert Hume exemplified the partners' close involvement, which extended well into the 1870s. Even after he had broken from the original partnership to establish his own cannery at Cathlamet, Washington, Robert continued to work on the canning line. His workday was long and arduous. The salmon typically ran in large schools for several weeks, and the catches of many tons that were landed at the cannery would spoil within little more than twenty-four hours. Since Robert attempted to serve double duty as proprietor and line worker, his day began at four in the morning and continued to ten or eleven in the evening. After the day's work, bookkeeping kept him busy until midnight. He recalled:

> I became so exhausted during the season, from want of sleep, that while working at the bench, soldering the bottoms on the cans, having a crew in front of me making the other part of the cans, and another crew behind me packing fish into them, kept me on the jump to keep up; and in order to keep awake [I] would go and put my head in a tank of cold water, which was running down from a stream in the mountains; while my head would be wet I would keep awake, and when it dried from the heat of the stove [which heated the soldering irons] in front of me, [I] would fall asleep, and the soldering iron would fall out of my hand; sometimes by hurrying [I] could get a little start on the men; my wife would come to the cannery and I would lie on the lounge in the office while she would watch and let me sleep for five minutes; sometimes she would pity me so much that she would steal a few minutes for me, then I would rush back and push forward [on] my work.[17]

Robert Hume had taken his experiences under the earlier Hume and Hapgood partnership as a guide for a very intimate style of cannery management. Even in 1870, after substantial growth in their enterprises, the Humes listed themselves as "foremen in fishery" or "can makers" in the census, not as cannery owners or proprietors.[18]

Their mark on the industry persisted; the processing techniques they developed set the basic industry pattern for decades. The partners, for the most part, eschewed major shifts in their way of canning. Instead of developing new methods to increase production, they simply expanded on the tried and tested. Their outright rejection of new methods symbolized their reluctance to change—a reluctance that at once made it possible but improbable for them to hire Chinese. In 1869, Robert Hume claimed to have developed a can-making machine, yet his elder brothers' resistance prevented its use. They condemned his "experimentalist" style and scrapped the machine. Instead of investing in what they viewed as more risky fixed capital, they chose to expand production. This, they hoped, might yield a steadier and more reliable flow of cash. Their decision not to employ new technology remained consistent with the partners' style of management. Once a practice became established in the Hume canneries, only the most extreme conditions prompted changes. Into the 1890s, as one author has noted, the Humes's "conservatism was reflected in their annual boast that they still packed salmon in the old-fashioned way."[19]

As the split between Robert and the elder Humes revealed, personal conflicts among the partners, not between employers and workers, seem to have been the major problem. During their second year on the Columbia River, for example, a rivalry between Robert Hume and Andrew Hapgood split crew and owners alike. Hume had, by his own account, surpassed Hapgood's skill in can making. Among the crew members, two sided with Hapgood and "began to impose" on Robert. When the hostility of the crew and Hapgood's jealousy "became too unbearable" for Robert, he withdrew from the partnership. In the year after the split, Robert offered jobs at his new cannery to workers who had sided with him in his battles with Hapgood. When Robert, for lack of funds, came back to work in the original cannery, Hapgood and his crew continued to make life difficult for the ambitious young man. In that small-shop setting, workers' identification with owners limited or diverted class conflict; early cannery workers lined up behind, rather than against, the various owners.[20]

Yet the partners ran their plants in a forceful, even antagonistic, style. At any sign of insubordination, they acted abruptly and decisively. Well known for his "summary action with malcontents," William Hume prided himself on being a "man of deeds, not words." When a fishing crew complained about the food, William simply paid off the cook for the season and told the crew members they could cook for themselves. He even wore a pistol to intimidate the men. Still, the early owners and crews maintained some common identification. When Columbia River fishermen went on strike, William Hume armed his cannery crew and continued operations. Hume and his crew identified more closely with one another than did the crew with the fishermen.[21]

Expansion, Competition, and Internal
Labor-Market Segmentation

Despite their efforts to stave off change, the partners faced problems stemming from expanding operations, severe limitations in the local labor supply, and competition from new canneries that required shifts in cannery management and staffing. In their first year on the Columbia, the partners canned four thousand cases of salmon, twice that of any Sacramento River effort—the result of large salmon runs and ironing out the basic canning techniques. By 1868, production had leaped to eighteen thousand cases and in 1869 to twenty-eight thousand cases.[22] Some of the growth can be attributed to several years of trial and error in processing the salmon or to larger Columbia River runs of salmon, but a portion also came through the addition of a second plant and more employees per cannery.[23]

Encouraged by the Hume and Hapgood success, two other entrepreneurs tried to establish canneries. The increase in the number of canning enterprises, though the two new plants employed only forty-two people, intensified local demand for labor at a time when, according to one early canneryman's recollection, "the packers had a hard time to get and keep help." In 1869, F. M. Warren built a cannery a few miles down the Columbia River at Cathlamet, Washington Territory, and John West put up a cannery across the river at Westport, Oregon. Of the two, Warren's plant put more strain on the labor supply near the Hume and Hapgood plants. By 1870, Warren employed fourteen men at his cannery and four fishermen—a small but significant proportion of the workers in the area. The eighteen men represented nearly 14 percent of Wahkiakum County's men of working age, over 19 percent of the cannery workers, and 22 percent of the county's laborers and fishermen.[24] John West's cannery across the Columbia River in 1870 employed twenty-four men, women, and children. While the cannery workers at Westport constituted nearly 30 percent of the town's residents (the town existed because of West's business), the cannery created no labor problems for the owners at Cathlamet or Eagle Cliff.[25] Poor and irregular transportation put the few potential cannery workers on the Oregon side of the river at too great a distance to work as commuters for the Humes and Hapgood, or for Warren.[26]

Warren and the Humes and Hapgood had located in Wahkiakum County, where the labor supply was so limited that canners could not staff their plants fully except by recruiting outsiders. The Hume and Hapgood canneries stood three miles from any neighboring farm. Cathlamet, not much more than a trading post at the time and the nearest center of population to their operations, was approximately twenty miles away and held few potential workers. Astoria and Portland, nearly equidistant, were the only options in their search for laborers.[27]

Astoria, the smaller of the two, but substantially larger than Cathlamet, boasted only a single wharf, a "wheezy old mill," and fewer than seven hundred residents. In 1874 one visitor commented that it was "in a chronic state of dilapidation" and in "the rudest Western clearing you ever saw. . . . [I]f you step off the [wooden] pavement," he continued, "you will go deep in mud."[28] Another caustically noted: "It didn't take a prophet to forecast that the languid place would never be a commercial hub."[29] In the 1860s and early 1870s, the only enterprises of note in the town were its customs house and the large hotel near the Pacific Ocean that catered to wealthy Portlanders escaping the summer heat.[30]

Portland, with 2,571 residents, was the largest local population center, but few roads or trails connected it with the canneries. The "regular" steamer traveled between Portland and Astoria only once every three weeks. But the partners looked to Portland, not Astoria, for additional labor. In 1868 and 1869 they ran advertisements in the *Portland Oregonian* for "men and boys" to work in the cannery. Their search for labor in Portland must have attracted applicants of a very different ethnic background than that of the New England-born partners, for despite its image as "a somewhat westernized recreation of a New England commercial city," Portland had a substantial foreign-born population. In 1870, nearly half its population was immigrant or of immigrant stock. Irish and Germans, the two largest groups of foreign-born in Portland, formed 31 percent and 24 percent of the city's foreign-born, respectively, or a total of 56 percent.[31]

A similar ethnic mix existed near the cannery. In 1870 the foreign-born constituted 37 percent of Wahkiakum County's residents. In addition, 24.3 percent of residents born in the United States had one or more parent of foreign birth. The percentage of foreign-born working males was even higher. In 1870, among those twelve years and up, the foreign-born made up 51.4 percent. Irish and Germans together formed the largest group of working age, with a total of 13.1 percent of the county's population.[32]

The Hume and Hapgood canneries reflected the regional ethnic mix. Of the seventy-two people identifiable as cannery workers, the census lists forty-one of foreign birth and an additional six with at least one foreign-born parent. The fifteen Chinese at George Hume's cannery made up the largest foreign-born group at 36.6 percent. Ger-

mans and Scandinavians ranked next at 12.2 percent each, followed by
Irish at 9.8 percent, and finally the Scots and English with a combined
total of 7.3 percent. The remaining 14.6 percent were of northern and
central European or Canadian birth.[33]

In hiring such an ethnically diverse crew, George Hume had clearly
moved beyond his earlier workers. The Humes and Hapgood considered themselves of solid New England "settler" stock and proudly ac-
claimed their Scottish heritage, which further bolstered tendencies
toward regionalism and ethnocentrism. Since the Scots and Irish had
a long history of antagonism, and the Robert Hume–Hapgood dispute
involved Austro-Hungarians who lined up with Hapgood against
Hume, it is not surprising that the cannery owners later spoke of the
Columbia River workers as undesirable criminals and riffraff.[34]

Tensions between workers and owners illustrate the beginnings of
a two-tiered internal labor market[35] in the canned-salmon industry. In
the upper tier, the earlier entrants held close relations with the company owners, received good wages, and had an opportunity for mobility within the industry. Newer hires were increasingly distinct in their
ethnicity from the owners and upper echelon of workers. Also they
received lower wages and had less opportunity for occupational mobility than those hired before them. Economists, sociologists, and historians debate the nature of immigrant incorporation into the economy of
the host country.

Two reigning paradigms mark the boundaries of the discussion.
Proponents of the orthodox interpretation hold that new immigrants
enter into the economy at the bottom because they lack the human
capital—on-the-job training, education, language facility—necessary
for positions beyond the most menial tasks. Once they acquire enough
human capital, they are able to attain better jobs and upward social
mobility. Later entrants to a country, particularly in an expanding
economy, automatically enter on the lowest rung but eventually can
move up in social rank.[36]

Critics of the orthodox position in the past decade have begun to
rally behind the segmented-labor-market theory (sometimes also referred to as the dual-economy theory) as a better device to explain the
economic position of immigrants and later generations in the economy.[37] Supporters of the theory argue that human capital alone does
not explain mobility and that ethnicity, at least in the United States,
has had a great influence on where immigrants enter the economy. The
economy, according to the theory, is composed of two sectors: primary
and secondary. The former is characterized by large, near-monopolistic
(oligopolistic) firms that offer to employees stable and secure jobs,

good wages and good working conditions, and mobility opportunities in an internal job ladder. Costs associated with the provisions for labor are passed on to consumers because the firms have near-absolute control of the industry. The secondary sector of the economy, by contrast, is made up of smaller firms in a highly competitive economy, often with dramatic seasonal production. Employers seek all possible means to lower their production costs, and the result is poor wages, high labor turnover, and extremely limited opportunity for any upward movement within the industry.[38]

While the segmented-labor-market theory explains developments since the 1930s fairly well, most of the literature contains little discussion of the causes of labor-market divisions in the nineteenth and early twentieth centuries. Ewa Morawska has suggested that turn-of-the-century firms exhibited characteristics of both the primary and secondary labor markets. She proposes that in certain companies "an ethnically split secondary internal labor market" emerged in which national origins and ethnicity were more significant factors in determining workers' potential mobility than was human capital.[39]

This was true in the canned-salmon industry. The division of the internal labor market into two segments was not, as some sociologists argue, a way for owners to divide workers against each other.[40] Instead, the hiring of Chinese eased some tensions that had existed between the crews and managers and benefited owners and the upper tier without at first radically remaking labor relations.

Had the Humes and Hapgood hoped to exploit ethnic diversity in their labor force to split their crews and keep labor costs low, they could have easily hired Chinese long before 1870. In California the Humes and Hapgood had been aware of Chinese immigrants, for they set up their Sacramento River cannery directly opposite the Sacramento Chinatown. In 1860, four years before cannery operations began, Sacramento's Chinese numbered 988, and 1,737 lived in surrounding Sacramento and nearby Yolo counties. Sacramento's Chinatown served as an economic hub for the Chinese in the area, and by 1870 its population had grown to 1,371.[41] It became known as *Yifo*, second city, ranking behind only San Francisco in importance to Chinese immigrants. The partners had contact with Chinese fishermen on the Sacramento River, Robert Hume even supplementing his income by selling to Chinese fishermen the fyke nets he knitted.[42] Yet even with a sizable and highly visible Chinese population in the region, the partners felt no compulsion to hire them to can fish and were loathe to move outside their original circle of family and friends. The same relative scarcity of quality salmon that prompted the move to the Columbia River also obviated any great labor demand.[43]

George Hume finally hired Chinese for his Columbia River cannery because the local labor scarcity forced him to seek them out. Uncertain of Chinese workers' merits, he hired only twelve for his crew, two as tinsmiths, and one as a cook. The twelve represented slightly more than 10 percent of the total employees in Hume's firm, a relatively safe proportion of his workforce if Chinese should somehow prove inadequate for cannery employment. Cheap labor was not his prime concern, nor was some desire to drive an ethnic wedge between his workers to impede any impulse to organize.[44]

Percentages aside, Hume may not have been able to find more than twelve Chinese to work for him. Until the late 1860s, Chinese had no particular reason to migrate to the Columbia River area. A few passed through the region in the late 1850s and early 1860s on the way to the mines, first in southern Oregon and then in Idaho and British Columbia. The few who remained in the area worked in the fledgling iron, paper, and woolen industries near Oregon City on the falls of the Willamette River outside Portland. In 1867, the Oregon Iron Company at Oregon City employed eighteen Chinese workers, but the fire that destroyed the works in 1868 put a temporary hold on Chinese employment.[45] Oregon's iron mines remained rather small; even so, in 1874 some 150 Chinese found work in the Oswego Iron Company mines.[46] Near Oregon City in 1867, a small paper mill employed Chinese, but no record of their numbers is available.[47] The Oregon City woolen mills in 1868 had room for twelve Chinese.[48] Oregon City's canal works also provided a few Chinese with jobs, while some other opportunities, mostly clearing land, were available in Oregon for Chinese agriculturalists. These opportunities drew only a small number of Chinese immigrants to the region. Only 461 Chinese lived in Portland in 1870, the largest concentration in an urban setting near the canneries.[49]

Outside Portland, railroad construction significantly added to the region's Chinese population. As early as 1868, Wa Kee and Company in Portland entered into a contract with the Oregon Central Railroad to provide a crew of approximately a thousand Chinese. Between 1868 and 1872, these Chinese worked on the four railroad lines under construction in the extensive Columbia River drainage.[50]

Railroad work—together with most other Pacific Northwest agricultural and manual jobs available to Chinese in 1870—was available only on a seasonal basis. The heaviest periods of employment occurred between March and September, thus increasing local demand for labor exactly when the canneries needed workers. From 1873 to the early 1880s, however, railroad building in the region was erratic and by the late 1880s had dropped off sharply. By then, salmon canneries had come to provide seasonal but regular employment to Chinese. By 1870, the railroads had drawn enough of them to the Pacific Northwest to make it possible for George Hume to consider their employment.[51]

The presence of Chinese did not guarantee their availability for cannery work. Indeed, Hume offered relatively low wages in comparison to the high pay the Chinese had come to expect as a result of the demand for their services. In 1868, for example, Chinese employed by the Oregon Central Railroad received $36 a month.[52] Hume employees averaged $46—a figure that includes the wages of the European American fishermen, skilled workers, and even the partners.[53] Pay rates, though not broken down by skill or race in the extant records, varied in the canneries. For example, fishermen earned about $5 a day, and Robert Hume in 1871 made $8 a day as a can maker for Andrew Hapgood. Wages such as these surely boosted the average in the Hume canneries and suggest that Hume paid the other employees much less than the going rate for railroad workers (and 60 percent less than West and Warren paid their workers).[54] High demand and high prices for Chinese labor, together with Hume's comparatively low cannery wages, may also have been no small factor in limiting the size of Hume's Chinese crew.

No less important a determinant in the number of Chinese was Hume's reliance on Sam Mott, his Chinese cannery cook, as recruiter. The cook, who had earned Hume's trust, spoke Chinese and probably had contacts within the small Chinese community in Portland that allowed him to recruit workers not under obligation to Chinese contractors or tongs (who also acted as labor suppliers). Since cannery employment was new and relatively inconsequential, none of the large labor recruiters moved to control access to those jobs, leaving them to individuals like Sam Mott. That opening, in conjunction with the short time he had to recruit and the marginal wages that Hume authorized him to offer, must account, in part, for the small size of the crew.[55]

Also limiting the crew size was the work itself. Even into the early 1870s, salmon canneries remained new and uncertain operations. Relatively few people, let alone any Chinese, had worked in them. Not until the mid-1870s did the plants on the Columbia become an "institution," an industry, which promised at least a modicum of security and stability. Instead, jobs as domestics and servants, cooks, laundry workers, railroad men, miners, and agriculturalists in the Pacific

Northwest and California promised more certainty for Chinese than cannery work.[56]

Once hired, Chinese in George Hume's workforce seem to have acted little different from earlier workers. When Robert Hume returned to the crew after his falling out with Hapgood, he worked with a Chinese crew member repairing leaky cans. Robert was unable to keep up the pace of work; Hapgood, his followers, and his Chinese coworker ridiculed him for his poor performance. The first Chinese, so few in number and working alongside the cannery owners, fit into the preexisting small-shop relations.[57]

When the early canners tried to increase their productive output and new investors built increasingly large plants on the lower Columbia River, they drew on precedents set by the Humes and Hapgood, including the employment of Chinese. The rush of cannery construction in the 1870s coincided well with the slackening of railroad construction and made possible the hiring of many Chinese for the cannery crews in the ensuing years. By mid-decade, Chinese crews had become the industry norm. Encouraged by their availability and performance, owners concentrated on increasing the size of their crews, not mechanization, to increase output. As a consequence, the newer canneries immediately bypassed small-shop production and had large crews that pushed owners away from the direct and intimate contact with the daily process of canning and management characteristic of the early Hume and Hapgood operations.[58]

The financing of new canneries by absentee owners, ranging from San Francisco investors to midwestern meatpacking companies, not only helped tie the industry into a market network that stretched beyond the region but also added significantly to the distance between owners and crews. George Hume's reliance on Sam Mott to recruit his Chinese crew hinted at the first major modification in the hierarchy of authority at the canneries. Hume's interjection of Sam Mott as the "boss," or foreman, of the Chinese crew lessened his involvement with the workers. As newer owners hired managers to supervise their plants, Chinese middlemen took on even greater roles in the day-to-day supervision of canning. The splitting of the workforce along racial lines actually lessened owner–worker tensions by creating a semiautonomous sphere for Chinese labor. As detailed in the chapters that follow, Chinese foremen utilized ethnic bonds to encourage high levels of production. When those failed, they did not hesitate to bully and threaten their crews through a "drive" system. In other industrial settings foremen sometimes became identified as part of management,[59] but in the salmon canneries, owners did not include Chinese middlemen and foremen as part of management.

In spite of the potential for exploitation by Chinese in positions of power, the mutual identification of Chinese at the canneries helped them create and maintain a distinct work culture. A separation of spheres did not automatically create hostility between Chinese and non-Chinese workers. The lack of substantial evidence forces speculation, but since Chinese labored in the bottom tier of cannery tasks— nonfishing and nonmanagerial, with the exception of foremen—they displaced few non-Chinese workers. Non-Chinese cannery workers, rather than lose their jobs, earned promotions to higher positions. Instances of such elevations occurred in other businesses as well, such as the Central Pacific Railroad.[60] The relatively few complaints registered and the only halfhearted participation in anti-Chinese campaigns by European American cannery employees indicate their acceptance of Chinese labor. They realized that their livelihoods as fishermen, skilled mechanics, and managers depended on canneries staffed by Chinese crews.[61]

Although in the 1870s "an ethnically split secondary internal labor market"[62] emerged in the canned-salmon industry, ethnicity was not a divisive wedge until owners delegated authority to others, making ethnicity more significant in determining one's position. When investors from outside the region established new plants, they bypassed the evolutionary process that the founders had followed in obtaining their workforce and went wholesale for the use of ethnically distinct Chinese crews for their inside work.

Organizing the Bottom Tier

Chinese were by no means an indistinguishable mass. Even among the first Chinese crew, evidence of a hierarchy is visible. Sam Mott's role as a labor recruiter put workers under an obligation to him for their jobs and foreshadowed the rise to power of Chinese labor contractors. In China, as well as the United States and other end points of the Chinese diaspora, individual Chinese commonly acted as labor recruiters for their non-Chinese employers. In the United States before the establishment of the canneries, Chinese recruitment for railroad work had almost always been arranged through contractors.[63] Sam Mott took advantage of the situation and acted as might any aspiring immigrant. The arrangements seemed to satisfy all parties.

Neither company nor census records reveal the specific tasks at which the first Chinese crew worked, but age, personal wealth, and

date of immigration influenced relationships among workers and contributed to hierarchies outside Hume's control. Age, generally considered an important element in Chinese interpersonal and familial relations, marked off some of the crew. Deference to elders permeated
nearly every level of nineteenth-century Chinese society, even in the
United States.[64] Among the first crew, Ah John was the eldest at forty
and fourteen years older than any other Chinese worker at the cannery,
including twenty-six-year-old Ah Ching. With relative certainty, one
can assume that the Chinese cannery crew, which on average was 22.5
years of age, deferred to Ah John. Of the others, six, or slightly more
than half, were between the ages of twenty and twenty-six. In addition
to his age, Ah John was the only possible member of the crew old
enough to have been part of the first wave of Chinese immigration
inspired by the discovery of gold in California. His many years in the
United States must have made him a valuable resource on immigrant
survival tactics and deserving of respect from the newer immigrants in
the group.[65] The others probably came in the late 1860s, prompted by
railroad construction, western mining booms, the ratification of the
Burlingame Treaty in 1868 (which allowed citizens of the United
States and China to emigrate from one country to the other), and socioeconomic turmoil in south China.[66] There is little doubt that the
relative youngsters of the group—Ah Wook at fifteen, Ah Lou and
Gee Fook at seventeen, and Ah Sing at eighteen—were far too young
to have been in the United States for more than a few years.[67] As early
as 1868, Chinese began to sail directly from Hong Kong to Portland,
and the younger members may have been among these newcomers.[68]

Those able to accumulate a cash reserve in the face of the difficulties of immigrant life received much admiration, too. Substantial personal property also very likely indicated an ability to send money home
to villages or to amass savings for eventual investment in the United
States or China. In this, Chinese differed little from other immigrants.
Ah John and Ah Ching reported to a census enumerator the largest
holdings of any in the crew. Twenty-six-year-old Ah Ching had $300
in personal effects with him at the cannery, while Ah John had $275
worth, more than double the crew average of $138 each. Recruiter and
cook Sam Mott had only $180 in money and personal possessions.
Comparatively, the value of Chinese miners' personal estates in southern California was about the same as that held by Ah John and Ah
Ching. Chinese miners in the productive northern California region
amassed several times more personal wealth than the most well-off cannery worker.[69] The relative poverty of the 1870 crew reflected the marginal position of the Pacific Northwest in global labor migration. The

Pacific Northwest thus may have attracted only immigrants with the least to risk. California, an important point for international migration since the gold rush, attracted more immigrants and allowed them to amass greater personal estates than in the Northwest.

The age of crew members also indicated the lowly place the work had in the minds of Chinese immigrants. In 1870, Chinese in Wasco, Multnomah, and Clatsop counties, Oregon, averaged about 26 years of age, somewhat lower than the average of 28.44 years in a survey of a third of San Francisco's Chinese population.[70] That sample reveals the mean age of the city's Chinese merchants was 32.24 years. Chinese entrepreneurs were of similar ages. Fish peddlers had a mean age of 37.67 years, while vegetable dealers came in at 34.05 years, barbers at 30.58, and tailors at 29.36. Those merchants and entrepreneurs—generally assumed to be at the peak of overseas Chinese society—were significantly older than cigar makers, shoemakers, cooks, and servants, who had respective mean ages of 22.41, 22.38, 22.98, and 16.13 years. San Francisco's Chinese cigar makers, shoeworkers, and cooks in 1870 were virtually the same average age as the Chinese in the Columbia River cannery. Cannery work, like San Francisco's industrial jobs, provided Chinese with minimal chances of upward mobility because white owners, managers, and workers reserved the better jobs. Aspiring Chinese immigrants who tried to move into some combination of mercantile activities, farming, labor contracting, or the vice industry needed capital, something that low-paid industrial workers seldom obtained quickly. The youngest Chinese immigrants at first filled the ranks of these rather undesirable industrial jobs, but when possible moved on to better fields of endeavor, though even those were severely limited by larger economic and social constraints.[71]

Among Chinese in the Pacific Northwest in 1870, cannery workers tended to be younger than those in other occupations and areas. During 1870, Chinese in the eastern Oregon mining regions averaged thirty-three years of age; those in the Portland and Oregon City areas averaged twenty-seven years old.[72] Miners and entrepreneurs, not workers in small industries, made up the bulk of eastern Oregon's Chinese population. Their high average age indicates that Chinese may have viewed mining as preferable to jobs in the small industries of the Portland area and that cannery work ranked lowest of all.

By 1870, canners and their workers had established three central and lasting features that would characterize the industry over the next seven decades: internal labor markets largely distinguished by ethnicity; a lower tier within that labor market in which cannery workers provided

structure and organization, in which they established their own informal hierarchy; and financial, marketing, and labor recruitment practices that tied the industry into a larger global system. The original
canners made a huge mark on the industry. Their risk taking in starting
the venture, in moving to the Columbia River, and in hiring Chinese
inspired others to follow them. Yet, without markets, the businesses
would have failed. Without additional labor, they would not have expanded. Cannery owners' ever-widening recruitment for labor outside
their original circle of families and friends eventually, but not inevita-
bly, led them to the Chinese. The key difference was that, unlike Ah
Shing and that first crew, the Chinese who followed them increasingly
found cannery work an important regular source of income and took
even greater pains to shape relations at the canneries in the decades
that followed.

2

"Satisfaction in Every Case": Cannery Work and the Contract System

IN THE LAST quarter of the nineteenth century, the canned-salmon industry gained increasing attention as an important regional enterprise. Local papers regularly reported the size of the fish runs, the establishment of new plants, and the use of new machinery. Area boosters also treated visiting journalists from across the nation and around the world to tours of the canneries to extol the virtues of the industry and the resource-rich Pacific Northwest. Yet despite the extensive press coverage, Chinese workers appear only in passing as colorful figures in the backdrop of those stories. "At nearly every cannery on the Columbia River," noted one writer for the *Weekly Astorian* in 1874, "the chief reliable form of help seems to be based upon the Chinese, and the fellows appear to ply their several vocations skillfully, with limited instruction."[1] Similarly, in 1899 a visiting reporter from Ohio told his readers that "all work is done by Chinese. It is said that it is possible to conduct a cannery successfully only by the use of Chinese labor."[2] If observers paid any more than passing attention to Chinese, they did so in terms more dramatic than factual. In 1888, the peripatetic Rudyard Kipling noted of his visit to a Columbia River cannery: "Only Chinamen were employed in the work, and they looked like blood-besmeared yellow devils, as they crossed the rifts of sunlight that lay upon the floor. . . . Chinamen with yellow, crooked fingers, jammed the stuff into the cans."[3] Kipling gave Chinese credit for their ability to handle the fish quickly, but his primary focus was on the plant and its setting.

> I was impressed, not so much with the speed of manufacture, as the character of the factory. Inside, on a floor ninety by forty, the most civilised and murderous of machinery. Outside, three footsteps, the thick-growing pines and the immense solitude of the hills. Our steamer only stayed twenty minutes at that place, but I counted two hundred and forty finished cans, . . . ere I left the slippery, blood-stained, scale spangled, oily floors, and the offal-smeared Chinamen.[4]

Most contemporary authors cast Chinese as little more than one-dimensional, alien shadows.

25

An examination of the cannery work culture[5]—that body of formal and informal rules that guided the behavior of laborers, managers, and owners—dispels that shadowy image, for it places Chinese as participants in shaping labor relations in the industry as immigrants able to overcome, to some degree, larger constraints caused by a myriad of discriminatory practices levied against them as well as numerous individual "human capital"[6] barriers such as language facility. The work culture they built provided organization in an industry that by its seasonal nature and poor pay tended toward disorganization.[7]

Chinese Labor in a Seasonal Industry

Even though George Hume set a precedent in hiring Chinese crews, investors in canning enterprises had to wait until 1873 before there was enough Chinese labor in the Pacific Northwest to support their efforts. Most Chinese drawn to the area in the late 1860s and early 1870s had come largely for railroad work, leaving few for the canneries. The outbreak of anti-Chinese violence in California, which drove many Chinese into other states or to urban centers, changed that. Also important to the increase of Chinese cannery labor were the Panic of 1873, Jay Cooke's financial failure in railroad building, and, in the immediate area of the canneries, the completion of the Tacoma–Kalama spur of the Northern Pacific Railroad. With the end of construction on the Tacoma–Kalama, for example, only a few of the approximately seven hundred Chinese workers continued on as section hands. Casting about for work, they often ended up in Portland, the recruiting center for the canneries. After 1873, the canneries grew in direct proportion to the availability of Chinese.[8]

The predominance of Chinese in the nineteenth-century canneries proved to be the most telling characteristic of the industry. Only four years after George Hume hired that experimental crew, cannery owners employed "almost entirely" Chinese. By 1874, only one of thirteen Columbia River canneries had an entirely non-Chinese crew.[9] For reasons that cannot be discerned, William Hume employed no Chinese workers "on principle" until 1885, when he hired them only as strikebreakers. Nevertheless, from the original thirteen, the number of Chinese workers by 1881 soared to more than four thousand in thirty-five Columbia River canneries.[10]

Cannery work did not provide year-round employment. Salmon runs began in the spring, grew large in the summer, and tailed off quickly in the fall. The availability of the raw material for this extractive industry determined the level of operations. Cannery owners tried to find uses for their plants in the off-season; between 1874 and 1877, they attempted to can beef, mutton, vegetables, and fruit, but high transportation costs incurred in shipping the raw materials to the canneries, combined with unsuccessful marketing attempts, yielded few profits. During 1888, several canners again tried packing fruit, with the same results. One canner unsuccessfully tried to convert his cannery into a sawmill in the off-season, and another advertised his "facilities for storage" of unspecified goods "at very cheap rates." Packers eventually let their plants sit idle, with the result that Chinese cannery employment largely was limited to salmon canning. Seasonal labor requirements engendered a sense of impermanence among owners and workers that encouraged the use of migratory labor. Canners felt that Chinese labor fit their needs well.[11]

Processing the Salmon

Bound to income from the limited salmon-canning season, canners concentrated on methods of processing the fish and recruiting and managing the Chinese crews calculated to earn as much as possible on their investments. In the nineteenth century, most technology employed in the canneries simply "enhanced" hand labor because the employment of large numbers of Chinese workers remained more attractive than the relatively high costs of inventing and coping with new machinery. Technological innovations were important, but none in the nineteenth century radically changed the industry. The approach to processing developed on the Columbia River by the Humes and Hapgood, along with other early canners, served as the model for the rest of the industry.[12]

On the Columbia, as in other regions at later dates, preparations for the season might begin as early as December and January but more often began in late February and early March. An "early" crew of about twenty Chinese tinsmiths—nearly half of a full crew—cut and soldered can lids and bodies. Even after ready-made cans became available in the 1890s, canners continued to manufacture some cans themselves in order to keep a small crew "in hand and ready for the process of packing" in case of an early run of salmon. Alaska operators generally used prefabricated cans when those became available. Because ships could not reach the plants in the foul winter weather, Alaska canneries had much less preparation time, and prefabricated, machine-made cans freed up workers. Even so, the use of ready-made cans was not extensive until the development of a seamless "sanitary can" in the 1910s that eliminated soldering and encouraged canners to abandon hand-made cans and Chinese tinsmiths.[13]

During the canning season, Chinese crews on the Columbia River averaged from 70 to 100 men, with some reaching 350 or more. Full crews arrived in late March, several weeks before fishing began. They passed the time readying the cannery and arranging their living quarters. Canning began slowly as salmon ran in small quantities. In late June, July, and early August the runs peaked, then rapidly dropped off in late August and September. Most canneries operated only into the late summer months, but some remained active through the fall salmon runs and employed smaller crews later in the season. The very few Chinese who remained for another month or two after fishing stopped labeled and cased the last of the canned salmon for shipment.[14]

While the Hume and Hapgood enterprise on the Sacramento and Columbia rivers had ironed out the basic techniques involved in the canning of salmon with European American workers, beginning in the 1870s Chinese handled the fish at every step. The process began with unloading the fish from a scow onto the dock with a "pew," a two- or three-pronged pitchforklike tool. Either in the scow or on the dock, one or two workers generally sorted the salmon by size, quality, and type. Still others filled two-wheeled carts and took the salmon to the butchering tables.[15]

At the butchering tables, two-man gangs handled the salmon. One worker lifted the fish to the table, and the other removed the fins, tail, head, and entrails. He tossed waste down a chute, or a hole in the cannery floor, to the river below and threw the dressed salmon into a large tub of salt water. Another Chinese worker washed and then scraped the fish with a knife. This latter step, known as "sliming," removed the mucous covering, some of the scales, and any blood or offal from the salmon. A second saltwater bath and another scraping and washing followed. A final once-over with a whisklike brush removed any other foreign matter.[16]

Using a gang-knife with multiple blades, a Chinese worker then cut the salmon into sections the same length as the height of the cans. By 1874, gang-knives had replaced earlier techniques of measuring the salmon with a notched stick, scoring the fish at each notch, then slicing through the fish at each scored spot with a large knife. Typical of technological changes in the nineteenth century, gang-knives did not displace workers but increased their productivity by making the work easier. Even with the gang-knives, salmon still had to be handled extensively. From the gang-knives, workers carried the sections to fillers, who cut them into three pieces: one large enough nearly to fill the can and two small ones to bring the can up to the proper weight. They packed each can, trimmed off any excess meat, and passed it to the "patchers," who weighed it and, if necessary, topped it off with small fragments of salmon. Another worker then spread salt over a two-piece jig that added exactly one-quarter ounce of salt to each can and made the work flow much faster than the Humes' earlier method of adding salt to each can by hand.[17]

Next, Chinese tinsmiths partially soldered the lids in place and sent the cans to be boiled in large cast-iron vats to exhaust any air. Afterward, they drew solder around the edge of the can with a pointed soldering copper (or iron) heated from a small charcoal stove and applied a second soldering copper the shape of the can top to ensure an airtight seal. Two men with a block and tackle then lowered nets or trays of cans into a bath of hot water. They watched for telltale bubbles released from improperly sealed cans, pulled them from the vats, and resoldered and retested those cans.[18]

A different set of workers then dumped the cans into large vats for an initial cooking of about an hour, then pulled the cans out and passed them to venters, who punctured the cans with a small awl or nail and mallet to release internal pressure. A Chinese tinsmith quickly resealed those cans with a drop of solder. Workers stacked the cans on a small cart and wheeled them into a large pressure cooker known as a *retort*. Salmon cooked in the retort for another hour and a half at 240°F, which thoroughly cooked the contents and softened the bones. Canners did not move to a single cooking method until the late 1890s, in an attempt to increase the speed of the canning line and adjust for a labor scarcity.[19]

The second cooking completed, "retortmen" unloaded the trays and put them into a lye bath to clean any grease and dirt from the cans. They wiped the cans with rags and then laid them on the cannery floor to cool overnight. Swollen from the internal pressure, the cans contracted slowly, and the night watchmen "enjoyed hearing [the cans] a'poppin' all night long" because the noise signaled an airtight seal.[20]

Canners worried tremendously about properly sealed cans and wanted skilled workers to test the cooled cans once more for leaks. The tester gently tapped each can with a small hammer, or a tenpenny nail, listening for the appropriate sound to signify an airtight can. Faulty cans, about 10 percent of the total, had to be redone, but during big rushes canners simply set them aside to spoil.[21]

To prepare the cans for shipment, Chinese applied a protective coating of paint (later lacquer) and often wrapped cans in tissue paper to prevent rust and corrosion. They then applied the appropriate labels, for canners usually had several labels, either directly on the can or on the tissue paper. In the final steps, workers nailed wooden cases together, filled them with labeled cans, and stacked them in the warehouse to await shipment.[22]

A hierarchy of cannery tasks emerged out of the interplay between the owners' perceptions of the tasks and those of workers. Cannery owners supervised most closely and paid best those workers most important to the quality of the final product. Can makers, fish butchers, and can testers received the best pay and highest status. Chinese can makers were essentially skilled tinsmiths, well versed in the shaping and soldering of tin for the cans. The success or failure of each cannery depended on its being able to produce properly soldered can bodies and lids. Improperly made cans or lids not completely sealed had to be reprocessed. If workers did not catch defects in the testing procedure, or if they improperly resoldered a can, the salmon spoiled, and the cannery stood to lose its product, profits, and good name.[23]

Tinsmiths received relatively high wages for their work. Data on wages in the canneries is sparse, but in at least one instance Chinese can makers earned only about 5 percent less than the few skilled European American tinsmiths in the same cannery.[24] Solderers and can makers earned nearly double the wages paid to "common labor" in the canneries. The early-season arrival of can-making crews at the canneries also assured them of a longer working season, which gave them larger incomes than the others who followed.[25]

Although they worked fewer months out of the year than can makers, Chinese salmon butchers held one of the more privileged positions in the canneries. Efficient and skilled butchers were essential to a cannery's success. One highly talented Columbia River butcher could behead, defin, and eviscerate between seventeen hundred and two thousand fish a day—fifteen to eighteen tons. In early spring, larger canneries took in five to ten tons of fish daily, but the big runs later in the year might bring as many as a hundred tons a day for a week or more. Canners relied on butchers to get through the waist-high stacks of fish on the plant floor before unprocessed fish spoiled. One worker remembered that it was "not so much like men struggling with innumerable fish, as like human maggots wiggling and squirming among the swarms of salmon."[26] The speed of the entire line depended on the ability and stamina of the four or five butchers to carry out their task. Speed was not the only requirement, however, because canners demanded that the butchers not cut too far down from the salmon's head, or collar, lest meat be wasted. With the rising prices paid to European American fishermen by the canners throughout the nineteenth century, the efficiency of the cut became as important as the speed.[27] Most of the time, the butcher lived up to management's expectation.

Chinese regarded butchering as hard work, and not all aspired to become butchers. The butchers' tasks began earlier in the day than those of the rest of the crew because they had to butcher a quantity of fish before packing began and lasted until they had sharpened their knives at the end of the day. The work itself was exhausting. The crew handled pieces of salmon reduced to the same size by the gang-knives, but butchers worked with salmon of varying sizes and had to adjust their rhythms in order to keep the rest of the canning line on an even pace. Smaller spring salmon forced butchers to handle more fish per case than the fifty-, sixty-, or even eighty-pound "spring hogs," huge Chinook salmon that ran in June and July. During the summer months, the number of fish dressed per hour declined, but cutting through the heavy vertebrae of the big Chinook in one blow of the knife created "exhausting strains on the wrist." Fatigued joints commonly "failed" butchers. In later years, as the Chinese Exclusion Act reduced the number of Chinese workers available and contractors attempted to staff the crews with as few people as possible, butchers had to work without assistants.[28] Lifting heavy spring hogs that might be five feet long added to the burdens of the job. One former Chinese butcher remembered: "A dirty trick was to shove the [bigger] fish to the other guy, you know. . . . You pick you the little one and kick the big one to him and then you get cussed out [if caught]!"[29]

Butchers ranked high in status within the crew, and their pay, from 25 to 50 percent higher than for other tasks, reflected the importance of butchering to the canner and the difficulties of the job. They had more opportunities for extra income than most cannery workers. Butchers could pilfer prime pieces of salmon during the day for their own use or for sharing or selling among the crew. From salmon heads collected during the day, some cut out the salmon "cheeks" after work and sold them fresh to local non-Chinese for 25 cents a bucket—about 10 to 15 percent of a day's pay. Butchers might also salt salmon cheeks or roe to give to family and friends or to sell in nearby Chinatowns after the season. By the late 1890s, even though canneries on the Columbia River began to process cannery waste into fertilizer and oil, all parties understood that Chinese butchers had the right to take what they wanted, sometimes even whole fish. Neither cannery managers, Chinese contractors, nor foremen dared refuse butchers this prerogative for fear of work stoppages.[30]

Butchers protected their valued positions by limiting access to on-the-job training. Like master craftsmen, butchers had the responsibility of caring for their implements; butchers shaped and filed the standard seven-inch blade down to just the right length. "You cut them down to suit yourself," one remarked, "because you can't afford to be swinging a big knife around" for hours on end. Butchers' knives also had to be sharp enough to cut through the flesh of the salmon easily but strong enough to pass through the bone and cartilage without chipping, breaking, or excessively dulling the blade. Often butchers honed their knives in secret to prevent others from learning their special skills.[31]

When they did pass on their skills, it was through an informal apprentice system in which assistants at the butchering tables dressed salmon during slack times or gave butchers a breather during large runs. Butchers colluded with contractors to control access to these apprenticeships by selecting certain members of the crew to be their assistants or by denying training to others, as skilled craftsmen had done for centuries in China.[32]

At the other end of the canning line, can testers also occupied special positions. A properly sealed can tapped with a nail made a distinctly different sound than an improperly sealed can. Striking a nail against a can might not seem a skilled task, but testing as many as forty thousand cans a day required a unique ability. Canners paid testers well for this work because they depended on the tester's skill as a final quality-control measure. Each cannery had but one or two testers; usually those who had worked for a number of years or those with the closest ties to the Chinese contractors worked at this light and high-paying job.[33]

Skilled workers formed the top tier of a crew's internal hierarchy. They gained their positions and status by honing their abilities and courting the favor of contractors, as well as through the cannery owners, who focused on certain critical stages in processing. Below the upper tier of tinsmiths, fish butchers, and can testers existed a second echelon of semiskilled workers—graders, slimers, and fillers—who received slightly better pay and had a somewhat higher status than the "common" cannery laborers.

Graders sorted the fish on the docks by type and quality. At first, canners packed only Chinook salmon, but by the late 1870s, Columbia River canners put up other kinds of salmon, which necessitated skilled graders. The progressive impact of intensive fishing and a vastly increased human presence in the Columbia River drainage affected the number of Chinook available for canning, but more important in the shift to other kinds of salmon was new competition from Canadian and Alaskan canneries. These enterprises put up lower-grade salmon and undercut prices for Columbia River Chinooks. Columbia River canners successfully carved a niche in the market for more expensive Chinook but also began packing other grades for the lower-priced markets. Consumers of salmon also grew more knowledgeable and discriminated on the basis of price and type of canned salmon. On the Columbia by 1883, Chinook salmon made up only 58 percent of the pack, and in the following years the percentage declined steadily.[34]

The move to canning other kinds of salmon and an increased attention to quality depended on the grader's ability to identify the salmon in a split second. Cannery owners kept a watchful eye on graders and placed them under great pressure to sort quickly and accurately through the tons of fish that came into the canneries. Sorters stood for hours, "eyes wide as plates," watching for minute clues that distinguished the grades of salmon. Repetitive and fast paced, the task also involved heavy work. With gaff hooks in each hand, graders flipped salmon into the appropriate bins or chutes, which required great strength and stamina. They were often among the largest and strongest of the crew. High pay and responsibility gave sorters some degree of status in the eyes of the Chinese crew and cannery owners, but most workers avoided this heavy and tiring task.[35]

Slimers also had important jobs. Their ability to remove quickly the blood next to the salmon's vertebrae with a special knife or scraper and then rapidly finish cleaning the fish affected the speed of cannery operations. Since improper sliming led to an inferior product, owners and managers insisted on fast, thorough work. Slimers handled many fish during the course of a day. They, and others in the canneries, donned light cotton gloves to make handling the slippery fish easier and to protect them to some extent from cuts and scrapes. They often wore out two or three pairs of gloves in a single day. Their job was the wettest in the cannery. In the early plants, they worked with the fish in bins of salt water. Owners later installed pipes that released a constant spray of cold, fresh water into a trough. In this environment and covered from head to toe with blood, scales, and mucous from the fish, many developed skin irritations caused by bacteria in spite of protection from gloves and oilskin aprons. Some slimers sought a way out through a rotation to some drier spot in the canneries, but most remained locked into the position. Slightly higher pay than common labor and a chance to get off work just after the butchers made sliming only a bit better than common cannery jobs.[36]

Like slimers, fillers worked at a fast pace and under pressure from the cannery owners to produce a high- and consistent-quality pack. Sales of canned salmon depended on the appearance of the fish in the

can. Filling was relatively light work but not easy. Ramming and jam-
ming fish into cans at the rate of about a thousand cans a day created
many discomforts for the workers. In addition to stiff and sore hands,
fillers easily contracted fish poisoning. Bones, can edges, and section-
ing knives frequently caused cuts and infections. As a result, fillers commonly suffered from swollen wrists and fingers, skin rashes, and fevers.
Severe cases, though rare, resulted in hospitalization and in the loss of
fingers or even a hand. From the earliest days, canners demanded that
fillers keep their hands clean to prevent foreign matter from getting
into the cans. Fillers had orders to wash their hands every half hour,
which made the work nearly as damp and uncomfortable as sliming.[37]

To some degree, consumers' notions about Chinese prompted this
drive for sanitation. Canned salmon found a national market just as
anti-Chinese sentiment gained fever pitch. A great many journalists,
travelers, and other observers had written with a sense of wonder
about the canneries and Chinese. While they were impressed with the
speed at which Chinese worked, many felt uneasy about eating a product handled by them. According to one reporter, Chinese cannery
workers were "sweet scented hogs in human form and filth . . . [who]
put salmon in the cans with their opium-scented hands and long-nailed
fingers." To counteract negative publicity, canners loudly proclaimed
the cleanliness of their workers and the sanitation measures in their
plants.[38]

In spite of such protests, cannery owners continued with Chinese
fillers. They marshaled the typical nineteenth-century arguments used
to justify the hiring of Chinese: They did work that whites refused and
remained on the job better than whites.[39] But the canners added that
Chinese were particularly well suited to the task. Like many nine-
teenth- and early twentieth-century industrialists, cannery owners believed that women performed fine, fast, and repetitive work, like
stuffing salmon into cans, better than men.[40] The slightly built southern Chinese immigrants they employed, though, were even better than
women because, as one canner explained, they had "hands as nimble as
a woman's, and . . . the power in [their] . . . fingers and wrists of a
man."[41] Nimble, strong hands can be found among both sexes and
all races, but the combination of characteristics canners attributed to
Chinese further legitimized their employment and demonstrates how
tightly racial and sexual prejudices were intertwined.

Even common labor required specific skills, usually acquired on
the job, and carried varying degrees of difficulty and danger. For example, fish pitchers, who had the hard work of unloading the scows, were
in constant danger of slipping while they stood among the salmon or

of injuring themselves with the pitchforklike pews. Owners pressured them to spear the fish in the head, not the body, so as not to damage the flesh. Pew marks appeared as an unsightly brown blemish in canned salmon. In addition, pitchers had to unload quickly to supply fish to the canning crew.[42]

Gang-knife operators, too, played an important role. To keep the fast pace demanded by owners, they had to develop a certain rhythm of work. The gang-knife operator's assistant had to get a whole fish quickly into place as the knife opened. As the blades came free from the cut sections, he had to clear the knife bed and then slide another fish in place, keeping fingers, hands, and arms away from the blades. The man cranking the gang-knife had to synchronize the cut with his assistant and apply pressure on the crank at just the right time. It also took a "muscular man" to force the knives through the fish, especially when the blades had been positioned to cut sections for the smallest cans. Depending on the size of the cans, the gang-knife had from five to twenty blades. Smaller cans required more blades than larger cans and made the knife more strenuous to operate. One worker recalled, "A man could take that gang knife and swing it down with all his might. Even then it did not always work. The knives [set for half-pound cans] were hard as hell to use because there were so many blades."[43] Gang-knives often jammed, and work stopped while the operator and his assistant pounded the blades free.[44]

At the other end of the canning line, retort workers struggled at common jobs characterized by periods of intense heat and humidity followed by cool and damp as they pushed and pulled the cars of cans in and out of the retorts and then dipped the cans into the lye wash. Cold and flulike symptoms in this stop-and-go position must have been common. Since retort work involved mostly strength and little training (non-Chinese "engineers" monitored the steam pressure), only the youngest, strongest, and least-skilled men worked the retorts. Retortmen also doubled in the "bathroom," by far the least desirable position in the cannery. There they dipped the cans into lye baths and then wiped away any remaining grease. The lye often splashed, causing skin irritations and burns as well as destroying clothing. Like the men in the bathroom, can venters also were burned and scalded as vented cans shot jets of boiling hot "salmon juice" under pressure "out ten, twenty feet." Chinese looked on retort, bathroom, and venting positions as having few redeeming attributes.[45]

Other workers performed the less hazardous but more menial jobs of carrying raw salmon or cans from one station to the next and of stacking the cans before and after cooling. Still more sent can bodies and lids quickly down chutes from lofts to canning lines below. Tedious and unrewarding jobs at best, these rounded out the lower echelons in the hierarchy of cannery tasks.

Although much like common labor in terms of the work itself, postseason labeling and casing were valued jobs for a select few. Canners had a great many labels for their products and some special labels for large customers. In spite of many long hours workers kept during the season, they did not label and case all the pack then because heavy runs required all available labor to pack the salmon. Many orders came in after the canning season ended. As noted earlier, owners kept a small crew during the off-season to label, case, and sometimes renovate rusted cans. Chinese desired these off-season jobs for the few extra months of employment, but the labeling and casing seldom involved more than a dozen people at each cannery. Often the can makers and butchers, because of their already high status and connections with the labor contractor, remained for these jobs. Canners kept a close eye on them because consumers bought salmon on the basis of the quality of the label and the condition of the can as often as on the quality of the fish inside. Badly labeled cans sold poorly. Improperly nailed cases broke open in transit, and the damaged cans proved hard to sell. Most canners refused to compromise the reputation of their product and demanded a high quality of work from these off-season employees, who in return earned additional money for their labors.[46]

During the last quarter of the nineteenth century, canners made relatively few adjustments in labor-intensive techniques. Since Chinese met with such consistent work conditions, they coined the idiom *yu sup* to describe it. *Yu*, Cantonese for "fish," and *sup*, a phonetic equivalent of "shop" (factory or plant) but meaning "wet," conveyed much more than simply "fish shop." That the Chinese used the character that generally denotes fish, rather than *gwai yu*, for salmon is not surprising. Cannery owners, managers, machinists, and fishermen all referred to salmon as "fish." Any other "scrap fish" they simply ignored. Among Chinese workers, fish and salmon were also synonymous.[47]

All in the industry referred to salmon as fish, but Chinese workers who called the plants *sup* revealed their understanding of cannery employment. *Sup* literally means "damp" or "wet" or "humid" but is used most commonly in conjunction with other Chinese characters to describe various rheumatic afflictions.[48] Its use to represent "shop" was fitting, especially when the conditions under which butchers, slimers, fillers, retortmen, and indeed all Chinese cannery workers toiled are considered. The description of the canneries as *yu sup* carried with it the full meaning and recognition of the strenuous and damp conditions in salmon canneries.

Recruiting and Managing Crews

Workers' and owners' perceptions of processing constituted one aspect of the Chinese salmon-cannery work culture, the recruitment and management of Chinese labor another. Labor contracting, sometimes referred to as the *padrone* system, was widespread and used by many European and Asian immigrant workers to find jobs and provide some structure within a labor market.[49] As in California agriculture, Chinese labor contracting helped stabilize and organize labor recruitment and management.[50] Such was also the case in the canned-salmon industry.

Although by the late 1880s access to cannery work and placement in the various jobs came to depend on Chinese contractors, recruitment and management of Chinese cannery labor went through at least three initial stages before the piece-rate system of contracting—typical of the late nineteenth and early twentieth centuries—came into being. First, a brief period of indirect recruitment through cannery employees occurred. The entrance of full-fledged Chinese contractors who paid workers by the day or month marked the second phase. In the third, a mixed piece- and day-rate system of contracting prevailed. That mixed system gave way to the fourth and final stage in which piece-rate contracting prevailed industrywide with only a few exceptions. Columbia River developments illustrate the origins of contracting in the salmon-canning industry and the stages through which it passed.[51]

Labor contracting was not original to the salmon canneries. In the Pacific Northwest railroad builders had relied on it long before canners sought out contractors for help in staffing their plants. Indeed, early salmon canners purposely avoided relatively high-priced contract labor and tried to recruit individual Chinese with the help of an employee, as Hume had relied on Sam Mott. The indirect recruitment and management of Chinese laborers remained difficult for the non-Chinese-speaking owners. They turned to the "China Boss" at the cannery to relay orders to the crew.[52] As outside investors, effectively absentee owners, poured money into larger canneries along the lower Columbia River, they opted for less direct and more reliable recruitment methods. The new owners and their managers made few attempts to recreate the kind of relations that the Humes and Hapgood had established with their first cannery workers. Convinced that they must rely on Chinese crews and aware that they had few common ties with which to control them, the owners turned to Chinese labor contractors.[53] The latter were willing to expand into the industry because of the large number of workers required and profits promised and because of temporarily high unemployment among Chinese workers after 1873 with the completion of the Tacoma–Kalama rail line.[54] Mutual interests propelled cannery owners and labor contractors toward each other.

At the cannery, the contractor or his foreman supervised the crew, which allowed owners and managers to concentrate on gaining access to raw materials and markets and to deal with non-Chinese employees. Managers continued to supervise the non-Chinese fishermen, machinists, and clerks on an individual basis, a division of responsibilities that further strengthened racial segmentation within the industry's labor market.[55]

As early as 1875, contractors provided laborers through a day-rate system for the canneries. Canners paid contractors set wages by the month for the skilled and semiskilled laborers—butchers, tinsmiths, fillers, and slimers—but for unskilled workers only $1 for each day worked. Early in the season or during poor runs, canneries might not operate every day or perhaps only a few hours a day. The unskilled among the crews worked "as wanted. . . . Only the time in which they are actually engaged being counted." Owners benefited immensely from this arrangement. They paid no wages during down times to the bulk of the crew and only partial wages during slack times. Labor costs for unskilled workers under the day-rate system thereby remained elastic.[56]

Contractors must still have made money from the arrangement, for presumably they would neither have entered nor continued without the promise of profits. In later years, most profits came from various forms of worker indebtedness created through controls on off-season working and living arrangements, fees for finding work, disciplinary fines at work, and extra charges for supplemental food, alcohol, and drugs during the season. The relationship among workers and contractors in the early years remains obscure, but contractors must have dictated much of the terms of work.[57]

Workers received the least from day-rate arrangements. While skilled and semiskilled workers devised various methods to protect their jobs, among them the informal apprentice system for butchers, unskilled laborers had little assurance of steady work, and even when they were employed, their pay remained the lowest in the canneries. They did not remain passive but took direct action to protect their employment. As early as June 1875, approximately 150 Chinese workers at the large Booth Company plant in Astoria refused to work when the contractor failed to pay their wages on time. Only after assurances by the owner that their pay was forthcoming did they return to work.[58] The following year, Chinese crews struck again at three different canneries for higher wages. In April 1876, at F. M. Warren's Cathlamet cannery, "a large number" of the Chinese workers walked off the job and sailed to Portland to look for other employment when Warren refused to meet their demands.[59] The next month, at two large Astoria canneries, Chinese also called for pay increases but were less successful than their fellow countrymen at Warren's cannery. After sitting out a day and a half, they "returned to work without accomplishing their purpose."[60] In addition to work stoppages that targeted distant owners or contractors, Chinese foremen also bore the brunt of worker violence. At one cannery in 1878, the Chinese workers "came nigh mamalusing [mauling] the celestial [*sic*] foreman," apparently for pushing the crew too hard or for failing to pay wages promptly.[61]

Ad hoc work stoppages and violence formed an important part of the work culture and allowed laborers to push for changes in the system. Workers' attempts to control the plant floor made owners aware of the necessity of keeping them at least minimally happy, for they could ill afford work stoppages at the peak of the season. Chinese crews worked "well," owners believed, "if they have a good overseer."[62] Canners told government observers that when dissatisfied, Chinese workers were "the hardest class in the world to manage."[63] Consequently, they pressured contractors to provide pay promptly to keep the workers from striking because ethnic solidarity did not prevent Chinese workers from openly resisting contractors. Tensions among cannery owners, contractors, foremen, and crews forced significant changes in labor contracting within the industry.

None of the parties remained satisfied with the day-labor system for long, and by 1878 a piece-rate system emerged. Owners favored the piece-rate over the day-rate system because their costs reflected the actual amount packed, whether high or low. They paid contractors money for each case packed, regardless of the number of workers employed or hours worked.[64] During the late 1870s and early 1880s, contractors' incomes soared because of large packs, but skilled workers received only monthly wages, and common laborers got their money in a lump sum at the end of the season. Differentiated wages solidified the stratification within crews and made it less likely for workers to strike as a group. Indeed, as long as salmon runs and packs remained at high levels, workers offered less overt resistance than they had under the day-rate system.

Canners, contractors, and workers did not convert immediately to piece rates, since both day- and piece-rate systems coexisted through the mid-1880s. By 1885, 68 percent of the Columbia River canneries still operated under the day-rate system and the remainder under the new piece-rate system. While one industry observer noted a steady trend toward piece-rate contracting that came "into favor more every year with cannery men and those who supply the laborers," during the mid-1880s Chinese contractors nonetheless remained flexible to whichever system appealed most to owners. Sit Que, labor contractor and Astoria agent for Chinese commission merchants Wing Sing and Company, in local advertisements promised "reliable cannery hands furnished—piece work or by the day. Satisfaction in every case."[65]

The piece-rate system fostered the widespread use of "drive" techniques of labor management found in other industrial settings. Cannery work had always been fast paced, and a local reporter in 1874 posited that there was "no room for drones at a Columbia River cannery."[66] But under the piece-rate system, contractors had a greater incentive to seek the most for the least. They tried to balance the size of the crew with the potential productive capacity of the cannery. With the fewest number of workers producing the greatest number of cans, the contractor made his greatest profits.

Such balancing acts encouraged contractors to use the drive system. By 1885, "responsible Chinamen . . . employ their own helpers, pay them by the piece, and then drive them as with the whip. Each subordinate supervises his squad of men and works himself like a Trojan, and is held responsible for faultless results. The work of canning," continued the Bureau of Fisheries investigator, "exceeded in rapidity anything I have ever seen, outside the brush-making establishments in the East."[67] Despite the intensity of the drive techniques of the piece-rate system, the stratification of Chinese workers on the basis of skill and method of payment lessened overt resistance, and workers began to adopt more indirect tactics, to be detailed later.

Events of the early and mid-1880s chiseled away at mixed day- and piece-rate contracting in the canneries. The Chinese Exclusion Act of 1882 and regional anti-Chinese violence in the mid-1880s resulted in a smaller potential pool of labor for the canneries.[68] At the same time, fishermen's strikes, poor fish runs, and poor market conditions lowered the pay of Chinese working under day- and piece-rate systems because they worked fewer days and packed fewer cases of salmon. By the end of the decade, a new, modified piece-rate system had all but replaced the older practices.[69]

The new system differed in two key areas: seasonal and daily pack guarantees, and provisions for hiring extra workers. The new arrangement also held benefits for all parties. It lessened the application of drive techniques and provided more secure seasonal pay for workers. Contractors eased up on workers because they, too, had assurances of minimum seasonal incomes. Finally, owners, though most had been satisfied with the earlier arrangements, found themselves better equipped to handle large runs of fish at lower costs than before. All seem to have been in rough agreement over the benefits of the changes, for arguments arose only over fine tuning, not the system itself.

Laborers and contractors both pushed hard for seasonal pack guarantees. During the poor salmon runs of the mid-1880s, "in every cannery groups of disconsolate" Chinese workers watched "with hungry eyes the few salmon tossed on the dock." When the newly formed fishermen's union struck for higher fish prices, Chinese found themselves "lounging around the streets [of Astoria] out of a job."[70] Working a few hours a day, or not at all, severely limited their incomes. At the same time, rather low market prices of canned salmon prompted cannery owners to cut back their operations and Chinese employment. Contractors also suffered losses from the slump in the industry. Contractors, no doubt encouraged by workers concerned about their earnings, demanded that cannery owners provide a guaranteed minimum seasonal pack, regardless of the size of the actual pack. In this way, contractors and workers received assurances of at least some small income. Owners, fearful of losing their Chinese crews, agreed, but tried to keep the season guarantees as low as possible, while, contractors argued for higher figures.[71]

Canners conceded to minimum seasonal guarantees but only on their own terms. First among their qualifications came the demand for a lower price per case on packs above the minimum. This provision reduced production costs and increased profits for the owners. For contractors, this arrangement reduced potential income to a degree but was a small price to pay for the security of income with a minimum seasonal guarantee. Workers suffered most because they earned only small bonuses for much extra work. In the rare instances when a company failed to meet the minimum guarantee, its managers complained that they were "paying something for nothing." In the year following a failure to meet a minimum pack, the company fought desperately to reduce seasonal guarantees to even lower levels to avoid any repetition of the problem.[72]

As a second contingency for approval of seasonal minimums, owners required of contractors a guaranteed minimum daily pack if the "fish were on hand." Canners sought high daily guarantees to assure that all salmon bought from fishermen might be packed and not left to rot on the docks. Contractors argued for low daily minimums in order to keep their crews from resisting speed ups and to keep crew sizes as small as possible in order to maximize profits.[73]

In providing crews under contracts with seasonal and daily minimum guarantees, contractors consistently promised to supply crews of "first class and skillful men" who performed their labors "in a good and workman like manner."[74] But as early as the mid-1880s, canners complained to contractors of "all the scrubs and opium smokers" in the crews. Although he operated on the Fraser River, Benjamin Young had learned canning on the Columbia River, and his dealings with Lee Coey typified owner–contractor relations of the 1880s regardless of cannery location. Young, in July 1887, angrily wrote to Lee Coey regarding the Chinese crew:

> Some twenty-five men came down here yesterday, and they are some of the most miserable, God-damnable damn Chinamen I ever saw in my life. . . . Such horrible looking opium-smokers I never did see. Suppose there should come a big run of salmon, they could not pack a hundred cases a day. . . . You can never have [my contract] again. You had better come down here and see some of the specimens you have sent down. I suppose we will be able to get along if I stay here and look after everything myself.[75]

Young's assessment was no doubt overdrawn, but his argument centered on the notion that Lee had not provided workers in sufficient number or quality to fulfill his contractual obligation. Young remedied the situation by threatening to hire additional workers himself and to charge them against Lee's account. In this instance Lee provided the necessary men, albeit at a slower rate than the obstreperous Young demanded.[76]

Almost completely buried under Young's abusive and confrontational rhetoric stood an important qualification to owner concessions regarding minimum-pack guarantees, that of "extra hires." Contractors not only tried to keep crew sizes small to maximize incomes but also had increasing problems recruiting Chinese from an ever-smaller pool of immigrants after the 1882 Exclusion Act. Crew shortages had not been a problem in the days of open immigration, but by the late 1880s canners began complaining of a dearth of qualified laborers.[77]

So acute was the shortage that contracted crews sometimes failed for weeks at a time to keep up with the pack during normal runs. Young's problem of a potential crunch in a "big run" became commonplace. In 1890 Andrew Hapgood, of the original Sacramento and then Columbia River partnership, claimed that for his Columbia River canneries he could not "get Chinamen for love or money" from his contractor.[78] After nearly a month of badgering Wing Sing and Company of Portland to provide more men, Hapgood wrote to a non-Chinese contact in Portland:

> We want you to see if you can get us four young [non-Chinese] fellows from 18 to 25 years old to work in the Cannery; we would give them $25 per month and their board. We want them right off immediately. Perhaps you know some young fellows and if not go to some intelligence office. . . . Do not go to Kinkaid, he is no good.[79]

Canners and contractors by 1890 and perhaps earlier, as the comment on Mr. Kinkaid's abilities indicates, had come to the tacit agreement that a failure to provide adequate help justified hiring additional non-Chinese workers at the contractor's expense.

Increasingly after 1890, the "extra hires" were women and children from the families of local European American fishermen hired at piece or hourly rates. By the early 1900s, clauses covering extra hires became a regular part of the contracts, and in the 1910s, extra hires constituted as much as a quarter of the people in the cannery labor market at the peak of the season. Packers benefited most from the extra hires. Such additional laborers allowed the big runs of salmon to be packed at no extra cost to the owners. Contractors disliked extra hires because their wages cut into profits but conceded because of the relative scarcity of Chinese laborers after the mid-1880s. Forced to accept them, contractors nonetheless tried to keep the extras' wages at a minimum, which partially explains the emphasis on women and children, who, contractors and owners agreed, could be paid less than men.[80]

Unlike the contractors, Chinese crew members must have looked favorably on extras, since they seldom displaced Chinese workers. (Contractors invariably gave first preference in jobs to their countrymen.) Because the extras worked for such a short time, usually two to three weeks, they acquired only rudimentary knowledge of the more specialized tasks and therefore posed no threat to skilled Chinese workers. When they did perform the same labors as Chinese, extras usually worked in lines temporarily added for the rush and hence at peak times lessened the impact of the heavy runs on the contracted crew. Only as the effects of the exclusion policies became apparent did non-Chinese begin to make significant headway in entering the cannery labor market. Well into the twentieth century, Chinese capitalized on their skills and scarcity to create a labor aristocracy and through the contractors controlled access to the best jobs.[81]

After the provisions for extra hires and minimum guarantees were in place, contractors and owners wrestled with the details of the agreements and searched for an advantage, but the parties did not attempt any radical overhaul of the basic system. Negotiations centered on the price per case, implementation of new technology, and changes in company organization. After the Exclusion Act, contract prices rose sharply. In 1886 and 1887, contractors received 35 to 38 cents per case, and between 1890 and 1892, canners paid as much as 44 to 50 cents per case. The relatively rapid price increases forced canners to approach negotiations with care. Workers' wages, however, did not advance at the same rate.[82]

Shifts in marketing strategies and the implementation of new technology further complicated negotiations. Canners moved away from packing Chinook salmon exclusively in one-pound "tall" cans to a variety of salmon in several different can sizes. At first, these changes caught contractors and cannery workers unaware. Flat cans, in particular, drew the highest prices on the fancy markets in which so many Columbia River canners tried to compete. One canner commented that flat cans "are nasty things to put up, [are] hard to solder, take . . . the best part of the fish, [cost] extra for labor, and [are] lots of bother."[83] When Hapgood and Company switched in mid-season to flat cans from talls, Chinese workers "raised great objections" and demanded that Hapgood "pay them double price per case."[84] Unfortunately for the crew, the contractor at Wing Sing and Company had failed to include any such stipulation in the contract. "We carefully reread our contract," Hapgood wrote to the company, to "make doubly sure that we were not in error and were in the right. . . . It did not say talls, flats, squares or oblong, simply 4 doz. 1 lb. cans. When we made known this fact to *Lang Bone the Boss*[,] they went to work grumblingly."[85]

By the end of the decade, contractors, for their own sake and probably under pressure from disgruntled cannery crews, made certain that owners specified in writing the price per case for each type of can. In their bids, they also tried to set the prices. In 1899, Wong Get submitted a typical bid to the Columbia River Packers Association (CRPA) in which he offered to pack

> One pound Tall cans 28 cents per case
>   each of 4 dozen cans
> One pound Flat cans 32 cents per case
>   each of 4 dozen cans
> One-half pound Flat cans 28 cents per
>   case each of 4 dozen cans

> One pound Oval cans 75 cents per case
>   each of 4 dozen cans
> Two pound Tall cans 20 cents per case
>   each of 4 dozen cans[86]

Half-pound flat cans, like ovals, were hard to pack, and contractors usually figured the prices on the basis of eight dozen cans to the case so that Wong's price per case of half-pound flats was actually 56 cents per standard case. By 1900, Wong, as well as other contractors, learned that he had to differentiate between hand and machine-soldered cans in his bids, especially for the oval cans for which a new soldering machine had been developed. Although most of Wong's bid prices remained the same, he charged 10 cents more per case for hand-soldered oval cans than for those done by machine.[87]

Contractors kept abreast of technological changes in the industry and required cannery owners to inform them about all machinery employed in the canneries before they entered into an agreement. For example, Suill Duck, general manager of Wing Sing, Long Kee and Company in Portland, wrote to the CRPA, which had approached him regarding a contract:

> Before answering your request . . . as to a contract to furnish you with a crew for next season[,] I would like you inform me of . . . how many and what kind of machines you have: whether you have a topping machine, washing machine, filling machine, labeling machine, lacquering machine, fish cleaning machine and butchering machine. Please state how many of such machines and of what kind you have. When I am in possession of these facts I will then be in a position to talk to you about a contract.[88]

Like extra hires, the new technology largely supplemented Chinese labor. By the turn of the century, cannery owners on the Columbia used a variety of machines, depending on the size and location of the cannery. Contractors had to be aware of the capacity of the plant to make an appropriate bid without risking huge losses. Many contractors folded after several years because of miscalculations and an inability to fulfill contractual obligations.[89]

In the 1890s a nationwide push toward company mergers affected contractors and their crews as much or more than newly applied technology, extra hires, or individual contractor skills. From the mid-1880s to 1905, the number of canneries on the Columbia River dropped steadily from thirty-seven to fifteen.[90] Increased competition drove some companies out of the business, but many others merged. Cannery mergers began outside the Columbia River with the 1893 formation of the Alaska Packers Association followed by other mergers in Alaska,

British Columbia, and the Puget Sound.[91] On the Columbia River in 1899, a handful of companies merged to create the CRPA. While the merger on the Columbia was not the first, it illustrates the impact on Chinese.[92]

In the first several years after the CRPA's formation, bids from competing Chinese contractors flooded into the CRPA office in Astoria. The merger involved eight companies that had consolidated operations and closed several plants. Fewer canneries and companies with the same number of contractors drove contract prices down and initiated an intense competition among contractors. Between 1899 and 1905, fifteen different Chinese contractors offered a variety of prices. CRPA managers disregarded some applicants out of hand but asked those they believed capable for references. Of the latter, they invited a select few for further discussions. By 1905, CRPA officials had settled on two or three contractors to handle labor recruitment and management for all their canneries on the Columbia and in Alaska. In spite of recurring disagreements over the contracts, the company worked with the same contractors for the next three and a half decades.[93]

The CRPA's decision to utilize only two or three contractors forced the remainder either to negotiate with other companies or to quit the business. Ju Guy, for example, had made substantial sums supplying Chinese to Columbia River canners before the CRPA merger; after its formation, his contract business failed. When he borrowed money from his friend Wong Wu to reestablish himself as a cannery contractor on the Puget Sound and subsequently failed, Wong took him to court to recover the money. The incident came to a close when the sheriff in Astoria seized Ju's property to cover the debt.[94] Company mergers stranded many contractors and workers.

To start up a cannery contracting business early in the industry's history had required little capital, but it did require considerable skill, connections with cannery owners and Chinese workers, and a healthy measure of luck. After the mid-1880s, with the combined impact of the Chinese Exclusion Act and overexpansion and competition in the industry, opportunities for new contractors to break in or for better-established contractors to expand business occurred only with the establishment of new plants or changes in cannery ownership. Once satisfied with a particular contractor, owners most often retained the same person, family, or company year after year, as did the CRPA.[95]

In the last quarter of the nineteenth century, Chinese provided much more than color for curious visitors to the salmon canneries. Chinese workers, foremen, and contractors with non-Chinese cannery owners created a flexible system of labor recruitment and management centered on the canning process. That system withstood major political and market changes. Formal power and authority came to be represented in the written agreements between owners and contractors. Increased specificity and detail in the contracts illustrated each party's efforts to gain an upper hand. Although owners had the greater power, contractors had the ability to affect the course of events. In the formal arrangements, Chinese workers fared worst but managed to exert an influence through physical disruptions and work stoppages. Their centrality in getting the salmon packed and their efforts to bend arrangements to their advantage gave them a place in determining the system that had evolved. Perhaps contractor Sit Que's 1885 claim that his crews provided "satisfaction in every case" was not too far off the mark.[96]

After the mid-1880s, Chinese workers had a vested interest in maintaining the status quo. Labor-intensive processing techniques, not significantly altered by mechanization in the nineteenth century, helped create a hierarchy within the labor force. As Chinese workers became fewer in number following the Exclusion Act, they became more valuable assets to canners and contractors and accordingly demanded and received better wages.[97] Assured of reasonably steady work and adequate pay at the top of the hierarchy, they had little reason or desire to revamp the system. As a result, their efforts to exercise power became less direct and more subtle than violence or strikes. Instead, they moved toward constructing communities beyond the cannery buildings, unspecified in the written contracts, to enhance their working lives.

3

Cannery Communities, Cannery Lives

DURING THE winter of 1909–1910, the owners of the Columbia River Packers Association (CRPA) investigated the possibility of establishing a cannery at Chignik, Alaska, because, in the words of part-owner Samuel Elmore, "Columbia River fish are practically fading away. Competition is growing stronger, profits less."[1] Elmore cited the consistently plentiful supply of high-quality salmon that ran for a comparatively long period as Chignik's foremost advantage over the Columbia River as well as other Alaska locations. To that line of argument he added: Companies used traps extensively in the area, which put the cost of salmon lower than that bought from fishermen; the cannery site was "on the Pacific side" of the Alaska Peninsula and was "free from extreme cold and ice"; it had "direct communication once each month by steamer and [had a] telegraph station near at hand"; fresh water was in plentiful supply; and the proposed site was situated on a "bay and harbor easily navigated," making possible "discharging and loading direct in the cannery [and] to and from ship[s]."[2] Other partners in the firm concurred that Chignik "has advantages which no other point in Alaska has."[3] In early spring 1910, the CRPA erected a cannery at Chignik.[4]

The CRPA's deliberation was typical. Beginning with the first salmon-canning venture of 1864 on the Sacramento River, eager exploiters of Pacific salmon built canneries where the salmon ran from the Monterey peninsula to the Alaska coast along the Bering Sea. Their prime concerns were plentiful salmon, navigable waters, a long canning season (determined by fish runs and weather), and ample fresh water.[5] The practice of drawing on a floating, ready supply of labor in the American West that included European American and Native American fishermen and Chinese cannery hands allowed owners to give little thought about building next to population centers that might supply workers. A great many salmon canneries stood in the most remote and isolated locales, giving rise to seasonal bunkhouse communities. Some operations were near to population clusters, however, and as the industry grew in the last quarter of the nineteenth century, several large cannery towns emerged on the coast. Canners built still other plants near existing small towns that had at the center of their economies timber, mine, or agricultural enterprises or transportation and communication, not canning.

Chinese lived and worked in the three settings—bunkhouse village, cannery town, and small-town cannery. There they experienced a relatively consistent pattern of labor recruitment and management by coethnics and of work routines inside the canneries. They lived and worked in a truncated society made up of seasonally contracted immigrant "bachelor" workers locked into particular positions in the industry by virtue of their ethnicity. Those factors, limiting as they may have been, gave the workers an opportunity to create common patterns of interaction. Yet because the cannery settings varied tremendously, Chinese faced very different circumstances outside the plant. Their efforts to shape their experiences within each community speaks to their ability to manipulate the constraints placed on them as international labor migrants in the U.S. West.[6]

Bunkhouse Villages

Within the bunkhouse villages, Chinese developed patterns of behavior to cope with the physical hardships of that environment. Outside observers often drew rosy pictures of these villages. One local editor in the 1870s romantically portrayed isolated Columbia River canneries as "invariably built out over the water on piles. Back of these on the banks of the river are clustered a few dwellings, with generally a pretty cottage, where the proprietor, or foreman resides. Back of these are high bluffs, covered with evergreen trees, mostly spruce, hemlock and fir."[7] Ironically, the editor neglected to mention the rough bunkhouse that probably stood between the "pretty cottage" and the plant. From the editor's distance, the buildings may have looked pretty, but closer inspection of any cannery would have revealed structures made of rough-cut lumber with large gaps between the planks to facilitate cleaning and reduce construction costs. The "China house" at the Tyonek cannery on Cook Inlet, Alaska, was, according to the superintendent, "just like a barn, with up-and-down boards and a wood floor."[8] The only source of heat in these large, one- and two-room structures was a single wood- or coal-burning stove. Workers pasted paper over the cracks to cut down on drafts and make the quarters more livable.[9] Owners adjusted their buildings to suit the particular environment, not to accommodate workers. At the CRPA cannery at Chignik, Alaska, vertical space was limited. The plant stood on a ten-foot-high gravel spit for protection from high tides, but strong winds kept the height of the structures at one low story.[10]

The quarters were spartan at best, and Chinese were left to supply what comforts they might want or need. All in the industry referred to the living quarters as "bunkhouses," but some had no bunks, only sawhorses with boards placed on top. Chinese had to provide their own bedding and furnishings. A three-gallon bucket—often the most versatile, functional, and only furnishing available—served as a suitcase, bathtub, and stool.[11] Owners did make some provisions for workers. The CRPA cannery at Chignik, for example, had a bathhouse with tubs and showers and a laundry with six tubs, but the superintendent consented only to supply hot water and steam. Chinese workers were responsible for its upkeep. Owners had function in mind when they built privies over small creeks so that the water carried away waste. Latrines placed on bridges must have been difficult and uncomfortable to use at night, especially in cold and windy weather, and no amount of paper pasting would help.[12]

For privacy in the one- and two-room enclosures, Chinese might make partitions. At Chignik, each worker "built himself a kennel out of the bunks" in the twenty-by-fifty-foot bunkhouse.[13] In a few plants, owners constructed eight-by-ten compartments that held four to eight men. Privacy in such rooms was difficult, for they were "like rabbit hutches."[14] Few bunkhouses had separate rooms until the 1920s when many of the original bunkhouses fell into such disrepair that new ones had to be built. Regardless of location, the bunkhouses always seemed crowded.[15]

Even though workers had no vested interest in the cannery structures, they kept their quarters as livable as possible. The National Canners' Association's sanitary surveys, conducted in voluntary cooperation with cannery owners in the 1910s and 1920s, generally listed Chinese living spaces as "exceptionally clean" in spite of the failure of owners to provide janitorial services. No evidence suggests that such was not also the case in the nineteenth century.[16]

These young "bachelors," while able and perhaps even willing to tolerate such living conditions as an unfortunate by-product of their position as immigrant laborers, immediately recognized that the bunkhouse communities lacked the social complexity of their home villages or even U.S. Chinatowns. First among the shortcomings was the virtual absence of Chinese women and families. Men predominated in Chinese immigration, but the male-to-female ratio at the canneries was even more lopsided than in other Chinese settlements. The 1880 census listed nearly 31 percent of the Chinese cannery workers on the lower Columbia as married, but none had wives with them.[17] Even into the twentieth century, only a few small-scale contractors/foremen lived with their wives at remote canneries.[18] Owners discouraged the presence of families and only reluctantly accommodated contractors and foremen, who lived separately from the crews.[19]

In the absence of Chinese women, bachelors attempted to interact with women of other groups, especially those hired as extras. Few European American women were at the plants, and because the majority population was intolerant of miscegenation, they rarely entered long-term relationships with Chinese men. Chinese workers more frequently established ties with Native American women.[20]

The location of the cannery was a key element in creating the opportunity for such alliances. Years before canning began on the Columbia River, European American diseases had decimated the Native American population so that Chinese men encountered Native American women at canneries most distant from European American settlements. In the Puget Sound and British Columbia, such relationships developed frequently, but even those were dampened by the intense competition between Chinese and Native Americans in agricultural labor, particularly in the hop harvests, where violence among pickers made social interaction difficult.[21] The large-scale employment of Native Americans in southeastern Alaska did not create direct competition for the Chinese crews but provided relief labor during heavy runs. Census records suggest that setting determined the frequency of interracial unions.[22] Settlements at remote plants were seasonal, though, and Chinese–Native American couples and their children who remained in the territory lived in small towns, not at the remote cannery sites.[23]

Deprived of families, many Chinese bachelors drew on the real or fictive kin networks that had aided them in their immigration to the United States. In their settlements they often formed groupings around common surnames and sometimes more formal clan associations. At the canneries, surname groupings occurred as well, but to a lesser degree. The manuscript population census reveals that before exclusion, surname groupings figured significantly in the smaller plants, though none had a crew in which all members possessed the same surname.[24] The scarcity of surviving lists of nineteenth-century crews makes it difficult to determine the extent to which Chinese utilized kinship networks.[25]

In addition to these networks, Chinese drew on an established practice from the villages of south China to improve their bunkhouse experiences. There, many villages had bachelor houses, sometimes attached to ancestral or clan halls, in which an average of forty to fifty young men resided. They went there to relieve crowding in their family dwellings and to remove themselves from families with girls coming "of age." Entrance into the bachelor house served to mark one's passage into manhood and ended only with marriage or departure from the village.[26]

Boys enthusiastically anticipated the communal life of the bachelor house. It provided them with an opportunity to spend what leisure time they had away from the family's work routine, in male social activities like gambling, drinking, talking, and going on swimming and fishing outings. They also engaged in ordinarily taboo discussions of sexual matters. Youths at the houses also came into contact with adults; guests on temporary stays from other villages and the "confirmed gamblers, drunkards, opium addicts, and the like" who continued to reside in the bachelor quarters as long as they did not fall "into such disgrace as to be barred from the village." Bachelor houses also sheltered men whose wives were "in confinement" during and after pregnancy and men on vacation from their normal duties. In the mixing of men and boys, the youths learned from their elders' experiences about how to deal with future challenges.[27] Cannery owners, of course, had no intention of facilitating passage into adulthood or communal life among their employees, but the workers very likely recognized in the bunkhouse an opportunity to re-create the experiences of village life in the homeland.

The 1882 Exclusion Act dramatically altered the bunkhouse communities. Instead of housing young men in their mid-twenties, they became home to workers who, by 1900, averaged nearly forty-five years of age.[28] The bunkhouses served less as a socializing institution than as a reminder of the lack of social mobility for Chinese in the United States. They had achieved a high status within the cannery ranks, but they had also remained locked into a two-tiered, ethnically segmented internal labor market with white workers occupying positions that held relatively greater potential for advancement than Chinese, who were essentially limited to jobs on the cannery line.[29] Their discussions must have centered on a life past, not one to come. By the turn of the century, then, the bunkhouse community no longer served as a rite of passage, though it did continue to provide an opportunity for sharing common concerns. Nonetheless, both before exclusion and after, the predominant characteristic of the bunkhouse was that it was built for the advantage of the cannery owner, not the social well-being of the workers.[30]

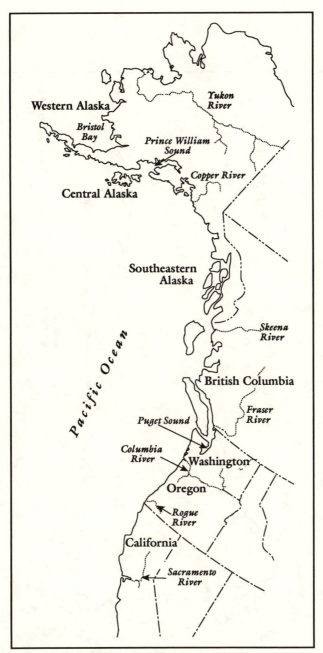

Salmon canning regions of the Pacific Coast

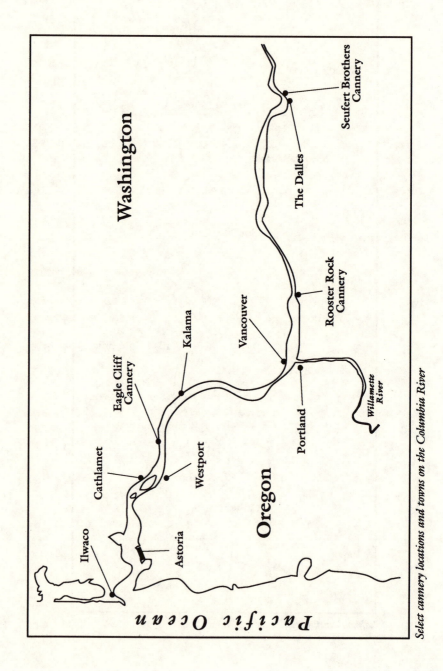

Select cannery locations and towns on the Columbia River

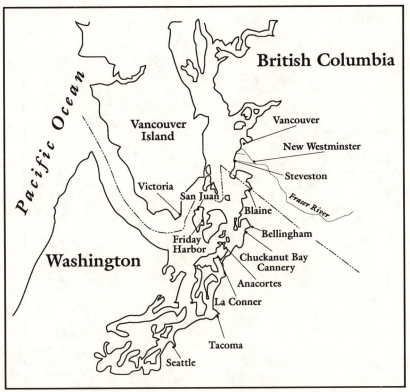

Select cannery locations and towns in northern Puget Sound and southern British Columbia

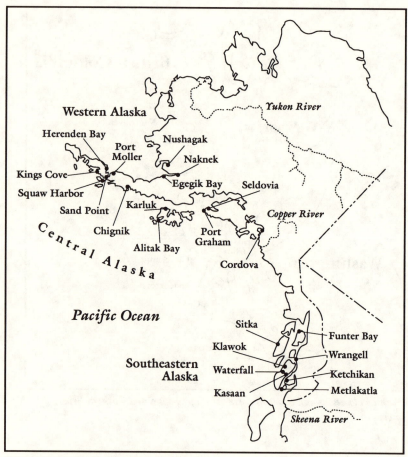

Western Alaska

Herenden Bay

Port
Moller

Nushagak

Naknek

Kings Cove

Egegik Bay

Seldovia

Squaw Harbor

Sand Point

Karluk

Chignik

Central Alaska

Alitak Bay

Port
Graham

Copper River

Cordova

Yukon River

Pacific Ocean

Sitka

Funter Bay

Klawok

Wrangell

Southeastern
Alaska

Waterfall

Ketchikan

Kasaan

Metlakatla

Skeena River

Select cannery locations and towns in Alaska

At Astoria, Oregon, in the mid-1880s, Chinese worked at every stage of the canning process (West Shore, June 1887, Special Collections, University of Washington, negative no. 14788)

Early version of the "Iron Chink" of the 1910s staffed by Chinese workers, with a Chinese "fish pitcher" at right (Special Collections, University of Washington, negative no. 9422)

The "Iron Chink" of the late 1910s slowly made its way into the canneries despite the claims of its manufacturer that it replaced many workers (Curtis Photo, Special Collections, University of Washington, negative no. 58156)

Filling cans was one of the few tasks open to women in early twentieth-century plants (Special Collections, University of Washington, negative no. 221)

While Asians and Asian Americans worked on the canning line, in the twentieth century, Native Alaskan women worked primarily as can handlers and fillers, and their children sometimes handled cans as well (Special Collections, University of Washington, negative no. 14787)

Union organizers for the Cannery Workers and Farm Laborers Union Local 7 drew upon their diverse ethnic backgrounds to build a strong union (Unidentified men, Box 40, Cannery Workers and Farm Laborers Union Local 7 Records, Manuscripts Division, University of Washington)

This was true of other aspects of cannery life as well. Food was served in a common mess hall provided by the owner, rather than in the family setting as in south China. Contractors supplied the fare and hired the cook. In return, they received a daily per capita sum from the cannery owners for provisions. This arrangement allowed contractors an avenue to control workers and gain profits from owners. In one fairly typical arrangement, during 1908 Seid Chuck received approximately 20 cents a day for each worker's board (nearly $2,000 for the season) at the small Seufert Brothers Cannery near The Dalles, Oregon.[31] Since contractors served relatively inexpensive rice, tea, and salmon or "scrap" fish from the cannery, they kept significant proportions of that money. In addition, some contractors bought the supplies through their own import–export businesses, which generated even larger profits for them.[32]

Workers perennially complained about their food. Contractors responded by selling extra supplies to crews, promoting gardens kept by workers, and encouraging them to gather plants and shellfish in their spare time. Many contractors stocked "slop chests" with special items and had the foremen at the plants sell the goods to workers at high prices on credit.[33] In the 1910s and 1920s, and presumably during the nineteenth century as well, though the record is unclear, contractors deducted large proportions of workers' wages for purchases from the chests. In 1902, at least one company, rather than the contractor, controlled sales of extra food.[34]

With the Chinese crews of the nineteenth century, contractors depended more on workers' initiative in keeping small gardens and gathering food to keep down complaints about food rather than on sales from slop chests. At the beginning of the season, contractors would send two or three men to prepare a small plot near the cannery. They worked for several days and then left it in the care of the Chinese cook. The contractor controlled the garden through the cook but relied on volunteers from the crew to plant, water, and weed. Usually five or six men kept the garden "just like a big farm." Charlie Koe, a former cannery worker and contractor, remembered his as a "kind of a community garden, everybody work on it and we all eat on it, it's just like a big family in those days."[35] Not only did the efforts of the cannery hands supplement their diet, but for some it recalled experiences of their homeland.

Live hogs and occasionally chickens kept at the canneries also provided sustenance, as well as a distraction. Contractors supplied hogs and chickens for the crews, and cooks fed them discarded fish and table scraps. The butchering of hogs every several weeks was preceded by a festive occasion of pig chasing that was followed by careful dressing of the meat under the watchful eyes of the crew and a few days of fresh pork at meals. The cook then salted down the remainder and doled it out sparingly for several weeks until the next butchering day. The chickens provided eggs and occasional holiday meals. Still, most of the cannery workers' protein came from fish. They regularly ate the perch, flounder, sole, and low-grade salmon caught by fishermen or themselves. In addition to being a social diversion and dietary supplement for workers, hogs, chicken, and fish lowered contractors' provisioning costs and crew tensions.[36]

Contractors seldom provided more than a basic subsistence. As a result, an important part of workers' activities at the bunkhouse villages involved gathering additional food. Wapato, *Sagittaria latifolia*, and a bulbous root long used as a staple by Native Americans grew in great quantities along the tidal flats of the lower Columbia River. Throughout much of the year, Native American women dug the roots out of the mud, loaded them in baskets, and carried them back to their villages. There they dried the wapato for several weeks and then boiled or roasted them. The cooked plant resembled a potato or turnip in consistency. The Chinese harvested and processed wapato in a similar fashion, loading them into baskets suspended from shoulder poles and bringing them back to the cannery where they steamed the root. Wapato is related to the *Sagittaria sagittifolia*, or swallow's tail (*yanwei cao*), cultivated in the shallow-water ponds and irrigated fields of China. Wapato certainly must have reminded the workers of familiar foodstuffs, but it is just as likely that they became "very fond" of wapato because gathering it provided an opportunity to socialize with the area's few Native American women.[37]

Although not as socially stimulating as the wapato harvests, the collection of seaweed from coastal waters was another familiar task. Chinese use dried seaweed in soups for its flavor and medicinal qualities. Near the mouth of the Columbia River, they ventured out to get seaweed so frequently that one favorite spot became known as "China Beach" among the local European American residents.[38] Depending on cannery location, Chinese also gathered freshwater mussels and saltwater clams. Food and its preparation carry much cultural importance for all Chinese, and each dish supposedly has its own special medicinal qualities.[39] In the canneries, where the food varied little and was often inadequate, it is no wonder that workers went to great lengths to keep gardens, harvest wapato, or collect seaweed and shellfish to supplement meager diets.

Chinese also developed a variety of coping mechanisms, including gambling, smoking opium, drinking homemade gin, and homosexual relations.[40] Gambling allowed the men to while away the time and gave them an opportunity to make money quickly. While informal, friendly games took place, quite often contractors or their foremen ran the games or hired professional gamblers on percentages.[41] Until 1909, the use of opium was legal; some Chinese workers appear to have been casual smokers, but others were heavily addicted: Long days of standing in the damp conditions probably led a number of workers to lean on opium to ease their aches and pains. Actual levels of usage are, however, impossible to determine.[42]

It is probable that among so many men at the isolated cannery communities, the incidence of homosexual relationships would be higher than in the society from which the men emigrated and perhaps even higher than in urban centers in the West. Reports from the 1920s and 1930s indicate that some contractors and foremen sent male prostitutes to the canneries and took a percentage of the money they earned.[43] By those decades, however, owners and superintendents frowned on pimping and male prostitution, largely for fear that the spread of venereal disease might affect the quality of fish packed and the productivity of the crews.[44] Evidence on homosexual relationships or male prostitution is very sketchy. Workers seldom discussed it with outside observers, and present-day informants avoid the topic or take great pains to distance themselves from it.[45]

Drug use and male prostitution, in particular, have been cited as evidence alternately to explain the depravity of Chinese laborers or their extreme exploitation by contractors and owners,[46] but such activities occurred among all workers at the canneries—fishermen, managers, and workers. The Chinese found additional ways to relieve tensions. Building and flying kites in the steady winds at Pacific Coast plants was a favorite, and the Chinese constructed all types of kites. Among them were some that emitted musical notes and others so large that they took a dozen or more men to handle the lines.[47] Chinese also tried to celebrate accustomed holidays, but the demanding cannery schedule only occasionally allowed them time off. Most often, they got a break during U.S. (or Canadian) holidays.[48] On their single day off during the week, they celebrated holidays, flew kites, and engaged in activities that must have been all the more enjoyable because they were outside the direct control of contractors, foremen, and cannery owners.

Cannery Towns

Of the three kinds of communities, bunkhouse villages were the most isolated. Crews were cut off from outside contact and confined to the cannery locale, but not all Chinese were burdened by such conditions.

Those who worked and lived in cannery towns led less monotonous existences. Two cannery towns—Astoria, Oregon, and New Westminster, British Columbia—provided some social, political, and economic opportunities. By the 1880s, Astoria had earned a reputation as "the Gloucester of the West," sustaining a large seasonal population of Chinese workers and a smaller, more stable core of entrepreneurs. Before the canning boom of the mid-1870s, however, only a handful of Chinese lived in the town. Between 1870 and 1874, they found employment as cooks and dishwashers in the local resort hotel, as servants in European American families, or as wood choppers and levee builders.[49] Astoria had fewer than a thousand residents, and its economy supported few domestic and day-labor jobs.[50] The potential growth of any sizable Chinese community seemed unlikely, but after 1874 the canneries provided the catalyst for the formation of an Astoria "Chinatown."

Caught in a competitive struggle over how to exploit the salmon runs most effectively, owners moved their plants to Astoria at the mouth of the Columbia River to gain first access to salmon and shipping facilities. Early canners on the river had believed that salmon congregated in the greatest numbers twenty to fifty miles from the river's mouth. As competition among the canners grew, they found that the canner who could first catch, can, and market the fish gained a small but significant edge over the others. The location of plants at Astoria allowed company fishermen to catch salmon just as they entered the river and to transport the fish quickly to the cannery. By locating their plants at Astoria, owners also saved shipping time to consumer markets. Portland, ninety miles upriver from Astoria, had been the original shipping point, but with the absence of rail connections between most lower Columbia River plants and Portland, owners found that shipments from Astoria reached important foreign markets first. The mill at Astoria, from which canners bought box shooks for casing the salmon, made it an even more logical spot for new canneries.[51]

The first Astoria cannery opened in 1874 and the second the next year. After the 1875 season, the *Weekly Astorian* proudly announced that the "success of the Astoria canneries establishes the fact that Astoria is the place for fish canneries." By 1876, the town had five canneries, a total of eight in 1877, and fourteen in 1880.[52] Owners of the new plants followed George Hume's practice and hired Chinese labor. Between 1874 and the mid-1880s, the Chinese settlement in Astoria grew in direct proportion to the number of canneries. By 1880, census enumerators listed 2,122 in Astoria and registered more than three-fourths of them as cannery hands.[53] Since owners built their plants side by side on the waterfront with the Chinese bunkhouses in a row behind the canneries, the living quarters were crowded into a very small section of the town. Several hundred Chinese entrepreneurs—merchants, restaurateurs, saloonkeepers, tailors, pawnbrokers, barbers, clothiers, gardeners, and laundry operators—hoped to benefit from transactions with the workers and settled nearby (see Appendix, Table 1).[54]

A second concentration formed around a smaller core of canneries that opened a mile upriver from the first Astorian plants. Although this section of town, known as Upper Astoria, housed 712 Chinese workers in 1880, no ethnic service economy served it. Only fifteen other Chinese lived in Upper Astoria: a woman with an unspecified occupation, four cooks, three laundrymen, six shoe-factory workers, and one merchant. Upper Astoria was little more than a satellite community of cannery workers.[55]

The prejudice of European American residents, added to the canners' placement of the bunkhouses, severely restricted Chinese settlement patterns. In 1879, the editor of the *Weekly Astorian* declared that "we cannot possibly colonize the Chinese in any one place in the city, but it should be done if possible; allowing that this is *such* a free country."[56] The desire to "colonize" the immigrants in a particular location reflected the informal boundaries imposed by European Americans on Chinese communities and epitomized an "internal colony" of reserve labor on which owners drew. Owners forced contractors to keep workers nearby, ready to respond to calls for work. By keeping crews small for as long as possible, canners lowered their labor costs and found themselves relieved from supporting workers. While Chinese awaited cannery jobs, they had to rely on their own savings, some contractor's largess, or noncannery employment.[57]

The Astoria Chinese community depended on the canneries for its economic base. In 1880 some 1,639, or 78.1 percent, of Astoria's Chinese worked in the plants.[58] Exclusion policies ultimately curtailed the possibility of sustaining high levels of Chinese employment in the canneries, but news of the pending legislation prompted a sudden emigration from China to the United States. A temporary surplus of Chinese labor delayed the act's impact. Many recently immigrated Chinese found their way to Astoria, where 40 percent of them reported to federal census enumerators in 1900 that they had immigrated during the two years before the Exclusion Act.[59]

Many of the American West's European Americans read the apparent abundance of Chinese immigrants as a failure of the Exclusion Act. In the mid-1880s, frustrated by a slow economy, they renewed their anti-Chinese activities. The 28 Chinese coal miners killed September 2, 1885, at Rock Springs, Wyoming, along with the 15 wounded and approximately 550 expelled, provided the first spark. Within two weeks, whites directed violence at Chinese in north-central Washington. From late September to early November, Puget Sound Chinese suffered at the hands of rioters.[60] Chinese left those troubled spots in large numbers; some returned to China, while others headed for safe havens in large California Chinatowns and Astoria.[61] In 1886, the *Weekly Astorian* reported that "probably" three thousand Chinese had crowded into Astoria seeking shelter. The town was "a sort of jumping-off place . . . and they congregate here in the same fashion and for about the same reason that they cluster in San Francisco—because they are driven off elsewhere and have no place else to go."[62] Many Astorians refrained from anti-Chinese activities because they believed the laborers might abandon the canneries, thereby causing the collapse of the local economy.[63]

Still, the town had some incidents of anti-Chinese activities. A small but vocal minority formed societies and in an occasional public speech or newspaper editorial urged the Chinese to leave, but they took no direct action against the Chinese. The only major anti-Chinese incident took place outside the auspices of the anti-Chinese societies. In 1885, the *Weekly Astorian* lamented the "race war" in the streets.

> Last Tuesday morning two drunken men on the roadway near [the canneries] upset two Chinamen. The Chinamen got some of their crowd together and made it equally unpleasant for the two men. The Chinamen then took refuge in their headquarters. Their assailants increased in numbers, made another assault upon the Mongolian stronghold. The descendants of Zengis Khan [*sic*] sallied forth with knives and clubs; their opponents mustered for the fray when Messrs. Tallant and Smith [both cannery owners] got between the belligerents and succeeded in calming their angry passions. The fire still smolders and may yet be quenched in gore.[64]

Open race war never ignited in Astoria as it did in other western locales. Instead, the town served as a relatively safe haven and attracted those who might not otherwise have come. Their presence only added to the number of workers available for the canneries.

After the mid-1880s, neither the number of Chinese nor canneries in Astoria continued their meteoric ascent. Exclusion discontinued immigration and reduced the labor supply just as canners on the Columbia felt the crunch of destructive competition among themselves and with operators in other canning regions. Whereas up to 1887 several thousand Chinese worked in the town's nearly two dozen canneries, between 1889 and 1892, only five hundred to six hundred labored in eight canneries.[65] By 1900, several more canneries had closed, with the remaining plants employing only 332 Chinese, or 59.2 percent of the workforce total.[66] A temporary increase in the number of canneries in the town around 1910 failed to stop the downward spiral in Chinese cannery employment; in that year, only ninety-one, or 50.2 percent, directly depended on cannery incomes.[67] Even that number dropped by half over the next two decades. Cannery work always remained important to Astoria's Chinese but never regained the position it had occupied before the late 1880s.[68]

Inside the Astoria plants, Chinese faced conditions similar to those at the bunkhouse villages, and they transplanted many of their behavior patterns. They took what fish they needed from the canning line or fished from the cannery wharf. The potential markets, however, were much greater in Astoria than at an isolated cannery. One Chinese worker recalled earning more on his breaks by selling the fish he caught with a net from the dock than he did for a full day of cannery work. Still, he continued both "jobs."[69] Others moved beyond individual activities to small partnerships. In the 1880s several enterprising Chinese tried to set up fish-drying operations atop their living quarters. Their efforts were short-lived because the other residents of Astoria complained vociferously about the "stench" until local officials shut down the business.[70] The tons of waste dumped by canneries, which sat on the mud flats at low tide or washed up at high tide and then rotted on the banks, generated only mild complaints from European American residents dependent on the canneries for the survival of their town.[71] Ethnic enterprise, especially that of the Chinese, garnered little support outside the ethnic community.

Although there were similarities between the bunkhouse villages and the cannery towns, the lives of cannery hands were qualitatively different in the two locations. In the towns, Chinese supplemented their food with vegetables and meat bought from Chinese truck gardeners and merchants. The gardeners at first maintained small plots in Astoria, but as real estate values increased, European American residents objected to the night soil that gardeners used to fertilize their crops and the free-roaming hogs they kept, and they forced gardeners to the outskirts of town.[72] The move made it less convenient, though still possible, for cannery employees to buy from them. While workers could purchase food and goods from merchants, contractors withheld cash payments and extended credit to them at local businesses in which they had an interest.[73] As a result of such practices, contractors needed no "slop chests" to maintain their hold on laborers' purse strings.

Workers in cannery towns had more opportunities for social activities than those at bunkhouse villages. One difference was the presence of many more Chinese women. In 1880, twelve of the twenty Chinese women in Astoria lived in households of two to four adult women without any spouses present. They averaged twenty-nine years of age, ranging from twenty-one to thirty-five with the exception of a thirty-nine year old and a sixty-four year old. Based on similar data for Chinese prostitutes elsewhere in the West, the former were of a "prime" age to be prostitutes in a small town dominated by industrial wage earners, while the latter two may have been madams or maids.[74]

Chinese female prostitutes in the West drew on three distinct clienteles. The healthiest and prettiest women often lived in isolation from all but their wealthy masters within the confines of the Chinese community; whether or not some were concubines, rather than prostitutes, is not revealed in census records. Others, whose masters catered to Chinese only, lived in poorer conditions. The least healthy and fortunate served all comers in the "cribs," or street-side brothels.[75] In Astoria, with its community of wage laborers, prostitutes of many ethnic backgrounds came specifically for the canning season. In all likelihood the Chinese prostitutes during the 1870s and 1880s worked in the cribs or sought patrons among bachelor Chinese. The *Weekly Astorian* noted in 1879 that one Chinese woman "stood in the doorway of a den on Chenamus street soliciting patronage."[76] A long-time resident remembered in his boyhood seeing women who "sat bare-naked from their stomachs up waiting for loggers, fishermen, and sailors" in the cribs of the waterfront district adjacent to Chinatown.[77] Local police only occasionally bothered to arrest or fine the town's prostitutes. Portland newspapers looked askance at Astoria's social atmosphere, commenting that the town "affords every opportunity and allurement of vice in its lowest forms. . . . During the fishing season it is perhaps the most wicked place on earth for its population."[78]

Not every Chinese woman in Astoria was, or remained, a prostitute. In 1877 Ah Bock, a "slave girl" held for "nefarious purposes," was transported from San Francisco and sold into prostitution in Astoria. Lim Sam, her lover, filed in local court for her freedom, and won, but he failed to stop her former owner from kidnapping her. Lim Sam freed her again by unknown means, and the two married in Astoria. In a rare moment of toleration, the local paper commented that the wedded Lim Sam and Ah Bock were truly "Chinese with a Christian heart."[79] Possibilities for romance and even marriage to another Chinese, though remote and difficult, made life in the cannery town much different from in the bunkhouse villages.

Lim Sam and Ah Bock did not appear in the 1880 census, but three of the twenty Chinese women who did appear lived with their husbands but without children present. A Mrs. Ah Kow was married to one of the major nineteenth-century contractors for the canneries. Mrs. Ming Ching and Mrs. Seid Lin were both listed as married to cannery workers. Their husbands may have been cannery foremen or skilled laborers able to afford to maintain a wife or concubine in Astoria, but it is also possible that the two held the women in prostitution. In Astoria during 1880, only a major cannery contractor could support a wife. Most contractors and merchants viewed early Astoria as a hinterland to be occupied seasonally and kept their main residences in Portland or San Francisco, perhaps with wives and families or mistresses. The remaining Chinese women in Astoria, though outnumbered by men at a ratio of over a hundred to one, provided Chinese cannery hands with a more favorable ratio than at the remote plants.[80]

The data on women for 1900 illustrate the tremendous change under way in the community. Thirteen of the eighteen adult women resided with their husbands or children. Among those outside nuclear or extended families, one fifty-six-year-old woman lived without her husband and gave her occupation as merchant. The four remaining women appear to have been directly or indirectly involved in prostitution because of their living arrangements and ages. These included a sixty year old and a thirty-eight year old, who appear in the census as "laborers." They may have been madams or servants in the brothels. Thirty-year-old Le Mo was the head of her household, living with two other women servants aged thirty-six and thirty-nine. Le Mo's retinue of servants suggests that she may have been a mistress or was in a more exclusive brothel than her counterparts in 1880. Other Chinese women may still have worked in the cribs, but census takers enumerated none.[81]

Of the married women, six had married the elite of Astoria's Chinatown and had their children present. Their husbands included a contractor, four merchants, and a tailor. Typical was Mrs. Lop Wy, who married a merchant and had five children, all of whom were born in Oregon. In these marriages a great discrepancy in age separated many husbands and wives. Hong Sing was twenty years younger than her forty-nine-year-old merchant husband. They had been married only two years and had one child born in Oregon.[82] So few Chinese women were in America that most frequently only the most wealthy and powerful men gained access to marriage partners. The discrepancy in ages came about because it took men years to become well enough established to get married; even then, they went into debt.[83] The high cost of marriages ruled out such opportunities for a great many cannery employees.

Surprisingly, in view of the costs of maintaining a nuclear family, four women married men specified in the 1900 census as "laborers." Servant Chun Linn and her laborer-husband boarded with the family of merchant Lum Dong in a household of six people. The remaining three married women lived alone with men, whom enumerators recorded as husbands, and had no children. Whether the men were pimps or husbands cannot be determined.[84]

The 1910 census listed only ten adult women, eight of whom were married to contractors or merchants and only one to a laborer. The remaining woman, Mrs. Go Sing, was married and had no husband present but boarded with a merchant and seven other lodgers in an extended family all with the surname Go. Similar to the practice a decade earlier, unions between Chinese in Astoria tended to be between younger women and older men. Lules Q. Wong's marriage represents the greatest age discrepancy. She had married a tugboat worker twenty-six years her elder. Mrs. Ju Sam was twenty years younger than her merchant husband and was apparently his second wife. Two of the adult women were born in Oregon and mark the long-time settlement of Chinese and the arrival of a second generation. Quon T. Sing had been in Astoria raising her family since 1891, when she married a tailor, Sing Wah. By 1910 Quon had given birth to seven children.[85]

The formation of nuclear families represented a shift in the character of the community from one of many young migrant bachelors catered to by a few prostitutes to a smaller community with nuclear families. The powerful and economically prominent members of the Astoria Chinese community who established families were primarily contractors who, by the turn of the century, had become more numerous in Astoria and had lived there long enough to build an economic base.[86]

Chinese in Astoria had more opportunities for a range of social activities than workers at isolated plants. During the canning season, they celebrated holidays and festivals with "great pomp and ceremony" and demanded and received "one-half day off each for . . . sports, ceremonies, feasts, etc."[87] Even though the Chinese (Lunar) New Year occurred before canning started, seasonal cannery hands and year-round resident Chinese made extensive "preparations for a big time" they expected at the festival, especially with their "detonation of bombs and firecrackers."[88]

Beyond "traditional" holidays, Chinese took advantage of all occasions that offered a respite from the plants. As in the remote canneries, they flew kites, but in Astoria they often flew them as part of such American celebrations as the Fourth of July. In the late 1890s, when Astoria began to celebrate its regatta, the town's annual event marking the importance of the canning industry, Chinese took part in the festivities. Chinese merchants in the town donated to the regatta fund, and in 1910 Chinese residents borrowed a dragon from Portland for the parade. Even cannery employees received the day off to enjoy the activities. At remote plants, these holidays passed with only minimum disruptions in the daily schedule.[89]

The concentration of Chinese in Astoria also attracted a Chinese theater troupe. As early as 1881, Chinese operas ran "full blast every night to big audiences . . . for two weeks" during the canning season in a rented hall.[90] By 1883, Astoria's Chinese had built a theater of their own. The settlement supported this venture only a few years after the larger Portland Chinese community had established its year-round theater for Cantonese opera and San Francisco's Chinese had opened a Cantonese opera school.[91] When the theater closed because of the declining population after the 1880s, Chinese in Astoria found other entertainment. With no theater of their own, they attended shows in the big opera house, though they sat in "China Heaven . . . way up above" the European American crowd.[92]

Deaths also reveal the differences between the lifestyles of Astoria's Chinese workers and those at remote canneries. When Chinese died at outside plants, their bodies were shipped to Portland or Astoria with dispatch. The prospects of dying at such locations troubled workers because it reminded them of their own fragility and the great distances to either their immigrant communities or their homeland. In Astoria, Chinese seemed better able to handle such crises. When one laborer died there of blood poisoning during the 1888 season, a very elaborate ceremony ensued. "His friends," reported the local paper, "scattered the usual assortment of tissue paper on the route of the defunct, and the remains go to Portland for temporary internment [*sic*]."[93] Chinese traditionally offered paper money to spirits in places frequented by the deceased to help in the afterworld. In Astoria such ceremonies were "usual."

Overseas Chinese commonly buried the dead for five or six years and then exhumed the bones and shipped them to China to be interred in the family grave. Men like Hong Too, the "general bone gatherer for the Sam Yup Co.," traveled on a regular circuit through the West. In 1886 he passed through Astoria, Portland, and The Dalles, collecting bodies of "his gang" for shipment back to China.[94] Another "Chinese company" sent its representative to Astoria and other key points in the Pacific Northwest later that same year.[95] As early as 1882, the remains of 225 Chinese lay in Astoria cemeteries awaiting shipment home. The town's service as a regional center for temporary burial pays tribute to its importance to these immigrants.[96]

Life for cannery workers in Astoria held a much more immediate connection to Chinese American social and cultural activities than those at the bunkhouse villages. The availability of options for Astoria's Chinese, in spite of the preeminence of contractors, made possible the building of power bases from which they might exert an influence on contractors. The formation of tongs, political parties, and religious organizations in Astoria created some chances to voice dissent.

"Tongs" included a vast array of social, political, and cultural associations among Chinese immigrants. Most often these organizations have been viewed by scholars alternately as protective protoclass organizations or as managers of the vice industry and exploiters of common Chinese immigrants.[97] Astoria reflected that variety, with at least one family association and several other social–political organizations. It also had tongs that depended heavily on the vice industry for income. Keeping Chinese laborers in a perpetual state of indebtedness through gambling, drug trafficking, and prostitution assured those who controlled these activities of their revenues. Nonetheless, the tongs could also act in workers' interests.[98]

Tong activity began quite early in Astoria. By 1876, both the Hip Sing and Bing Kung tongs had established branches there, and over the years as many as four to six more followed. The Hip Sing, Bing Kung–Bow Leong, and Suey Sing tongs formed the three largest. They also dominated and sometimes fought one another for control of the local vice business. In 1888, for example, violent confrontations among the Suey Sing, Hip Sing, and Bing Kung tongs in the West manifested themselves locally in the competition for gambling in Astoria. The struggle wracked the town until the Chung Wa, forerunner of the Chinese Consolidated Benevolent Association, helped to mediate a truce. During the remainder of the nineteenth century, no more significant intertong antagonisms erupted in Astoria.[99]

The highly visible vice industry and open conflicts among the tongs received much more attention from the Astoria press than the tongs' labor guild activities. In order to recruit and retain members, the tongs in Astoria attempted to control cannery hiring by coercing or encouraging contractors to become members and then pressuring them to hire from within the tong membership. Tong control over cannery labor was neither immediate nor complete. In 1880, observers noted that in most canneries "each [Chinese] is employed directly without the intervention of the six companies or any other persons."[100] After the mid-1880s, when contractors monopolized the labor market, the tongs began to move in; by the twentieth century, contractors commonly secured laborers through the tongs. In Astoria, the Bing Kung–Bow Leong Tong was strong enough to force the major contractor for the Columbia River Packers Association (CRPA) to join. Wong Kee Brown, another contractor in Astoria, held membership in two such organizations.[101] Contractors in Astoria were not alone in this relationship to the tongs. In Seattle, for example, Goon Dip was forced to join several tongs because of his contracting for Alaska and Puget Sound salmon canneries.[102] The tongs were less effective in preventing contractors from assigning family members and friends the best cannery jobs, thus revealing their incomplete influence over the labor market.[103]

The power of the tongs weakened in the first decades of the twentieth century, and they shifted their orientation to more social activities. During this time contractors regained positions of power. Scholars have noted a similar decline in the influence of San Francisco's tongs, especially in the vice industries, but have debated why. Some hold that the balancing of the sex ratio pushed residents to want a more settled and stable lifestyle.[104] Others point to the recognition by merchant and tong leaders that crime cut into tourism—the new economic base of the San Francisco Chinatown.[105] These do not serve to explain the situation in Astoria, for the gender ratio there remained heavily skewed, and tourism never supported the community's elite. Yet, except for one brief eruption in 1922, organized crime and violence diminished.[106]

Astoria's shrinking population of transient salmon fishery employees, not limited to Chinese, did not promise much revenue for those involved in organized crime, so the tongs had no reason to retain their old ways in the town. Just as important, the Chinese community relied to such a great extent on the salmon canneries for its economic base that contractors and workers feared continued crime might result in the loss of their jobs. The impetus toward less-violent tong activities in Astoria grew out of the contractors' attempts to court cannery owners.

In the nineteenth century, owners had been concerned only when drug use or addiction or other vices lessened their laborers' productivity. When in 1893 the *Astoria Budget* claimed that Chinese were "sweet-scented hogs" with "opium-scented hands and long-nailed fingers," owners did not respond directly to the charges.[107] In the first decade of the twentieth century, as the public grew increasingly intolerant of the conditions exposed by Upton Sinclair in the meatpacking industry, canners felt compelled to demonstrate that their plants, and their products, were sanitary. Ordered by owners to supply "clean" workers, contractors countered by playing a visible role in eliminating the vice industry and changing the local image of Astoria's Chinese settlement. In 1916 Chan Ah Dogg, the most prominent Astoria cannery contractor, joined others in a campaign to "rebuild" Chinatown and assured European American residents that he and his fellow Chinese were "eager to serve and become of value to the community."[108] Their efforts were rewarded when the editor of the *Astoria Budget* announced that the Chinese "understand the human race, love their children, are painstaking in their work, clean in their homes, and proud of their ancestors," a far cry from the paper's stance in the previous century.[109]

The opening in 1904 of a branch of the Bow On Tong for American-born Chinese in Astoria, like those in Portland, Fresno, Santa Clara, and Los Angeles, reflected the change from tongs as controllers of the vice industry to tongs as social organizations. Similar to the Native Sons of the Golden West in California, an organization that argued against the intermixing of ethnic groups, the Bow On Tong had as its purpose the representation of American-born Chinese interests, not necessarily those of immigrants. It no more sought control of the vice industry than it did the recruitment of cannery labor. Its programs catered to a broad class coalition among the American-born who were seeking a place in the larger Astoria community.[110]

The waning of tongs and their influence on contractors marked the end of one avenue of resistance that had served workers' interests, but others were emerging. As the Qing Dynasty crumbled and reformers and revolutionaries proposed alternative governments in China, the Chinese in the United States took stands of their own. In Astoria, the debate over imperial reform or the establishment of a republican government framed the discussion and provided cannery hands with a chance to oppose contractors, at least in politics. In the summer of 1900 a branch of the Chinese Reform Society formed in Astoria with the ultimate goal of restoring Kwang Hsu to the throne. "Hundreds" of flag-waving Chinese attended the opening speeches, noted the *Daily Astorian*. Those "in favor of the emperor are wearing photo buttons of him and seem to be very proud of them." They include "some very ardent reformers among the better class here in Chinatown," contractors and merchants among them.[111]

At the other end of the political spectrum were the Chinese who supported Sun Yat Sen. In the first decade of the twentieth century, Sun "secretly" went to Astoria while on tour in the United States to raise money for the establishment of a Chinese republic. He discovered that not all followed the political line of the "better class" in the Chinese community, for a number of its residents threw their support to his organization. The community split was brief, however, and in 1913 Astoria's only political organization was a branch of the Kuomintang (*Guomindang*), or Chung Hwa National Club, as it was known in Astoria, that represented Sun's new republican government. The "ardent reformers" who had supported the emperor formed no countering organization and dropped from the public eye. The political debates had touched Astoria only for a short time and gave limited opportunities for dissenting. Still, in the bunkhouse villages, political agitation other than that espoused by the contractor would have been next to impossible given the tight rein held by his representatives, the foremen.[112]

In addition to tong and political organizations, religious institutions in Astoria gave Chinese opportunities not available at remote canneries. The town's European American residents mistook the small shrines to patron deities in the tong headquarters for "joss houses" or temples. While some Chinese communities had Buddhist and Daoist priests and temples, there is no evidence that Astoria had anything but small shrines.[113] As early as 1880, though, individual Chinese Christians sought to save the souls of their countrymen through street-corner preaching. They appear to have had little effect.[114] Not until the proponents of the Social Gospel reached Astoria in their attempts to reform immigrants through home missions did Christianity begin to make headway in the Chinese community. In 1888 a "Chinese missionary," who was "the latest in the matter of saving souls," set up a Salvation Army barracks in the residence of a deceased contractor.[115] The missionary's progress is unknown, but by the early 1890s the Presbyterian and Baptist missions were teaching English in night schools that were "numerously attended."[116] The schools' popularity among workers may have grown out of the belief that the acquisition of English might help them find a way out of the canneries and helps explain why attendance at the night school did not automatically result in conversion to Christianity. As the Chinese community in Astoria shifted from one primarily of immigrants to one of settled families, the churches switched their focus. By the 1920s, the Christian churches in Astoria, especially the First Baptist Church, had their most significant impact on the American-born Chinese. Children of many ethnic backgrounds participated in its programs, and that brought their parents into contact with each other.[117] Such intermingling broke down some of the racial barriers in Astoria. The nineteenth-century mission schools and the twentieth-century congregations expanded the range of institutions that lay outside direct contractor control.

For as much as Astoria offered to Chinese workers, it also meant contending on an ongoing basis with a substantial European American population that became hostile whenever the two groups competed for jobs within the industry. The earliest contention emerged over fishing for salmon. A "Chinaman dare not fish in the Columbia," federal fisheries investigator George Brown Goode observed, "it being an understood thing that he would die for his sport."[118] David Starr Jordan and Charles H. Gilbert, who worked with Goode, concurred. "There is no law regulating the matter," they wrote for Goode's report, "but public opinion is so strong in relation to it, and there is such a prejudice against the Chinamen, that any attempt on their part to engage in salmon fishing would meet with a summary and probably fatal retaliation."[119] In the next decade, though, prejudice and discrimination did not prevent Chinese entry into commercial salmon fishing.

During the 1880s, a few Chinese found employment as "helpers" on Columbia River gill-net boats, on fish wheels, and on fish traps. Owners often ran their own fishing boats, wheels, and traps and felt that Chinese, hired out of Astoria for less than others, might reduce the cost of salmon at the dock. Independent fishermen, too, sought to lower their operating expenses and in a few cases hired Chinese assistants to help row the two-person boats and pull in the nets. Their efforts meshed with Chinese aspirations to expand their employment opportunities. As early as 1884, canners began staffing their boats with Chinese, and by 1888, Chinese in the boats numbered ten.[120] In that same year, three others found jobs on traps or fish wheels.[121] Chinese employment outside the canneries might have increased had it not been for the establishment of the Columbia River Fishermen's Protective Union (CRFPU). From the founding of the organization in 1886, CRFPU members accepted Chinese employment only in the plants, not on the boats. Owners obliged the CRFPU because the cost of salmon was always the greatest expense in canning and they feared that organization might drive the price of fish too high. To assuage the CRFPU, after the late 1880s the companies ceased to give positions on the boats to Chinese.[122]

Inspired by the same general conditions in the industry that prompted owners and independent fishermen to hire Chinese as fishermen's assistants in the 1880s, canners looked to Astoria's Chinese to knit gill nets during the off-season as a means to shave costs. Each year companies "let out" thousands of fathoms of twine to the fishermen and Chinese on credit. The knitters then sold the nets back to the canneries as they finished the task. Knitting gill nets, which on the Columbia River ran up to 250 fathoms (1,500 feet) in length, was a tedious and laborious task but required the outlay of little cash because no heavy machinery was necessary. Chinese, neither housed nor fed by the cannery companies during the winters, had to maintain themselves through advances meted out by the cannery to Chinese labor contractors in Astoria. For them, knitting provided additional income and relief from indebtedness to contractors.[123]

As early as 1880 and through the decade, Chinese knit nets for less than half the price white fishermen charged.[124] In spite of lower labor costs, Chinese did not monopolize the task because canners also let out twine to European American fishermen in order to trap them into a cycle of indebtedness that bound them to the company. With each advance of twine or cash against their knitting, they became obliged to fish for the cannery in the spring. If they resisted company orders during the fishing season, owners might privately chastise and publicly embarrass fishermen for the failure to repay debts incurred in knitting the nets. If moral suasion failed, owners did not hesitate to blacklist fishermen or to press law officers and courts to pursue those who absconded without paying debts incurred knitting nets.[125]

The formation of fishermen's unions made the canners more cautious about hiring Chinese to knit, but did not end the practice. In 1909 CRPA secretary George H. George wrote to the Rooster Rock cannery superintendent, "in your entry of knitting . . . you say [a net was] knit by Ah Chow, which is all right but . . . we don't want these men [non-Chinese fishermen] to know that it was knit by a chinaman [*sic*], consequently cut the reference to this out of their account." The cannery was located nearly a hundred miles up the Columbia River in territory where the organization of fishermen in unions was not yet firm. Still, the employment of Chinese had to be kept secret to avoid repercussions from the potentially contentious fishermen.[126]

Chinese fishermen and knitters tried to push beyond the usual boundaries of their cannery employment, but that was possible only in Astoria where Chinese had a sizable presence. At the cannery villages, Chinese worked only in processing. Yet even in Astoria, the inability of Chinese to maintain fishing positions and the necessity of keeping their role in knitting hidden stands as testimony to the power of European American prejudice and their determination to set employment boundaries.

The Chinese were not completely at the mercy of those who might act against them; the labeling process stands as a case in point. Once the Chinese were employed regularly in canneries, they labeled and wrapped all the cans. In 1876 a Columbia River canner began using a machine to apply glue to the labels, which led to a reduction in his Chinese labeling crew. In a backhanded compliment laced with the racial stereotypes of the time, a local reporter noted: "Apropos of the imitative genius of the Chinaman, it was curious to note how readily a heathen mastered the intricacies of this really complicated machine."[127] The growth of Astoria's European American population, more than mechanization, led canners to replace Chinese labelers with "the deserving class" of local residents—the wives and daughters of fishermen and other European American residents. According to the *Daily Astorian* in 1878, these women and girls performed their duties to the "full satisfaction of their employers."[128]

In the era of open immigration and a plentiful supply of Chinese, the owners had no reason to fear that denying Chinese labeling jobs would bring about any labor boycott of the plants. Consequently, throughout the 1880s and into the early 1890s they continued to hire "little girls" who "speedily and neatly place[d] upon [the cans] the proper labels, handling from 2,000 to 4,000 each per day."[129] A decade after the passage of the Chinese Exclusion Act, however, canners faced a labor scarcity in spite of the contraction of industry on the Columbia. Chinese contractors and workers took advantage of that scarcity to demand the return of labeling positions. In 1893, canners responded by discharging the girls, despite the protests of some of Astoria's European Americans, and rehiring Chinese.[130] By the end of the decade, local papers reported that the Chinese again "monopolize[d]" labeling and left "very few women so engaged."[131] In labeling, as in fishing and net knitting, owners at first dictated the terms of employment, but changes in the availability of Chinese enabled workers to reshape some aspects of cannery employment to their advantage.

In spite of the influence the owners exerted, the most visible source of power in laborers' lives was the contractor, whose control varied with the influence of the exclusion legislation and the particular canning locale. During the highly fluid labor market of open immigration, contractors for Astoria's relatively large canneries could not rely solely on surname or district association ties for the recruitment and control of workers, as they did in smaller, remote canneries. In Astoria, though the surnames Wong and Lum frequently appeared on lists of cannery workers, no single surname was dominant. The heavy flow of new Chinese immigrants and the reputation of cannery employment as a reasonable alternative to other jobs in the 1870s and early 1880s drew a diverse group of Chinese to Astoria. At one local cannery, a census enumerator found that 160 Chinese in one bunkhouse spoke "three different and distinct Chinese dialects," which nearly "paralyzed the enumerator and interpreter."[132] Each emigrant district in south China had its own dialect, and the presence of three in a single cannery indicated that contractors did not rely on surname ties in their recruitment.

Without a mutual identification based on common district origins, contractors used other means of control. Indebtedness and immigrant institutions, such as the tongs, provided two alternatives. One contractor, Ah Kow, attempted another: He tried to move into the ranks of cannery capitalists. In the late 1870s he was Astoria's only resident contractor and "the leading spirit among the Chinese." In 1878 he arranged for a ten-year lease on a waterfront lot and planned to build a wharf and cannery on the site. He postponed building the plant until after a visit to China. An inability to finance the cannery or his death in 1879 cut short his entrepreneurial aspirations.[133]

Had Ah Kow succeeded, he might have had a greater influence over workers in his various roles as owner, contractor, and fellow countryman. Outside Astoria, only a few others attempted to take up the course of action Ah Kow had begun. In 1917 Chinese businessmen on the Monterey peninsula opened a cannery, but stiff competition and inconsistent salmon runs so far south forced them to close.[134] More frequently, Chinese with money to invest looked to prospects that required less capital than canneries, such as import–export businesses, truck gardens, laundries, or restaurants. Investments in such enterprises in cannery towns helped contractors recoup some of the wages they paid to workers and also acquire a measure of indirect control over them.[135]

Ah Kow was exceptional, not only for his grand scheme, but also for his early residence in Astoria. At first, most contractors lived permanently in Portland or San Francisco and only temporarily in Astoria. Competition and mergers between the late 1880s and the early 1900s eliminated many Columbia River canneries and drove Chinese contractors out of business, encouraging those who remained to take up residence in the cannery towns in order to monitor the work more closely. CRPA records indicate a dozen or more active contractors on the lower Columbia during the 1890s, but only six survived the mergers at the turn of the century. In the smaller, postexclusion cannery town made up of families instead of seasonal laborers, contractors developed stronger ties to workers and cannery owners. Cannery owners increasingly relied on key individuals to supply crews and tried less often to play contractors one against another. Their goal was to maintain a steady source of labor. Residents of the Chinese settlement also relied more heavily on contractors to represent their interests to the European American community, which helped confirm the social leadership sought by the contractors.[136]

Chan Ah Dogg, Astoria's premier contractor, supplied hundreds of laborers to the CRPA and other companies on the Columbia River and in Alaska.[137] Chan contracted with the CRPA for nearly four decades until the unionization of the canneries eliminated contracting just before World War II. Known to the European American community for his "honesty and reliance" and as Chinatown's unofficial "mayor" and "spirit of progress," he also possessed considerable influence in the Chinese community. He was at one point superintendent of the Chinese school in Astoria and remembered as "nearly a millionaire . . . by Chinese standards."[138]

Chan and the other contractors enhanced their standing within the community by hiring family, friends, and community residents first for cannery jobs, especially off-season positions. Even the children of the Astoria Chinese families, though under age, found cannery employment through the contractors. Unlike rural California, where Chinese gardeners and tenant farmers formed the "social nuclei" of the community, in Astoria contractors stood at the center.[139]

Astoria's mercantile partnerships demonstrate the networks through which contractors could exert influence. In 1924 the deputy commissioner of immigration in Seattle described these partnerships: "Perhaps twenty members pay in $500 each. They do not work in the store, but when they want to bring in a son, they have a salary assigned to them, and they come to the store for a while to prove that they are merchants."[140] By the turn of the century, Chinese efforts to circumvent the exclusion policy, which allowed merchants but not laborers to enter the country, led to the establishment of so many partnerships that the *Astoria Herald*, tongue-in-cheek, opined that "there are in Astoria today about 800 Chinamen, 780 of whom claim to be merchants."[141]

U.S. Customs Service officers kept registers of the partnerships, including those in Astoria. Contributors to the Duck Lung Company partnership, three of whom were contractors, each paid in $500 to the business. Seventeen of eighteen partners in the company shared a common surname. Thus, business and extended clan relations bound cannery laborers and contractors together, as this list of contributors reveals:[142]

Wong Duck	Works in cannery at Coquille[, Oregon]
Wong Lung	In China; went last year, manager
Wong Kee	Contractor and foreman in cannery

Wong Hing	Runs employment agency
Wong Chew	Contractor and cannery boss occasionally
Wong Poon	Working in cannery at Astoria
Wong Hawk	Working in cannery at Astoria
Wong Hop	Working in cannery at Coquille
Wong Yit	Was canneryman laborer, now in Chicago
Wong She	Employed in store as porter
Wong Mo	In China—went this year—workman in cannery, Astoria
Wong Lum Lup	Gardener in Astoria
Wong Lew	Bookkeeper in store
Wong Yung Chin	Gardener in Astoria
Wong Hung Bun	Contractor and cannery boss at Astoria
Lew Ah Jun	Runs employment agency
Wong Sing	Workman in Coquille Cannery
Wong Lip	Cannery [worker], Saiuslaw[, Oregon]
S. H. Gain	Manager, Duck Lung Company [not a partner]

Chinese workers could exert pressure on contractors by invoking informal familial obligations or more formally by requesting assistance through the clan associations, but more likely such ties provided Chinese contractors with another means of control. In addition to Duck Lung Company's store, customs officials reported that the "firm owns building but leases ground. Operates the whole place—one room on ground floor devoted to fan tan game and one for lottery. Quite extensive facilities for washing and cooking. Rent rooms (about six) for about $3.50 per month—about 15 or twenty men."[143]

Duck Lung Company's combination store, casino, and boarding-house rented out rooms to cannery hands in the off-season or to young bachelors who might work only irregularly in the canneries. In spite of the more or less equal contributions to the partnerships, contractors' control of cannery employment helped them maintain an upper hand in the community. The availability of such partnerships also reveals how different the cannery towns were from bunkhouse villages.

Since the mid–1870s, Astoria consistently had offered a greater range of economic activities for workers than the remote cannery sites. Before exclusion, an ethnic economy (trade solely within the Chinese community) supported slightly less than 3 percent of the Chinese in Astoria—small businessmen, professionals, and skilled workers. Their activities in the ethnic economy also employed a small corps of clerks and helpers. The remaining Chinese enterprises in Astoria depended on European American customers for a substantial portion of their income. Laundrymen, gardeners, cooks, and domestics all relied on transactions with the larger Astoria community.[144]

Open immigration and the canning boom did not engender stability in Astoria's ethnic and local economies. Only small Chinese crews stayed during the off-season to label and box cans, to make cans for the next season, or secretly to knit nets. Exact figures are unavailable, but local newspaper accounts suggest that Chinatown's population expanded and contracted dramatically with the canning season.[145] Only with great difficulty did Chinese entrepreneurs attain any year-round success in the ethnic economy. Even for those who traded with, or worked for, non-Chinese, Astoria held very little promise in the off-season. The same seasonal surges in population occurred among European Americans, making business opportunities scarce for all in the winters.[146]

By the turn of the century, the ethnic and local economies had stabilized enough to support a core of small-scale entrepreneurs throughout the year. As a result, small businessmen, laundrymen, and gardeners survived the decline in Astoria's Chinese population far better than did any of the professional, skilled, or common-labor groups. Chinese merchants fared best between 1880 and 1910 and increased on both a numerical and proportional basis (see Appendix, Table 1). In 1880, twenty-seven merchants made up 1.3 percent of the population. By 1900, because of a larger permanent population and perhaps because of the provisions of the exclusion policies, merchants numbered thirty-one and in 1910 thirty-four, or 5.5 and 18.8 percent, respectively, of the Astoria Chinese population.[147]

A smaller Chinese population limited growth opportunities for Chinese who catered to an ethnic economy, but the death knell to such businesses came in 1899 with the completion of the rail link between Astoria and Portland.[148] The rail line made the trip to Portland easy, brief, and inexpensive for Chinese in Astoria. It also made it nearly impossible for Chinese professionals and merchants to compete with those in Portland. Consequently, Astoria became a kind of satellite community of clients for Portland's Chinese. Barbers, for example, dropped in an almost direct proportion to the shrinking Chinese population in Astoria.[149] Skilled workers among the Chinese either moved on after 1880 or opted for employment in the canneries. Cooks and domestics nearly disappeared by 1910, in part because of a growing balance in the sex ratio in the town. In 1890 Astoria's men outnumbered its women by more than two to one (2.2 men for each woman).[150] In 1910 the ratio had dropped to 1.58 men for each woman.[151] Over the same time span, Astoria's population increased dramatically from 2,803 in 1880 to 6,184 in 1890, some 8,381 in 1900, and 9,599 in 1910.[152] Those increases came largely through an influx of working-class families, a group unable to support many Chinese in service occupations.

Of the small businesses still open at the turn of the century, only truck gardening and laundries grew in proportion to the size of the community, these two occupations being supported and sustained by a larger European American population. Chinese in those occupations catering to the ethnic economy dropped from sight, with only those able to serve the larger local economy surviving.[153]

As employment and business opportunities disappeared, the contractors' control of the Chinese community's capital allowed them to monopolize the surviving stores. Some they ran themselves; others they financed. They also maintained their positions, much like merchants in other urban centers, through easy access to the West's Chinese communities and even China. Contractor Jew Mock (Chew Mock) commuted between Astoria and San Francisco and later Oakland, to be near the canneries and workers with whom he contracted during the season, but during the remainder of the season he lived nearer his California enterprises.[154] Likewise, CRPA contractor Chan Ah Dogg traveled between Astoria and China, sometimes taking his family with him. His trips to China involved more than visiting relatives, for he was said to have business "interests" there. His ability to reinvest in China boosted his status among Chinese in Astoria, and his journeys gave him a special conduit to laborers' villages and families.[155] In spite of shrinking opportunities and the increasing power of contractors in the town, workers continued to prefer Astoria jobs to those in bunkhouse villages, for the cannery town offered them a much richer experience.

The Chinese settlement in New Westminster, British Columbia, closely rivaled Astoria in what it offered Chinese residents as a cannery town. It had become the center of Fraser River canning in much the same fashion as Astoria had become the key point on the Columbia: Early canners put their plants in an area they felt most conducive to fishing. New Westminster, in 1884, had British Columbia's second largest Chinese community. With 1,680 Chinese residents, only 87 fewer than Victoria, New Westminster came to be known as *Erbu*, or "second port," among Canada's Chinese. Victoria was *Dabu*, or "premier port."[156]

New Westminster was a cannery town, but it had a much broader economic base than Astoria. Chinese employment patterns reflected that diversity. New Westminster's Chinese relied heavily, but not exclusively, on the canneries for employment. Cannery workers represented 31.4 percent of the unskilled, semiskilled, and service laborers within the community and 23.2 percent of the town's entire Chinese population (see Appendix, Table 2). Farm workers accounted for 32.2 per cent of laborers and 23.8 percent of the total; sawmill workers for 15.3 percent and 11.3 percent, respectively; and ditch diggers for 12.6 percent and 9.3 percent, respectively.[157]

The nature of the Fraser River salmon runs also contributed to the town's relatively small proportion of cannery workers. The plants relied primarily on Sockeye salmon, which ran on a four-year cycle. The runs peaked in the fourth year, were smallest in the third, and were only slightly larger than the third in the other two years. Moreover, the runs were very brief, with the heaviest period lasting only several weeks. Chinese employment reflected that variability. For example, in the large 1897 run, one Fraser River cannery ran from April to June with forty-five Chinese. During these three months, they canned salmon for an average of seventeen days out of the twenty-six possible days each month. In July, 155 men worked an average of 16 days, and in August, 159 men averaged 23.25 days each. Presumably, the run began in the second week of July and continued through most of August. In September, the canner discharged 106 laborers, and the remaining 53 logged an average of 20 days each. That season, workers put up 39,131 cases of salmon, or 4.1 cases each per day.[158]

In 1900, the smallest run in the four-year cycle, the same canner employed only twelve Chinese in April for 2 days; thirty in May for 21.5 days; thirty in June for 9.5 days; sixty-three in July for 6 days; eighty-five in August for 16 days; and none in September. For 1900, the cannery produced only 6,105 cases, or 2.67 cases per person per day. Even with a smaller crew than in 1897, the contractor had overstaffed the plant. Such fluctuations occurred regularly on the Fraser River, but canners could not predict the runs with any accuracy beyond the knowledge of a "big year" every fourth canning season.[159]

Although the size of canning crews varied from month to month and year to year, a small core of Chinese "regulars" returned annually. Others came in only at peak times from Victoria or Vancouver, as well as New Westminster. Members of supplemental crews saw their jobs as short-term and relatively high paying. A great many others preferred more regular employment in the coal mines, sawmills, and agricultural fields.[160]

By 1900, New Westminster still had canneries, but the locus of Chinese activities in the industry had shifted to Vancouver because the latter had surpassed Victoria as the province's major port, and it offered Chinese a relatively large range of job possibilities. As of 1902, the Vancouver community, with 2,053 Chinese, had outstripped that of New Westminster, which had dwindled to 748.[161] Despite the six canneries still operating in New Westminster, Vancouver became the major supplier of cannery labor. In 1902, Lee Cheong, president of the Victoria Chinese Benevolent Association, enumerated 551 Chinese cannery laborers in Vancouver, or 26.8 percent of the community— about the same proportion as in New Westminster during 1884.[162] Cannery work never became as important a source of livelihood in New Westminster or Vancouver as it was in Astoria.

Small-Town Canneries

Astoria and New Westminster, in terms of Chinese labor, were the most significant nineteenth-century cannery towns on the Pacific Coast, yet other settlements also housed many Chinese cannery hands. Chinese workers at the small towns with canneries had economic and social opportunities more akin to those at bunkhouse village settings than those at cannery towns. Still, several canneries stood near sizable Chinese settlements, like that at The Dalles, Oregon. During the 1880s, up to four canneries operated near The Dalles, about 180 miles from the mouth of the Columbia River. In the 1890s, they were consolidated into a single cannery only three miles from the town. The town's location near the rapids of the Columbia, which prevented further navigation upstream, made it the major shipping point for rail and river traffic through the Columbia River gorge. Transportation, not canning, formed the base of the local economy.[163]

The Dalles, in 1880, had 2,232 residents; by 1910, its population had nearly doubled to 4,880. The figures for Chinese in the town do not reflect that trend. In 1880, railroads employed about seven hundred Chinese, or 65 percent of those in Wasco County, where The Dalles is located.[164] The 1890 census identifies only 205 Chinese in the county.[165] The end of railroad construction, as well as the reduced size of the county after the state redrew its boundaries, accounted for some of the drop. In 1900 only 138 Chinese lived in the county, and by 1910, their number was down to 93.[166] While the Chinese population in the county declined steadily, in The Dalles it fluctuated. In 1880, for example, 116 Chinese lived in the town, but only 79 did so in 1890. As of 1900, the number had climbed to 109; then it fell to 77 in 1910 (see Appendix, Table 3). Although the timing of the census enumeration explains some of the swings, seasonal employment opportunities in eastern Oregon's mines and agriculture were also a factor.[167]

In the nineteenth century, The Dalles's Chinese depended on jobs in the railroad-based economy, but the end of railroad construction forced them to rely on employment that catered to the European American community. The completion of the railroads not only spelled unemployment for construction crews but also reduced jobs for laundrymen and cooks who had relied on those workers' patronage. Some jobs remained for section hands, and for a time, an economy less dependent solely on railroads prolonged the life of the Chinese settlement. The Dalles had a small Chinese community that provided greater opportunities than the bunkhouse villages but nothing approaching the social, political, and economic complexity of Astoria.[168]

A decline in railroad work by Chinese contributed to the shrinkage in the Chinese population of The Dalles. The expansion of production in the Seufert Brothers Cannery, however, led to an increase in the number of Chinese employed there, from fifteen in 1900 to thirty-one in 1910. The 1910 crew represented 40 percent of the Chinese in the greater area of The Dalles.[169] The distance from the cannery to the town did not hinder workers' access to the community, for unlike the situation on the lower Columbia, road and rail connections between the cannery and town made transportation easy. Chinese found it possible to enter The Dalles and patronize Chinese businesses if they so desired.

Easy rail access from the cannery to Portland, as well as The Dalles, made it possible for the contractor to earn profits from activities usually intended for cannery hands. At the Seufert Brothers' plant, the Chinese foreman and several workers took control of the garden. Francis, the son of one Seufert brother, commented that

> the Company never said anything about a China boss who kept one or two cannery Chinamen busy in the garden. . . . [F]rom about July on, the China boss would ship several hundred pounds of Chinese vegetables by express to Portland six days a week. Whatever the China boss received for these vegetables was none of the Company's business. This was just one of the sidelines the China cannery foreman had going for himself.[170]

The cannery garden became the contractor's and foreman's truck garden, not a place for supplementing the workers' fare and evoking remembrances of home. Competition with the contractors' garden might also have accounted for the decline, from ten to two, in The Dalles's Chinese truck gardeners between 1900 and 1910.[171]

The "China boss" controlled other sales in the local market. Francis noted: "When the Indians wanted salmon heads they went to the China boss and bought as many as they wanted for 50 cents a sack."[172] Extra income and gardening activities in the bunkhouse villages, in contrast, were too insignificant to attract contractors or foremen. In cannery towns, they fell to specialists, but wherever possible, the contractor or foreman took over the enterprises if any sizable profits could be had.

At Ilwaco, Washington, across the Columbia River from Astoria, the establishment of a small cannery in the first decade of the twentieth century created employment for approximately two dozen Chinese. In the last decade of the nineteenth century the town had five hundred to six hundred residents, but no Chinese appeared in the census until 1900. In that year, ten Chinese immigrants lived in Ilwaco: a domestic servant for a farmer, a saloon worker, a cook for a boardinghouse, two laundrymen, and five gardeners.[173] As in many of the West's numerous small towns, they relied on the service sector for their employment. By 1910, thirty-one Chinese—including twenty cannery hands, a cannery foreman with his wife and four children, a laundryman, and four truck gardeners—lived in the town. The market for fresh vegetables kept several Chinese in business, but gardening did not attract the contractor's attention as it did in The Dalles.[174]

Ilwaco cannery workers remained separate and had infrequent contact with other Chinese in the town. According to the contractor's son, the Chinese did not "go into town for a show," and only one of them went weekly to pick up the mail for the entire crew. For diversion they cared for the cannery garden, talked among themselves, read newspapers, played cards, and some took "a puff, couple puff of the opium pipe," or made "their own [whiskey,] but mostly for cooking or a little for themselves." On rare occasions, several workers rowed the four miles across the Columbia to the Astoria Chinatown.[175] Only the possibility of travel to Astoria set these Ilwaco cannery hands apart from those in bunkhouse villages.

In other plants near small towns where income from gardening did not prove great enough to attract contractors or truck gardeners, cannery workers occasionally profited. At Cathlamet, Washington, which had a permanent population of three hundred to five hundred and an average of two dozen Chinese at the cannery each season in the first decade of the twentieth century, one man, known only as "China Jim," worked in the local cannery and moonlighted as a gardener and day laborer. China Jim fertilized his garden with manure from the stables in town and, according to local accounts, brought his "produce to town . . . suspended from a yoke on his shoulders."[176] China Jim gained a degree of celebrity status among Cathlamet residents. He helped them with their own gardens in addition to selling his goods, but most of all, his generous supply of lichee nuts and candy and his passion for flying kites made him immensely popular with local children. China Jim also made his mark by consistently interacting with local European American residents. Although he stayed in Cathlamet only a few years and locals are not certain where he went, China Jim remains in the town's historical annals as "ambitious, friendly, and polite," a far different collective memory of the Chinese immigrant than is to be found in most small towns with nearby canneries.[177]

Despite the favorable memories that Cathlamet residents had for China Jim, the town's small European American population supported few Chinese outside the cannery. As of 1900, it had only a single truck gardener and five cooks in logging camps or private homes.[178] The population did not increase much in the first decade of the twentieth century, and in 1910, only 352 people resided in Cathlamet.[179]

While Cathlamet's early twentieth-century residents accorded China Jim special status, during the nineteenth century they had tried hard to segregate the few Chinese in their community. Their efforts were reflected in the structure of the cannery bunkhouse. "There was a high board wall around what can only be described as [the] courtyard" of the bunkhouse, explained a long-time Cathlamet resident. "This protective wall was due to early violence on the Columbia River against the Chinese." The remainder of the bunkhouse was "almost windowless," another attempt to prevent harm to workers.[180] Cathlamet's physical barriers hemmed in Chinese residents, just as the clear, though informal, boundaries did in Astoria.

The development of southeast Alaska's fishery, mining, and timber industries contributed to the growth of small towns populated by European Americans. At the turn of the century, the village at Loring, Alaska, consisted of several hundred "permanent" residents. In addition to a cannery, the town also had a trading post, a sawmill, and two fish-oil processing plants. Loring's employees lived at the cannery but could go into the town.[181]

Contact between Chinese and Native American residents in Alaska was similar to such interactions in other regions. While Chinese at The Dalles sold fish heads to Native Americans, Chinese in Alaska sold *Sam Shu*, "Chinese gin," at inflated prices to Native Alaskans, other local residents, and the non-Chinese cannery laborers. The beverage, which in San Francisco cost 90 cents a gallon, sold for $8 a gallon in Alaska, in part because it was illegal in the territory. Some of the gin trade was on a small scale and carried out by individuals. With a relative lack of enforcement of the prohibition statute, large-scale sales also took place, and just as in the states when an enterprise promised substantial gains, contractors probably took control of it.[182]

Of the Alaska canneries, those in Ketchikan held the greatest opportunities for Chinese. During the first decade of the twentieth century, the town had more than a thousand residents and several sawmills
and canneries. While Ketchikan bore a resemblance to the cannery
towns, it had no Chinese community. Instead, by 1910, it had a small
Asian population of three Chinese, nineteen Japanese, and two Filipinos. While the level of interaction among these Asians, who worked as
cooks, laundrymen, and common laborers, remains unknown, chances
for Chinese to meet other Asians existed at Ketchikan, something not
available at places like Loring. Wrangell and Juneau also had small
Asian populations. These clusters of Asians further reduced the relative
isolation for Chinese at nearby southeast Alaska canneries. Those Asian
populations were very small, usually only a handful of households, and
had nothing akin to the complex Asian American social and cultural
milieu available to Chinese in the cannery towns of Astoria and New
Westminster.[183]

Industrywide, Chinese formed social units that reflected the setting in
which they toiled. At the bunkhouse villages, the isolation, the cannery
structures, the owners' cost-cutting strategies, and workers' positions
as "bachelor" laborers gave Chinese few materials with which to work.
They fashioned relationships among themselves in those bunkhouses
and gardens, or at the water's edge that reflected familiar patterns. In
the several cannery towns along the coast, by contrast, their actions
did not center so heavily on the cannery. They did have to contend
with contractors who sought to establish themselves as the social nuclei
of the communities, but on the whole they found fewer restrictions in
their social and economic activities than they did at the bunkhouse
villages. Life in the cannery towns was richer, but no less challenging,
since Chinese also faced larger and often hostile European American
populations. Between the two extremes were the canneries on the social and economic periphery of small towns. There, contractors' control and workers' opportunities varied. Of the three cannery settings,
this was perhaps the most difficult. Workers had no real opportunities
outside the control of the contractors or foremen, and they still came
into contact with potentially hostile local populations. Yet a few, like
China Jim, managed to survive. In the West's urban oases and in a
seasonal, extractive industry, Chinese adapted and survived by fabricat-
ing communities out of their immigrant work experiences.

4

Competitors for the Chinese

RATHER THAN use Chinese laborers alone to pack salmon into the cans by hand, "we will do nearly as well as the previous years by using filling machines during the heavy part of the run." So Carl A. Sutter of the Fidalgo Island Packing Company (FIPC) explained to his financial partners in British Columbia on the eve of the 1907 season.[1] He observed that even though "reliable" Chinese demanded higher rates than before and that company managers could "get Rail Road [*sic*] Chinese contractors at anything we may ask, . . . to let the contract to such parties [is] certainly out of [the] question."[2] Sutter urged his partners to pay extra for experienced Chinese contractors and laborers who "understand the cannery work."[3] FIPC managers thus faced a dilemma common at the turn of the century—how to cope with a growing labor shortage in the midst of tremendous industrial expansion. Partial automation of its lines and the placement of thirty Japanese alongside seventy Chinese in the plant resolved the immediate problem for FIPC managers.[4] Arriving at such a decision was not easy, for many cannery owners hesitated to spend large sums on machinery that ran on a seasonal basis and clung to the notion that only Chinese could adequately perform cannery tasks.[5] As the FIPC solution indicates, canners overcame their resistance to mechanization and the utilization of non-Chinese workers.

While new applications of technology and the creation of a multiethnic internal labor market separated the experiences of nineteenth- and twentieth-century cannery workers, the unremitting efforts of canners to exploit Pacific salmon drove the changes. The dramatic increase in the number of plants dotting the banks of streams and bays, from 91 in 1890 to 165 in 1900 and ultimately to a high of 306 during the boom years of World War I, illustrates the rate at which canners pulled salmon from the waters.[6] To contend with that expansion in an era of shrinking labor supply, canners explored new technology while they pressured contractors to continue to staff the canning lines. Once company owners found that contractors might effectively recruit Japanese and later other ethnic groups, they chose to rely on a flexible labor supply and labor-intensive processing techniques rather than trying to achieve full automation, which required great capital investments.

The new ethnic groups transformed the industry's labor market from the two-tiered structure with European American fishermen in the upper echelon and Chinese cannery hands in the lower to one in which the lower rank was divided, but in which Chinese established a "labor aristocracy" over the newer Asian and nonwhite entrants.[7] How Chinese came to achieve their place of privilege, how new ethnic groups sought to strengthen their positions, and how and when owners decided to apply new technology illustrates the abilities of immigrants to organize their working lives amid tremendous ethnic fragmentation and competition.

The Foray into Mechanization

Before the 1890s, a ready supply of relatively inexpensive Chinese labor did not encourage canners to replace Chinese with costly, often experimental, technology. Instead, owners most frequently installed machinery that enhanced labor-intensive processing techniques. For example, power gang-knives introduced in various forms after the 1890s made the task less taxing physically than the hand-cranked apparatus and raised workers' productivity. They also kept the processing lines running more smoothly because the belt-driven knives jammed less often than the hand-cranked ones. Further, the size of the cut could be adjusted as easily with the power knives as with the hand crank. Hand-cranked gang-knives continued to be used in the smaller plants for many years, but most owners readily employed some form of machine-powered knives.[8]

Other innovations necessitated larger crews. Cooking was the lengthiest step in processing. To quicken the pace, owners used stronger retorts and heated the full cans only once. Single cooking replaced the older method of cooking, venting, resealing, and recooking the cans and cut in half the time spent on the task. These changes increased productivity in the canneries without eliminating positions and may even have demanded larger crews as a bottleneck in production was overcome.[9]

Nonetheless, some machines did displace laborers. As early as 1881, Chinese at one British Columbia plant walked off their jobs at the peak of the season because a soldering machine led to the elimination of skilled tinsmiths. The strike forced the owner to set aside the machine that season, but in the following year he and the contractor arrived at an agreement that permitted machine soldering.[10] Still, as late as 1901, workers were protesting the machine's use. In that year, owners of a British Columbia plant hired Chinese "to finish up the tail end of the pack." The laborers understood their job to be soldering, but the canners wanted them to operate the machines. "As soon as it was understood that most of the work was to be done by the machine," noted a San Francisco newspaper, "without a sound [the Chinese workers] picked up their belongings and fled out of the cannery."[11] Most workers' protests were ad hoc, since the uneven application of new machinery gave contractors the luxury of shifting skilled workers to plants that had yet to adopt the technology.[12]

Hand and machine soldering coexisted until the early 1910s when the introduction of the "sanitary" can, really a process in which the cans' ends and lids were crimped together and an airtight seal guaranteed by the use of a rubber sealing compound or paper gasket, made moot the question of using skilled Chinese to seal cans. The application of this latest sealing technology reflected owners' desires to capitalize on the value of the raw material by eliminating waste more than efforts to replace workers. Leaky cans had always been a problem, and the new can nearly eliminated spoilage, formerly expected to run as high as 10 percent of the pack.[13]

Sanitary cans represented the canners' twentieth-century drive for efficiency and the search for machines that replaced labor-intensive activities. Proponents of the much-heralded "Iron Chink," or automatic fish butchering machine, claimed it required only two operators and eliminated the need for ten to twenty men. The manufacturer capitalized on the popular lore that the inventor had devised the machine specifically to displace the Chinese, who were unworthy recipients of cannery wages, but the heavy reliance on anti-Chinese rhetoric failed to bring many immediate sales. Owners responded slowly to the use of the machine because they were reluctant to forego hand butchering. Hand cuts wasted less meat, and skilled butchers easily adjusted to different-size fish. Such was not the case with machines.[14] Of 156 canneries on the coast in 1904, a year after the Iron Chink's introduction, only 5 companies used twenty-three automatic butchers; of those firms, 2 had 19 of the machines and focused their efforts on packing a lower grade of Alaska salmon.[15] In the following year, seven firms used twenty-nine units.[16] According to regional newspapers, by the end of the 1907 season the Iron Chink still had not made "any particular inroads into [the Chinese workers'] vocation of fish cleaning."[17]

In the 1910s, more companies used the automatic butchering machines but placed them only in canneries where the salmon runs and type of salmon packed justified their use. The Columbia River Packers Association (CRPA), with plants in Alaska and along the Columbia River, put different kinds of machinery in each cannery. In Alaska, the company used machines for the bulk of the pack because the short, heavy salmon runs encouraged concentration on lower-grade salmon put up in uniform lots of one-pound tall cans.[18] At Astoria, it used some machines, but large portions of the pack continued to be processed by hand. There the longer and steadier flow of salmon past the plants, the great variations in the size of Chinook on the Columbia, and the availability of labor (contract or otherwise) led the company to concentrate on high-priced, hand-butchered, hand-packed Chinook salmon and to continue its reliance on labor-intensive techniques.[19] At its small Rooster Rock Cannery, nearly a hundred miles upriver from Astoria, the company relied solely on hand butchering and employed only the machinery cast aside by superintendents at the company's other plants. While part of the rationale for this strategy was the same as at Astoria, the smaller and erratic catches at Rooster Rock meant that heavy mechanization would not have been economically profitable.[20] Regional variations in the application of technology reflected owners' strategies for effective extraction, processing, and marketing. The sales of butchering machines increased in the canning boom of World War I because of huge government contracts for uniformly packed, low-grade salmon. Those who brought in the machines to reduce waste remained disappointed until the 1920s when improvements in the machinery "practically eliminate[d] waste of raw material."[21]

The Scarcity of Labor

Although owners only slowly adopted the butchering machine before World War I, they were interested in it from the outset as an alternative to increasingly scarce and uncooperative Chinese labor. With industry expansion in the 1890s, contractors tried to recruit beyond their accustomed networks, but that weakened their hold over the new laborers. In San Francisco, Chinese workers took advantage of the strained ties and new demand for their services to ask for advances up to $200 (half a season's wages). Some enterprising workers even went to two or more contractors for advance money and then failed to appear when the ships were ready to depart for the north. In 1902, when Congress renewed the legislation that excluded Chinese, San Francisco newspapers estimated that several hundred laborers had absconded with their advances, far more than in any previous season.[22]

Beleaguered contractors tried a variety of methods to control their losses. In San Francisco some hired the Morse Detective Agency to "assist" them in forcing workers to show up at the ship on time;[23] one contractor posted notices in Chinatown offering $20 to anyone who brought runaways back to him;[24] and a few threatened legal action in local courts, perhaps hoping to discourage those who feared deportation from absconding.[25] Even the most prominent contractors were not immune to workers "stealing themselves." Chew Bun, labor supplier for canneries and farms, lost $20 to $200 each from workers who ran off with their advances. Chew Bun did not rely on the court system but administered punishments himself. One local paper explained that he was "merciless when he detected a breach of faith," but the journalist neglected to explain what action might have been taken.[26]

Detectives, rewards, legal suits, and violence did little to solve the problem, and in 1904 the contractors adopted what they hoped would be a more effective policy. They tried to entrap workers by reducing significantly the amount of the cash advances and hiring only those who purchased unnecessary dry goods and clothing at inflated prices on credit against their season's wages. When workers returned from the canneries, they found themselves deeper in debt, for contractors had cut wages for common laborers by 40 percent, and some failed to pay at all. The small cash advances and limited wages fostered indebtedness and dependency among workers. By mid-decade, the resources for escaping the northward trip were no longer available.[27]

At least some Chinese workers tried to counter contractors by forming unions. In 1904, Chinese in British Columbia established the short-lived Chinese Cannery Employees Union in response to contractors' failures to pay wages at the end of the season, but it made no headway with the contractors or the canners in British Columbia.[28] In 1905 the *Portland Oregonian* reported that in Astoria Charlie Lee, a "walking delegate . . . [and] representative of the Chinese labor union," had lodged a protest on behalf of Chinese whose wages for the previous season had been withheld. The paper's use of the term "walking delegate" to describe Lee indicates a possible link to the International Workers of the World (IWW), whose organizers traveled from site to site to bring workers into one big union, and though records are scarce, some of them were Asians. Regardless of Lee's association with the IWW, canners and local law officials blocked his efforts, and the workers never received their back pay.[29]

Canners and contractors had no tolerance for union activities among Chinese. In 1904 one British Columbia packing company paid its contractor, Lee Coy (also known as Lee Coey), extra to assure that workers would not join a union or strike during that season.[30] In 1906 Columbia River contractor Sit Que wrote to the CRPA that he was "willing to inform" on any workers and contractors associated with the "Chinese Union" because he "hated unions." In exchange for such services, he demanded that the CRPA retain him as its contractor and pay an additional, but modest, increase in the per case contract price in order to ensure nonunion Chinese crews. The CRPA rejected Sit's offer because its managers believed their present contractors were able to prevent union activities among the workforce.[31]

The combined effects of industrial expansion and declining Chinese numbers after the exclusion laws made futile workers' attempts to abscond or organize unions. The situation only encouraged owners and contractors to look outside the Chinese community for additional workers. In 1905, the year after Congress made Chinese exclusion permanent, contractors for the Alaska Packers Association (APA) introduced non-Chinese workers on a large scale and retained only the most essential Chinese employees. In 1904 the company had hired through contractors 3,132 Chinese for its canneries, but in 1905 it employed only 1,236.[32] It allowed contractors to fill the remainder of the crews with workers from other ethnic backgrounds. The precipitous drop in Chinese employment prompted severe criticism of contractors by Chinese leaders in San Francisco. They feared that the community's capability to provide relief to the unemployed might be overtaxed if contractors failed to hire their usual quota. Community leaders established a committee to meet with the ten San Francisco contractors and encouraged them to hire only Chinese.[33] In 1906, APA contractors largely ignored those requests and hired roughly the same number of Chinese (1,413) as the previous year. Thereafter, they employed even fewer, and by 1921, the company workforce included only 282 Chinese.[34]

As the number of Chinese shrank, those remaining developed closer ties to contractors, who cultivated those connections by rewarding loyal workers with better assignments, a task made easier by the staggered application of technology. In the first two decades of the twentieth century Wong On, a prominent cannery and agricultural contractor, sent older, skilled Chinese workers with whom he had the best relationships to coastal Oregon canneries that relied heavily on hand labor and had a relatively slow pace of work. For his Columbia River crews, he hired experienced Chinese from the Northwest's cities and towns. Finally, he staffed the crews to be sent to isolated and mechanized Alaska plants with the youngest, least-skilled Chinese, as well as non-Chinese, from San Francisco. Even in the Alaska crews a contractor might "feather bed" and hire older workers for lighter cannery jobs such as clean-up or "supervision." Since all such positions depended on good relations with the contractor, workers found that their efforts to resist rewarded them with no employment or with jobs in the worst places.[35]

Local Labor Sources and Regional Variations

The willingness of contractors to hire non-Chinese but retain a corps of skilled Chinese helped canners use a mix of men and machines to exploit the salmon runs to the fullest. It also enabled Chinese to establish an "aristocracy of labor" with themselves at the top and newcomers at the bottom. While the transformation in the labor market united Chinese, the new entrants fell into two groups: Native Americans and European Americans living in the vicinity of the canneries and immigrants from abroad.

Canners found Native Americans desirable because they fed and housed themselves, thereby freeing owners of that cost. Their residence near the plants made it possible for companies to hire them by the day as needed. Owners also hoped that the reliance on wage labor created by employing women and children in the plants might discourage men from striking for higher fish prices. Finally, companies tried to recoup wages paid to families through company stores just as they did with other non-Chinese employees. Bringing Native Americans into a monetary economy through the canneries encouraged a dependency among Native Americans that immensely benefited owners.[36]

But in spite of lower costs, canners remained reluctant to rely solely on Native Americans. They wanted workers "willing to give their labor at all times," but Indian men had little desire to give themselves over to company control.[37] One federal investigator noted that an Indian man was too frequently "seized with the desire to leave; he must hunt, or he must fish for his family, although his wages for a day will purchase more fish than he can catch in a week; still he must go, and he goes."[38] The canners could not depend on men who refused to sacrifice their independence completely. In locations where several companies established plants, problems with Indian labor were compounded by workers playing the companies against each other. As a result, canners used Indian men to supplement "outside" fishermen transported to the plants.[39]

Owners were more pleased with Native American women, to whom they attributed an "immemorial instinct" in handling salmon, particularly in the task of sliming. Canners also believed, though, that women's "intelligence only warrants giving them some work."[40] Few in the industry conceded that women were capable of attending machines, doing heavy jobs like handling trays, or performing skilled tasks. As long as Chinese labor was plentiful, canners employed Indian women primarily as a means of gaining leverage with contractors. In 1887 Benjamin Young threatened to hire "clootchmen"—Native American women—to replace the Chinese crew if his contractor, Lee Coey, failed to provide adequate help.[41] At the beginning of the twentieth century, contractors themselves needed to hire women to supplement their dwindling crews. This led to competition for their services. At the FIPC Ketchikan, Alaska, cannery in 1912, the superintendent complained: "The other contract[ors] are enticing our Indians away and paying more wages than Seid Back can possibly do [*sic*]." Seid nevertheless responded with similar wages because failure to supply enough labor would eventually lead a company to seek a new supplier.[42]

The differing availability of Native Americans for cannery work from region to region affected their place in the canneries. In British Columbia, the relatively large Indian population created strong competition within the labor market, and they rivaled the Chinese in power and influence. The strong divisions that emerged in the British Columbia canneries between Chinese and Native Americans, and later among them and European Americans and Japanese, hindered unionization. It took cannery workers in British Columbia a decade longer to organize a union than their counterparts in the United States.[43]

In southeast Alaska, the employment of natives was at an even higher rate than at other U.S. canneries. In the nineteenth and early twentieth centuries, most plants in the district averaged twenty to forty Indians. Only at Klawak and Metlakatla did solely Native American crews pack salmon—temporarily at Klawak and under special circumstances at Metlakatla. At Klawak, one of the first two cannery sites in Alaska, cannery operations began in 1878 with Native American labor, not Chinese. Until 1896, company owners employed Native Americans, but between 1896 and 1900, owners brought in contracted Chinese crews because of a growing rift between Indian workers and managers.[44]

At Metlakatla in the late 1880s, a missionary, the Reverend William Duncan, helped transplant a Christian utopian community of Native Americans from Canada. In 1890 the community-run plant operated with only Native American labor. Duncan and other church leaders believed that the cannery should provide for the economic and spiritual well-being of the community. While the wages paid to Metla-

katlans were one-third more than those at nearby canneries relying on
the prevailing contract system, half of it was in coin and the other
half in script redeemable only at the company store. That arrangement
effectively halved the cost of their labor and made the venture
profitable.[45]

In other U.S. canning regions, only plants in northern California
relied heavily on Indian labor. Owners in Del Norte County proclaimed that they hired local Indians as day laborers because of "a
strong objection to the employment of Chinese in the county."[46] Canners must also have been reluctant to support contract crews for the
small and erratic operations in northern California. For the same reasons, Chinese seemed to avoid the area because it provided them with
no steady income. Though staffed by Native Americans, the northern
California plants played no significant role in the industry.[47]

In the canneries of central Alaska, owners also tried to hire Indians
from nearby villages to supplement their crews, but the limited Native
Alaskan populations and intense competition for local labor meant that
canners could not count on Native Alaskans as a steady source of workers. To draw them in, owners and contractors devised strategies for
recruiting Indians. At the APA Alitak Bay Cannery, Chew Mock and
cannery managers arranged for the villagers' transportation to and
from the cannery.[48] Transplanting the entire village next to the APA
plant made it difficult for other companies to draw on the residents for
their operations. Only on heavily populated Kodiak Island did canners
find it relatively easy to recruit Indian and Creole laborers.[49]

Canners also tried to attract Native American workers by providing medical care. The annual arrival of company fishermen and contract crews introduced many diseases to Indians, particularly influenza,
measles, gonorrhea, and syphilis. While large companies like the APA
and CRPA dispensed free care, their purpose was to maintain a ready
supply of healthy, productive workers. Similarly, owners condoned
missionary and educational activities, especially those of their managers, with the intent of attracting Indians to the cannery locale. CRPA
superintendent J. S. Osmund and his wife helped establish a school
near the company's Chignik cannery. The Osmunds hoped to instill in
the members of the Chignik community personal hygiene and work
habits as well as new religious beliefs. CRPA managers thought that
the school would not only draw Indians to the site but also "helps us
out considerable [sic] with the Territorial government."[50] The canners
needed to maintain good relations with the territory in order to continue mining salmon from Alaska waters. For similar reasons, the APA

supported the establishment of schools.[51] Political favor thus played no small role in canners' provisions for Native American laborers.

In western Alaska, the competition among canners for Indian labor was even more intense than in central Alaska. At Nushagak, where as many as ten canneries operated in a given season before the 1930s, the small Native American population of several hundred provided few workers per cannery. At the CRPA plant, for example, no more than four Native Americans worked "inside," and only twenty fished for the company. The cannery location, nearly thirty miles from the village, also severely limited the company's ability to recruit workers. Sparse population and the clustering of canneries near major streams made the CRPA's experience typical for western Alaska.[52]

Puget Sound canners had different options. In the nineteenth century they had created a dependency for wages among Native Americans like that encouraged by operators in British Columbia and southeast Alaska. By the first decade of the twentieth century, the European American presence in small towns along Puget Sound had increased dramatically. Shared ethnic backgrounds with those new residents encouraged canners to hire what they believed to be the "more deserving" European American women in their plants. Just as with Native Americans, employment of wives and daughters of fishermen helped canners use the entire family to control its overall fish and labor costs. In the 1920s and 1930s, canners also cultivated the favor of these workers for political battles with state and federal governments, which attempted to restrict commercial fisheries.[53]

Aside from a close identification with European American "settlers" and the political advantages of their employment, Puget Sound canners also moved away from Indian employment because their plants, built in the late 1890s, utilized the most modern and mechanized canning lines of the day to put up the brief and heavy runs of Sockeye salmon headed for spawning grounds in British Columbia. They believed Native Americans incapable of operating these machines, and by the turn of the century Indian employment in the Puget Sound canneries had virtually ceased, leaving only Asians and European Americans.[54]

Owners of coastal Oregon and Washington plants during the nineteenth century had also employed a few local residents. Robert Hume, the "Salmon King" of the Rogue River, in 1896 allocated for Chinese labor five times the amount he paid to Native Americans and ten times that for European Americans.[55] This ratio slowly changed. In the first two decades of the twentieth century, Washington's coastal canners took the lead in employing local whites rather than Chinese or Indians.

Between 1890 and 1910, anti-Chinese sentiment along the Washington coast ran high among local residents, who drove away all Chinese but those in the canneries. In 1905, one Washington newspaper editor noted that during the fall salmon run "this part of the year is the only time that Chinese labor is employed [in Aberdeen], all being at the cannery." For the rest of the year, he continued, "not even a Chinese laundry is tolerated."[56] Grays Harbor boosters had great hopes that the bay might become a major Pacific shipping port. The lumber and salmon industries fed their aspirations for a time, and the local population grew dramatically. As on the Puget Sound, owners hired local white residents. By the 1910s, Washington coastal canners were employing mixed crews of Chinese and European Americans. In 1915 the Barnes Packing Company at South Bend even began the season without its "regular complement" of Chinese labor and instead employed "local talent." Still, Chinese were not entirely out of the running, as the community newspaper noted: "It is possible that the regular crew of Chinese will be put on later."[57]

Coastal canners used nearby residents as a bargaining tool with contractors. In 1911, the Kurtz Packing Company broke with its contractor over his "unreasonable demands" and ran its cannery with local labor. Apparently the contractor had tried to change the terms after the original agreement had been signed. Much of the dispute centered on the company's desire to add filling machinery to the canning line. The contractor and his Chinese crew wanted to retain hand packing because the coastal canneries had become a special province for older, skilled Chinese. The contractor lost and the company added machines. While the managers of Kurtz Packing Company publicly lamented increased costs associated with inexperienced local labor, the new mechanization allowed for greater production and lower labor costs. Managers also pointedly announced that its new strategy would "be the means of supporting from 20 to 40 more [European American] families."[58] The Kurtz Packing Company thus played on local boosterism and appeared the hero to local anti-Chinese forces while skirting Chinese demands for contractual changes and resistance to mechanization.

Similar changes also undermined the Chinese position in Oregon's coastal canneries. In 1888 only sixty-one (14 percent) of the cannery employees were white. By 1909, the number of coastal cannery employees had dropped from 440 to 292, but the percentage of white workers had risen to 25 percent.[59] In the next decade and a half, the trend accelerated, but by the middle and late 1920s refrigerated trucks traveled on the new highways that connected the coast with the fresh fish markets of the Willamette Valley's towns and cities. Better prices for fresh salmon in those new markets put an end to most coastal canning and consequently Chinese employment.[60]

Japanese Arrivals

While the number of Chinese and their job opportunities declined between 1900 and 1920, canners were not able to staff all their plants with Native American and European American workers, and they continued to rely on Chinese contractors. They in turn drew on a growing supply of migrants and immigrants arriving in the U.S. West. In particular, the Japanese came to form an important segment of the cannery labor market.

Before 1900, relatively few Japanese made the journey to the United States. Frequently, they were political refugees fleeing the new Meiji government or were "schoolboys"; the latter were an admixture of those seeking education outside Japan but unable to finance it without working and those intent on learning English as an avenue to success in some small-scale entrepreneurial activity.[61] Beginning in the mid-1890s, a wave of Japanese labor immigrants from Hawaii and Japan surpassed the earlier arrivals in number and significance. Between 1892 and 1910 alone, some eighty thousand Japanese entered the United States. By 1900, California, Oregon, and Washington had Japanese populations of 10,151, 2,501, and 5,617, respectively. By 1910, Oregon's Japanese residents increased their number to 3,418, Washington to 12,929, and California to 41,356.[62] Washington was an important destination, especially the Seattle area, which in the first two decades of the twentieth century had the largest Japanese population among the Far West's urban centers. In 1910 it had 3,212 Japanese to San Francisco's 1,781, and in 1920 it continued to maintain its lead with 7,457 to San Francisco's 4,518.[63]

Large-scale emigration from Japan grew out of the government's push for rapid industrialization, which was meant to help ward off European and American imperial designs on the nation and to assist in the establishment of a Japanese empire. While industrialization strengthened the nation-state, it did so largely at the expense of the agricultural sector. Beginning in 1873, the government switched from taxes payable in kind and based on production to a more stable land tax paid in currency.[64] While the new tax program gave the Meiji state a more predictable income, it had the effect of forcing farmers into debt to pay taxes, particularly in years of poor harvests. Moreover, the government's deflationary monetary policy and fiscal retrenchment of the 1880s ultimately forced a great many peasants into tenancy and wage labor. Although it was possible for residents in eastern Japan to seek employment opportunities in the new industries in places like Hokkaido, which was under heavy development, western Japanese who lived on small marginal plots had few alternative sources of income. Government legalization of emigration in 1885 and the assistance officials gave Hawaiian sugar planters in recruiting laborers in western Japan facilitated the labor immigration to Hawaii and subsequently the U.S. mainland. Once the Japanese established networks of fellow villagers and family members abroad, the process was self-sustaining as long as income was needed and employment was available.[65] The waning of Chinese immigration to the United States in the midst of the American West's burgeoning extractive enterprises made the supply of western Japanese laborers all the more critical.

Japanese worked in salmon canneries as early as 1874, but three factors kept their numbers low before the turn of the century: the relatively plentiful supply of Chinese labor before the 1882 Exclusion Act, the ability of Chinese to limit entry into cannery jobs, and Japan's limitations on emigration before 1885.[66] Nineteenth-century Japanese immigrants who found employment in the industry worked as fishermen in British Columbia, and a small minority were engaged in Puget Sound plants among a sea of Chinese. By 1900, a new trend in Japanese employment had begun. One Chinese contractor sent a crew of fifty Japanese to a Bristol Bay cannery in western Alaska. The owners had encouraged the contractor to hire them on an experimental basis and hoped to avoid high-priced Chinese labor.[67] Elsewhere in the territory, only one or two worked at any given cannery, most often as cooks for fishermen or cannery managers. Managers of plants with Japanese laborers complained that the new immigrants "were not only lazy and worthless, but were constantly raising a disturbance."[68] While their greater number in these canneries may have encouraged Japanese workers to protest conditions, they remained a small and isolated percentage of the crews.

Through immigration, Japanese made an even larger showing in Puget Sound canneries than they did in Alaska plants. In 1900 some 153 Japanese worked in five cannery crews at Fairhaven (later part of Bellingham). Ninety-six percent had immigrated in 1898, 1899, or 1900; 69 percent in 1900 alone.[69] Tremendous growth in Puget Sound mills and railroads provided many jobs and stimulated the growth of large new communities. In 1890 Seattle had only 125 Japanese, but as it became the major northern port and rail link, its economic base provided for 2,990 Japanese residents in 1900. That growth in Seattle was mirrored in other cities and towns on Puget Sound and all along the coast.[70]

With such a ready source of new laborers, companies and their contractors rarely resorted to overseas recruitment. The only exception was the APA, which in 1903 and again in 1906 tried to recruit Japanese plantation workers from Hawaii. It found few employees for its efforts, but repeated its program in 1911 and 1913, only this time to induce Hawaiians and Filipinos to emigrate.[71] The APA's intermittent recruitment program was an anomaly in the industry. The newer immigrants provided a pool of labor on which most canners, through the contractors, drew. In the Pacific Northwest contractors had to make only minimal efforts to hire Japanese. In 1905 cannery contractors went to the dock in Tacoma, Washington, and enticed away Japanese brought to the country for work on the railroads.[72]

At the turn of the century, most cannery owners still believed Chinese to be far superior to other workers. They pressured contractors to provide crews of "first class and experienced men" and that prevented contractors from hiring only Japanese at lower wages. Between 1900 and 1910, Japanese usually made up about a quarter of contract crews. In a typical season the CRPA Nushagak, Alaska, plant had eighty-three Chinese and twenty-two Japanese. The company's contractor Chew Chew had to promise the CRPA that he would hire Japanese only "in the case that Chinese laborers are scarce."[73] Once the regular crews had been filled, however, canners did not discriminate. In 1902, for example, the CRPA wrote to one cannery superintendent about the necessity of hiring additional workers during a rush period: "Tell your boss Chinaman there that he must get a half-dozen more men, either Chinamen or Japs."[74] The managers of the CRPA, and of most other companies, quickly came to the conclusion that the addition of Japanese in the crews was "all right so far as it goes," as long as the contractor satisfied "the terms of . . . the contract."[75]

Contractors hired these new workers at the lowest wage levels. Canners attempted to take their share of the labor savings rather than simply allow a contractor to put "more money in his pocket" by supplying cheaper workers. In 1904 the FIPC warned Hop Chong Lung Kee and Company: "Remember we do not pay any fares on Japs, as there are lots of unskilled labor [*sic*] at Ketchikan."[76] In 1906 the CRPA demanded that Chew Chew and Chew Mock pay half the transportation costs for Japanese who had shipped out of San Francisco. By 1908, the company had altered its policy and forced the Chews to hire Japanese only from Portland in order to save the firm money.[77]

Owners could not be assured that the preferential hiring of Chinese would guarantee good crews. Early in the 1902 season, the superintendent of the CRPA Nushagak cannery complained to company managers: "I endeavored to Pack the King Salmon by Hand Filling, but found that but one Chinaman and one Jap knew anything about the work."[78] In 1909 the CRPA notified Lam On that in the crew of thirteen Chinese and ten Japanese at its small Rooster Rock plant on the Columbia River, "the Japs are of very little use and . . . some of the Chinese are not much better."[79] In spite of managerial mumblings, at least a few Japanese acquired canning acumen very quickly and moved into skilled positions. In 1911 a coastal canner bragged that he had "one of the most experienced fish handlers on the coast, a Japanese."[80]

Chinese made efforts to guard the canning skills they had acquired by trying to keep certain aspects of the tasks secret. They hoped that this would prevent owners or contractors from displacing them with their less expensive Japanese competitors. They had limited success in this endeavor because they could do little to prevent determined Japanese from observing them. In addition, the implementation of mechanized butchering and filling by the 1920s destroyed the foundation on which the Chinese had built their labor aristocracy. Before mechanization displaced most skilled workers, Japanese had already begun to make headway into the better cannery jobs, as the increase of Japanese wages relative to those of Chinese reveals. In Oregon and Washington canneries during 1901, the average Japanese earned approximately two-thirds of what a Chinese worker made.[81] By 1909 that gap closed to within 5 to 10 percent less than Chinese wages. In that same year, a few Japanese in two Columbia River canneries earned more than some Chinese.[82] As of 1912, skilled Chinese and Japanese in Oregon canneries received the same pay. Skilled Japanese laborers, however, numbered 45 percent fewer than Chinese.[83]

In the Alaska plants, Japanese wage and occupational advances lagged behind those in Oregon and Washington. The distinction between skilled and common workers was greater, and canners depended heavily on the few remaining Chinese to process a small portion of the pack by hand. They hired a few unskilled Chinese, together with large numbers of Japanese, for the part of the catch packed by machines. The Immigration Commission reported that in 1909 "Chinese do the most skilled work, and are the highest paid employees."[84] Yet the overall trend in the labor market after 1910 was toward wage equity among all ethnic groups. No clear pattern of wage discrimination against Japanese persisted past the first decade of their employment.

As Chinese continued to dominate the industry until the 1920s, wage discrimination became overshadowed by favoritism shown to Chinese in assignments. Regional variations in the proportions of the contracted crews filled by Japanese illustrate the practice. Among the canning districts, coastal Oregon and Washington had the lowest proportion (28.8 percent) of Japanese (see Appendix, Table 4). The contractors' favoritism played only one part in Chinese dominance of the coastal labor market. As late as 1921, the superintendent of the Macleay Estate Company cannery on Oregon's Rogue River informed contractor Wong On that a replacement butcher "must be a Chinaman, not a Japanese."[85] Some owners, particularly those in small, owner-operated plants, still insisted on retaining patterns of employment in their canneries that closely resembled nineteenth-century practices.[86]

On the Columbia River, Japanese never fully displaced Chinese. The residence of contractors and Chinese in Astoria strengthened their positions, but more important, when canners opted to replace Chinese with other workers, they looked to local European American residents. In the first decade of the twentieth century, Japanese made some headway, and though some had acquired the necessary skills, canners continued to hire them for common labor positions at the most mechanized plants. In 1909 in Clatsop County, Oregon, Japanese made up 48.8 percent of the cannery crews. The county had the most highly mechanized plants on the river, and its principle city, Astoria, had several hundred Japanese residents. In the canneries of Multnomah County, Oregon, near the substantial Portland Japanese settlement, 38.2 percent of the workers were Japanese. In the more remote, often less-mechanized canneries on the river the proportion was lower. In Pacific and Wahkiakum counties, Washington, Japanese made up 32.2 percent of the workers. In Wasco County, Oregon, far from Astoria or Portland, canners employed Japanese for only 19.5 percent of the crews.[87]

The control that Chinese contractors wielded over cannery jobs and the growth in the European American population along the Columbia, as well as the Japanese preference for work in other industries, led to a reduction in Japanese participation. In the mid-1910s they made up only a little more than 27 percent of the contracted crews and only 4 percent of all cannery workers on the river.[88] Other industries employed far more Japanese than did the canneries. In 1920 in Clatsop County, for example, 159 Japanese worked in the timber industry, which offered better pay and longer employment than canning, while only 37 labored in the canneries. In that same year, 418 lived in the county, including 342 men, 38 women, and 38 children.[89] Even though their population was roughly equivalent to the Chinese in the county, Japanese workers exerted much less influence in the canneries. State investigators commented that Japanese immigrants on the lower Columbia River were "unobtrusive and little noticed" by other residents.[90]

In the first decade of the twentieth century, Japanese participation in Alaska canneries was also restricted by Chinese contractors, who showed favoritism to their countrymen by sending them to canning regions with better conditions and wages. In 1909, southeast Alaska canneries employed roughly the same proportion of Japanese (38.9 percent) as those on the Columbia River (39.1 percent). The relatively long season and smaller canneries there encouraged Chinese to retain their positions. By contrast, the isolated conditions and more highly mechanized plants of western and central Alaska discouraged Chinese. As a consequence, Japanese and Chinese employment in central Alaska stood at nearly equal levels, 48.6 and 51.4 percent, respectively. In western Alaska, Japanese formed a majority (57.3 percent) of the contracted crews.[91]

Employment shifts in southeast Alaska during the 1910s reveal the ability of Japanese to establish themselves more firmly in the labor market. In the second half of the decade, roughly 59 percent of Japanese in Alaska canneries worked in the southeastern section of the territory.[92] In some cases, as at the FIPC Ketchikan cannery, Japanese outnumbered Chinese. Yet numbers alone obscure continued Chinese influence. In 1915 at the FIPC Ketchikan plant, contractor Seid Back sent thirty Chinese and forty-five Japanese to the cannery. The entire Chinese contingent, but only five Japanese, made up the first crew, which arrived early in the season to set up the cannery and begin packing. The forty additional Japanese arrived much later in the season. Those in the first group earned pay for eight months, while those in the second worked only four months. Under this hiring policy, and in spite of their numerical superiority, most Japanese earned less for the season than Chinese, even though they got the same monthly pay.[93]

Close to Seattle (a major port of entry for Asians in the twentieth century) and to a number of smaller Japanese immigrant communities, the Puget Sound canners in 1909 employed Japanese for 48.9 percent of their crews. The 1909 data, however, reflect a "big year" run in the four-year Sockeye salmon cycle.[94] Japanese employment dropped significantly in slack years as Chinese contractors retained their skilled countrymen rather than Japanese. After 1913, the usual fluctuations were further complicated by road blasting at Hell's Gate on the Fraser River, which nearly blocked the passage of salmon to their spawning grounds during that peak year. The wartime canning boom and subsequent postwar slump created additional strains in the Puget Sound. Japanese most often supplemented a smaller, more stable core of Chinese and local European Americans.[95]

The level of mechanization also affected Japanese employment in the Puget Sound plants. Whatcom County had the largest and most mechanized canneries on the Sound. In 1909 Japanese there made up 43.6 percent of the crews.[96] While not particularly remote or isolated, Skagit County canneries were less mechanized and smaller than those in Whatcom County. Accordingly, Chinese maintained a stronger presence there, and Japanese constituted only 13.6 percent of the crews.[97] The only exception to the pattern was at Friday Harbor on San Juan Island. In that cannery, the contractor split the crew into equal gangs of Chinese and Japanese, though the record does not indicate why or how this was done.[98]

Cannery life in the Puget Sound held special challenges for Japanese. As early as 1905, signs of tensions between Japanese workers and local non-Asian townspeople appeared in a deadly conflict at Blaine, Washington, near the Canadian border. Angry Japanese chased a white worker into the streets of the town after he had stabbed one of their own with a fish pew in a cannery scuffle. The town's European Americans came forward to protect the white worker and forced the Japanese back into the plant, injuring four. The Japanese consul in Seattle called for the protection of the immigrants, and Washington's governor promised an investigation. White workers threatened a walk out, but Japanese beat them to it. Meanwhile, Chinese refused to support their Japanese coworkers in the conflict and continued on at the cannery, even though the burden made them "half-dead with fatigue."[99]

Amid the swirl of accusations and activities, ethnic competition in Puget Sound canneries continued. The most striking incident occurred in 1915 when 350 whites, largely those hurt by layoffs in local sawmills, met in Anacortes and called for canners to discharge all Japanese. Owners at first rejected the demands, claiming they employed Japanese because whites refused to do the work. In an open show of support for the anti-Japanese forces, the town's police moved into the canneries and seized all weapons found among the Japanese. Fearful of armed clashes that might paralyze production, the owners defused the situation by agreeing to hire local whites whenever new positions became available.[100]

Shortly after the Anacortes incident, anti-Japanese proponents turned to terrorist tactics. They blew up one of Blaine's water mains and posted a sign nearby that read: *Put out the Japs or there will be*

something worse than this happen.[101] European American residents
agreed that Japanese cannery employment in Blaine and the earlier Anacortes strife had prompted the bombing. State Labor Commissioner
E. W. Olsen found it politically advantageous to initiate a special investigation of the incident. Federal officials had urged Olsen to keep a low
profile because they feared diplomatic pressure from Japan. Nonetheless, Olsen made certain that the newspapers knew about his efforts to
supply "American labor" for the canneries.[102] The Blaine and Anacortes incidents themselves did not force Japanese out of Puget Sound
plants, but the activities of state officials and pressure from local European Americans eventually encouraged canners to move away from
Japanese employment. For their part, many Japanese looked to other
forms of livelihood in the timber industry, in agriculture, or in some
entrepreneurial activity as alternatives to cannery work so that by the
late 1920s Japanese only occasionally toiled in Puget Sound canneries.[103]

Those who remained in the cannery labor market during the 1920s
witnessed substantial changes. Significant Japanese employment became increasingly limited to Alaska through two major, separate recruiting centers. The canning companies with headquarters in San
Francisco dominated the industry in western Alaska, and to a lesser
degree that of central Alaska. Most contractors in the Bay Area were
Chinese; they drew on the relatively large population of their countrymen first and then, almost indiscriminately, on many other groups for
additional laborers. Japanese made up only a small proportion of the
latter. Seattle emerged as the secondary center for the Alaska canneries,
and contractors there supplied workers mainly for the southeastern
region. A handful of Japanese contractors had established themselves
in the city and drew on its sizable Japanese immigrant community.[104]
Consequently, the employment of Japanese relative to that of Chinese
differed dramatically in various regions of Alaska. Between 1921 and
1930, an annual average of 476 Chinese worked in western, 267 in
central, and 339 in southeast Alaska; Japanese averaged 192, 366, and
589, respectively.[105] The ratio of Chinese to Japanese, particularly in
southeast Alaska, marked the "arrival" of Japanese as an important contingent in the labor market.

While Japanese were second only to Chinese in their influence in
the contracted crews of Alaska canneries in the 1910s, the labor market
also included others. Mexicans and Mexican Americans made up the
largest group of these new workers, at times outnumbering Japanese.
Mexican employment grew dramatically during World War I so that
by 1917, nearly fifteen hundred worked in Alaska canneries. Through-

out the 1920s, their annual total stood between 1,000 and 1,300, with the exception of 1923 when 1,749 labored in Alaska plants.[106] The growth in the American West's commercial agriculture and the exclusion of most Asian immigrants fueled a great surge in Mexican labor migration to the United States. Contractors, especially those in San Francisco, did not have to look far for additional laborers for their western Alaska crews.

Mexican tenure in the canneries was brief and eventful. Contractors sent the vast majority to western Alaska where conditions were the worst in the industry. At the end of the World War I, the Mexican consul in San Francisco filed complaints of abuses in international labor recruitment and the poor treatment of Mexican citizens in Alaska canneries.[107] His accusations stood alongside investigations by the Oregon, Washington, and California Labor Bureaus, which revealed systemic exploitation in the industry.[108] Bad press and pressure from these institutions brought only limited improvements for Mexicans and Mexican Americans and did little to discourage their employment. The telling blow came with the broad push for their repatriation during the Great Depression. Between the 1929 and 1930 seasons, the number of Mexicans and Mexican Americans in Alaska canneries dropped nearly 40 percent, from 1,178 to 721.[109] From 1930 to 1935, an average of 822 worked each year, but for the remainder of the 1930s, the annual total dropped to 567.[110] In spite of their reduced number, Mexican and Mexican American patterns of employment in the most trying plants continued. Throughout the 1930s, 91 percent worked in western Alaska, 7 percent in central Alaska, and 2 percent in southeast Alaska.[111]

Other ethnic groups also entered the Alaska labor market. Filipinos, Koreans, Hawaiians, Portuguese, Puerto Ricans, Peruvians, Chileans, and "Arabians," as well as American blacks and a few U.S.-born European Americans followed much the same pattern as did Mexican workers. They were relegated to the least-skilled tasks and least-desirable canneries and were the first to bear the brunt of market and political fluctuations. With the exception of Filipinos, covered in subsequent chapters, no fellow ethnics served as contractors to protect their interests and the governments of their homelands did not have enough power to bring pressure that might improve conditions for their citizens involved in international labor migrations.[112]

Nonetheless, these unprotected immigrants struggled to make the best of the situation. During 1910, one group of seven Korean immigrants lived next to the Taku Cannery in southeast Alaska. Of the seven, U-Park headed the household and lived with his wife (listed only as Mrs. U-Park) and seven-year-old daughter, Alice. With them were four roomers, all Korean-born men between the ages of eighteen and forty-three. Since all seven had immigrated to the United States in 1906, presumably from Hawaii, they seem to have come in a group. All, except for Alice, must have found some work in the cannery, for it was the only source of income in the immediate vicinity. They may well have found temporary work in the plant, perhaps through another Korean immigrant, nineteen-year-old Sam Young, listed as a laborer in the contract crew.[113]

Aside from Young, the crew consisted of twenty-three Chinese and six Japanese who had secured regular jobs within the cannery. The Parks and their boarders were only tenuously connected to the plant and relied on family and immigrant networks to sustain themselves near the Taku Cannery. Without fellow ethnics as contractors, neither the many Mexicans nor the few Koreans achieved the security in the labor market held by Chinese and later Japanese and Filipinos.[114]

In the last decade of the nineteenth century and in the first two decades of the twentieth, owners tried to adjust their processing techniques to suit the limitations of the salmon runs and the availability of labor: neither embracing nor eschewing fully the use of new technologies. A brief and intense shortage in contract labor at the turn of the century convinced them that Chinese alone could no longer fill their labor needs, and as a consequence, they expanded their recruitment efforts to others. Rather than rely on overseas recruitment for labor, canners and contractors had only to look to Native American, European American, or Asian communities. Their labor supply guaranteed, owners then concentrated on the combination of laborers and machinery that best aided them in exploiting the salmon runs. Contractors allocated their skilled workers and fellow countrymen to canneries that retained labor-intensive techniques for at least a portion of their pack. They and their favored workers were largely unaffected because of the staggered mechanization of the canneries and rapid expansion in the industry. Contractors' arrangements with owners did change to reflect the use of new machines, and canners tried to take a share of the savings associated with cheaper labor, but most large contractors remained secure.

Ethnic competition within the labor market was the most visible change. The scarcity of Chinese workers, their connections to contractors, and their on-the-job training gave them an aristocracy of labor. For the first decade of the twentieth century, their position buffered them from many technological and market shifts. By the 1910s, however, Japanese became better established in the labor market and offered Chinese significant competition for control of cannery jobs in the upper tier. The regional allocation of labor according to ethnicity suggests at least partial success on the part of Japanese to wrest power from Chinese workers and contractors. Many other ethnic groups had also entered the labor market, but before the 1920s, they were not able to compete against the long-entrenched Chinese and the newly established Japanese bases of control. Nonetheless, even the least-protected laborers sought to stabilize their employment and the conditions of their work. Mexican laborers called on the consular offices of their homeland to protect them, while Koreans relied on immigrant and family networks.

By the end of the 1910s, then, the cannery labor market had fragmented into three large divisions: in British Columbia Asians, Native Americans, and European Americans competed with each other for jobs; in continental U.S. canneries European Americans steadily pushed out Asians and Native Americans; and in Alaska Chinese and Japanese struggled with each other for preeminence while other ethnics and Native Americans supplemented the crews. Through it all, the canners managed to maintain a steady supply of laborers.

5

"Fecund Possibilities" for Issei and Nisei

IN THE FIRST three decades of the twentieth century, Japanese posed the most significant challenge to Chinese in that segment of the cannery labor market recruited and managed by contractors. At first, Japanese entry into the labor market bolstered Chinese and allowed owners the luxury of a very flexible labor supply. Yet, as they increased in number, acquired a canning acumen, and developed direct ties to canners through coethnic contractors, Japanese chiseled away at the Chinese labor aristocracy. Ethnic competition forced a reconfiguration of the labor market from its earlier two- and three-tiered structure in which workers below Chinese had no representation among contractors to one marked by increased complexity. Workers without fellow ethnics as contractors continued to find themselves in the lower echelons of the labor market. They could only hope that some force outside the contractors or even the industry, such as state or federal agencies or their home governments (as was the case with Mexican workers in the era of World War I), might intervene on their behalf.[1] Even with external influences supporting them, up to the mid-1930s workers without coethnic contractors had limited influence in the industry. Japanese and Filipinos—though later and to a lesser degree—strove to break out of the lowest tier of jobs and influence through vertical ethnic identification with their "own" contractors, as Chinese had before them.

As similar as Chinese and Japanese strategies to exert influence in the industry's labor market may have been, their experiences proved different on at least three counts. First, Chinese had entered the industry at a time when the labor recruitment and management system had not yet jelled. Japanese had to conform to the well-established system that the Chinese helped create. Second, the Japanese migration to continental North America included a greater proportion of women than did the earlier Chinese movement.[2] In certain canning locales, the presence of Japanese men and women strengthened ethnic solidarity and inhibited class-based alignments. Chinese in the nineteenth century had no such gender considerations relative to cannery work. Finally, the presence of numerous Issei women contributed to the establishment of a much larger American-born (U.S. and Canadian) generation among Japanese than among Chinese. While American-born Chinese did work in the canneries, their numbers never matched the huge influx of Nisei into the industry in the 1920s and 1930s. Multiple generations in the plants added another complicating dynamic that Chinese had not faced: The means by which Japanese immigrants established themselves in the industry, interacted with other workers in the cannery communities, and how their children came to play an important role in the industry demonstrates that immigrants participate in fashioning the contours of their daily working and living environments.

The System of Subcontracting

To achieve a status other than that of supplemental or extra workers, Japanese first had to gain access to positions of power in the industry's labor recruitment and management system. They did so initially through subcontracting. Although Chinese contractors had sought out secondary labor recruiters through their own countrymen in the 1890s, and canners had drawn Native Americans to the plants through village headmen, Japanese quickly overshadowed those earlier efforts. As early as 1901, Tsureyoshi Kikutake and Kosuke Sakamaki acted as subcontractors for several Chinese firms. Kikutake had supplied Japanese for the Pacific Northwest's booming railroad and timber industries, and that fact encouraged Goon Dip, a prominent Chinese cannery contractor, to draw on Kikutake's services.[3] Others moved up from the ranks of workers employed by Chinese contractors. For example, Goon Dip hired George Nishimura as a personal driver. Nishimura then used that favored position to bring greater numbers of his fellow Japanese immigrants into the industry and earn a tidy profit for himself. Personal gain and assistance to countrymen were not mutually exclusive.[4]

The "system" was relatively simple. Contractors promised subcontractors commissions for each person recruited and then paid the workers through the subcontractors at the end of the season. Subcontractors bore responsibility for the behavior of the men they brought to the contractor, and a written document specified the terms of the relationship, much as owners did with contractors. If members of subcontracted crews should "refuse to obey orders . . . , institute a strike, or . . . by any other manner cause unnecessary trouble or expense to the [contractor]," the agreement stipulated that the subcontractor, as the responsible party for the men recruited through the system, pay a fine of up to several hundred dollars.[5] Because the Alaska canneries were so distant, contractors seldom visited the plants, and consequently they inserted very specific clauses to restrict subcontractors and their crews. Contractors deducted, through the subcontractor, 50 cents for every hour a man refused to work. Such fines might easily surpass workers' daily wages after only a few hours. Contractors also penalized the subcontractor $200 for any member of his crew who sold liquor to Native Alaskans. The money was deducted from the balance of a worker's unpaid wages. Contractors must have hoped that by penalizing workers they could bring greater pressure to bear on the subcontractor, who needed to retain good relations with his crews if he hoped to continue to recruit them in future seasons. The experiences that Chinese had in negotiating with owners helped them design very detailed agreements to cover nearly every contingency.[6]

Japanese subcontracting grew out of a labor scarcity, but Chinese contractors remained selective, and not all recruited Japanese. In 1905 one Portland contractor refused to make a subcontract with the Japanese Labor Association for work at Columbia River Packers Association (CRPA) canneries.[7] The contractor declined, no doubt, because he had access to plenty of Chinese workers who had been displaced by the decision of the Alaska Packers Association (APA) to hire non-Chinese for its crews. Further, the formation of a union among Chinese workers in that year must also have made him leery of any "labor association." Nonetheless, during the first decade of the twentieth century, Japanese entered the industry through the subcontract system in great numbers.

Subcontracting added another layer of authority to the cannery hierarchy, since a great many of the early subcontractors augmented their commissions by serving as foremen for their crews. Some continued as foremen for many years; others hired another Japanese as foreman when their subcontracting operations grew. Whether subcontractor or hired hand, a foreman for the Japanese crew was a new component. In plants with ethnically mixed crews, a Chinese foreman answered to the superintendent and the Chinese contractor and was responsible for the crews of Chinese and Japanese as well as extra hires. Foremen for subcontracted crews oversaw only Japanese workers. They were under great pressure because cannery superintendents, contractors, and Chinese foremen scrutinized carefully their every action.[8]

Issei (first-generation immigrant Japanese) workers bore the brunt of the Japanese foreman's tenuous position. One laborer remembered: "As soon as work began, the foreman's eyes became sharp. Our foreman, whom until that moment I had not disliked, suddenly changed into a slave driver. His face looked like a devil to us."⁹ Foremen drove the crews hard, and if tough looks failed, brandished their "lotus roots" (pistols) in front of the crews.¹⁰ Some foremen did not stop at threats. In 1914, when one Japanese cannery hand allegedly "voiced dissatisfaction over his contract" at a Dundas Bay, Alaska, cannery, he "was visited by [the foreman] Ito and two helpers." Ito's assistants held the worker as "Ito took his life with a long sword."¹¹ Three years earlier, in San Francisco, subcontractor S. Sasaki arranged Alaska jobs for fourteen of his fellow Japanese and gave them advance money. One of the crew, K. Tabagashi, reportedly "gambled it away" and demanded of Sasaki an additional $40. An argument followed in which Tabagashi brandished a pistol, and Sasaki responded by shooting him dead.¹² While deaths by sword fights and pistols duels provided high drama for the European American press, it obscured the everyday bullying under which Japanese workers must have suffered. One Issei summed up that treatment by explaining: "Of course there may have been some ideal foremen, but unfortunately I've never met one."¹³

Japanese workers had several avenues of resistance open to them in the face of such treatment. When Jimmy Kiyohara, a subcontractor in Anacortes, came to the bunkhouse "in an ugly mood," he first berated the crewmen "for drinking and not being on the job." Not satisfied with the results of his verbal assault, he took up a knife and stabbed one worker in a scuffle. Four of the crew chased him down and fatally wounded him with four shots from a pistol. The action was not a spontaneous response to an isolated incident. The workers several days earlier had agreed among themselves to "take no more orders from Kiyohara" because of his aggressive behavior.¹⁴ That Japanese workers took similar action in other instances no doubt made Japanese foremen and subcontractors wary of pushing them too far.¹⁵

Some Japanese workers openly resisted subcontractors and foremen, but others responded more subtly. Those taking a less overt route relied on a shared Japanese cultural heritage to dampen the fiery behavior of foremen. The *oyabun–kobun* (parent–child or superior–inferior) relationships among the subcontractors–foremen and workers helped prevent foremen from "unilaterally exploiting the boys."¹⁶ Shizu Mamizuka, the wife of a Japanese contractor, believed that "foremen and contractors were a kind of *oyakata* [surrogate parent] . . . of the regular workers."¹⁷ In exchange for workers' loyalty, those in positions of power were to protect and provide for those below them. While the relationship was frequently lopsided in favor of the contractor, laborers expected these norms to be followed. Mamizuka recalled how that relationship manifested itself after each canning season:

There were always more than thirty boys loafing around. They were hangers on. In our basement there was a sumo corner and a judo floor, and one corner was given over to a kitchen. Since there were foods—rice soy sauce and canned goods—left over from the cannery seasons, the boys could stay there without worrying about where the next meal was coming from.[18]

The segregation of responsibilities and work in the canneries along ethnic lines reinforced that cultural value and helped Japanese establish a distinctive and separate sphere of influence in which common ethnicity bound workers and foremen together.

The opportunities for exploitation and the insecure position of many subcontractors, however, frequently strained that alliance. Many smaller-scale subcontractors found their positions so tenuous that they devised schemes to make quick profits at the expense of all other parties involved. In the first two decades of the twentieth century, Japanese subcontractors often absconded with preseason advance money or the balance of workers' wages at the end of the season. In 1910 the *San Francisco Chronicle* noted that labor contractors were "at their wits' end" because among Japanese "more than one sub-boss had decamped with the advance money."[19] Japanese subcontractors who departed with advances left Chinese contractors unable to fill their contractual obligations and companies without full crews. To protect their interests, canners in the first decade of Japanese contracting began to require surety bonds of the contractors and subcontractors.[20] This eliminated preseason frauds, but at the end of the season subcontractors disappeared with money that contractors had given them for the workers' wages. In San Francisco after the 1908 season, for example, Sotaro Okuda, subcontractor for the large Chinese firm of Quong Ham Wah and Company, had to explain to "a turbulent crowd" of workers that they would receive no pay because foreman K. Iriye had run off with several thousand dollars in gold coin meant for them.[21]

Exploitation of cannery workers reached its nadir under subcontractors. Some Japanese subcontractors and foremen found absconding to be profitable, but there were no opportunities for sustained income from such activities because subcontractors could only hope to violate the trust of their crews and the contractors once. Most subcontractors found substantial profits came their way simply by charging inflated prices for clothing before the cannery ships sailed north and for "luxury" food such as coffee and doughnuts during the season or by running gambling tables. Beginning in the first decade of the twentieth century, the shrinking pool of available Chinese labor under the exclusion laws led to the entrance in the cannery labor market of workers and subcontractors of many ethnic groups. That diversity in turn fostered competition among the groups and contributed to the exploitation of workers because no single group other than Chinese had any representative above the rank of subcontractor to whom they could look for protection. Japanese subcontractors appear to have varied little from the norm; Kikutake helped shanghai men when other recruiting tactics failed. In the midst of protests about the treatment of workers, Chinese contractors claimed no responsibility for the actions of their subcontracting agents and bent ethnic divisions to their own advantage in order to continue preferential treatment for Chinese workers. They successfully shirked any responsibility as managers of the subcontracted crews.[22]

Breaking into the Ranks of the Contractors

Unlike workers from other ethnic backgrounds, who got cannery jobs only through subcontractors, Japanese eventually broke free of such arrangements and established themselves as contractors. As early as 1910, Japanese began to arrange contracts free of obligations to Chinese. In that year, Kikuzo Uyeminami, proprietor of the A. B. Japanese General Contractors in Seattle, secured one of the first direct contracts with canners. By mid-decade, he was recruiting workers for a half-dozen companies. He maintained those business relationships for the next two decades. In the mid-1920s, according to his own letterhead, he provided "first class help . . . to railroads, mills, camps, restaurants, ranches, dairies, and hotel[s]" as well as workers for as many as eight canneries. His was the largest Japanese contracting enterprise in the Northwest.[23]

The timing of their entry and the presence of their countrymen in great numbers in the labor market allowed Japanese contractors to establish themselves firmly. The domestic market for cheap grades of canned salmon in the 1910s and World War I government contracts led to the establishment of many new plants, especially in southeast Alaska and the Puget Sound. By the late 1910s, seven or eight Japanese had agreements with companies to provide laborers, most often at newly opened canneries or at those that operated with extra lines during the war. In 1916 the small Lummi Island and Friday Harbor canneries on Puget Sound let contracts to Japanese for their entire crews. During the war, the Fidalgo Island Packing Company (FIPC) contracted with Kikutake and Uyeminami for its plant at Herendeen Bay, Alaska. In 1919 the company also contracted with Uyeminami for a small Japanese crew to operate an additional canning line at its Anacortes cannery but simultaneously maintained its agreements with its Chinese labor agent, Seid Back.[24]

By the beginning of World War I, Seattle had become the focus of Japanese recruitment for the canneries. Many of the new canners had set up offices in the city because it was relatively close to Alaska, had good rail connections to the rest of the country, and held an important position in the region's timber and railroad industries, as well as agriculture. Once there, the canners drew heavily on the large Japanese settlement in the city. In the aftermath of World War I, though, a precipitous short-term decline hit Japanese contractors harder than Chinese because as they struggled to secure contracts they very often lost out to better-established Chinese labor suppliers. Companies neglected to reopen wartime canneries or ran with fewer lines. One member of a cannery owner's family recalled: "I remember the night the Japanese [contractor] called on us, he brought me a beautiful tea set. . . . They would come and talk over and tell you how many good workers they could supply, what wages they would expect, what you were supposed to do, to have a house for them to live in, how they would be taken care of, and different things."[25] Still, after gifts and much discussion, Chinese won more cannery contracts than Japanese. While Japanese contractors continued to supply workers to canneries in the 1920s, they did so on a smaller scale than in the 1910s, and Chinese contractors continued to supply the majority of workers. The postwar slump even forced some Japanese contractors back into subcontracting.[26]

Nonetheless, Japanese subcontractors and contractors captured a substantial portion of the labor market in a time of great growth in the industry, and as a result their countrymen benefited. The experience of one worker, K. Mori, illustrates the pattern and significance of cannery employment for Issei. Twenty-one years old on his initial arrival in the Northwest from Japan in 1907, Mori worked for three months in a shingle-bolt mill. Either attracted by slightly higher wages or at a contractor's behest, he left for a two-month stint of cannery work in southeast Alaska. Something about that experience prompted him not to return in the following season but to take a job in a sawmill. After two years there, he shipped once more to an Alaska cannery, but this time as a foreman, not as a common laborer. Mori had probably developed a close association with the contractor in order to attain that position. Such mobility was not typical, for relatively few Japanese became foremen. Mori's new income allowed him considerable flexibility. Some years in the fall and winter, he returned to Washington's shingle mills;

other years, he relied only on his cannery income to, in his words, "loaf around Seattle all winter and spend money."[27]

Mori's foremanship represented the height of mobility for most Japanese in the industry, since Chinese contractors tried to limit competitors, and Japanese jealously guarded such positions once they had them. Shut out of further advancement, he took employment in Montana with a railroad section crew—probably as a foreman—and for two years he kept this year-round job. Isolated though it was, railroad employment provided a more steady and secure income than seasonal cannery work.[28]

Perhaps because of the isolation in Montana, Mori returned again to an Alaska cannery but only for a single season. He then went to work in Washington canneries, first supervising a crew at an Anacortes plant and later at a Grays Harbor firm. Proximity to more established communities and the greater length of the canning season in Puget Sound and at coastal plants made work at those locales more attractive than in Alaska. By securing the position in Washington, Mori had achieved a small advance up the cannery hierarchy and enough income to bank against six months of unemployment between seasons.[29]

When Japanese contractors lost business in the postwar contraction, Japanese workers also felt the crunch. Mori survived the sharp swings in the industry by returning to the mills, and by the mid-1920s, his employment pattern no longer included the canneries. Not too distant from his last cannery job, he found a position as a foreman in a southwest Washington sawmill. Mori's intermittent cannery employment exemplified the place that cannery work held for Issei. In many ways, the Issei position as migratory laborers in the American West in an era of unrestricted immigration made their experience very much like that of Chinese before 1882, but Issei never gained the relative security in their cannery positions that Chinese enjoyed. Whereas an increasingly large percentage of aging Chinese came to depend solely on cannery work for their support, Japanese more readily found employment on railroads and in mills when market fluctuations created a scarcity of cannery jobs.[30]

While immigration restrictions levied against Japanese after 1908 curtailed their presence in the industry, Issei nevertheless continued to work in the industry until their wartime incarceration in 1942. Their representation by contractors and their relatively large, continuous presence in the labor market led to the creation of new cannery communities. The ethnicity of the contractor, not necessarily the proximity to a town, became the central determinant in how workers viewed the twentieth-century plants. Two cannery communities thus emerged, known as "Chinese" and "Japanese," even though they were ethnically mixed. At Chinese canneries, Issei faced difficulties. While some Japanese believed that mixed crews "worked in harmony," most registered complaints. Even in crews in which Japanese outnumbered Chinese, Chinese workers received better treatment. Japanese had to eat Chinese dried or salted vegetables and fish softened with water and fried in lard. In comparison to typically light Japanese food, such fried fare turned many Japanese stomachs. It had "an indescribably bad smell, cooked with cheap oil," noted one Issei. "It was just terrible," remembered another, "probably even 'coolie' meals were better than ours."[31] Chinese also complained about cannery meals, but Chinese cooks and contractors gave them special consideration in the type and quality of dishes served, a courtesy not accorded to the Japanese.[32]

To contend with what they perceived as inadequate food, Japanese workers sometimes "ran away from the Chinese group, had a different meal cooked, and ate [it] separately." They also brought their own pickled vegetables to the cannery and, with goods pilfered from the plant, stored them under the floorboards in their bunkhouses. They consumed most of the pickled items themselves and sold or gave away the remainder. Others caught crabs and octopi, dug clams, or fished and hunted, which provided additional nutrition as well as leisure activities.[33] As another strategy, some Japanese tried to establish good relations with the cooks for the Asian cannery or the European American fishing crews in the hope that they might get better food. Some of those cooks, much like some foremen, used their positions to exploit workers. More than one kept back the best food and sold it on the local "black market." Not all cooks had supplies to spare, and workers had to rely on the "slop chest" maintained by contractors and their foremen. They might also buy candy, doughnuts, and bread at the company store. One Issei explained: "[We] could get any kind of food, as much as we wanted," but procuring that food often created considerable debts by the end of the season.[34]

Ethnic antagonisms between Chinese and Japanese compounded problems with cannery fare and indebtedness. Those conflicts often surfaced in the bunkhouses, and as early as 1903, Puget Sound canners provided segregated living quarters for the two groups. Chinese bunkhouses most often included an office for the foreman or contractor, a kitchen, and a mess hall in addition to the sleeping area. Since Japanese crews were smaller and arrived later in the season than Chinese crews, and they were not represented by a contractor, only some of their bunkhouses had attached mess halls. For the same reasons, most were also considerably smaller than the Chinese bunkhouses. With the waning of Chinese numerical dominance in the crews after 1905, canners found that by building smaller compartments designed to house eight to sixteen workers within the larger bunkhouses, they could segregate the crew members without having to build and maintain separate facilities. As workers of ethnic backgrounds other than Chinese and Japanese entered the labor market in the 1910s and 1920s, the bunkhouses with these compartments reinforced the fragmentation of the cannery work culture into ethnic subcultures. Only occasionally might workers from different groups live together in the same room.[35]

Canners or contractors may have consciously devised compartmentalized living arrangements as a managerial "divide and conquer" strategy at mixed canneries, as did some Hawaiian sugar plantation owners, but no direct evidence supports such a conclusion.[36] While the canners were not against playing one ethnic group against another in the case of work stoppages, most separate facilities appeared because owners feared that ethnic conflict might threaten the productivity of their crews. They had to make little effort to divide early twentieth-century laborers already fragmented by their ethnic differences.[37]

That splintering of the labor market into ethnic subdivisions meant that Japanese never attained the degree of influence within the industry that Chinese held in the nineteenth century. Yet at specific canneries, staffed mostly by Japanese workers and overseen by a Japanese contractor, Issei workers created their own versions of the bunkhouse community that, though it differed only outwardly from that of the Chinese, allowed Issei to fare better than at plants run by Chinese. Instead of fried Chinese dishes, they ate Japanese rice, *miso* (a soup), dried sea slugs, various pickled vegetables, and dried *daikon* (radish) as well as *fu* (a light cake made of wheat gluten)—all very different from Chinese cuisine. Some saved rice from their meals or stole it from the kitchen and made unrefined sake in spite of regulations against its manufacture at the canneries. Even when the food was familiar, some workers charged that Japanese contractors oversalted preserved items sent to the canneries and encouraged cooks to salt heavily what they served in the mess house in order to dissuade workers from eating too much.[38]

During their leisure time in the bunkhouses, the laborers mulled matters of "commonplace life" by which they meant "women, alcohol and dirty stories." Low-grade sake and far-ranging talk, however, did little to make up for an incomplete social life at the worksite. In the male-dominated canneries, particularly those in Alaska, Japanese workers interacted first among themselves and then with other workers, for even at "Japanese" plants they seldom made up the entire workforce.[39] Among Japanese in the canneries, and Chinese as well, the probability of homosexual relations ran high. Indeed, contractors or foremen, Chinese and Japanese alike, may have exploited the situation by making prostitutes of certain men in the crews. Homosexual activity in the canneries has been viewed by some observers as evidence of the depravity of the workers and their extreme exploitation.[40] Instead, more might be understood about interpersonal and interethnic relations at the canneries if the extent of homosexual activity could be quantified to the broader context of their immigrant societies. Probing into that activity is, however, nearly impossible because homosexual behavior among cannery workers remains buried beneath a great many cultural taboos and was seldom discussed by the workers themselves.

Japanese and Chinese, when at the same plants, faced the problem of contending with their conflicting nationalisms. In the late nineteenth and early twentieth centuries, larger international events such as the Sino-Japanese War (1894–1895) and the Twenty-one Demands made by Japan on China in 1915 strained divisions that had already been reinforced by the occupational hierarchy and ethnic fragmentation. On some special occasions, however, Chinese and Japanese did join together. In 1921, when a great famine struck China, Chinese and Japanese in canneries on the Columbia River donated roughly equivalent portions of their incomes to a relief fund. In spite of a common experience as immigrant laborers participating in the West's industrial transformation, however, no strong pan-Asian identity emerged among Chinese and Japanese. Job competition, discrimination among the contractors, and international politics all fostered ethnic antagonisms.[41]

An age gap also separated Chinese and Japanese. Issei during the first decade of the twentieth century were substantially younger than the Chinese. In 1910 in Alaska, Japanese workers averaged twenty-nine years of age; Chinese, forty-eight. Slightly more than half of the Japanese (50.4 percent) were between twenty-five and thirty-two years old, while a similar proportion of Chinese (50.1 percent) were between forty and fifty-four. Only 8.3 percent of the Japanese were older than forty, compared to 76.9 percent of the Chinese.[42]

The expectations of the younger Issei immigrants differed markedly from those of the middle-aged and older Chinese. To the Japanese, cannery work was a means to relatively good pay but not a steady and long-term source of income, as K. Mori's employment history suggests. The predominance of Chinese contractors and frequent layoffs caused by downswings in the industry limited cannery prospects for most Issei. The exploitation of the West's resources that had begun in the last half of the nineteenth century grew to immense proportions in the twentieth century. To maximize their annual income, Japanese had to seek work in a migratory cycle that spanned numerous industries and territories. Their agricultural, mill, and mine employment carried them throughout the states of the Far West and even into the Southwest.[43] Chinese workers, in contrast, found that Chinese contractors provided somewhat better protection for them in the canned-salmon industry, and as a consequence, Chinese workers depended on cannery incomes more heavily.[44]

Rather than look to the Chinese, Japanese cannery workers most often found opportunities for companionship with Native American women, especially those in Alaska and to a somewhat lesser degree in the Puget Sound area, where Japanese could meet Native American women during agricultural harvests, particularly hop picking, which was an important part of the seasonal cycle for Japanese and Indians.[45] Casual, short-lived summer romances dominated much of the contact between Issei workers and Indian women. The partners often paid a heavy price for their interactions—incidences of venereal disease ran high. Cannery doctors treated such cases for a fee, but many times workers would not, or could not, pay and suffered as a result.[46] Most often, the women bore the greater burdens. A number of Issei looked on them as a means to satisfy immediate desires, only to be set aside at the end of the season. Issei had, among their cannery slang, pejorative labels for native women indicating a general lack of respect. In 1907 Japanese workers at an Alaska plant reportedly "raided" a nearby village for its women, suggesting that even rape, as an avenue to sexual gratification, was not unknown.[47]

Japanese attitudes and behavior combined with their temporary stay at the canneries left a great many women pregnant at the end of the season and without spouses during the winter. One former Japanese worker remembered: "Every year when a cannery boat goes up to Alaska, to unload these cannery workers, there will be Eskimo or Indian women with little babies looking for papa."[48] Even if the cannery workers remained with their new families, the woman's relatives did not always happily provide support for the couples. One of the "cannery children" bitterly recalled: "My mother . . . had some relatives in the Indian village, but they didn't like her for a long time because she married a Japanese."[49]

Some Issei and Native Alaskans did establish stable and long-lasting relationships. These families found a home in the woman's village at times, but they might also live year-round in the growing small towns of southeast Alaska. A small number of Issei brought their wives and children back with them at the end of the season to the continental

United States. Issei society outside Alaska looked on these mixed marriages with even less enthusiasm than did Native Alaskans, with the
result that the families often lived in isolation from the Japanese community.[50]

Gender Relations

In the first decade of the twentieth century in most canning areas, and
throughout the first half of the century in Alaska, a majority of the Issei
worked as bachelor immigrants, their sporadic contacts with Native
Americans notwithstanding. In the 1910s, the increasing presence of
Issei women transformed the character of Japanese American society
from one of bachelors to one that included many nuclear families.
Some of the women worked in the canning industry with their husbands. Chinese and Korean immigrant women also found employment
in the plants but were so few in number that their impact was negligi-
ble. Issei women were numerous enough that they added a new element to labor relations in the industry.[51]

From the mid-1890s to World War II and beyond, the settlement
of Japanese men and women at Steveston, British Columbia, represented the greatest level of Japanese family involvement in the industry.
Unlike most cannery operators on the Pacific Coast, British Columbia's canners employed Issei men as fishermen, relying on men and
women from various ethnic groups for labor within the canneries. The
concentration of canneries at Steveston led to the growth of a Japanese
community dependent on fishing.[52]

The Japanese settlement at Steveston began as a temporary residence for bachelor fishermen. In the early 1890s, only a few Issei lived
and fished seasonally in British Columbia, returning to Japan at the
end of each season.[53] After 1893, when European American fishermen
formed the Fraser River Fishermen's Protective Union, canners sought
out Japanese as an alternative source of labor; by 1896, British Columbia had nearly a thousand Issei fishermen.[54] Competition with U.S.
companies on Puget Sound and the formation of the British Columbia
Fishermen's Union in 1899 encouraged canners to hire even more Japanese. In 1901 on the Fraser River, nearly four thousand Japanese
worked the salmon boats, and they constituted upward of a third of
the commercial fishermen there. By the turn of the century, their great
numbers sufficiently weakened the influence of the European American
fishermen, which served the canners' interests but also allowed Japanese to form their own protective organization, the Fishermen's
Benevolent Association. From 1900 on, canners manipulated competi-

tion among Japanese, European American, and Native American fishermen to keep fish prices low.[55]

When Japanese fishermen established more permanent residences and brought their families to Steveston in the first two decades of the twentieth century, owners took that opportunity to employ Japanese women alongside European American and Native American women. In the U.S. branch of the industry, Asian and Asian American workers identified with coethnic contractors but stood very separate from the European American fishermen. At Steveston, the presence of Issei women in the plants and Issei men on the boats fostered an ethnic solidarity among Japanese. When Japanese men struck for higher fish prices in 1913, for example, Japanese women supported the strike, but the men of the other ethnic groups continued to fish, and non-Japanese women continued to pack salmon.[56] Those divisions persisted until World War II when the Canadian government deemed the Japanese a threat and removed them from the coast. Not until 1945 did workers in the province begin to overcome those ethnic divisions and form broader collective bargaining organizations.[57]

Japanese women's immigration and participation in British Columbia canneries contributed to ethnic competition, but it also helped the Japanese establish a more permanent settlement at Steveston. So many Japanese lived and worked in the town in the first half of the century that it ranked second to Vancouver in the number of its Japanese residents. The town's Japanese came from many districts, but the vast majority came from Mio in Wakayama prefecture.[58] "There aren't many people left in [Mio]," reflected Umanosuke Suzuki, "they all moved here" in the years before World War II.[59] Such chain migration to immigrant fishing villages on the West Coast was not unique to Steveston. Japanese communities in Monterey and Terminal Island in California also centered on fisheries (sardine instead of salmon) and relied heavily on emigration from a small district in Japan. The members of those transplanted fishing communities often retained strong local dialects and traditions, which set them apart as "rustics" to the citified Japanese residents of Vancouver, San Francisco, and Los Angeles. Yet the bonds they formed enabled them to develop friendship and family networks within their community that lasted long after economic and political forces spread members over a much wider geographical base in the postwar era.[60]

In Steveston, the men operated the cannery boats, and some worked inside the canneries while the women worked mostly as slimers and fillers and were hired by contractors. As in other regions employing women, canners paid Issei women on an hourly basis for sliming and on piece-rate wages for filling. Chinese foremen kept track of each slimer's pace by issuing tickets for every half-case of cans packed. Women redeemed the tickets through contractors or foremen at specific intervals during the season but sometimes had to wait until the end of the season.[61] Like other immigrants, Steveston's Japanese relied on the income of these women. The women sought employment virtually the moment they landed on Canadian soil. "When I came . . . I was almost six months pregnant," recounted Moto Suzuki of her arrival at Steveston early in the century. "It was in July, fishing season, so I started work in the cannery almost right away."[62]

The involvement of several hundred Japanese women in the gender-divided workforce at Steveston between 1910 and 1940 made possible the development of a Japanese women's subculture of work that contributed to their families' earnings, helped ease the burdens of wage labor, and imparted greater meaning to their employment. Just as black women in Chesapeake oyster houses and Chicanas in California's vegetable canneries made their work a social and socializing center of their lives, so did Japanese women at Steveston.[63] In all those cases, the women came together daily at the plants, and that allowed them to visit, discuss problems, and educate younger women in the ways of adult life. Their working lives were not like those of urban women domestics, who were often dominated by their employers and who labored in isolation, enjoying only occasional contact with other domestics.[64]

While piece rates and ethnic divisions among women created a competitive atmosphere, the social aspects of their jobs contributed to a cooperative spirit. The care of children is a case in point. In Japan, working women might rely on their extended families to watch the children, but at Steveston child care was a pressing issue. The women had to contend with an inconsistent work schedule as well as the lack of older children or other relatives who could help take care of the youngsters. Since neither cannery owners nor Chinese contractors provided facilities at the plants, the women were left to their own devices. Some women solved the problem temporarily by strapping an infant or small child to their backs with special sashes (*ombu*).[65] This was possible as long as the children were small and relatively inactive, but as they grew older, other solutions became necessary. Owners only tolerated in their plants children strapped to their mothers' backs or those who performed at least some very basic and repetitive task. Without a place for young children at the canneries, the burden of solving the child-care problem fell directly on Issei women.[66]

Irregular work hours made solutions difficult. Moto Suzuki, an Issei woman at Steveston, explained: "Sometimes we worked one hour a day, sometimes five hours, sometimes ten hours a day."[67] To deal with such unpredictability, Japanese women established a *mori* house, or informal day-care center, at which working mothers shared the responsibility of caring for the children. Pregnant women and those with young children contributed more time to the effort in order that they might not have to work in the cannery during a difficult period and so that the other mothers might earn greater incomes. While lost wages from sharing the burdens of child care limited individual incomes, such cooperation placed the good of the community above that of the individual.[68]

Even in areas where Issei women's employment was significantly less than at Steveston, the women organized similar systems to assist each other. In 1926 at Astoria, nine Issei couples worked in the CRPA Elmore Cannery. The women earned incomes as fillers and slimers and the men worked elsewhere in the plant. During June, July, and August two women, identified in the records only as Mrs. Hanaoka and Mrs. Ikagami, worked alternate days. The regularity of their work patterns suggests a shared responsibility for child care between at least two households and an arrangement much like the *mori* house in Steveston. They may also have extended their services to the other Japanese families in the area.[69]

Shared ethnicity and problems of immigrant life contributed to cooperation among Japanese women, yet the work environment also fostered fragmentation. The size and placement of the filling tables, one to each processing line, forced women into groups of about a dozen. Canners and contractors tended to let workers determine the makeup of the table. Issei women at Steveston divided up on the basis of familial and friendship networks. The CRPA Elmore Cannery employed an average of seven Japanese women each month (five to eight depending on the point in the season)—too few for them to discriminate among themselves. Among the European American women the luxury of choosing workmates was more likely, since the number employed averaged eighteen (with a range from twelve to twenty-four). Assignment of workers to tables in the plant was based primarily on ethnicity, with other considerations secondary. Japanese women thus formed one unit, and European American women several others. The three Chinese women, Irene and Constance Wong and a Mrs. Chan, were too few in number to work at their own table.[70] Since Chinese immigrants and their children in Astoria by the mid-1920s had become involved in the town's public schools and Protestant churches, they had more in common with non-Asian than with Japanese women and probably worked with European American women. Although less distinct than at the filling tables, a similar self-grouping among women also took place along the sliming troughs.[71]

Women carefully guarded their positions, allowing in new people only with the consensus of the group. Those from a different social or ethnic group were not accepted. Owners and managers condoned such behavior, for they recognized that productivity and quality of the pack at the tables depended on good relationships among workers. Women at the filling tables developed strong small-group identities. When men approached to bring fish or cans, they were met with silence from the table. Further, women developed an informal hierarchy that included a "first" and then several lesser tables. The status of a particular table depended on the quality and quantity of salmon brought by conveyor, trough, or tray to the table; by the ease and frequency with which the packed cans were sent back into the canning line; the abilities of the workers; and the stability of employment (extra tables might be added during a rush and were staffed by temporary workers). In all but the Steveston canneries, Japanese women relied on ethnic bonds first; when there were too few coethnics to occupy all of a filling table or section of slimers, they had to find ways to work with European American women, much as the Chinese women did at the Elmore plant.[72]

Generational Changes

Whereas Issei women and then their daughters continued to work in the canneries of Steveston until World War II, in the United States no significant number found employment in the industry. Very few Issei fished commercially for salmon in the United States, and the owners failed to provide residences for families, as the canners did in British Columbia. When Japanese in the United States established families, they did so around small urban businesses or rural agricultural pursuits.[73] The preference U.S. canners had for hiring European American women also worked against the large-scale employment of Japanese women. During the 1920s, it would be the sons of Japanese women who moved into U.S. canneries, particularly the Alaska plants. Seattle, because of its large Japanese population during the first three decades of the twentieth century, its seven or eight Japanese contractors, and its proximity to the Alaska canneries, became the focus of Nisei cannery employment. Japanese contractors there sent to southeast Alaska school-aged Nisei boys in the "second" crews that departed after schools were out, arrived at the plants for the rush season, and returned in time for fall classes. While Seattle Nisei had advantages in gaining entry into the canneries, boys from central California also labored in the canneries, though they had to travel to Seattle to get the jobs through one of the Japanese contractors.[74]

These "boys of summer," as one Nisei has labeled them, saw their cannery employment as a rite of passage into manhood. Before their Alaska jobs, Seattle's Nisei boys and girls, and their mothers, often spent the summers in the strawberry fields on Bainbridge Island and in the White River Valley. Berry picking supplemented the family income and provided a community service for Issei agriculturalists in need of labor. At the more distant farms, the families might stay in bunkhouses for as long as two or three weeks, but the presence of their mothers and sisters allowed the boys no sense of independent adventure. At ages twelve to fifteen, the boys began their cannery employment and ventured away from their families for the first time. That the work was tedious, repetitive, and held only limited opportunities for advancement mattered little. After all, this was a grand adventure, perhaps repeated for a few years with a group of friends through their college years. They assumed that college graduation followed by white-collar employment would bring an end to their cannery days. They had no compulsion to speak out against the rough conditions in the bunkhouses and canneries, which seemed to them only temporary burdens.[75]

While cannery work provided a sense of adventure for the boys and a new source of labor for contractors and canners, it did not detract from family expectations for their sons. Issei parents believed that they must provide an education for their children and saw the canneries as one way to finance that endeavor. By the late 1920s, the trend of summer employment for school-aged Nisei took on such great proportions in Seattle that the *Japanese American Courier* noted that cannery work held "fecund possibilities of becoming an institution of the academic-minded intelligentsia." Indeed, the editorial continued, cannery crews staffed by relatively highly educated workers made them "ideal institution[s] for [Nisei] students."[76]

In addition to promoting the formal education of their sons through cannery work, Issei parents believed that the contractors or foremen would watch over the boys, and that fact comforted them. Families usually arranged cannery employment for their sons through contractors with whom they had familial, friendship, or community ties and expected them to be responsible for the boys. Those same connections between the parents and the contractors eliminated the most ruthless treatment of the boys and placed constraints on the amount of "adventure" in which the boys might engage. The *oya-bun–kobun* relationship among Issei workers and the contractors was thus extended to Nisei.[77]

During the 1930s, Nisei began to fear that their assumptions about mobility might not be accurate and their "boys of summer" attitudes began to fade. Older Nisei, who had graduated from colleges and professional programs in the 1920s, had captured the few white-collar jobs available for Japanese Americans, mostly in the ethnic economy.[78] The second cohort of Nisei, who passed out of high school and college in the 1930s, retained notions of upward mobility out of the canneries, but the near-monopoly on jobs held by elder Nisei together with the depression exacerbated the dismal prospects for younger Nisei. George Taki, one of the prominent Nisei leaders in the emerging union movement, commented:

> There just [were] not any employment opportunities for the bulk of the Nisei after they got out of college. It was quite difficult for the Nisei to get decent jobs with Caucasian companies in Seattle because these companies would not hire orientals. . . . The great majority were doomed to disappointment and [were] forced to work at menial jobs in the Japanese community . . . and the future did not look too promising.[79]

Instead of landing professional jobs, many of the college educated had to fall back on the family business or farm or continue their association with the canned-salmon industry.[80]

At least some Nisei recognized the uncertainties that faced them. Daiki Miyagawa, brother of prominent Nisei unionist Daisho ("Dyke") Miyagawa, tried one of those menial jobs in the Japanese produce row along Seattle's waterfront. "It looks sort of picturesque," he commented, "but it is not fun for a person to work down there. . . . I was legally underpaid." Daiki worked long hours for very limited pay under difficult circumstances. "I was always being imposed on and asked to put up with [it] . . . because jobs were scarce and there were family obligations," he remembered. "My employer was a fellow church member and a friend of the family so he took advantage of me. . . . It may have been the system in Japan, but I could not take it so I went back to work for my father [in his restaurant], much as I disliked that work."[81] Such prospects disappointed Seattle's Nisei. Albert Ikeda, a Nisei in Los Angeles, noted: "[They] were pretty bitter about being pushed down. . . . They worked hard and they were still hopeful that someday they would be able to make some advancements altho[ugh] this dream was fading pretty fast."[82] Opportunities for Nisei during the 1930s were dismal all around. George Akahoshi of California recounted: "Jobs in those days were so scarce . . . [that Nisei] had to cling to any kind of job they could get in order to keep body and soul together."[83] Soon what had amounted to little more than summer camp for teenage youngsters became central to Nisei livelihood, but even that shrank before their eyes as wage levels dropped from roughly $50 a month in 1929 to about $30 in 1933. Although discouraged by the reduction in their paychecks, Nisei had few options outside the canneries for any income.[84]

Nisei cannery employment was also threatened by the entrance of Filipinos into the labor market. Filipinos began working in Alaska during the 1910s, and by the late 1920s, they outnumbered Japanese (Issei and Nisei) in Alaska by a ratio of nearly three to one.[85] Competition with Filipinos pushed some Issei and Nisei toward greater dependence on Japanese contractors for jobs. They feared that Filipinos might gain control of the labor market, either through the few Filipino contractors who had managed to establish themselves in spite of the intense competition from Chinese and Japanese or through exclusively Filipino union locals begun in the early and mid-1930s. One Nisei pointedly remarked: "We wanted to keep the Filipinos from getting too much power . . . because then they could kick the Japanese out." Many feared either the loss of their jobs or extreme exploitation, like that which non-Chinese in San Francisco faced under Chinese contractors and the subcontract system.[86]

A small core of Nisei believed that even the contractors could not protect their jobs. Unlike the elder Nisei leaders, who sided with business interests and the Republican party, the younger Nisei leaned toward the Democrats and sympathized with organized labor. The latter looked at the growing union movement among Filipinos with concern and hope. They found Filipinos' first efforts at ethnically segregated unionization troubling but recognized that Filipinos sought to combat the contract system that underrepresented them. Like the Issei and Nisei before them, these young liberal Nisei sought to capitalize on change. Rather than oppose an exclusively Filipino union that might leave them without cannery employment, prolabor Nisei tried to involve Japanese in the union movement to keep their cannery jobs open, to resolve some of the problems in the industry's labor relations, and ultimately even work to remedy some of the larger dilemmas they faced as a minority in American society.[87] The dynamics of those organizing efforts balanced against the concerns of a particular ethnic group are the subject of the ensuing chapters.

From the turn of the century to the 1940s Japanese modified existing patterns in labor recruitment and management to establish themselves in the canned-salmon industry. They interacted with other workers in the cannery communities and developed their own communities, and they and their children learned to cope with rapid economic and social change. Based on the timing of their entry into the labor market and their numbers, Japanese managed to secure positions first as subcontractors and then as contractors. Although Japanese were secondary to Chinese in power, the beachhead that the contractors provided gave Japanese the continued possibility of jobs and influence. That influence became evident in the "Japanese" canning communities they established. Especially in the Alaska canneries, these were simply Japanese versions of Chinese bunkhouse communities, but from the 1920s, the northward journeys of young Nisei took on new meaning: More than a means to immediate economic livelihood, they considered cannery work a passage to adulthood and a potential avenue for upward mobility. In continental U.S. canneries, a few Issei women added to their families' incomes and found that the relationships established in the plants allowed them to share concerns and responsibilities among themselves and hence to establish a women's work culture. At Steveston, British Columbia, the Japanese settlement contributed fishermen and cannery workers. Ethnic, rather than occupational, divisions reigned supreme, but gender lines did separate fishermen and women. In the plants, Issei women relied on familial and friendship ties to ease the burdens of their employment and give it greater meaning. Japanese established themselves in the industry, but just as they did so, competition from contenders and the economic woes wrought by the Great Depression altered their approaches to cannery work.

6

From Factionalism to "One Filipino Race"

BORN IN 1905 in the Ilocano region of the Philippines, Ponce Torres, along with a group of his schoolmates, emigrated to the United States via Seattle in 1925. Within two weeks of his arrival, Torres had signed on with a contractor recommended to him by townmates who had arrived in Seattle several months earlier. Seattle's Chinatown, he explained, "was the center of job employment to go to Alaska [because] . . . the offices of those Japanese, Chinese . . . , and Filipino contractors" were there.[1] By the end of the decade, the continual circuit of summer work in Alaska salmon canneries and fall apple harvests in Washington's Yakima Valley prevented him from consistently attending college—a dream he had held from his earliest thoughts of emigration. The onset of the Great Depression further exacerbated his plight, and by 1932 the frustrated Torres plunged into union organization as an alternative to his earlier endeavors. Many of Torres's fellow countrymen thought he "was crazy" to bring up unionization publicly in Seattle's Chinatown, virtually in front of the contractors' offices.[2] Torres responded: "We are but [a] laboring family that would belong to one class, that [we] are brothers rather than . . . Visayans or Ilocanos or Tagalog[s] or Pangasinan[s] or any sectionalist feeling. That . . . [is] the hardest part for us to do, to make ourselves understand that we are one Filipino race."[3]

Torres, like most Filipinos, entered the cannery labor market relatively late. Chinese and Japanese were so well entrenched in the labor recruitment and management system that despite Filipinos' numerical dominance in the cannery crews by the late 1920s, very few found positions as contractors. As a result, upward mobility was severely limited. Opportunities outside cannery employment were largely in seasonal agriculture or domestic service, so the chances for the additional schooling Filipinos believed would give them mobility seldom materialized. Ultimately, the depression curtailed remaining avenues to which Filipinos had looked for advancement. The centrality of cannery work to Filipino immigrants led some of them to fight for greater representation in the industry's labor recruitment and management

125

system, particularly through unionization. By the mid-1930s, the "warming" of organized labor toward Filipinos and other "ethnic" laborers, and the political climate of the New Deal, gave enough support to the unionization efforts that Ponce Torres and other Filipino unionists achieved their goal of uniting most of their fellow immigrants behind their organizing efforts.[4] How Filipinos first approached cannery work and then departed from established practices in the new labor organizations illustrates the persistence of ethnic loyalties amid class-based activities.

Late Entries

In the years before World War I, Filipinos who immigrated to the United States and its territories most often went to Hawaii. Plantation owners recruited them to supplement Chinese, Japanese, and Korean laborers already there.[5] Of the few Filipinos who ventured to the United States after Americans occupied the islands in 1898, most came as students.[6] Not until the end of World War I and the passage of the 1921 and 1924 immigration acts that forbade Asian immigration and restricted many Europeans did Filipinos begin to journey to the United States in significant numbers. Classified as United States nationals, they traveled with United States passports and were not affected by the ban on Asians.[7]

After their contracts with planters expired, Filipinos often migrated to the United States. Of those entering California in the 1920s, 56 percent came from Hawaii. Before mid-decade, that percentage ran high; in 1923 alone, 84.6 percent migrated from Hawaii. To plantation workers, the U.S. labor market promised greater choice and freedom of action.[8]

Direct migration from the Philippines took on a greater role by the end of the decade. Regular, direct steamer travel to Los Angeles, San Francisco, and Seattle made available relatively inexpensive steerage rates for emigrants.[9] The steady commercialization of agriculture on the archipelago until the mid-1920s also contributed to the number of Filipinos seeking passage out of the islands because it created a corps of wage laborers among the peasantry. Displaced peasants together with urbanites extended their search for employment to the American West. Many Filipinos, influenced by American teachers in the islands, migrated as laborers but had higher education in mind as the ultimate purpose of their relocation. For them, earning money in seasonal or domestic work was a means to attend American schools. Ramon Tancioco, like many others, left simply because there was "nothing to do in my town."[10] In 1928, with well-established travel routes and plentiful encouragement to leave the Philippines, 57 percent of all Filipinos arriving in California had embarked from Manila, while only 35.4 percent came from Hawaii.[11]

Whether they came from Hawaii or the Philippines, Filipinos immigrated with increasing frequency. In California from 1920 to 1922, an average of 618 annually entered the state from overseas. From 1923 to 1925, the average annual number jumped to 2,535, and then from 1926 to 1929, it leaped to 5,408.[12] Although the data reflect Filipino immigration only to California, the increase in Filipino employment over the decade in the Alaska canneries can be taken as a sign of their greater presence in the United States. In 1921, nearly a thousand Filipinos worked in Alaska, where they outnumbered Chinese by nearly a hundred and Japanese by more than three hundred.[13] Filipinos had competed with other "new" ethnics, including nearly fourteen hundred Mexicans and Mexican Americans, for those positions. The Mexican presence in Alaska peaked in 1923 and then waned as Nisei and Filipinos began to push them out of the canneries. So many Filipinos found work in the industry that in 1925 the *Juneau Gateway* aptly remarked: "Very seldom will you meet a Filipino along the Pacific Coast who had never been to Alaska."[14] The "Alaskeros," Filipino cannery hands who made the journey north, by 1928 numbered 3,916, compared to 1,065 Chinese, 1,445 Japanese, and 1,269 Mexicans.[15]

Filipino immigration to the United States thus supplied sufficient workers without any significant effort on the part of canners or contractors to recruit overseas. Instead, familial and friendship networks among the immigrants helped integrate them into the West's migrant and seasonal labor markets. Relatives and friends in the United States, already knowledgeable about job opportunities, greeted the newcomers. Those without relatives or friends would be met "right at the docks" by some of the more ambitious contractors. If they "did not realize that going to Alaska [was] one good source of income" when they first arrived, explained Ponce Torres, they learned that it meant "quick," though not "easy," money.[16]

Cannery jobs were a part of a large migratory circuit along which Filipinos trekked in the Far West. Work in lumber mills, for railroads, and on ranches and cash-crop farms of the West, as well as domestic service positions, was available to Filipinos, as it had been to the Chinese and Japanese before them. By the 1920s, however, the continued capitalist transformation of the entire American West forced Filipinos into far-flung searches for employment. Many followed the crops, taking seasonal jobs in Oregon, Washington, Idaho, Montana, California,

Arizona, and Texas. Transportation routes unavailable to Chinese and
Japanese and the availability of credit allowed Filipinos to purchase
cars to follow that wide circuit. Some of the immigrants were very
creative in obtaining autos. Toribio M. Martin noted: "Some boys
have cars . . . , but the cars don't even belong to them. . . . They pay
down on a car, you know. When [they are] unable to keep [up] on the
payment the [car dealership] goes down there [to California] and
pick[s] it up."[17]

Not all Filipinos defaulted on loans but instead pooled funds in
the small groups of family, friends, and fellow villagers in which they
traveled to help meet car payments and pay for fuel, food, and lodging.
Small-group affiliation and cooperation marked significant aspects of
the Filipino immigrant experience that helped them cope with their
positions as international labor migrants in the American West. In the
unionization of the canneries, the small group was both an asset and a
hindrance, as we discuss later.[18]

Cannery Employment

The agricultural labor circuit, supplemented with various urban jobs
throughout the year, provided Filipino immigrants with only enough
income to survive. As Toribio P. Madayag explained: "You can't make
no money in California."[19] Cannery employment proved an exception.
"We could depend on one job, and that is the Alaska [cannery] jobs
[sic]," remarked John Castillo.[20] Those prospects drew Filipinos to Seattle's "International" District, which housed a variety of immigrant
and ethnic groups. There they waited out the months of deepest winter
before cannery ships sailed north. The Alaskeros lived most of that
time in Seattle in rooms owned by contractors or friends of contractors. George Nishimura, who had started off as one of Goon Dip's
Japanese subcontractors in Seattle and later became a contractor himself, "used to hire a house for the Alaskeros," explained Zacarias Manangan. "Supposedly those that will go to Alaska should [stay] free."[21]
Nishimura did not deduct rent from workers' wages, but the Filipino
foreman he put in charge of running the boardinghouse charged Filipino residents a fee. He also put on airs and acted like a "big shot, . . .
rich guy."[22] Nishimura made no effort to develop the same *oyabun–kobun* (parent–child or superior–inferior) relationships with his boarders
that he shared with his fellow Japanese. Neither did his Filipino
foreman.[23]

Doubled up in their hotel and boardinghouse beds and dependent
on advances doled out by Chinese and Japanese contractors for "a job

in prospect," Filipino workers often accumulated considerable debt before the canning season began.[24] Aside from cash and credit advances for rooms, Chinese and Japanese contractors issued meal tickets redeemable at the restaurants they owned. While the extension of credit helped workers short on cash, who for a 15- or 20-cent ticket got a meal and dessert, it also put them in debt for as much as a month's wages. Contractors also forced workers to buy clothes, bedding, and rubber boots at inflated prices from their stores. Workers had no particular use for some items, such as the dress clothes, and sold them to pawnbrokers to get some cash. Jose Acena commented that Seattle's Japanese pawnbrokers did well because "Pinoys [Filipino immigrants] would go there in the pawn shop to get [money] . . . to gamble,"[25] but many did so to redeem part of their advances in cash to spend or save as they saw fit. Aware that the workers had funds, the proprietors of Chinese gambling houses offered free meals to attract hungry and bored Filipinos waiting to go north.[26] The entrepreneurial success of Seattle's Chinese and Japanese communities depended heavily on Filipino clientele, coerced or not. Like business enterprises in the Chinatowns in Sacramento and in the San Joaquin River delta area, Seattle's Chinese and Japanese businesses were "parasites" feeding off these workers' incomes. Local contractors were also deeply involved in these businesses. If a Filipino complained too loudly about the circumstances, he found it difficult to land a cannery job in subsequent years.[27]

Such practices created much resentment. Many Filipinos retaliated by flocking to the pool halls, restaurants, and boardinghouses run by other Filipinos, who had scraped up the capital to open small businesses. Even though the few Filipino contractors were involved in these small businesses, ethnic ties to the workers prevented extreme exploitation. Bibliana Castillano recalled no coercion in her husband's contracting and merchant activities. He was "so charitable he almost supported the whole town," she contended. When Alaskeros bought goods from him, they purchased only "what they want and can afford."[28]

Filipino workers felt little animosity, particularly in the 1920s, toward their countrymen who had established themselves as contractors and businessmen. The contractors admitted that they made "a little money" in the arrangement, but workers like John Mendoza concurred that the three or four Filipino contractors in Seattle "were all pretty good" to their Filipino crews.[29] Like Chinese and Japanese before them, Filipino contractors, subcontractors, and most foremen gave favored treatment to members of their own ethnic group. Each "boss," Teodolo A. Ranjo explained, gave special treatment to certain people, who in turn remained loyal to him.

> I was not really discriminated upon by the contractor. . . . Pedro Santos, we call him Panyell, he used to favor the students. He would hire [Filipino] students before he gets somebody else because he knew we were struggling for better education and he believe[d] we were good workers. I had a nice job from Pedro Santos every time I went to Alaska.[30]

Whether contractors favored students because they admired their aspirations for a better life or because they considered them more pliant workers is not clear. But what is clear is that Filipino contractors tried to protect at least some of their countrymen working for them, just as Chinese and Japanese had done.[31]

Not many Filipinos became contractors, however, because of the oligarchy of Chinese and Japanese. Owners tended to retain Chinese and Japanese contractors with whom they had dealt for years, and that practice contributed to a minority rule in the labor market. Filipino workers believed that Chinese and Japanese contractors did not represent their interests and even set them against each other, as the boarders in George Nishimura's boardinghouse testified. Nonetheless, they persisted in their attempts to gain access to cannery jobs. Some tried to break into the industry by playing on the owners' prejudices. In 1931 a group of Filipinos represented by Lee P. Root, a "white" contractor, submitted a bid to the Fidalgo Island Packing Company (FIPC) for the 1932 season in which Root promised "an ample supply of Filipino labor headed by competent foremen."[32] Root differed from Asian contractors by telling the owners that dealing with him would mean doing "business with a reliable *white* man."[33] Filipinos in Root's crew may not have known the language he used in communicating with the company, but they must have hoped that the common ethnicity shared by Root and the owners might bring them jobs.

Even those favored by the existing system at times tried to bypass the contractors. When the FIPC's main Chinese contractor Seid Back died in 1932, members of the Filipino Students' Association at the University of Washington hoped to take advantage of the situation by negotiating with the company themselves without the help of a contractor. The students submitted a bid that was 5 cents per case lower than the industry average and assured the company that "[we are] blessed with two very capable foremen . . . [and have] just the right men for your canneries."[34] The company promptly and politely turned down the request the next day. Company managers preferred to select workers from established contractors rather than from upstarts like the students.[35] Their failure aside, the students' decision to act through a small group was in line with their cultural norms.

Filipinos ordinarily broke into the ranks of contractors only under special circumstances. When, in the midst of negotiations with the FIPC for the 1932 season, Seid Back died, the company hired two separate contractors, dividing its business between another Chinese, a relative of Seid Back, and a Filipino, Pio De Cano, who ran the most extensive Filipino contracting and subcontracting business in the Pacific Northwest and had previously supplied Filipinos for the company as a subcontractor. Discussion about changes in labor recruitment and management practices had been under way in the company since the late 1920s because of declining product prices. Managers hoped that the move would save them money and make the handling of crews easier. They also avoided the problem of relying on untried parties like those represented by Root or the Filipino students. The managers were not ready to break new ground in their labor recruitment and management practices.[36]

While a few Filipinos, like De Cano, managed to become contractors, canners' preferences for experienced labor provisioners allowed most "aspirant" Filipinos to rise only to the position of foremen. Owners, and Chinese and Japanese contractors, believed that Filipinos worked best under "bosses" from the islands. They thus delegated the responsibilities of recruitment and management to Filipino foremen, who in turn received relatively high remuneration and special treatment. Sylvestre A. Tangalan's experience reveals just how much becoming a foreman meant to Filipino immigrants. Tangalan had worked during the 1930s in the canneries to finance his education in architecture at the University of Washington. When he graduated, he received two job offers, one as an architect in Manila and the other as a foreman in Alaska. Unfortunately, he reported, the position in Manila "was a little dismal compared to what I could get as a foreman in Alaska."[37] He took the Alaska job because it offered better pay and more responsibility, but ultimately lost it in a dispute with the Cannery Workers and Farm Laborers Union, which was to target foremen as remnants of the old contract system after 1939. Tangalan's choice reveals the importance with which Filipino immigrants viewed the position of foreman.[38]

In spite of their shared ethnicity, Filipinos in positions of power, especially foremen, took advantage of their countrymen. Nishimura's foreman squeezed rents out of workers. Others demanded half a month's pay or more just for the promise of a cannery job. For example, Romero Alin recalled that "sometimes you have to give about $25 to the foreman so you can get a job."[39] Still others bankrolled gambling tables on the ships and at the canneries. According to Alin, foremen asked workers: "Can you gamble, or do you gamble?" "If you are not a gambler," he explained, "they will not hire you."[40] The narrow access to cannery jobs forced Filipino workers to depend on those who might take advantage of them.

Foremen also acted as overseers at the cannery. They resorted to a "drive system" to a far greater degree than had Chinese or Japanese. Cannery work had always been fast paced when fish reached the plants in large numbers, but by the 1920s and 1930s, as Filipinos entered the industry, the mechanized nature of the work had greatly accelerated the pace. Ponce Torres explained: "We got to work fast" to keep up with automated canning lines.[41] Chinese and Japanese contractors gave better-paying, lighter work to their countrymen and placed Filipinos in the more demanding jobs. Contractors felt justified in making these ethnic divisions of labor because Filipinos were generally stronger than the older Chinese and Issei, as well as the school-age Nisei. Among Filipino workers, an inability to keep up with the pace meant no job the following season. For foremen, it meant confrontations with disappointed cannery superintendents and contractors. To keep their own positions, Filipino foremen pushed their crews hard.[42]

Alaskero Life

Filipino workers kept up the pace, for the most part, because they were young and strong. "It's pretty good work," noted Mike Castillano, "it's not bad, it makes you strong."[43] Alaska was a romantic adventure, a proving ground for men such as Castillano, much as it had been for many Nisei. To be an Alaskero was to be a survivor, a toughened veteran of the canneries. Filipinos so desired to be a part of that select group that a few stowed away aboard steamers headed for Alaska. In the 1930s, Toribio M. Martin was one such adventurer. He sneaked onto a steamer, in his words, to go "visiting" in Alaska. He and fifteen other stowaways were discovered en route and put ashore at Cordova, Alaska. There they "stole" from cannery kitchens with the help of Filipino cooks who gave them handouts; toward the end of the canning season, they got jobs as "extra hires." Martin had no regrets about the hardships of his Alaska voyage.[44] While the stowaways were not typical, they illustrate the strong lure of work in an Alaska cannery.

Among Filipinos, Chinese, and Japanese, life at the canneries did not vary significantly. All provided their own bedding for bunks made of planks nailed together without springs or mattresses. The bunkhouse, according to John Castillo, might be "nothing but a big empty room . . . [in which] you can make your own partition to have a little privacy."[45] At older plants, Filipino workers lived in mixed bunkhouses with Chinese and Japanese, but in the newer facilities they lived in segregated quarters. In 1919 at the Columbia River Packers Association (CRPA) plant in Chignik, Alaska, the company provided one twenty-by-fifty-foot structure dubbed the "China Quarters" for twenty-six Chinese and three Japanese workers and a two-room, twenty-by-fifty-foot "Phillipean [*sic*] house" for its thirty Filipino employees. The company also provided separate quarters for the Chinese foreman, Native Alaskan workers, and European American fishermen.[46] As with the Japanese earlier, cannery owners found it beneficial to segregate new workers. While the action lessened overt ethnic conflicts, it helped perpetuate segregation among the mixed crews.

Work schedules and leisure time were also little different for Filipinos than they had been for Chinese and Japanese before them. Filipinos occupied themselves after a day in the cannery with Ping-Pong, horseshoes, volleyball, and card games.[47] When they tired of messhouse meals of rice, salmon, *pindang* (also *daing*), or jerked scrap fish, they went on picnics, tried to "hook some trout," and even (illegally) hunted deer. They also gathered crabs, mussels, and berries and kept gardens and raised pigs to supplement the cannery fare.[48]

Filipino immigrants had a penchant for dances and music, making certain to bring musical instruments, phonographs, and records to the plants. They took great pride in their "orchestras," which played at cannery dances on Saturday nights and holidays. So important were music and dance to Filipinos that in the late 1930s and early 1940s in their union contract negotiations with companies, they demanded phonographs and a supply of popular records.[49] Other workers at the plants were less enthusiastic about the dances. Older Chinese and Issei retreated to their own activities in the evenings, but Nisei attended the dances, although few took the floor. Most were intimidated by the dashing, daring moves of Filipino workers as they danced with Native American and occasionally European American women from the canneries and nearby settlements. Nisei danced, too, but only the brashest of the schoolboys risked their reputation on such activities.[50]

More than Chinese or Japanese workers had done, Filipinos married Native American, African American, and European American women.[51] The cannery dances were only incidental to that phenomenon. Most Filipino immigrants were fluent in English or had considerable facility in the language, and that made it easier for them to communicate with the women. The growth of small communities in southeast Alaska by the 1920s also afforded young Filipino immigrants more opportunities to meet women at the canneries than had been available to Chinese or Japanese earlier in the century. In one such case, Romero Alin met the Tlingit woman who became his wife in Ketchikan.[52]

Some Filipinos believed that they could become a part of American society through marrying a European American woman, a faith based on images of the United States supplied by American educators in the Philippines. When Salvador del Fierro married a woman from an Italian immigrant family he met during the 1920s in a Ketchikan, Alaska, cannery, he may have been influenced by such assumptions.[53] Nonetheless, by the end of the 1920s, many dated and married other persons of color and avoided courting "white" women because of the hostility that such relationships generated. With few reservations, the Filipino community welcomed women of color as new members. Their cosmopolitan perspective helped Filipinos in their relations with others in the United States.[54]

With only minor exceptions, then, Filipinos fit into the industry much as Chinese and Japanese had in earlier decades. They found employment through contractors, most of whom were not Filipinos. At the canneries, their outward behavior marked them as somewhat different from other groups, but for the most part they adapted to preexisting patterns. They seemed able and willing to cope with what limitations existed for them in the industry. Yet the onset of the Great Depression significantly altered Filipino perspectives on cannery work and their immigrant experience. They were transformed from youthful, adventurous, and romantic Alaskeros to hardened workers scratching for survival.

"Improvement Should Be Done"

The impact of the depression affected Filipinos in short order. Between 1929 and 1933, wages for unskilled cannery positions occupied primarily by Filipino workers dropped by 40 percent.[55] What had been in the 1920s "a good source of income" no longer provided even a minimum for survival. Outside the canneries, they faced lower pay in other migratory jobs.[56] In 1933 when some Alaskeros went from their cannery jobs to pick hops near Yakima, Washington, they barely earned enough in the twenty-day hop season to pay for the 165-mile trip to Seattle, where they hoped to spend the winter. Apple picking in Washington's Wenatchee Valley, formerly a regular part of the migratory harvest cycle, went to hard-pressed "local" European American help given preferential hiring by orchardists.[57] One Filipino cannery worker, Ramon Tancioco, managed to find a winter job at a farm near Gresham, Oregon, but earned only 15 cents an hour. Tancioco indicated that he would not ordinarily have considered the job, but at the time he was in no position to refuse it. Even on that small amount he might have fared well enough, but his employer paid him in wood to burn in his stove rather than in the cash he needed to buy food.[58]

The depression also shattered the dream of a formal education held by Filipino immigrants. Quite simply, according to Ponce Torres, "when there was no job we could not go to school, there was no money."[59] Before the depression, Filipinos' hopes for education had seemed possible. Between 1920 and 1925, an estimated two thousand of them (about 15 percent of the total Filipino population in the continental United States) attended school, and by the end of the decade, the number had increased dramatically. In 1928 alone, approximately a thousand enrolled in classes. The depression took its toll; in 1932 only eight hundred matriculated, in 1935 just five hundred; by 1939, the number had fallen to three hundred.[60] Declining cannery incomes forced Filipinos to find other seasonal jobs, which extended their work season and left little time for school. The upward mobility they hoped might come to them through cannery work disappeared in the depression.

For Filipinos, the earlier adventure and romance of Alaska had been transformed into an unattractive reality. "As we grow older in the cannery," recounted Ponce Torres, "then we learn that we are being abused and improvement should be done."[61] How improvements should be made, however, was not immediately clear to them.

Filipino workers had several options. They could attempt to rally behind an individual or small group, as they had with Lee P. Root or the Filipino Students' Association, or look to organized labor. Efforts at the former had yielded little in the previous years. In the latter, they had the example of the Cannery and Agricultural Workers Industrial Union (CAWIU) formed in 1930. The Trade Union Unity League, sponsored by the Comintern, had joined with the ethnic fraternal orders of California field workers to organize the CAWIU. Its initial efforts were among Mexican migrant agricultural workers, but within several months it incorporated Filipinos as participants in work stoppages throughout California. The CAWIU urged Filipinos, Mexicans, and European Americans to recognize that "a boss is a boss" and to join in "working-class unity" against contractors and ethnic middlemen who promoted a "nationalistic unity" and "fake unions" as an alternative to the class-conscious action urged by the CAWIU. The CAWIU made some headway but dissolved after 1934 when the Comintern moved away from attempts to form competing labor organizations to joint action within a united front against fascism. For locals up and down the coast, the dispersal of its members into other labor organizations provided important leaders who pushed for class action amid narrow ethnic interests. Some attempted to bridge the ethnic divisions among various workers in the unions that emerged in the mid-1930s. During its tenure, the CAWIU provided support and assistance to Filipinos in agricultural jobs but did not organize workers in the salmon canneries.[62]

The CAWIU was not the only organization for agricultural workers. In the Pacific Northwest, Filipinos toiling in the fields and orchards near Seattle in 1930 formed the Filipino Laborers' Association (FLA). Instead of serving as an example of a multiethnic alliance like the CAWIU, the FLA pitted Filipino workers against Japanese growers. It did not extend to the canneries, and its emphasis on ethnic exclusiveness epitomized the initial stages of the subsequent unionization effort among cannery workers in the Pacific Northwest.[63]

Organizing a Union

Not until the winter of 1932 did efforts at unionization among Filipino salmon-cannery hands in the Pacific Northwest begin. Ponce Torres recalled that only "a few people [met] to plan something to improve ourselves."[64] They congregated in secret for fear of reprisals by contractors and canners. Torres explained that they could not "possibly get many people at one time. . . . We have to do it between school days."[65] Planning around school schedules indicated the central role played by students in the effort. More than other Filipinos, students felt the constraints on their expectations for social mobility during the depression, which explains their interest in changing the labor recruitment and management practices in the industry. Nonetheless, this early cabal barely included a dozen members.[66]

The small group of planners concluded that "the only solution to the problem is to be organized," and in June 1933 they held a special public meeting of the Filipino Laborers' Association to discuss affiliation with the American Federation of Labor (AFL). The "big crowd" of seven Filipino union officers and nineteen others listened to C. W. Doyle of Seattle's Central Labor Council, carefully discussed the issue, and voted in favor of affiliation. On June 19, 1933, the Filipinos entered the AFL as the Cannery Workers and Farm Laborers Union (CWFLU), Local 18257.[67] Although the reasons for AFL endorsement of the local are unclear, CAWIU successes in organizing California field laborers may have jolted the AFL into action to head off what it perceived as a communist-led insurgency.[68]

The newly affiliated local stressed goals that revealed the barriers to be overcome if the workers were to improve their condition. The union pledged to foster the attainment of higher skills and efficiency among its members. Although unions invariably used such language, Filipinos did need to cultivate their canning expertise in order to make possible their movement into the specialized tasks monopolized by Chinese and Japanese. The local also proposed shorter working hours, which would either bring greater overtime pay in rush periods or force the hiring of larger crews and thus provide more jobs for unemployed Filipinos.[69]

To achieve its goals, the local also had to unite a divided Filipino community. This proved no easy task. In Seattle, for example, most Filipino immigrants were Ilocanos, but the community also had Tagalogs, Pangasinans, and Visayans—each group with its own dialect—as well as other ethnic associations. In 1923 Tagalogs in Seattle had founded a branch of the Caballeros Dimas Alang (its title originating from revolutionary Jose Rizal's pen name). In that political, nationalistic, and self-help organization, members conducted rituals and secret meetings in Tagalog to the exclusion of other groups. Not every Filipino association was based on ethnicity, however. In the late 1920s, students at the University of Washington had formed a Filipino Club that fostered their academic pursuits, helped with their social lives, and provided economic assistance. Contractors helped raise money to run the club, and they used that connection as an avenue to a labor supply. Small-group activity was symptomatic of the factions among Filipino immigrants. The manner in which Filipinos entered and worked in the industry further heightened their reliance on such groups.[70]

Before the depression, the use of family, friendship, and ethnic networks to gain employment had its advantages for Filipinos, who faced a Chinese and Japanese oligarchy over labor recruitment and management in the industry. That strategy also helped at the plants where Filipinos worked in the small groups characteristic of their immigration. Sylvestre A. Tangalan explained that at the cannery where he worked: "We were happy, mostly Bauanganians," fellow villagers from La Union.[71] Segregation at the cannery reinforced, rather than destroyed, Filipino ethnic and immigrant ties.

The elimination of cannery jobs and severe wage cuts caused by the depression threw these small associations into intense competition with each other. Trinadad Rojo recalled that there was "quite a struggle for jobs frequently."[72] Union organizer Chris Mensalvas tersely noted, "there . . . [were] too many organizations" to create any unity among Filipinos.[73]

To overcome factionalism, the founding members of the CWFLU made a vague promise to encourage friendship among Filipino cannery workers, but that did not carry much weight amid the intense competition for jobs. They made more progress when they agreed to allow foremen into their ranks as long as these men had no shares in the companies for which they worked. By this method, the local's leaders hoped to represent the various factions within the Filipino community and still maintain some measure of control over the foremen. Foremen were valuable potential assets to the union because they had historically held power over Filipino workers in the recruitment process and at the worksite and because they represented the highest Filipino position in the contracting hierarchy.[74]

Union officials could also have allowed contractors and labor agents to join their organization in order to represent factions in the community, but they did not. They believed that contractors might compromise the local in its negotiations with the companies and undermine the position of workers in ways that foremen would not. Instead, the local hoped to take from contractors the authority to set wages, thereby guaranteeing members' wages and increasing its appeal.[75]

In the 1933 season, after its affiliation with the AFL, the Filipino-led local made little progress, a problem that some attributed to an inability to attract foremen into the ranks. "We got no chance to employ our member[s]," lamented Ponce Torres, "because we were not foremen." The companies "did not recognize us," he continued, and the union was unable to provide many jobs for its members.[76] The local did manage to extract a promise from some Chinese and Japanese contractors to hire unskilled workers at $45 per month, $15 to $20 more than the going rate. Once on the boats, however, contractors and their foremen informed workers that the wage rate was $25 a month.[77]

Contractors' refusals to allow the Filipino-led AFL to recruit and the low wages they paid during 1933 led the leaders of the CWFLU to attack the contract system. Directly confronting contractors proved difficult for Filipino unionists. Many young Filipinos had relied on earlier arrivals from the Philippines for assistance in finding jobs and dealing with the frequently abrasive, even abusive, American society. Since elders, other family members, and fellow villagers had often steered them toward contractors, a web of mutual obligations tied these immigrants to the contractors.[78]

Rather than attack all contractors, officials in the local realized they had to be flexible because of the factionalism in the Filipino community. In their negotiations for the 1934 season, the local's leaders at first called for direct contracts between the local and canning companies, but the mass meeting in December 1933, at which Ilocano-, Tagalog-, English-, and Spanish-speaking interpreters explained the union program, illustrated the problems in uniting Filipino workers. To convince them of their unity, that they were "one Filipino race," officials of the local decided to target only Chinese and Japanese, not Filipino, contractors. The local's leaders, however, set aside the call for direct contracts until, as one leader put it, "the union will be stable financially."[79]

To foster that stability, officials of the local secretly wrote to contractor Pio De Cano about the necessity of cooperation among all Filipino workers, unionists, and contractors. The great changes taking place in America because of the depression and the desperate plight of Filipinos in the country made it imperative, wrote the secretary of the local "that we . . . get together to formulate a strategic plan by which we can accomplish our common cause and ultimate goal . . . the consequent and eventual control of our Filipino Labor and the Canned Salmon Industry itself."[80] Their conciliatory approach to De Cano signaled the officials' desire to place themselves on a level equal to that of Filipino contractors and to win their cooperation. In March 1934, their efforts came to fruition in a round-table conference of Filipino contractors, foremen, and the local's leaders. Contractors at the meeting promised to hire union members if possible. De Cano, at least, followed through on that promise and dispatched eleven union members to one Alaska cannery in late May.[81]

During these negotiations, union officials sent mixed messages to the National Recovery Administration (NRA). Virgil Dunyungan (president of the CWFLU) and Cornelio Mislang (secretary of the CWFLU), in a confidential memo to the NRA, blasted Chinese, Japanese, and Filipino contractors.[82] In his testimony before the NRA Codes of Fair Practice and Competition hearings in San Francisco, Dunyungan repeatedly called for the abolition of the contract system and the institution of written contracts between workers and companies, the contracts to be signed and the workers paid at union headquarters. Throughout his testimony, however, he did not once mention Filipino contractors, only Chinese and Japanese.[83] Clarence T. Arai, a prominent elder Nisei from Seattle also at the hearing, pointedly reminded those in attendance that there were Filipino contractors in the industry.[84] Pio De Cano's submission of a petition bearing 150 to 200 signatures of Filipinos favoring continuation of the contract system further confirmed the link between Filipino workers and Filipino contractors.[85]

Ethnic representation was at the heart of the issue, and the CWFLU demonstrated little willingness to include Chinese and Japanese workers in its membership. In January 1935 the local's membership voted "that Seattle Filipinos will be employed first in the canneries."[86] By implication, Chinese, Japanese, and all other workers ran a distant second in priority.

Neither AFL-sanctioned locals like the Filipino-led CWFLU in Seattle nor the ethnic Japanese Cannery Workers Association under Arai and the Filipino Cannery Workers Association under De Cano proposed a complete elimination of contractors. Instead, they sought to place their segregated organizations into the existing contract system as specialized recruiters and distributors of labor for their ethnic constituents. Their efforts were frustrated, however, by other organizations also competing for members. Seattle's Filipinos on the left were drawn away from the AFL local and into the Fishermen and Cannery Workers' Industrial Union (FCWIU). Sponsored by the Trade Union Unity League as a rival to the CWFLU before 1936, the FCWIU attracted many who had not benefited from contractor connections, were frustrated with the slow headway and narrow interests of the CWFLU, and were tired of only rhetoric about eliminating contractors. In 1935 the FCWIU dissolved under the Comintern's united front, and many of its supporters eventually joined the CWFLU. They entered the CWFLU as its unity splintered over the issues of the role and place of contractors in the organization and the degree to which the local should represent ethnic or class interests.[87]

After 1935, a small core of leaders in the CWFLU began to be more critical of the contractors, but the union also contained procontractor members frustrated with the lack of social and educational mobility in the union and the United States at large. John Ayamo, Seattle's premier Filipino lawyer and an activist in the first two years of the CWFLU's operation, sided with those who wanted to retain the contractors. As one of the few established professionals among Filipinos in Seattle, he had attained considerable social status. Neither membership in the union nor minor offices satisfied him, and early in 1935 Ayamo broke with the local to head the Filipino Labor Protective Association. CWFLU officials claimed that the association tried to profit at the expense of the workers by acting as the contractors had done and that it was composed of "destructive elements" who sided with contractors and companies against Filipino interests. Ayamo and the

Protective Association in turn accused Dunyungan of mismanagement of the local's funds, high-handed tactics in dealing with members, and collusion with company owners. Both sides had grounds for their accusations, and the rivalry deeply divided the already factionalized Filipino community in Seattle.[88]

The relationship between the camps was further exacerbated by battles between the Teamsters and Longshoremen, led respectively by Dave Beck and Harry Lundeberg (the latter an official of the Sailors Union of the Pacific and a close associate of Beck's arch enemy, Harry Bridges) over control of the waterfront. These wars pitted Seattle's labor organizations against one another. As each side sought allies, the leaders of the cannery workers' organizations were drawn into the struggle. Most workers, however, though aware of the hurricane that raged above their heads, focused on more immediate issues of personality conflicts within their own community, ethnic representation, and future jobs, rather than on the internecine warfare of the large labor organizations in the area.[89]

Desire for upward mobility splintered the Filipino community, and the factions included more than simply the CWFLU and Ayamo's Filipino Labor Protective Association. Aside from clearly contractor-backed organizations, like De Cano's Filipino Labor Association, non-union "aspriant agents" also tried to break into the ranks of the industry's labor recruiters and managers. S. M. Estepa of the Filipino Alaska Canneries Workers Association best represents such efforts. To the NRA, which was investigating the industry, Estepa argued that Chinese and Japanese, who constituted only about a quarter of the cannery crews, got substantially better work, food, and wages than did Filipinos, who made up three-quarters of the workforce. The result, he claimed, "is rather hard for Filipinos . . . , creating resentment." Estepa complained about Chinese and Japanese who had "a system of excluding any new aspirant contractors by emphasizing to the packing companies . . . th[ese] new aspirant[s'] unreliability." Government intervention to "prevent the monopoly of one or two men who enjoyed the friendship of the superintendents and foremen in the canneries" would relieve the problem. The NRA could police the system to "prevent monopoly" and force canners to rely on "competent aspirant agents" who would better represent the ethnic makeup of the industry's labor market.[90]

While the NRA proffered little help, Estepa's rhetoric about mobility, ethnic representation, and monopoly struck at the heart of the problem confronting the CWFLU. The local's inability to break the contractors' control over hiring discouraged Filipinos from joining. As late as 1936, the CWFLU could claim only 375 members who paid their dues on a regular basis, a rather small number in comparison to the nearly 2,000 who, through the contractors, paid "dues" only during the canning season. The former were committed members; the latter paid dues only as an employment fee.[91]

Attempts by the CWFLU to wrest control from contractors might have been more successful had government agencies been more supportive. Government officials were not unaware of the problem. John R. Arnold, a mid-level NRA bureaucrat, believed the contract system "gouged the workers employed under it, and has in all probability raised the price of canned salmon." Arnold estimated that contractors in 1933 earned an average profit of nearly $51 for each person they placed in a job. This charge for "services rendered," according to Arnold, made it "difficult to see . . . why [companies] have supposed the labor contract system to be economical from their own standpoint."[92]

In spite of Arnold's personal crusade within the NRA to eliminate contractors, the definition of "member of the industry" in the code remained vague enough to allow contracting to continue in a thinly disguised form. The canners, seeking stability and reliability, for the most part stood by their old contractors, who in most cases simply called themselves "labor agents" for the companies under the provisions of the NRA rather than independent labor contractors. The companies paid a per capita sum to the agents for each man recruited and a bonus of 3 to 5 cents for each case of salmon packed during the season. The former contractors still recruited laborers but turned the list of names over to the local along with the season's dues deducted in advance from the workers' pay. The union's position remained unchanged except for the additional dues it received. (It was the alleged favoritism and personal gain in disbursing the money from these dues that prompted dissatisfied union members to charge Dunyungan and other CWFLU officials with corruption.) The NRA's reluctance to eliminate contracting, according to Arnold, was because the "familiar phrase about oppressing small enterprises makes it impossible to eliminate . . . [the contractors] from the picture." The "tenderness," charged Arnold, which the NRA legal division held for contractors thus assured their continuation.[93]

But the NRA code also signaled the beginnings of the contractors' demise in the industry. Before the code, only a few owners had anticipated problems in the contract system. After years of bad press, the canners, under the auspices of the Association of Pacific Fisheries, met in 1933 "to discuss and adopt a constructive program re[garding] contract labor."[94] During 1934 and 1935, the Alaska Packers Association, which since the 1910s had been the regular recipient of negative press reports concerning workers' exploitation by the company's contractors and subcontractors, was one of the first packers to adopt the labor-agent arrangements of the NRA code. The Canned-Salmon Industry Inc., the business association for the owners, had urged packers to carry out the NRA code provisions "in good faith," to remember that "these employment agents are *your agent[s]*," and to keep in mind that "the industry wants no criticism." By accepting the NRA's role and modifications in the contract system, the canners began to moderate their relationship to contractors.[95]

Two NRA actions won over owners and helped assure that contractors could no longer act independently. The NRA consciously developed its alliance with the canners and kept them informed of its decisions at every step. While owners made some concessions, in the end they benefited from this federal intervention. For most industries, the NRA set minimum wages and maximum hours. While it accomplished the first in the canned-salmon industry, it refused to limit the weekly hours of work because canners (and agriculturalists as well) successfully argued that "the entire season is an emergency." Well aware of the NRA's activities and believing they had won a critical exemption, most canners tried to cooperate with the NRA's labor provisions.[96]

Those provisions transformed labor recruitment and management. The contractors struggled with an uncertain future. In 1934 Seid Sing, contractor turned labor agent for the Fidalgo Island Packing Company (FIPC), wrote to the company of the problems he faced. "At the present," he explained, "a lot of Filipino boys came to see me about jobs at the canneries, but I have not made much of a promise."[97] Unable to assure employment with any certainty, contractors like Seid lost credibility among workers.

Contractors lost power at the plants, too, as the code provisions shifted the emphasis of managing workers away from the contractors to the cannery superintendents. Vance Sutter, superintendent of a FIPC plant, complained: "That damn [code] pamphlet can be interpreted any way one would like it to read." Sutter's frustration resulted from his increased responsibilities.[98]

When the United States Supreme Court declared the NRA unconstitutional in 1935, contractors nevertheless faced the same problems. Canners continued to carry out the spirit of the NRA labor provisions because they were convinced that their new cooperative public image was valuable, particularly given prolabor sentiments during the New Deal era. Following the Court's decision, the National Canners' Association urged salmon canners "to continue present employment conditions" because "changes at this time would disturb conditions within the industry."[99] The FIPC concurred that "all packers contacted so far have signified their approval of continuing the present [cooperative strategy] . . . , particularly on account of the labor situation."[100]

Contractors increasingly had reason to cooperate with the Filipino-run CWFLU. In 1934 the CWFLU arranged jobs for members through six contractors (officially listed as "agents"). Two were Filipino; the remainder Japanese. By 1936, the local had increased the number of contractors to eight, among them Goon Dip and several smaller-scale Chinese contractors.[101] The commitment of workers recruited under these circumstances is difficult to determine because in this arrangement the contractors paid members' dues. Nonetheless, in that same year, the local managed to arrange with three large canning companies the direct hiring of its members. The ability to work its way into the labor recruiting process significantly enhanced the union's image, power, and membership.[102]

To compete with the contractors and aspirant agents even more successfully, the CWFLU adopted a series of social welfare programs for members. It gave $50 to a Filipino-owned cafe in exchange for the restaurateur's providing meals to "indigent active members." The local also loaned money to members. In 1935, for example, it approved a $50 loan to a Filipino who a year earlier had supported the local's efforts in a farm workers' strike near Seattle.[103] Such actions helped members avoid indebtedness to contractors and encouraged nonunion Filipinos to think seriously about joining. Allocation of the local's financial resources for any purpose other than supporting cannery organization, however, led to charges of favoritism and misuse of union funds. In spite of the charges, the local's efforts to provide meals and money for some of its members reveal that some money was returned to the rank and file.[104]

As the union's membership grew to several hundred in the first few years, it created its own job ladder, separate from that of the existing hierarchy of cannery tasks. At first, titles were awarded as recognition of service to the union and carried status only. Financial stability soon allowed the local to pay its officers for their contributions. The salaries for 1935 reveal the significance of income from a union position relative to the average cannery worker's $25–$50 a month during the canning season. The CWFLU monthly salary scale for officers was: president, $80; vice-president, $40; secretary, $60; treasurer, $40; trustees, $40; guard, $20; guide, $20. Their salaries also touched off resentment, especially when they voted raises for themselves.[105]

The local also became politically active in an attempt to achieve recognition as the voice of the Filipino community. Its appearance at the NRA code hearings marked it as an early advocate for the Filipino community. Elsewhere, the local's records indicate no activity concerning the Tydings-McDuffie Act (1934), which proposed eventual independence for the Philippines but also contained stringent immigration restrictions. The CWFLU did get involved in at least two other legislative actions at the state level. In 1935 the local sent a three-person delegation to Olympia to fight against antimiscegenation bills in the Washington state legislature.[106] Also, in 1937, the local protested a Washington state bill that would prevent Filipino immigrants from owning or leasing lands because of their newly acquired "alien" status under the Tydings-McDuffie Act.[107] Such highly visible political lobbying enhanced the local's status in the Filipino community. Among contractors, only Pio De Cano took up broader community concerns, challenging in state courts the application of antialien land laws to Filipino immigrants between 1937 and 1941.[108]

The local also cultivated community support through its public relations efforts. It gave to the *Philippine American Chronicle* a 4 percent interest loan as well as gifts of cash. In return, the CWFLU asked for a regular labor column in the paper. Thereafter, the *Chronicle* became for all practical purposes the local's official organ. This was no great concession for the paper because two officials of the local, Virgil Dunyungan and Cornelio Mislang, were the publishers. While the local's involvement with the *Chronicle* gave it a wider voice within the community, it also fostered deeper divisions because the other major newspaper, the *Philippine Advocate*, lined up against the local and the *Chronicle* and was backed by Ayamo's Filipino Protective Labor Association.[109]

Martyrdom and Its Effects

The CWFLU efforts to do more than negotiate for higher wages and better hours for its members and the larger community indicate that its leaders genuinely attempted to remedy problems confronting Filipinos. Yet in spite of its best efforts to unite the community behind a unionization drive appealing to ethnicity, the CWFLU made little headway. Charges of graft and corruption against Dunyungan and other officials made the local an easy target in a community with many factions. Only the murders of two top leaders and a concerted propaganda effort provided the essential, if temporary, cement to bring the Filipino community together behind the unionization movement.[110]

The motives and actions behind the killings in December 1936 of union leaders Virgil Dunyungan and Aurelio Simon, along with Placidio Patron (the nephew of a contractor), are shrouded in mystery. Apparently, during the summer and fall of 1936, Dunyungan, using Simon as a go-between, had been meeting with Japanese and Filipino contractors and Clarence Arai, perhaps the most visible representative for the Japanese cannery workers in Seattle at the time. The record is not clear on what transpired at these discussions. A few contemporaries accused Dunyungan and Simon of taking money from contractors who were trying to control the local. The increasing involvement of Japanese in the CWFLU beginning in 1936 lends some credibility to the possibility that Dunyungan may have been using the contractors and Arai to recruit Japanese workers into the local to eliminate a source of competition and conflict.[111]

On December 1, 1936, Dunyungan and Simon were to meet at the Gyokku Ken Cafe, owned in part by prominent Japanese contractor George Nishimura, and the usual contact place for clandestine meetings. The only point of consensus among those recalling the event was that Dunyungan, Simon, and Patron died there. Two scenarios of the shooting predominated. In the first, Placidio Patron shot Dunyungan and Simon. Dunyungan died almost immediately, and Simon, though mortally wounded, managed to kill Patron. The story accepted by the local police and local white press, which regarded the killings as interracial murders and thus inconsequential, was that Patron had acted out of his dislike for the CWFLU and the competition it offered his own "hiring hall."[112]

In the second scenario, after Patron had killed Dunyungan and Simon, a hidden assailant shot him to prevent him from revealing the motive for the murders. Contractors could have paid Patron to slay the two officials and then ordered Patron's death to eliminate any connections to them. Unionists favored this explanation.[113] Margaret Dunyungan, Virgil's wife, gave yet a third reason. She implied that hostile forces within the local itself wanted Dunyungan out of the way because the charges of corrupt activities against him were hurting the union program.[114]

Who killed Dunyungan, Simon, and Patron is still a mystery, but what emerged in the aftermath is not. The local took advantage of the situation to make martyrs of Simon and especially Dunyungan. Ponce Torres, secretary of the union, claimed that he arrived on the scene within five minutes of the shooting and that Dunyungan "said 'Ponc[e] . . . , continue.' . . . Then he started to stagger. . . . [He was] unable to speak to me . . . [and] died in my arms, so I let his head lay on the floor".[115] Officials within the local, whether involved in the killings or not, took every opportunity to make certain that the supposed call to "continue" was carried to all in Seattle's Filipino community. They stressed that the shootings were not the result of gang warfare among competing labor organizations or an interracial killing but were "the latest and most vicious attack made by the employers" against union forces; this was an attempt "to kill the union by killing or eliminating these leaders."[116] For a week, they put the bodies on display at the union hall and then arranged for a huge funeral parade. To serve as a continuing reminder of the two men's absence, leaders of the local established the Dunyungan-Simon Memorial Fund, though the available union records do not make clear its purpose.[117]

The Dunyungan and Simon killings together with the ability of the local's leadership to seize the moment closed the ranks of the Filipino community behind the union movement. Teodolo Ranjo mirrored sentiments in the community. "Naturally," he noted, "we blame[d] the contractors" for the deaths.[118] Most Filipino workers felt the incident "solidified the whole union" and "gave militancy and fury to the [Filipino] labor movement."[119] Those who had opposed Dunyungan found the source of their frustration purged and joined the new leaders in pushing the local's program. Although detractors of the union program remained among Filipinos, the lack of a clear target such as Dunyungan for their discontent made them no match for the newfound prounion sentiment within the community.[120]

Until the murders of Simon and Dunyungan, Filipino attempts to control some portion of the labor recruitment and management in the industry, had largely followed the lead of Chinese and Japanese. Filipinos did have less opportunity than Chinese, or even Japanese, to become contractors and often worked in more mechanized plants; yet, through the 1920s, most looked on cannery employment as a romantic adventure. Even the limited chances for mobility seemed not to discourage them.

The Great Depression shattered their world and left them with no money and no mobility. Faced with the dismal realities of the 1930s, they tried to open the industry in new ways. Fortunately for them, canners had begun to shift their stance on the contract system, and government agencies had started to provide some minimal support for change. By the mid-1930s, though, Filipinos were not united in their responses to the changes taking place around them. Small-group affiliations that had been helpful in their immigrant experience in earlier times no longer served their interests. Contractors, aspirant agents, and the CWFLU all proposed to represent them, but not until the "martyrs" fell did the Filipino community unite behind one larger group—the CWFLU. Following the Dunyungan and Simon killings, CWFLU officials moved to organize non-Filipinos, but their efforts to bridge the deep ethnic divisions among the workers was not easy and sorely tested the tenuous unity Filipinos had achieved.

7

Indispensable Allies

BY THE MID-1930s, the contract system had decayed so much that it provided neither services for workers nor a stable supply of labor for canners. Filipinos, in particular, but also Japanese and Chinese increasingly found no fair ethnic representation through contracting, mirroring the experiences of other ethnic groups during the first four and a half decades of the twentieth century. The precipitous decline in cannery wages during the Great Depression also set workers against contractors, who seemed unable to respond to the needs of their crews. Not only had contractors lost ground with their fellow ethnics, but they also came under fire from owners who, under combined pressure from the media, organized labor, and federal agencies, had shifted to a more conciliatory stance toward cannery workers. Contractors got caught in the middle, though they tried to work within the new system of labor recruitment and management that was emerging. Once Chinese, Japanese, and Filipinos recognized their common circumstances, they proved indispensable allies to one another in determining what should replace contracting.

The alliance drew on workers' ethnic identifications but moved beyond those to create a loose class solidarity among the cannery hands.[1] Ethnicity complicated the fabrication of a class-based association among workers, and that was further compounded by geographically distinct labor markets in San Francisco and Seattle, and international and national politics. Those two centers of recruitment created differential responses to the demise of the contractors, while in the political realms those interested in maintaining ethnic solidarity in opposition to class alignments used anticommunist "red-baiting" as a lever to further their programs. The competition between national and regional labor organizations for control of maritime and waterfront unions also influenced the shape and direction of the alliance as did the policies and actions of federal agencies.[2] How Asian and Asian American cannery workers capitalized on the decline of the contract system, contended with two different labor recruitment centers, and negotiated the labyrinth of ethnic loyalties, anticommunist sentiments, and interventionist federal agencies reveals the workers' abilities to "play" the larger structures to their advantage at critical historical junctures.

Unionization in San Francisco

The demise of the contract system had different implications for the Pacific Northwest and the San Francisco Bay Area because their labor markets as well as the ethnic divisions within them differed in important ways. While interethnic competition in Seattle encouraged Filipinos to form unions to combat the dozen or so Chinese and Japanese contractors, the less than half-dozen contractors in San Francisco held far greater control over the labor market. By the 1930s, only about six canning companies still operated out of San Francisco, and they depended heavily on three or four contracting firms for their large crews. This enabled contractors in the city to establish an oligarchy through which they controlled the labor market.[3]

San Francisco packers largely operated plants in central and western Alaska, where the salmon seasons were shortest. Consequently, they had invested heavily in technology to speed up and make the work process more efficient. These firms offered mostly unskilled and relatively low-paying positions. Chinese and Japanese contractors in San Francisco provided jobs in these companies for their countrymen, but the supply of the latter was quickly exhausted when they found agricultural and urban jobs in California more readily available and attractive than work in isolated Alaska canneries. As a result, San Francisco contractors recruited from many ethnic groups including Filipinos, Mexicans and Mexican Americans, Puerto Ricans, and blacks. Workers formed ethnic blocs, but unlike those in Seattle, they tended not to find much ethnic representation through contractors. As a result, they had little influence on labor recruitment and management practices in the industry.[4]

The ethnically diverse labor market in San Francisco led to the development of a particularly exploitative twist in the contract system. Mayer and Young was the most powerful combination among the contracting oligarchy in the city and best illustrates the extremes of the San Francisco situation. Between the 1910s and the mid-1930s, Mayer and Young teamed up with the Quong Ham Wah Company, headed by Lem Sem, to recruit an estimated fifteen hundred workers annually, mostly for the Alaska Packers Association (APA). Lem Sem filled his roster with Chinese first, giving them the better jobs, then turned to Mayer and Young for help in filling the remaining slots. In anticipation of the call for labor, the firm looked locally and sent "runners" to central and southern California to hire Mexicans and Mexican Americans as well as any others willing to trek to the Bay Area to wait for an opening in an Alaska crew. Once workers arrived in the city, the firm demanded that they buy unnecessary clothing and supplies at exorbitant prices. The firm also ran gambling tables during the season and then deducted so much from workers' wages after the season that some had only a few dollars to show for several months' work.[5]

Mayer and Young's practices had not gone unnoticed by the local press and the state government. As early as 1913, contractor-run gambling on cannery ships resulted in legal suits being brought against the canners in California courts, which ruled that packers were not responsible for the fleecing; the contractors were accountable, but since there were no laws against gambling on boats, nothing could be done. The courts also failed to regulate the prices of goods "sold" to workers. With no written promises of wages or conditions between workers and contractors or cannery owners, state courts found no grounds for convictions in spite of the muckraking press's coverage of the workers' plight.[6]

Public and judicial pressure did little to curb the activities of Mayer and Young. In 1918 the firm managed to get its officers deputized when cannery hands had "mutinied" on a vessel returning from Alaska. The protesters were arrested as International Workers of the World (IWW) suspects and possible draft dodgers.[7] Such incidents made the firm notorious. Myron Young, an early partner in the firm, claimed that any accusations were "a pack of lies—all lies. I have a legitimate business here. Big business men trade with me. And besides, business is business."[8]

That "business," carried out by additional family members in the ensuing years, continued unabated through the 1920s, but with the involvement of federal agencies in the industry by the mid-1930s, cannery workers fared better in the courts. A series of suits filed in 1934 by cannery workers and the newly formed Alaska Cannery Workers Union (ACWU) of San Francisco led to the indictment of Mayer and Young, along with the APA, for the illegal operation of a labor agency without a license, for nonpayment of cannery workers' wages, and for requiring workers to buy clothing in order to qualify for employment.[9] The individuals and organizations that attacked Mayer and Young represented a broad coalition, including the California State Labor Commission, the U.S. District Attorney, the Legal Aid Society, the Mexican consul in San Francisco, and the Associated Charities of San Francisco. An attorney for the workers charged that Mayer and Young had perpetrated "the worst case of slavery since the Civil War."[10] In March 1934 those of the Young and Mayer families with positions in the firm received sentences: Samuel Young and Emile P. Mayer got two-year terms; Arthur L. Mayer, Emile's son, earned an eighteen-month sentence; another major accomplice who was not a family member, served thirty days in jail.[11] In spite of public sentiment condemning Mayer and Young, by the end of the 1934 canning season the courts reduced the sentences for Young and E. P. Mayer to two years probation and a six-month jail term.[12]

The indictments signaled canners that previous patterns of outright exploitation would no longer be tolerated. Shortly after the initial sentencing, the APA announced that it would give up the contract system because of the poor public image it had earned in its association with Mayer and Young and because of the APA's desire to cooperate with labor and government in the face of the pending National Recovery Administration (NRA) codes. The APA's move away from an old system of labor recruitment and management was symbolic, rather than real, for it gave up only its Mayer and Young connections and negotiated directly with contractors, who under the NRA code called themselves "labor agents."[13]

Nonetheless, the disintegration of the Mayer and Young firm led to a scramble among those desiring to break into the oligarchy of labor recruiters in the Bay Area. Just as in Seattle, aspirant agents proposed to represent different ethnic groups, but in San Francisco they were cut off by the concerted efforts of unionists, who had formed an ethnically inclusive local. That effort had begun in 1934, the same year as the Mayer and Young trial, with the short-lived, radical- and white-led Cannery Workers Union Local 18893 under an American Federation of Labor (AFL) charter. Organizers Fred West and Julius B. Nathan were among the more militant unionists associated with the AFL in the Bay Area.[14] West was active in labor's battles over the organization of Bay Area longshoremen in the early 1930s and helped form the Proletarian party in San Francisco, a political faction slightly more radical than the Socialist Labor party but less so than the Communist party. Nathan was less militant than West and was "noncommunist," but he was committed to organizing migrant workers, made evident by his later efforts to unionize California farm laborers.[15]

West, in particular, took great pains to involve nonwhite representatives in the new organization. At his behest, longshoremen Willie ("Bill") Fong, a Chinese American; Karl Yoneda, a *Kibei* (an American of Japanese ancestry educated in Japan) and a Communist party member; and a Filipino, probably Eduardo Morris, joined West's efforts.[16] Like West, these three were deeply committed to organizing all in the labor market, not just those in one ethnic group. The local's organizers worked in concert to represent all cannery workers who shipped out of San Francisco, but the local's limited financial resources, and more important, its failure to gain company contracts led to its demise. Nonetheless, its activities set a precedent for the cross-ethnic representation of Chinese, Japanese, Filipino, and other cannery laborers.[17]

In 1934 and 1935 Chinese and Japanese contractors continued to supply labor to salmon canners. Not until late 1935 and early 1936 did Fred West of Local 18893 try again to establish a union to combat the contractors under a new AFL charter as the Alaska Cannery Workers Union (ACWU) AFL Local 20195.[18] The ACWU continued the earlier precedents of an inclusive organizational program and white radical leadership with the ascension of George Woolf to the presidency of the local. Woolf had been president of the Ship Scalers' local in San Francisco, held office in the radical Maritime Federation of the Pacific, and was active in the city's working-class politics. Once in the ACWU, Woolf quickly established himself as an important force nationally in his efforts toward the formation in 1936 of the United Cannery, Agricultural, Packing, and Allied Workers of America (UCAPAWA). Under UCAPAWA's loose organizational structure, Woolf acted as its de facto regional president from 1937 to 1950. From his various offices, Woolf consistently pushed for broad working-class unity.[19]

Local 18893's precedent and the ACWU's activities in pushing for inclusive unionization linked it with the Bay Area's Chinese and Japanese radical elements, Ben Fee and Karl Yoneda among them. The latter, though few in number, played an important role in aiding the union movement and at the same time helping their ethnic communities. Nonetheless, Asian American involvement in the locals remained small. In 1936, the ACWU had fewer than forty Japanese members (less than 3 percent of its membership). The two Japanese contractors in San Francisco at the time provided representation for many of their countrymen who went north from San Francisco and account, in part, for the small Japanese contingent in the union. That Japanese immigrants were suspicious of communist influences in Japan and in their own communities also explains their reluctance to associate with radicals. The Nisei preference for hiring out of Seattle for southeast Alaska canneries, rather than out of San Francisco for central and western Alaska canneries, further restricted the number of Japanese departing directly from San Francisco and reduced the numbers associating with the ACWU. Still, the presence of forty Japanese, despite the discouragements, signified that at least a few found merit in the union programs.[20]

Although Chinese were even less involved in the ACWU than Japanese, unionists did find some sympathetic ears in the Chinese community. Through its vernacular press and by word of mouth, the community was well aware of conditions prevailing in the canneries. Chinese workers had also absconded with advance money given to them by contractors or assaulted foremen as part of their fight against mistreatment. The new inclusive unions gave Chinese additional avenues for resisting contractors. Pro-Chinese Communist party (CCP) factions in the Bay Area also provided support for unionists. The Kuomintang (National People's party) ties of many of the community's elite, however, made it risky for workers to affiliate with organized labor because they often depended on jobs provided by the elite within Chinatown.[21]

The Great Depression made an increasing number of American-born Chinese, coming of age in the 1930s, painfully aware of their lack of potential mobility. Almost all recognized discrimination in American society. They also realized that the most attractive occupations in Chinatown's ethnic economy were already taken by Chinese immigrants and an older generation of Chinese Americans. Some young Chinese saw the control held by earlier arrivals and the elder American-born as symbolic of the oligarchic control and outdated ideas under which China itself suffered. Cut off from opportunity in the Chinatown and U.S. economies, they realized, too, that their knowledge of the Chinese language was generally not extensive enough to enable them to find employment in China. By the mid-1930s, the estimated five thousand American-born Chinese in San Francisco of voting (and therefore working) age, together with the many about to come of age, faced dismal employment prospects.[22]

Unions promised a new mobility, but the number of Chinese directly involved in union activities remained low. NRA officials commented that Chinese "felt they had been very fairly handled by the contractors . . . and were frequently dependent upon them for subsistence."[23] Many Chinese believed they had little to gain from opposition to the existing system, particularly since the demise of contracting would not become clear until late in the 1930s. Their patterns of behavior and association proved difficult to break, even after unions had eliminated contractors.

By 1936, though, at least a small core of Japanese Americans and Chinese Americans in San Francisco was ready to consider unions as an alternative to contractors. In that same year, the ACWU gained company recognition, and all but 280 cannery workers who shipped out of San Francisco carried union cards. Part of the local's success had come in its ability to gain recognition by canners located in the city and to negotiate successfully for a wage scale some $15 more per month than the NRA code's minimum $50 per month for the industry. The local had come close to a $35 increase over the NRA minimum, but the Cannery Workers and Farm Laborers Union (CWFLU) in Seattle had settled for lower wages, which forced the ACWU to accept less in order to retain jobs for its members.[24]

The ACWU managed to establish control of the San Francisco labor market even though it had to temper its program against the weaker position of the CWFLU in Seattle because only three canning companies still operated out of San Francisco by 1936, and they did not want to deal with small, fragmented, and divisive aspirant agents. Instead, they preferred to recruit through one stable source, even if that meant a union hiring hall. The great volume of canned salmon produced allowed owners to pass on any additional costs incurred in the use of union, rather than contract, crews to consumers by raising the price of each can only a little. The elimination of contractors' fees also held the promise of reducing labor costs enough to compensate for better wages paid to workers. Able to negotiate contracts and capitalize on the demise of Mayer and Young, the ACWU thus successfully became the primary labor recruiter for Alaska cannery labor in the San Francisco area.[25]

During 1937, international events bolstered the local's image among Chinese. Japan's invasion of China in mid-1937 pushed the Chinese Communist party toward the policy of a United Front with the Kuomintang against that invasion. That alliance in China also brought together diverse political factions in Chinese American society. In this cooperative context, the Chinese Workers Mutual-Aid Association (*Jiasheng huagong hezouhui*) formed to promote better working conditions and education for Chinese laborers and to encourage political activities among Chinese. The idea for the association was developed by a group of Chinese who, in a series of long talks aboard a cannery ship returning from Alaska in 1937, viewed such an organization as a way to involve hesitant Chinese in the labor movement.[26]

The organization's founders, including Ben Fee (a Communist party member trained in Moscow), Sam Young, and Bill Fong, at first attracted only a small group of workers. By the late 1930s and early 1940s, however, the organization's membership peaked at nearly four hundred. While cannery workers were numerous within the Association, its membership also included laundry, garment, agricultural, restaurant, and dock workers as well as seamen. The association cooperated with ACWU officials to include Chinese in cannery crews. As cannery wages rose under the combination of union negotiation and an improved economy, Chinese looked to the association as a conduit for cannery jobs, and Chinese affiliation with the union increased accordingly.[27]

The association also capitalized on Chinese nationalism for support. It joined the War Relief Association in boycotts of Japanese ships in San Francisco Bay.[28] In addition, union leaders recognized the need to foster cooperation, and organizer Karl Yoneda spoke as a union representative before the Chinese Workers Mutual-Aid Association at its first anniversary banquet. Yoneda delivered an impassioned English-language speech about the necessity for Chinese and Japanese workers to unite against "Japanese aggression" in China. He reminded them that Chinese and Japanese in the United States should cooperate, not compete, with each other.[29] While Yoneda's approach may not have struck a warm chord in the Japanese community, it certainly was popular among Chinese in San Francisco. Yoneda helped, in at least a small way, to bridge growing divisions between Chinese and Japanese in the city over the conflicts in the Pacific war.

As the ACWU tried to foster an "international" spirit among its Chinese, Japanese, Filipino, Mexican, and American-born members, it met with significant challenges. During the 1937 cannery season, the ACWU local, by a vote of 933 to 23, decided to go with the Congress of Industrial Organizations (CIO) and to affiliate with UCAPAWA as the Alaska Cannery Workers Union, Local 5. The most radical members of the old AFL local went into the leadership of the newly affiliated CIO local to join other prominent, radical waterfront organizers.[30] In response to the CIO affiliation, Edward Vandeleur of the AFL California State Federation of Labor reissued the AFL charter for Local 20915 to Fred West, an organizer who had been among the first to promote the earlier AFL local. West was reported to have had ties to Sugehara Sakamaki, a prominent Japanese contractor in San Francisco. The AFL local's connection to Sakamaki drew on ethnic solidarity. Its reticence to condemn Japanese aggression in China and its anticommunist stance helped the AFL local garner nearly six hundred supporters. That the AFL could muster less than half the membership of the CIO local is an indication of how well cannery workers in San Francisco felt the CIO-backed local would represent their interests.[31]

The AFL decision to charter segregated locals ultimately contributed to its failure to emerge as the bargaining agency for Bay Area cannery workers in the 1938 certification election sponsored by the

National Labor Relations Board (NLRB). AFL recognition of competing factions among workers encouraged groups such as the Filipino Independent Union (FIU) to vie for representation. The FIU was a separate and segregated ethnic organization opposed to CIO and AFL affiliation. Like earlier aspirant agents who had sought to break into the industry as contractors were being pushed out, Edward D. Mabon of the FIU told government officials that his organization believed workers "should be given the free and unhampered right to choose their own employers [and that] labor and capital should be working together in harmony and mutual co-operation."[32]

Like Lee P. Root of Seattle, the FIU drew on racial intolerance and antilabor rhetoric to compete with established contractors. Its leadership explained to Labor Secretary Frances Perkins that the "Communist Clique," which in the past had used "the AFL banner as a camouflage" and was now among the CIO forces, had duped and cheated the "unsuspecting simple-minded Filipino cannery hands." Treated as aliens in the United States and spurned by organized labor, Filipinos had been either "compelled to turn communist," despite the fact that communism was "absolutely foreign to the Filipinos," or compelled to form an organization to protect Filipino interests. The FIU, claimed its leaders, represented the latter course of action and "stands for all that is righteous, just, Christian-like, honest, fair, truthful and constructive." Its members were merely asking for "their God-given right to labor and earn an honest livelihood."[33] The FIU made little headway against the larger, better established AFL- and CIO-backed organizations because the canning companies wanted nothing to do with small, unpredictable labor suppliers.[34]

Nonetheless, during the heated 1938 spring certification election in San Francisco, nonunion separatists finally joined in a last-gasp effort to save what they could of the old labor recruitment and management system. "Several hundreds" of workers attended a meeting of the Combined Alaska Cannery Workers, where they drafted a petition to be sent to the NLRB and the respective leaders of the CIO and AFL locals, as well as the FIU. This document's drafters argued that "needless fighting and inter-union disagreements" cost jobs. To avoid the "ruin and disaster" that continued bickering might bring, the petitioners proposed that the three major parties—the AFL, CIO, and FIU—evenly divide the task of providing labor for the canneries. Of the eighty whose names appeared on the letter, 34 percent indicated that they were affiliated with one of the three locals (six listed an AFL affiliation, five had CIO ties, and sixteen came from the FIU), but the remainder were unaligned workers who had come to realize that the entrance of established labor organizations into the cannery labor market relegated them to the sidelines. Their efforts to foster cooperation amounted to little more than a belated jockeying for a position at the bargaining table, an effort that the NLRB and canners opposed.[35]

For all the tumult generated by the AFL and FIU, San Francisco cannery workers voted overwhelmingly for ACWU, CIO Local 5. The union's representation of the various ethnic groups in its hierarchy helped secure that victory. In this fashion, the CIO local subsumed separatist, nationalist perspectives under its broader, ethnically inclusive vision. The ACWU pushed hard for its vision. Because the companies relied on it for labor and because it had the support of other waterfront unions, its task was easier, but the confrontation among unionists and contractors in the Seattle area restricted the ACWU's headway.[36]

Unionization in Seattle

In Seattle, the demise of contracting and the rise of unions had taken a different path from that in San Francisco. The deaths of two major contractors, Seid Back and Goon Dip, in 1933 had not resulted in a power vacuum among the provisioners of labor, as had the destruction of Mayer and Young in San Francisco. The contractors' families continued the business.[37] In 1935, on the eve of the push for more inclusive unionization, the eleven contractors—three Chinese, four Japanese, and four Filipinos—provided workers with at least some rudimentary ethnic representation. The separatist organization of Filipinos in the CWFLU since 1933 simply offered greater representation for Filipinos, who formed a plurality in the labor market but who were represented by relatively weak contractors. Chinese and Japanese, as well as Filipinos before the killings of Virgil Dunyungan and Aurelio Simon, saw unionization as an effort to upset the ethnic balance among the various groups. The ability of the CWFLU to establish hiring halls in 1937 further exacerbated ethnic rifts because Chinese and Japanese feared the loss of their jobs.[38]

After 1935, though, some CWFLU leaders began to recognize that their organizing efforts solely among Filipinos might hinder the local. Accordingly, they began to recruit Chinese and Japanese. Seattle's Chinese, unlike those in San Francisco, had not created a Chinese Workers' Mutual-Aid Association, but among them was a small core of vocal union activists who had links with the CWFLU. Wayn Dong You, Charlie Chinn, Billy Woo, Wilson Mar, and Lee Way provided leadership among prolabor Chinese, and they eventually gathered under the CIO Local 7 banner.[39] Aside from those individuals, Seattle's

Chinese proved reluctant unionists. Hoping to prod them into greater activism, Wilson Mar publicly chastised his countrymen for not showing "any damn bit of interest in the cannery organized labor movement" in spite of their presence in Alaska "for numbers of years." As a remedy to that apathy, he urged Chinese to attend a union meeting. Mar's criticism earned him praise within the local as a militant union member, but his efforts produced few results.[40]

The Japanese became much more involved. The debate over AFL or CIO affiliation divided the Japanese community and allowed a new group of largely younger, "progressive" Nisei to articulate their interests. In the mid-1930s, Nisei took the most prominent leadership roles on both sides of the union issue as the battle lines formed.[41]

Clarence T. Arai was perhaps the most visible person among Japanese on the side of segregated, nationalist interests. Arai exemplified those Nisei who had come of age in the 1920s, found relatively good positions within their ethnic communities, and believed mobility in American society was possible. Born in Seattle in 1901 to a prominent Issei family, Arai had more access to social mobility than Nisei who matured later in the twentieth century or came from families less well off than his own. The first American-born Japanese to pass the bar, he was able to develop a professional career as an attorney, though his practice was limited to clients within the Seattle Japanese community, particularly the Japanese-speaking Issei. In spite of his position, he still had to struggle in a community that had limited funds available for legal services.[42]

Arai was also a leader in social affairs. He gained prominence in the Baptist church as a youth leader, Sunday school teacher, and deacon. At the University of Washington, he joined various student organizations. In 1928 he worked to resuscitate a political and social organization for Seattle's Nisei that was to be an early and important component in the formation of the Japanese American Citizen's League (JACL). His drive for leadership positions earned him a commission in 1931 as an infantry captain in the Reserve Officer Training Corps, which further refined his organizational skills. By the mid-1930s, Arai was an important and influential member of the Japanese American community.[43]

Arai was so visible that Congregational minister, theologian, and author Albert W. Palmer singled him out as a "typical and thoroughly assimilated Japanese."[44] Palmer had in mind a benign, linear progression toward a rather simple assimilation, but Japanese American cultural adaptations were much more complex than he imagined, as is evident in the activities that led to the formation of the JACL. One reason for its founding was that many inside and outside the Japanese community believed political activity as *the way* for Nisei to participate in American society and as proof of their voluntary assimilation. During the late 1920s, Arai tried to develop a graduate thesis on the "phases of the culture contacts of the second generation" in the Department of Sociology at the University of Washington. His approach to the topic reflected his thorough immersion in Robert Park's theory of a race relations cycle, which was emphasized by the department at that time. Arai believed that, by voluntarily joining in American society, Japanese, especially Nisei, might help remove discriminatory barriers, and he hoped that Nisei might be able to "skim the cream from both cultures."[45]

A second reason was that Arai and others wanted Nisei to vote in a bloc. Arai foresaw a "Pacific Era" in which the center of world civilization would shift first from the Mediterranean to the Atlantic and then, in the twentieth century, find its ultimate resting place in the Pacific between the United States and Japan. If Japanese Americans were to act as a cultural bridge and exert significant influence on local and national issues, Nisei had to coalesce in some organization where they could work to form a common set of social, political, and educational goals. In this way, Japanese Americans could achieve more "than the average American voter who climbs on the band wagon at the eleventh hour, not knowing what he is doing, and caring less."[46]

Arai's oratorical skills and political training put him at the head of the movement to promote Japanese solidarity and political activity, and he did not stop with the JACL. Arai became the local president of the Young Men's Business Club, was appointed to the executive council of the Republican Club and Young Republican League, and was a local committee member of the District Republican Club. He and Karl Yoneda (at the opposite end of the political spectrum) were the first Japanese in the continental United States to run, unsuccessfully, for positions in state legislatures.[47]

As a community representative, Arai had also been appointed to represent Japanese vegetable growers in their labor dispute with the largely Filipino field workers. Although Arai's legal work set him against Filipino laborers in that instance, he did not oppose their presence in the Northwest. In 1930 he denied that Filipinos were displacing Japanese and Chinese in the canneries, mills, and railroads. He stressed, instead, the benefits to small businesses of wage-earning Filipino patrons. Others in the Japanese community concurred. "Many of the small [Japanese-owned] shops," wrote the editor of the *Japanese American Courier*, "are practically dependent upon this race for trade."

Organized Filipino farm laborers, in contrast, threatened Japanese farmers.[48]

Arai continued to defend what he believed to be the interests of Japanese Americans as a whole, even when this meant supporting some form of unionization among Japanese cannery workers. At the NRA code hearings, as in the formation of the JACL, his goal was to encourage group solidarity and to give direction to Japanese actions. Arai's proposal to form an ethnically exclusive local to protect Japanese jobs met a receptive audience. Arai capitalized on the support he found in the community to begin a separate organization for Japanese laborers.[49]

Arai's influence among Japanese cannery hands increased steadily after 1934. Fearing that his separatist organization might undermine the position held by the Filipino-dominated CWFLU, after the 1936 season the CWFLU finally took action. Union members elected Robert Okazaki to the board of trustees. The local's leadership believed him the perfect counter to Arai. Although technically an Issei, Okazaki considered himself a Nisei. His flashy clothes and efforts to keep abreast of the latest fashions further set him apart from many Issei. In spite of his dress and demeanor, Okazaki remained tied to Issei interests. He worked as a translator for firms from Japan that did business in the Pacific Northwest and for contractors. In one instance, he even traveled to Japan as a "personal secretary," really more of a personal retainer, for a contractor. By using Okazaki's intergenerational position, his links to Japan and to the Issei, his visibility, and his bilingual abilities, the CWFLU hoped to win Japanese support.[50]

Okazaki's usefulness to the union, as it turned out, ended quickly. The deaths of Dunyungan and Simon had forced the local to abandon connections to contractors. In April 1937, when Okazaki was accused of enlisting men through contractors, union officials demanded that he appear before them. Okazaki left the CWFLU to head AFL Local 20454, with which Arai was associated. His days as a unionist were also brief. By the summer of 1938, Okazaki had moved to Los Angeles to pursue a film career. His abdication from the CWFLU and subsequent departure to Hollywood affected the CWFLU significantly. In his wake, a more potent and lasting core of leaders emerged from the ranks of younger Japanese. Those new leaders had the ideals and personality to combat Arai.[51]

George Taki and Dyke Miyagawa exemplified the combination necessary to tackle Arai and his supporters. Taki was energetic, outgoing, and well-known among Nisei. He took the reins of office as vice-president and served on the union's negotiating committee as a representative for Japanese within the pro-CIO faction of the AFL.[52] Miyagawa was much quieter but was noted for his integrity and commitment, and he performed the important role of policy formulator. Within the union he served in secondary but valuable positions: as a publicist writing for union, local, and Japanese newspapers and as a trustee.[53] Between them, Miyagawa and Taki possessed potent skills.

Taki and Miyagawa pounded the streets of Seattle for support, with some success. During the 1930s, many younger Nisei had become interested in the Democratic party, were sympathetic to organized labor, and were committed to notions of racial equality. Capitalizing on those sentiments, CWFLU leaders argued, with Taki's and Miyagawa's implied consent, that their local was inclusive while Arai's was racist. "Our union bars racial discrimination," stated one leader, and "[we must] cast away the confusion created by Mr. Arai in propagandizing and stigmatizing our Japanese group to make them an isolated race."[54] On a less positive note, the CWFLU warned that those who sided with Arai or other "labor agents . . . [were] jeopardizing their future chances to go to Alaska."[55] Taki and Miyagawa argued that Japanese involvement in the CWFLU was the only way to protect Japanese jobs and prevent Filipinos from completely taking over the labor market. Arai himself contributed to the CWFLU cause when he failed to attend a public debate on the question of affiliation with the CIO. CWFLU leaders proclaimed this as positive proof that Arai was in collusion with contractors and ran a "puppet union."[56]

Arai lost ground under this assault. From the mid-1930s, Japanese support for Arai became increasingly lukewarm. Many felt that his activities were no more than self-serving bids for power.[57] To capitalize on those negative sentiments, the CWFLU began the regular use of Japanese interpreters at its weekly meetings to assure that all Japanese members clearly understood its programs. This further isolated Arai. The local also picketed the "Japanese quarter" of Seattle, thereby threatening the income of Issei and older Nisei businessmen who depended on Filipino customers, many of whom were CWFLU members. AFL president William Green was correct when he charged the CWFLU with discriminating against Arai's local, but CWFLU leaders ignored the allegations because they believed that Arai's local undermined their efforts to include Japanese.[58]

The CWFLU's new Nisei leaders, its ethnically inclusive ideals, and its ability to promise future jobs convinced Japanese workers that it would best represent them. By late spring, 1937, Arai still had not firmly established his separatist AFL local. Hiroshi ("Monks") Shimabara, a union delegate at a southeast Alaska cannery during that season, astutely noted: "It seems that the Arai union has been checked this season, but as long as it has a charter and backing it will be a potential menace to the Union."[59] The CWFLU managed to keep the separatists at bay, but by the end of the season, it, too, stood at the brink of disaster.

Part of the crisis was external to the local. The Seattle Central Labor Council consistently blocked the CWFLU's participation in its affairs, and the AFL threw its support to locals "containing only certain nationalities," rather than the CWFLU. To make matters worse, the AFL charged that the CWFLU had improperly collected dues and had failed to pay its membership fees to the AFL. CWFLU leaders openly admitted that they "had not been abiding strictly by their Constitution or the Constitution of the A.F.L." and had violated them with the sole purpose of "benefiting the members of the Cannery Workers Union," not the national or regional bodies.[60]

Despite their defiance of the AFL, the local's members were not clear about the direction they wanted to take. Some of the CWFLU's Filipino members rallied behind the newly formed UCAPAWA organization. Conrad Espe, the Norwegian American business agent for the CWFLU who had resigned to go into UCAPAWA, returned to the local in August 1937 to urge an immediate affiliation with UCAPAWA.[61] Espe had long been involved with radical labor organizations. From 1933 to 1935, he had been an organizer for the Fishermen and Cannery Workers' Industrial Union; then in the fight against fascism, he joined the CWFLU. He had been instrumental in broadening the interests of the local's leadership, and when he returned to urge an affiliation with UCAPAWA, many listened to his call. His promise that UCAPAWA, under the CIO, would follow a policy of "non-prejudice" and "liberalism" attracted much attention, but the problem of money owed to the AFL and the uncertain future of UCAPAWA-CIO caused many of the local's members to balk at CIO affiliation.[62]

Those members who urged continued affiliation with the AFL for financial and security reasons were concerned that the local would go bankrupt if it affiliated with the CIO because the AFL threatened legal action to protect its funds from any faction that might break away. Rumors that the AFL might expel the CWFLU because of financial irregularities led some members to the conclusion that they must "clean house" before deciding on the affiliation issue. Questions about the immediate versus long-term viability of the CIO and UCAPAWA also bothered workers. While the "CIO is going on fire [now]," unionist Antonio Rodrigo explained, "[w]e have to go easy. . . . We may put on a new suit, but there are times that a man may like his old suit better than the new."[63] Delaying any decision seemed the best option to many in the CWFLU.[64]

If some in the local were ambivalent about CIO affiliation, others were dead set against it. They believed that UCAPAWA and the CIO were inappropriate because they presented "a new philosophy to the workers," one that was too far to the political left. Aside from their anticommunist sentiments, these unionists feared that CIO affiliation might bring mass deportations of supposedly "alien" members because of guilt by association.[65] Another small segment of the local's membership felt that neither the AFL nor the CIO were of any use. Both, they believed, failed to address fundamental problems in the industry. Foremen, for example, still showed favoritism and defied union directives. An independent organization not at the beck and call of a national affiliation might be better able to resolve issues that neither the AFL nor the CIO seemed able or willing to tackle.[66]

In stiff competition with locals that received ethnically based charters from the AFL and deeply divided within its own membership over the affiliation issue, CWFLU Local 18257 established a special committee of five to study the issue and make a recommendation concerning affiliation. The committee consisted of three Filipinos and two prominent individuals from the Nisei community, Dyke Miyagawa and George Minato.[67] While the committee wrestled with conflicting interests in the local, the AFL charged in the courts that the local had acted in a financially irresponsible fashion, that it discriminated against Japanese members, and that its program of union-sponsored relief, particularly the issuing of meal tickets at endorsed restaurants, was a racket to exploit union members. The AFL also asserted that Filipinos in the local were nothing but a "bunch of conflicting cliques" acting on the basis of "intensive sectionalism among themselves."[68] In some respects, the AFL was right. In the winter of 1937–1938, Filipino unity began to crumble after its high point following the Dunyungan and Simon murders. The AFL's activities were designed to split the Filipinos further rather than bring them together.

The AFL's legal action and public slurs stood in sharp contrast to the CIO's program of interethnic and interracial cooperation and equality. In mid-September 1937, the special committee recommended that the local avoid expulsion from the AFL by voting to "accept a charter" from UCAPAWA as the Cannery Workers and Farm Laborers Union, CIO Local 7. Conrad Espe assured the committee that the Maritime Federation, from which the CWFLU under the AFL had gained much support, would continue to aid the new local. Committee members viewed Espe as a "good man" and accepted his word. Making the decision in committee, however, proved easier than implementing it among the local's members.[69]

The special committee tried to keep the vote under wraps for fear that an immediate announcement might give opposition forces among Filipinos and Japanese time to divide Filipinos to an even greater degree before CWFLU began its negotiations with the companies for the 1938 season. As a union officer noted, "There is so much dessension [*sic*] among the Filipino group [that] . . . [d]eclaring our new affiliation will give the American Federation of Labor a chance to reissue Local 18257 to this . . . group who [*sic*] is trying to split the Union."[70] Committee members also hoped that by delaying the announcement until after the agricultural harvests began, enough dissenting Filipinos might have left town. The committee withheld the news for two weeks and then publicly announced its decision on October 1, 1937.[71]

As the leaders of the new CIO local feared, the AFL countered the announcement with a promise to maintain Local 18257 for all "oriental" workers, meaning in this case Filipinos, who wanted to remain with the AFL.[72] The AFL also renewed its support for Clarence Arai's leadership of the segregated Japanese AFL Local 20454.[73] CIO supporters charged that this tactic only created a "foreman [*sic*] clique" through which the AFL hoped to continue controlling cannery jobs. Despite the high level of AFL activity, the special committee's strategy of delaying the affiliation announcement worked in favor of the CIO-backed CWFLU. The referendum vote within the membership to approve the committee's action took place after many members, particularly Filipinos, had left Seattle to follow agricultural harvests. The members still in Seattle voted in favor of the CIO, but dissenters claimed that the CIO majority was "hardly 10% of our total membership."[74]

Since Filipinos formed more than half the membership of the CWFLU, their choice of affiliation was critical, but the CWFLU did not neglect Japanese and Chinese. The AFL's renewed support of Clarence Arai led George Taki and others to insist on a publicity program explaining the benefits of CIO affiliation to Japanese. Taki considered this necessary to counteract "the propaganda being conducted by Arai in Japanese papers" and "to educate our Japanese brothers along the lines of our policies and programs."[75] By November 1937, Dyke Miyagawa had quit his studies at the University of Washington and begun working full-time for the union "as a representative of the Japanese group" and publicist for the CIO.[76] Still, into March 1938, Nisei leaders in the CIO local had made few inroads into the Japanese community. Ethnic nationalism and international events detracted from the CIO's appeal to Japanese.[77]

From Japan's invasion of Manchuria in 1931 to its takeover of China in 1937, Clarence Arai had consistently appealed to Japanese nationalism.[78] Many within the community agreed with him. He had explained in Seattle that Japan was "forced through the violation of treaty rights" to enter Manchuria and that the Japanese puppet state there was "nothing more than a buffer state to prevent the spread of Communism in the Orient." The support of Japanese Americans for Japan's position in Manchuria against communist expansion, explained Arai, was an expression of American loyalty and patriotism. In a July 4, 1934, radio broadcast Arai told Seattle listeners that the "so-called foreign 'isms' should have no place in our [U.S.] government." Arai's argument that Japanese and American patriotism were not mutually exclusive struck a sympathetic chord among Issei and Nisei.[79]

Arai continued as an important leader among Seattle's Japanese up to their internment in 1942. His success hung on his ability to create a brand of nationalism that incorporated ancestral connections to Japan with residence in the United States. To do so he had to move away from his earlier affinity for Robert Park's theory of a race relations cycle. Arai still believed that assimilation occurred, but, unlike Park, Arai saw it as voluntary, rather than inevitable, and always incomplete. Assimilation resulted in a pluralism in which cultural nationalism could be tolerated. The United States was, he argued, itself a "League of Nations" in which the different ethnic and racial groups "all get along." With such notions Arai could easily reconcile his Americanism with his Japanese nationalism and link it to the AFL's separatist program.[80]

Arai and his AFL supporters used that nationalism to counter the CIO. They argued that if the CIO won the battle for industrywide recognition, "Japanese workers [would] be locked out from the industry." Such reasoning further convinced some Japanese that the CIO's antidiscrimination rhetoric was false. In their minds, the CIO was anti-Japanese because it did not allow for the separate organization of Japanese locals.[81]

Japanese nationalists also used the CIO's support of boycotts against Japanese ships in U.S. harbors as ammunition for their cause. In 1937 and 1938, Chinese in West Coast port cities turned out in large numbers to picket Japanese ships. While this constituted a great rallying point for the Chinese American communities and boded well for the relationship between some sectors of organized labor and Chinese, it convinced many Japanese that the CIO was against them. To widen the gap between Japanese and the CIO, Filipino leaders in the

AFL pandered to Japanese nationalism. During spring 1938, Joe Dulay of the AFL told a crowd of Japanese workers: "I really entertain a strict reverence to that great Empire of Japan as I would certainly like to see Orientals to look down on Caucasians just as Caucasians now look down upon the Orientals. . . . I really cannot understand how certain Japanese leaders could endorse a boycott of Japanese goods."[82]

At the same public meeting, George Taki tried to counter Dulay by claiming that Arai's associations with unions effectively amounted to his endorsement of the boycott. Unfortunately for Taki, public knowledge of Arai's anti-CIO and pro-Japanese activities combined with the separate efforts of AFL locals 18257 and 20454 to organize Filipinos and Japanese, respectively, worked against his argument and further discouraged Japanese affiliation with the CIO.[83]

At least some CIO organizers, like Taki, also tried to use nationalism to their advantage. Even those who were decidedly against Japanese imperialism were, at times, unwittingly painted as supporters of Japan. Dyke Miyagawa, himself as critical of Japanese imperialism as Karl Yoneda, but not so outspoken, was one such person. In the late 1930s, Miyagawa's father donated money to the Japanese war effort in Dyke's name. When the Japanese-language press published a list of contributors that included Dyke, he was furious, but by that time there was no way for Miyagawa to strike his name from the roll. Miyagawa's unwilling association with Japanese militarism allowed some to view him as a fellow nationalist, while his union activities allowed others to see him as a liberal. That flexibility could not have hurt the CIO local.[84]

Recognizing the high level of nationalism among Japanese, CIO leaders refrained from criticizing Japan's imperialism. Early in 1938 one executive board member noted that the local, "due to the composition of [its] members . . . , could not very well define publicly [its] stand on the issue."[85] While the CIO local condoned some mild nationalism, it fell far short of that espoused by the AFL local and Arai. The CIO local's failure to support Japan loudly and consistently in the international arena was an important factor in its inability to win over great numbers of Issei and Nisei.

CIO leaders could not be certain how much a factor nationalism was among Japanese, or among Chinese and Filipinos, until workers were forced to take sides. An NLRB audit in mid-April 1938 revealed that during the 1937 season, 1,597 workers had signed with the CIO, 685 with the AFL, and 504 with both. The NLRB also found that 1,252 workers got cannery jobs with no union affiliation whatsoever. With 44 percent of the workers holding no membership or dual membership, Robert M. Gates, regional director of the NLRB, warned that it was "not possible . . . [on the basis of the audit] to give a final determination" on the appropriate bargaining agency for workers.[86] Nonetheless, the CIO took its plurality as a sign that it was the sole representative for cannery workers. The AFL protested that the audit "did not adequately and truthfully represent the present sentiment of workers."[87] The AFL's claims had merit, since between the 1937 and 1938 seasons Arai purported to have enrolled as many as eight hundred Japanese members in his local alone. Under extreme pressure from the AFL, which believed it could win an election by as much as a two-to-one margin, and from canners, who wanted nothing more than an assured supply of labor, the NLRB set a consent election for early May 1938 to resolve the dispute.[88]

With only the month of April in which to campaign, competition for Chinese, Japanese, and Filipino votes rose to fever pitch. The CIO local stumped for Japanese and Chinese involvement in union affairs as it had never done before. Its leaders openly admitted that in the past they had "crucified a lot of . . . Japanese Brothers for having signed up with Arai" but were ready to "welcome them back in willing arms."[89] George Taki even aimed a blow at his opponents' masculinity, saying that retaining dual membership was "not the manly thing to do."[90] While Seattle Japanese supporters of the CIO stumped for their cause, the ACWU in San Francisco, newly affiliated with the CIO, sent aid. Karl Yoneda traveled up from San Francisco to distribute leaflets among Seattle's Japanese and pestered listeners on the main streets of Seattle's International District with pro-CIO rhetoric from a public address system mounted on a rented truck. Yoneda even brashly challenged Arai on the sidewalk, claiming that Arai represented the companies and former contractors more than workers. Yoneda believed that his publicity efforts aligned 60 to 70 percent of the Nisei solidly with the CIO local.[91] Taki placed support at about 50 percent. Higher proportions were difficult to gain, he claimed, because the editors of Japanese newspapers were hostile to the CIO because of its stance against Japan's imperialist activities. He also claimed that newspapers suppressed stories favorable to the CIO.[92] Both Yoneda and Taki were optimistic in their calculations, and other CIO officials came to believe the vote would be so close that they decided to keep Arai a hundred feet away from the NLRB polls for fear he might exert too much last-minute influence on Japanese voters.[93]

CIO organizers provided special translators to "win over Chinese brothers."[94] Wilson Mar and other long-time supporters of the CIO's efforts also did their share of work by carefully explaining the voting procedure to Chinese.[95] Barely a week after the consent election, several CWFLU members assaulted Mar at the Union Hall; though that violence occurred after the voting, it demonstrates the level of tension over Chinese participation in the local's affairs and the grudges some members still bore the Chinese.[96]

Just before the consent election, the CIO stepped up its organizing efforts among Filipinos. Aside from the divisions caused by aspirant agents, the CIO local had to consider the role of Portland's largely Filipino local. As early as 1935–1936, Dunyungan and George Woolf (president of the ACWU) had thought that the Portland local was "under control" and that there was little question of Filipino workers' support from that quarter. With its approximately eight hundred members, however, it was too large a bloc of votes to take for granted, and a careful organizing program among them assured support for the CIO.[97]

In Seattle and Portland, pro-CIO Filipino unionists worried about members who were "AFL at heart," even though they expressed support for the CIO. CIO proponents told Filipinos that the AFL was aligned with "ex-contractors, foremen, and California boys who had never been to Alaska before."[98] Contractor Pio De Cano's support of the AFL gave credence to the first allegation. As for the second, the AFL did indeed recruit Filipinos from California who had never worked in the canneries to boost its membership before the 1938 season. Filipinos from the Northwest feared they might be displaced by those new arrivals if the AFL won the election. To counter divisiveness among Filipinos and to defend against being undermined by newcomers to the labor market, CIO representatives in the Northwest received pledges of support from a variety of Filipino social and fraternal orders among Bananginians, Narvacans, Pangansinans, and Laoaginians. The memory of the Virgil Dunyungan and Aurelio Simon killings continued to provide a unifying influence in the Pacific Northwest, and this also assisted the CIO. Relative to Chinese and Japanese, then, the Filipino vote for the CIO in that region seemed fairly well assured.[99]

The very level of the CIO's organizing activity among Chinese, Japanese, and Filipinos demonstrates the AFL's influence. While the CIO could ill afford to alienate any potential supporters in its coalition, the AFL's strategy of separate organizations catering to ethnic nationalism and aspirant agents took much less delicate maneuvering. AFL organizers spent most of their efforts highlighting Filipino domination of the CIO local, which they charged would lead to discrimination against Chinese, Japanese, and perhaps even certain Filipinos, and stressing the "foreign 'isms' " of the CIO. Some AFL members claimed to have first joined the CIO but then subsequently quit it because of the organization's radicalism. Joe Dulay told cannery workers at a mass meeting before the consent election: "I spoke against communism because I don't believe it."[100] The AFL had a strong appeal with its promise of a continued balance among the ethnic groups that allowed for the expression of cultural nationalism.

A month of bitter struggle gave way to the contentious NLRB election of May 5–7, 1938. The opening and closing of the polls at odd times proved the greatest problem. The AFL charged that its members had not been allowed to vote and that the CIO was behind the irregularities. NLRB officials refused to hear the AFL appeals and stood by the final count that put the CIO on top with 1,560 votes to the AFL's 1,307; an additional 169 ballots were invalidated by the NLRB. In comparison to the NLRB audit of union affiliation in the 1937 season, which showed the CIO with 1,597 members and the AFL with 685, the AFL had made far greater gains than the CIO. That the AFL did not win stands as testimony to the efforts of Chinese and Japanese leaders in the CIO and their local's ability to counter nationalist sentiments sufficiently to give the CIO a clear edge. Indeed, they were indispensable allies in the effort for a more inclusive style of union organization in the salmon canneries.[101]

As soon as the election results became official, the AFL protested on the grounds that many of its members had not voted. By this time, however, officials in the NLRB had lost patience with the entire affair. The ethnic groups in the cannery labor market—Chinese, Japanese, Filipinos, African Americans, and others—noted one NLRB official, "will probably never be assimilated into the American strain at any time. . . . We believe that this element is always going to cause trouble . . . with complaints of unfair labor against some employer who is utterly helpless to protect himself."[102] The NLRB upheld the election results and planned to override by "legal fiat" and "rigid control" any future objections. The prime concern was that canners have a steady and reliable source of labor. Any search for the bona fide bargaining agent was secondary as long as workers were not dreadfully exploited. Asian cannery workers thus ranked far below business interests in the minds of NLRB bureaucrats.[103]

At least some in the NLRB believed that the AFL's deep-seated hostility toward Asian laborers was partially to blame for the AFL defeat. E. P. Marsh, U.S. commissioner of conciliation for the Department of Labor, commented: "Confidentially AFL leaders have a bull by the tail and cannot let go; I think they are sick of the problem of dealing with this class of Oriental labor . . . [and] they are fed up with the whole thing."[104] Marsh intimated that the only hope he had, along with labor leaders in the upper echelons of the AFL national organization, was that higher union wages might eventually attract enough "white" workers to displace that "class of Oriental labor."[105] Such a process had already been under way since the 1920s in the Puget Sound canneries, though high wages had not been the prime factor in the displacement of Asians by European Americans.[106]

CIO leaders could not have known what the NLRB or AFL planned for the future. From the moment of victory in the election, they had worried that the AFL would "maneuver . . . for a reopening of the elections on a plant by plant or company by company basis."[107] Had the NLRB decided to allow separate elections for each cannery, the AFL would have won half the plants, and the labor market would have remained fragmented on the basis of ethnicity. Ultimately, the CIO earned the right to act as the collective bargaining agent for Alaska-bound cannery workers. Although problems from the contract era persisted, after 1938 the system of labor recruitment and management in the industry was tied to unions, not contractors. Many Asian Americans had been very active in unionization, but it was the determined lobbying efforts of a few Japanese and Chinese, together with a corps of dedicated Filipinos, that gave the margin of victory to the broad and inclusive CIO vision of labor organization, rather than the AFL's narrow, ethnically based locals.[108]

8 | *A Fragile Alliance*

THE 1938 VICTORY for cannery workers seeking an ethnically inclusive union was momentous. Ethnic segregation in the labor market had characterized the industry up to that point, and it had taken no small effort to overcome the divisions. The 1938 election, while bringing the ethnic groups under the Congress of Industrial Organizations (CIO) locals, did little to change the ethnic makeup of the labor market or to smooth over antagonistic relations among the groups in the union. In the season following the election, the Alaska Cannery Workers Union (ACWU) in San Francisco and the Cannery Workers and Farm Laborers Union (CWFLU) in Portland and Seattle sent to Alaska 367 Chinese, 684 Japanese, 3,266 Filipinos, 380 Mexicans, 78 blacks, 87 Puerto Ricans, and 27 Hawaiians, as well as a total of 39 Koreans, Chileans, and Peruvians and several dozen European Americans.[1] Between 1938 and 1942, Asian and Asian American workers and union leaders in the two locals built and maintained a fragile alliance that struck a balance between workers' personal and ethnic interests and a broader, inclusive, class-based union ideal. Workers and unionists modified the labor recruitment system to suit those parallel but often conflicting considerations—a task made more difficult by the insistence of company owners that the locals continue to function much like the contractors had. To counterbalance the potentially negative effects of disciplining workers, the locals had to provide appropriate rewards and compensations for their members. The new set of practices that cannery laborers and union leaders created functioned for only four years. By 1942, two events external to the union destroyed it: the shift in company headquarters from San Francisco to Seattle, and U.S. involvement in World War II. Balancing ethnic and class concerns, contending with industrial change, and living in an era of chaotic international politics was as difficult as attaining the CIO victory in 1938.

Recruitment and Job Allocation

The first task for the locals was to gain control of recruiting and provide union members with jobs. The system they devised was straightforward. To determine who was eligible for positions in the canneries,

172

the locals issued special booklets to members. These "books" were stamped each time a member paid his dues. In late winter, workers approached locals in San Francisco, Portland, or Seattle for jobs just as they had under the earlier contracting system. Rather than rely on personal connections with some contractor to secure work, union members presented their books. Members in good standing received jobs first; the others had to bring their membership status up to date and wait for positions. When all members in good standing had received employment, the locals gave annual work permits to nonmembers. They issued them to counter company, government, and American Federation of Labor (AFL) pressures to retain an open shop, as well as to maintain some control over who entered the canneries. Men with permits who obtained jobs paid fees based on the particular positions they held, and they paid union dues for the months they worked, but they had no voting rights or seniority within the union.[2]

The books and permits served purposes other than those of union control. A union member who did not plan to go to Alaska might lend his book to a friend or relative. The borrower assumed the name on the book for the season and paid the dues. The regular crews and foremen often knew of these cases but accepted the practice as an appropriate way of maintaining a balance among the ethnic groups in the plants. Book loaning also worked as an informal recruitment device, for some of the borrowers, though discovered by the union, were allowed to become members because they had kept up the dues. In the first two seasons after 1938, as long as the work was done and the dues were paid, other workers in the crews, the foremen, and even some union leaders did not pursue the matter.[3]

By 1940, workers' efforts to make personal gains by lending their books outstripped any benefits to the union. A few members sold their books for the season to the highest bidder. The abuse of the system encouraged union officials to investigate cases and take disciplinary action against those who allowed others to use their books. The accused often claimed that their books had been lost or stolen, but if there was evidence suggesting otherwise, they had to prove their innocence or risk expulsion. If an offender was uncovered at a cannery, he was denied future work but still received his pay for that season.[4] Book loaning continued after the 1940 disciplinary hearings but on a much reduced and very informal scale. Officials seemed to ignore book loaning as long as it was used to fulfill informal ethnic quotas. They acted only when members tried to make money from such transactions.[5]

The locals retained the permit system as a compromise between union control and ethnic representation. Particularly in San Francisco, permits allowed Chinese workers, reluctant to join the union for fear of community sanctions, to continue their annual trips northward. The Chinese Workers Mutual-Aid Association, which had worked with the local before 1938, provided the essential link for the ACWU to the Bay Area Chinese community, and the local promised to give the association's members permits before any other nonmembers. While the arrangement helped Chinese keep cannery jobs, their links to the union remained tentative, and they were charged with "stringing along" with rival unions or "reactionary" elements of the old contract system more frequently than any other ethnic group. Further, in 1938 and 1940 union members sued the locals for failing to employ them before the permit holders. The suits represented a lapse in the union's ability to reconcile ethnic representation and union ideals.[6]

Once assured of a cannery job by virtue of owning or obtaining a book, or by purchasing a permit, a worker still had to contend with several lean weeks before his ship's departure. During that period, under the contract system, laborers had relied on various forms of credit extended by the contractors. They now turned for credit to the local unions. In Seattle, the CWFLU gave out meal tickets as a form of welfare and as advances on the season's earnings. Before unionization, critics had often targeted this practice as evidence of the abuse of workers. The potential for exploiting workers continued under the CWFLU. Several officials had invested in restaurants that accepted meal tickets and were endorsed by the local.[7] Whether they gained financially through the patronage of cannery workers is difficult to determine. Protests over their investments were minor, and abuses appear to have been few. One Nisei union organizer and publicist, Dyke Miyagawa, regularly welcomed cannery workers into his father's restaurant and gave them free food. Dyke's actions did not please his father, but none could accuse him of seeking financial gain at the expense of union commitments.[8]

In addition to meals, workers needed lodging. Before unionization, contractors had colluded with boardinghouse operators to foster indebtedness among workers, but preseason housing problems persisted even after union recognition. When the CWFLU failed to persuade canners to provide room and board, it responded as best it could to worker requests that the union itself build or rent housing. An outlay of cash for hundreds of workers was far beyond the union's means, but it did provide a few couches and beds to the most desperate members awaiting cannery ships.[9]

Compared to determining which workers would be sent to what canneries, the troubles with room and board were minuscule. In sending members to the canneries, locals had to balancing broad union goals against workers' narrower self-interests. In 1936 the ACWU in San Francisco established a hiring hall, and a year later the CWFLU in Seattle followed suit. By dispatching workers through the hall, leaders hoped to avoid the favoritism rampant under contracting. Union seniority, service on picket lines or committees, and individual skill levels were supposed to determine where workers were sent and what positions they held. The United Cannery, Agricultural, Packing, and Allied Workers of America (UCAPAWA) claimed that the cannery workers' locals showed "no trace of race prejudice in spite of the many nationalities employed."[10]

Dispatching became the battleground within the union between ethnic nationalists and those who espoused internationalism. CWFLU leaders complained that the "whole problem and mess arises from the desire of each group, each nationality, to have someone on the dispatching committee whom they can reach. Some members still don't know the difference between a union hiring hall and the contracting system."[11]

The CWFLU was reluctant "to play up the racial angle" to eliminate informal quotas. That made it difficult for workers to see a distinction between the union's dispatching program and that of the contractors. Contractors, especially those in the Pacific Northwest, had recruited through ethnic networks for specific canneries, and the local made no radical departure from past allocations.[12] The greatest change may actually have been the increase in special requests to place family members and friends. Hiroshi ("Monks") Shimabara, a staunch Japanese American supporter of the CIO's racially inclusive vision and himself a union delegate, saw no contradiction in asking leaders to secure cannery work for his younger brother, who had no previous cannery experience.[13]

Tolerance of old patterns gave dispatchers tremendous power, and some took advantage of their positions. A few demanded that workers pay them under the table to be assigned to one of the early crews, get certain jobs, or be sent to one of the canneries with better working and living conditions. By the end of 1937, the conflict between the union's efforts to insure an informal ethnic quota and dispatchers who sought personal gain or members who wanted favors had become all too apparent. Union members complained loudly about "[f]irst-time Alaska men" with no seniority who had received jobs before them.[14]

In response to such allegations, officials in the CIO locals tried to ensure that each ethnic group had a representative among the dispatchers. They also kept foremen, many of whom were union members but had earned their positions through years of contact with contractors, out of the dispatching process, for these positions presented too many opportunities for the continuation of the contract system's most troublesome features.[15] The locals also asked the Maritime Federation of the Pacific, an association of waterfront unions to which they belonged, to police dispatching. The federation sent observers to the hiring halls to insure fair play. When the observers were present, the process ran smoothly, but "the minute their back[s] [were] turned" dispatchers violated procedures. The National Labor Relations Board (NLRB) urged the Maritime Federation to take over the "Oriental dispatching problem," but the federation was "loath to step in too strongly on the union autonomy principle," and with the exception of sending observers, left dispatching up to the cannery workers' locals.[16]

In 1939, Eugene T. Dennet of the Washington State Industrial Council noted that "the biggest problem ahead is dispatching. Those that cannot get what they want will resort to agitation."[17] Repeatedly, officials in the locals called for reforms in dispatching in order to make "a clean break . . . , once and for all . . . , with representatives of the contracting system and of the underworld."[18] During spring 1941, the Seattle local admitted that it "replaced Japanese with Japanese" after 175 Japanese American members had volunteered for duty in the U.S. military. CWFLU leaders argued that to replace Japanese on the basis of seniority or with "other races . . . would be trouble."[19] Among those "other races" were several hundred Mexicans and Mexican Americans and a small, but growing, number of African Americans, who benefited from the locals' commitments to waterfront and agricultural workers and to ethnically inclusive labor organization.[20] Still, the locals had to rely on an uneasy compromise between established practices and newer union ideals.

Maintaining (Union) Discipline

As they had under contracting, owners demanded that the labor recruiter also be responsible for managing workers. This meant that the locals not only had to supply "the necessary experienced men" as specified in the contracts but also had to police workers' behavior at the plants. Maintaining discipline and affecting changes in behavior was not easy. During 1937, before the consent election, one unionist complained: "There are any number of members [who] do not seem to have any of the principles of Unionism. They seem to be satisfied to know that they have an agreement signed and let it go at that."[21] Discipline problems were not resolved with the 1938 CIO victory. In 1939

George Woolf, president of the ACWU, explained the difficulties: "We have had about 600 complaint cases heard in three years[;] it is about time to put our house in order and realize that this is a Union." Woolf admonished members for their "gun play, stabbings, fist-fights, hood-lumism, insulting and disregarding orders of foremen and delegates, etc., a general disregard of rules and regulations of the Union and unwillingness to cheerfully and honestly do a day's [work], and a desire to ignore the fact that we are cannery workers." The disruptive few were the "chronic[ally] dissatisfied curbstone philosophers who adopt a policy of sabotage, inefficiency, laziness and indifference, and who do as little as possible and who make conditions as miserable as possible in the canneries and on boats."[22]

Woolf's tirade read like a list of charges typically cited in discipline cases. Fighting, often a manifestation of ethnic tensions at the plants, had to be controlled to prevent the union from destroying itself. The local regularly fined and expelled members in an effort to resolve problems, but with only limited success. International tensions among China, Japan, and the Philippines added to interethnic tensions, and leaders had to work hard to keep tempers below the boiling point.[23]

The locals also had to contend with the uneasy relationship between their members—the outside crews—and Alaskan workers. In 1941 the union disciplined a Filipino member, Joe Prudencio, who was "caught fooling around" with Native Alaskan women. The union delegate at the cannery explained: "Well, it's too bad Prudencio was caught. Of course, all of us fool around with the girls sometimes, but Joe got caught, and he was supposed to be attending to his work." Prudencio received only a reprimand for failure to be on the job.[24] Other cases posed greater threats to the union and revealed the darker side of ethnic and gender relations. In a 1942 disciplinary hearing, the foreman at one Alaska cannery reported:

> I went next door and hear[d] a noise in the room that belonged to the Seattle crew. I opened the door, and went in. There I saw four or five men and one [Native Alaskan] girl. They had the girl on the table stripped naked. They were all having a carnival. Four were holding the girl, while the other was satisfying himself. . . . I broke it up [and] told them all to go back to work and the girl to get dressed, and not to say anything about it as it would only cause more confusion in an already badly confused gang. I thought it best for the interests of the Union and protection of the girl . . . that the whole thing not be repeated, or spoken of again, and that we let the whole matter drop.[25]

When asked why he had failed to report the incident immediately, the foreman responded that the men would not have gone to jail or been "because the women were natives. Nobody pays attention to ⌐ives."[26] Only a few such investigations were undertaken because, ⌐ne worker noted, too much publicity about such incidents would ⌐aise a stink on [*sic*] the Union."[27] Fearful of losing what limited support it found among Alaskan Natives and residents, the ACWU's executive council brought charges against the ringleader of the group, who raped the Native Alaskan woman, and suspended him for two years.[28]

The locals also battled continuously over another potential source of disruption for the union, gambling. George Minato, a union delegate for several southeast Alaska canneries, noted his frustration: "The only thing that worries me is this gambling that is going on," and "no one will cooperate."[29] The locals put antigambling clauses in the contracts, but to no avail. Workers were reluctant to discontinue a favored pastime or forgo an opportunity to strike it big. One foreman claimed that the crew "pestered" him so much for advances on their pay that he got $600 from the company so the workers would leave him alone.[30]

Policing gambling proved to be a difficult task. Union officials recognized that they could not stop or prosecute workers who participated in established leisure activities without undermining union support. Still, they had to be vigilant on the "question of rackets." The officials decided they "wouldn't prosecute a man for a friendly game, but for making a business of it." Following that line of reasoning, the executive board of Seattle's CWFLU decided that the foreman who had "borrowed" $600 from the company so that the workers could gamble was making "a business of it" and barred him from the union for two years.[31] Occasional suspensions did not stop gambling.

Disciplinary actions alienated some workers, but the locals' apparent successes in contract negotiations convinced most that the union was on their side. Whereas contractors had been most concerned with the price per case, in union contracts workers came to the fore. Each worker had a written agreement with the union and the company that specified wages and working conditions. Under the contract system, these matters had usually been the subject of verbal agreements. Under the unions, each worker received his pay directly from the company, not through an intermediary. These changes brought immediate support for the union.[32]

Workers' continued loyalty to the union depended on its ability to negotiate increasingly better wages. On the eve of unionization in 1932 and 1933, wages for common laborers ranged from $25 to $50 a month.[33] By 1939, unionists boasted that they were responsible for wages that ranged from $80 to $100 per month for common labor.[34]

The annual boost in wages by an average of 10 percent was not solely a result of the union's activities. In 1934 the National Recovery Administration (NRA) had set minimum wages at $50 a month for cannery workers.[35] The first adjustment thus came from government, not union, pressure. Economic recovery after 1933 helped canners reestablish their consumer markets and made it easier for them to accept wage increases. Labor costs remained well below 20 percent, usually 10 to 15 percent, of the total costs of canning salmon.[36]

Nonetheless, the locals made a yearly ritual display of their demands. In 1942, Steve Glumaz of the negotiating committee reported to members: "We are asking for a 65% increase in wages this year. . . . [We] should, with arguments at hand for demanding a good increase, get at least a 30% raise."[37] The wartime economy encouraged such high demands, but the strategy was consistent with earlier negotiations. The committees for each local demanded huge increases in order to gain support from its members. Still, the vast difference between wages in 1932 and those in 1939 was as much the result of the economic position of the canners and government intervention as it was the efforts of the union.

The cannery workers and their union representatives also lobbied for uniform wage rates across all canning regions. Under the contract system and early unionization, geographical distinctions in wages reflected decades-old perceptions of the canning regions. Negotiators for the companies had argued that the types of salmon packed in each region created important variations in the length of the season and the degree of mechanization, thereby necessitating different pay levels. By the late 1930s, however, most Alaska canneries were highly mechanized. The new and more sophisticated machinery, particularly for butchering and filling, made it possible not only to handle large quantities of salmon but also to produce a better-looking product than was possible with the canning machinery of the 1910s and 1920s. Technology had effectively homogenized the labor process to the point that the regional distinctions held relatively little meaning. Union negotiators pointed out that "the same effort and amount of work are exerted regardless of location. Production cost is proportionally the same all [the] way down [the Alaska coast,] regardless of any class of salmon[,] so that there is no basis for division of wage scales."[38] CWFLU vice-president George Taki put it more simply: "They make the same amount of profit. That's why I stand for a definite uniformed [*sic*] wage scale."[39] The locals were able to bring wage levels in southeast and central Alaska into conformity with each other, but not western Alaska, where the pay remained slightly higher.[40]

...ssification was also important. From 1937 to 1939, the ̣ained with companies for three job categories: A (skilled), ̣killed), and C (unskilled), based largely on the informal hierar- . tasks that workers and canners had created during the contract- era. In 1939 the locals eliminated the C category, placed skilled ̣d semiskilled workers in the new A classification, and put the un-skilled workers into the B rank[41] (see Appendix, Tables 5 and 6).

The union hoped that reclassification would increase workers' wages, but it did not. During the depression, sales of high-priced salmon had languished, while inexpensive machine-packed salmon continued to find buyers. When the prospects for war production revi-talized the industry, lower grades of machine-filled cans continued to make up the bulk of orders. In view of changes in the market for canned salmon, the job reclassification principally represented union-ists' efforts to save the pay scale of skilled and semiskilled jobs, rather than an effort to increase unskilled laborers' wages.[42]

At least a few union leaders recognized that the combination of wage increases, uniform wage rates, and job reclassification during the late 1930s only saved workers from losing ground. In 1941 Conrad Espe, UCAPAWA official and former business agent for the CWFLU, argued that "cannery workers, in spite of gains of actual wages in the contracts[,] have been getting less and less per season." Cannery wages had not kept abreast of consumer price increases, while technological improvements in the canneries had led to higher production and faster-paced work.[43]

The locals made even less headway with work hours. The NRA and the NLRB granted canners exemptions from eight-hour days be-cause the potential for any uncanned fish to spoil created an "emer-gency" situation; however, they agreed with the union that overtime rates should be paid for more than eight hours' work. From the mid-1930s, the bargaining issue was how much that rate should be. Pay-ment for overtime added substantially to the annual income of the workers.[44]

The locals took credit for changes in wages and overtime pay, but they could not take much credit for improving working and living conditions. Negative press in the 1920s had hurt consumer markets so much that by the 1930s most canners had already adjusted their plants and outbuildings to comply with the suggestions made by the National Canners' Association sanitary surveys. The NRA hearings revealed many problems in the industry, but relatively little was said about liv-ing and working conditions at the plants. By the 1930s, then, the worst problems associated with wages, hours, and conditions had been resolved. Most workers believed that union activities alone brought these changes. They had not, but the locals capitalized on that belief to impose a new union hierarchy at the plants that assured their control.[45]

Creating a New Union Hierarchy

Foremen constituted the most powerful obstacle to establishing the new union hierarchy. They might block union programs at the canneries and might even try to become labor agents. But the locals also needed to retain foremen's positions in order to help maintain the balance of power among the various ethnic groups and as a path for mobility. (Foremen held the highest position at the plants to which workers might realistically aspire after the demise of contracting.) Further, they needed the managerial experience foremen possessed. Karl Yoneda remembered the chaos that resulted when the ACWU tried to run crews without foremen: "Through our own inexperience we didn't realize that the food supply, except salmon, should be spread evenly to cover a three-month period. As a result we had shortages [and] numerous complaints."[46] The local learned the hard way that while its officers might be committed to workers' welfare, it had to rely on possibly hostile foremen to manage the crews at the plants.[47]

Having risen through the ranks under contracting, foremen resisted union control. During 1937 and 1938, their defiance was the strongest and most troublesome. They created havoc in the hiring halls when they attempted to take part in dispatching. At the canneries they were no better. When workers at one plant were unhappy with the foreman for showing favoritism to certain individuals, they threatened to report him to the union. "The Union is nothing," he bluntly told them, "it is a fuck union."[48] Ethnic rivalries complicated the issue. In that instance, the foreman was Japanese, and those who filed the complaint were Filipinos. In another 1938 case, the mixed Japanese and Filipino crew at New England Fish Company's Noyes Island, Alaska, cannery charged Dick Kanaya with misconduct and favoritism in work assignments. CWFLU officials heard the workers' complaints but excused the foreman's activities on the grounds that he was "an old timer in the industry under the contracting system [and] did not exactly . . . [understand] the benefits and good conditions that the union . . . [was] seeking."[49] In 1937 the local could not discipline resistant foremen because it needed them to help manage the crews, whereas in 1938 it did not want to put Kanaya "on the spot" because on the eve of the consent election, the CIO local could ill afford to alienate Japanese voters.

By 1939, the locals had begun to chip away at the foremen's power. In addition to removing foremen from dispatching committees, the locals instituted a screening process in which they assessed the applicant's canning skills and experiences and recorded his ethnicity. Those same points had been important under contracting, but the locals formalized the process and added the question: "Will you abide by union rules?" All applicants thus had to submit to union discipline to secure jobs. To control foremen, the locals fined them $150 for "frequenting" AFL meetings. (Common workers earned penalties of $25 for the same offense.) They also made recalcitrant foremen suffer "lecture[s] on the labor movement and on labor principles" to bring them in line with union policies.[50] In 1939 the AFL made an unsuccessful attempt to recruit foremen unhappy with CIO restrictions, but the locals had enough power to fend off such advances and to discipline foremen.[51]

In 1940 the officers of the CWFLU felt even more secure in punishing members they deemed "not faithful" to union ideals, particularly foremen, and they put into effect strict guidelines for limiting foremen's powers. By then, the fear of a counteroffensive by the AFL or an independent union had subsided. At one 1940 Seattle meeting of AFL forces, only forty Asians attended. Three times as many local whites, hostile to Asian labor, appeared. Of the Asians, five were Japanese, three of whom were unemployed foremen. The remaining two Japanese were CWFLU "confidence men" sent to spy. By that time, Asian foremen could expect cannery work only through the CIO local.[52]

Although the locals quickly established methods to control foremen, they continued to tolerate troublesome individuals because owners demanded that the union supply "qualified foremen acceptable to the company."[53] Through the new guidelines, the union made every effort to make foremen "the technical director of operation[s]" and not the virtual lords over workers they had been under contracting. To weaken foremen, the locals also increased other workers' responsibilities. Contractors had used assistants or subcontractors to represent other ethnic groups at the plants. The union institutionalized the practice by creating the position of "second foremen" at three-fourths the pay of foremen. At the cannery in Taku Harbor, Alaska, for example, it hired a Filipino foreman and a Japanese second foreman because the two groups had "requested representation in the cannery foremanship."[54]

The installation of second foremen raised the same issues as the appointment of foremen, so the locals created additional positions for delegates, timekeepers, union coordinating committee members, and department heads to counter the first and second foremen. Among them, delegates had the most power. They had been sent to canneries in 1937, but after the CIO locals won the elections, delegates' roles became better defined and more powerful. They took over the "personal problems" of the crew from foremen and acted as combination shop stewards and local union business agents. They kept and posted daily records on overtime and longshore work to insure fair rotation among workers, presided over weekly union meetings at the canneries, inspected the kitchens and bunkhouses to ensure that the companies upheld their contractual obligations, and sent written reports back to the locals. They also had the authority to request additional manpower at any given cannery. With foremen, they shared responsibility for "maintaining discipline . . . , peace and order among the crew,"[55] but alone were to "encourage wholesome recreational activities [such as] volleyball, ping-pong, boat racing, educational meetings, musical and literary programs, picnics, et cetera."[56] For their efforts, delegates received $25 a month more than the best-paid workers on the canning line. The union tried to "prevent delegates from becoming fault finders [and] using their position as a stepping-stone to foremanship." Delegates who pressed charges against foremen were ineligible for the positions. The stricture was designed to prevent conflicts of interest among those seeking advancement. The rule implied, however, that foremen remained more powerful than delegates.[57]

Still, delegates offered new avenues for balancing ethnic representation. Data on delegates are sparse, but in 1937 the Seattle-based CWFLU sent fifty-eight delegates to seventy-five canneries (some supervised several smaller canneries). Of those delegates, fifty-one were Filipinos. Their predominance reflected that ethnic group's larger presence in the local and a way for the union to adjust for their underrepresentation as foremen. Four prominent Nisei unionists were selected as delegates; the remaining delegate was Wilson Mar, a loyal and vocal CIO supporter among Chinese in Seattle. The Japanese and Chinese delegates each oversaw several canneries so that their influence was greater than that of a single Filipino delegate. Despite the predominance of Filipino delegates, the message to Chinese and Japanese workers was that they would be represented and that the local rewarded those who supported its program.[58] Once in the position, however, the same ties that bound workers and foremen sometimes connected delegates and foremen. Ponce Torres explained: "If the delegate . . . [is] a relative or friend of [the] foreman, the foreman controls him."[59] Old channels of influence persisted, and union officials continually struggled with conflicting goals of a broad union program and workers' self interests.

The creation of the positions of timekeeper, union coordinating committee member, and department head represented efforts to counter the power of foremen and police workers' behavior. Moreover, the positions increased workers' chances for representation and advancement within the union hierarchy. Timekeepers kept records of overtime and longshore work for delegates. Only larger canneries had timekeepers, and the locals used the position to reward supporters who might otherwise not have been able to find cannery work. For example, Dyke Miyagawa, instrumental in garnering Nisei support for the CWFLU, had been crippled by a childhood accident and was unable to perform canning tasks. The CWFLU appointed him as a timekeeper as a reward for his efforts on the union's behalf.[60]

Because canneries were several hundred miles from union headquarters, day-to-day matters had to be dealt with at the plants. To facilitate this, the union created unpaid positions on coordinating committees designed to "provide better understanding and harmony between the foreman and the delegate, and between the employer and the employees without sacrificing progressive unionism." Each was to be the "Executive Council of the crew." Through them, workers were educated in union ideals and entrusted to make their own decisions about discipline at the plants. Acting on such democratic principles gave workers more formal power to effect change at their workplace than they had had under contracting.[61]

Finally, the appointment of department heads formalized the authority of key workers along the canning line and in the warehouses. A large cannery might have as many as eight department heads: in the fish house with the pitchers and sorters; in the butchering department among the Iron Chink (automatic fish-butchering machine) operators; in the sliming department; in the can loft; along the line among filling- and sealing-machine attendants; at the end of the line with the can catchers and tray loaders; in the bathroom among the lye-wash workers; and in the warehouse where workers cased and stored the canned salmon. Staffing in the departments reflected an informal segregation based on ethnic and friendship networks. By appointing department heads, the union provided representation for each group.[62]

The Destruction of the Alliance

The new union hierarchy was awkward and unwieldy, but it functioned in spite of internal tensions. Changes in the industry, followed by wartime exigencies, however, strained and ultimately destroyed the alliance that workers had built in support of the union's system of labor recruitment and management.

The first blow came in 1941 when San Francisco packers shifted the base of their operations to Seattle. Once there, the canners recruited primarily from the Northwest, not San Francisco. Karl Yoneda claims that the canners made the move because they no longer wanted to negotiate with the militant members of the ACWU and hoped that they could deal more easily with the CWFLU.[63] The militancy of the San Francisco local cannot be denied, but the move to Seattle was predicated on other factors. The Merchant Marine Act of 1920, or Jones Act (named for its sponsor, Senator Wesley L. Jones of Washington), prohibited the shipment of any goods to or from Alaska in foreign vessels.[64] The act eliminated competition from two Canadian steamship lines that had rail connections in Prince Rupert and Vancouver, British Columbia. Only two other steamer companies served the Alaska trade, and both had their headquarters in Seattle. In effect, then, Seattle with its huge wharves and warehouses and excellent rail links became the gateway to Alaska and attracted canning companies there. Later departure dates from Seattle also saved canners money because they began the payment of wages once their crews boarded the ships.[65] More than the militancy of workers in San Francisco predicated the canners' northward moves.

The loss of jobs to Seattle workers left ACWU members in dire straits. Having dispatched no permit men for the 1941 season, the ACWU still had three hundred to four hundred book-holding members in good standing without jobs. The local appealed to the CWFLU to hire its members rather than Northwest permit men, but the Seattle local balked. One issue was the loss of CWFLU autonomy. Since the mid-1930s, the ACWU and the CWFLU had had an uneasy relationship, and each local believed its program should prevail over the other's. CWFLU officials and members were worried that the ACWU might try to control dispatching in Seattle. Further, the CWFLU doled out extra jobs to permit men to maintain ethnic representation among workers in the Northwest, and it was loathe to give up slots to the ACWU.[66]

Neither in 1941 nor in 1942 did the two locals arrive at a satisfactory resolution. Finally, in 1943, the two amalgamated. Members of the ACWU had no other option if they hoped to retain their cannery jobs, for the canners hired the bulk of their crews through the Seattle local in order to lower their labor costs. Nonmembers in San Francisco, many of whom were Chinese, were hit hardest. Amalgamation effectively eliminated the window through which they had entered the industry. In order to find a cannery job one had to be a full member from San Francisco or Seattle. The union continued to issue permits but apparently only to workers from Seattle, not San Francisco. Since permit holders had no voting rights within the union, they had no ability to change the policy. As a result, Chinese employment in Alaska canneries dropped precipitously from a scant 120 in 1940 to 42 in 1943.[67] Their employment further dwindled, and by 1952 fewer than twenty Chinese, among nearly twenty-five hundred union members, worked in Alaska canneries.[68]

Other factors contributed to the withdrawal of Chinese from the canneries. Alaska residents—Native Alaskans and European Americans—through their own union organizations had become a formidable political force and yielded enough workers to compensate for the loss of several hundred Chinese from San Francisco. The use of more sophisticated machinery for lower grades of salmon displaced skilled Chinese "old-timers" as well as Japanese and Filipinos. More directly, World War II opened new possibilities for Chinese in the military and defense-related jobs. After 1941, Chinese were no longer a significant part of the cannery workers' alliance.[69]

Whereas the canners' northward move and the subsequent amalgamation of the locals had virtually curtailed the Chinese presence in the industry, Japanese in Seattle briefly gained influence. Japanese had not relied on the permit system but had concentrated on gaining what they believed to be a fair share within the union, particularly the CWFLU. They demanded and received representation in various offices and committees and maintained a strong presence in specific canneries previously thought of as "belonging" to Japanese contractors. Japanese were concerned that Filipinos, by virtue of their substantial numbers, reaped greater benefits. In response, they formed a bloc to lobby and vote for programs and to support individuals who benefited them under the auspices of the *Nippon Kan* (alternately known as the Japanese Educational Hall, Japanese Educational Society, and Japanese Hall).[70]

The *Nippon Kan* began as a social gathering place for Japanese workers but by early 1939 had become much more when its officers collected dues from its members. Filipinos in the CWFLU accused the organization's members of being disloyal to the local, but George Taki reassured officials that the "Japanese Hall" was not "for dual union purposes" and was a "gathering place of the Japanese brothers so that they can be taken hold of promptly if they are needed to do something for the union."[71] At the hall, Taki explained, Japanese-language speakers could clearly explain the union's program. That the hall served such a purpose cannot be denied, but in it Japanese members also developed collective strategies for union meetings and elections. The local had no choice but to allow Japanese members to continue their activities in the hall. Officially, union leaders used Taki's explanation to justify the continued existence of the hall, but the threat that up to a quarter of the CWFLU's membership might withdraw if the local forced Japanese to close the hall gave them little choice. Consequently, the *Nippon Kan* continued but became the target of Filipino animosity and fears about competition from Japanese.[72]

Japanese continued to meet in the *Nippon Kan* for the next several years in order to develop an agenda that would allow them to vote in a bloc and thereby place Japanese in key union positions. They did so effectively until the bombings of Pearl Harbor and Manila in December 1941 put an end to their hopes for employment in the industry during the Pacific war. Immediately after the bombings, the union publicly announced that "Japanese Nationals will not be employable."[73] Japanese workers met in the *Nippon Kan* that winter to discuss the impending "welfare difficulties" caused by the loss of future cannery jobs. U.S. involvement in the war hurt more than the Japanese rank and file, since union officials lost their positions, too. Dick Kanaya, a trustee and member of the executive board, resigned, in his words, "for reasons beyond my control."[74] Dyke Miyagawa also stepped down from office but was careful to condemn the "militarist dictators of Japan . . . who . . . created the war." He asked union members and the American public not to associate Japanese in the United States with Japan's military and apologized to Filipinos for the destruction of their homeland.[75]

Neither the American public nor the Filipinos seemed to heed Miyagawa's words. By late winter, it had become clear that Japanese faced more than the loss of cannery jobs. A Seattle Japanese American newspaper announced that the March meeting of the *Nippon Kan*, "due to present circumstances," would be the last.[76] While the CWFLU stated explicitly that Japanese would not be employed in the canneries, it remained silent about Japanese internment. Whether the union simply failed to act or purged its files after the fact, no stance on the issue is evident in the records.[77] By all appearances, the CWFLU took no action in defense of its Japanese members. Once interned, most Japanese cannery workers remained estranged from the union. In June 1942, Tayasaburo Sekii wrote to ask about his status, but no evidence exists that the union replied.[78] Dyke Miyagawa penned several pieces for the *UCAPAWA News* in which he supported the American war effort and union concerns, but he and Sekii were exceptions.[79] Most Japanese were occupied with the turmoil and disruption of evacuation and internment, not with the union that had let them go in silence. After their wartime experiences, few Japanese returned to cannery work. The union's 1952 membership roll lists fewer than sixty Japanese members.[80]

The forced withdrawal of six hundred to seven hundred Japanese workers from the labor market created a shift of power in the industry in the favor of Filipinos. With the Japanese gone, positions as foremen, delegates, department heads, and line workers opened. For example, in 1942 Felix A. Narte took over the foremanship in the cannery at which he had been regularly employed. In that plant the foreman before him had been Japanese.[81] Within the union, new positions opened as well. Filipino workers brought in family members, friends, and people from their emigrant districts. Among Filipinos, this renewed old rivalries that had been subsumed by the larger goal of forming and then maintaining a union that had previously balanced Filipino interests against those of Japanese and Chinese.[82]

The war also provided opportunities for Filipinos outside the canneries. Many volunteered for military service. The CWFLU earned praise for its "outstanding [role] . . . in developing the First Filipino Infantry Battalion" through recruiting efforts at the union hall. As early as the summer of 1942, the union lost 500 to 600 Filipino workers to the army, 300 to the army transport service, and 250 to the navy.[83] While many had volunteered out of a sense of nationalism and patriotism, one official reportedly told fellow unionists: "I am going to the army because our Union is going to the rocks. There is no use sticking to it, I have a good chance of becoming a commissioned officer."[84] Still others deserted the canneries for better employment. With the help of the CWFLU, Filipinos found jobs in shipyards, aviation plants, and other industries boosted by the war. With union assistance, a few escaped the migratory agricultural work circuit and moved into a more secure sector of the economy.[85]

Throughout the West, Filipinos moved to take over lands formerly held by Japanese. The CWFLU encouraged and assisted them. The "imminent evacuation of Japanese," stated the executive council in late March 1942, means

> there will be chances for our members to take over leases to farm. For that reason the Union should adopt policies to see to it that the Gov[ernment] will take over leases of [Japanese] evacuees and no profits [will go] to the owners for the duration. Also that we have to get help for cooperative farming from our members from the Farm Security Administration.[86]

The executive council empowered a committee to poll its members as to who was interested in farming.[87] Going through government agencies and arranging leases was not new for Filipino immigrants because they had leased reservation lands from Native Americans in the past,[88] but movement onto Japanese American lands and the union promotion was.

To fill the vacancies created by the loss of Japanese workers, the union cooperated with owners to recruit Filipino and other workers from the California fields. With them in the ranks, the unionists felt they might actually be able to live up to the name of their local as the Cannery Workers and *Farm Laborers* Union. The CWFLU carefully guarded these new recruits from the companies because it feared that owners would use the shortage to gain control of the union hiring halls or bypass them completely. Such fears were unfounded, for canners continued to rely heavily on the union for labor recruitment. Even the combined efforts of the union and canners failed to meet wartime labor needs. Packers claimed it was "impossible" to get enough workers to their plants, especially those in western Alaska. The labor shortage led to a scramble to get ahead inside the union; favoritism increased dramatically, and old rivalries among Filipinos were revived. The notion that the union was "going to the rocks" was not too far from the truth.[89]

Filipino nationalism and patriotism were countervailing influences to that divisiveness. In April 1942, the industry's magazine, the *Pacific Fisherman*, carried pictures of several Filipino foremen. "These are the men who put the salmon in the cans," read the caption. "They're all set to can salmon to beat the Japs, and are determined to make it 'Food for MacArthur's Men' on the Bataan Peninsula, where some of them come from."[90] Filipinos had become the canners' new allies overnight. Companies capitalized on Filipino patriotism to pull foremen to their side whenever possible, hoping to regain some advantage over the union. They also used that patriotism to push crews to accept higher production levels and longer hours.[91]

Supporting the war effort gave Filipinos a sense of worth and proof of their good "citizenship" (even if they had been never been given the right to become U.S. citizens) as well as an opportunity to express Filipino nationalism. The CWFLU encouraged members to buy defense bonds in its name. Between December 1941 and the end of January 1942, the union had secured $1,500 in war bonds earmarked to help purchase a Boeing aircraft "to bomb Tokyo."[92] On December 15, 1942, union members organized a "Filipino Day" in Seattle during which they raised $48,050 for war bonds.[93] In 1944,

Trinidad Rojo, president of the CWFLU, claimed the union had helped members contribute $185,000 during the course of the war. According to Rojo, their fund raising and military service made Filipinos "the darling of the American heart."[94]

Within the canned-salmon industry, war brought a renewed focus on mechanization and the recruitment of other than Filipino workers. Wartime labor shortages brought the final impetus to mechanization. Canners who had not earlier done so now used machines that had been available since the mid-1920s. High-speed lines with sophisticated filling and sealing machines took up the slack as the labor supply shrank. Outside western Alaska, the industry also pushed for women's involvement in canning. The September 1943 issue of *Pacific Fisherman* carried on its cover a picture of women in the plants and the caption *Women at War—Doing the Work of Men.*[95] Even though women had long toiled in the canneries, the wartime labor shortage and the growth of European American communities in Alaska made it possible for canners to hire greater numbers of local women. The task of loading and unloading trays of cans from the retorts, which had earlier been done by two-man teams, was now done by four-women teams. Canners carefully cultivated women's patriotism and sense of self-pride in order to get them to work in the canneries. They claimed publicly, if demeaningly, that heavy cannery work was "traditionally done by men, but the girls glory in their ability to handle it satisfactorily."[96] Women may have felt pride in their work, but their participation made it possible for canners to begin a program of replacing Filipinos in the crews.[97]

Amid the voices calling for increased women's participation in the industry, a small minority also urged bringing in immigrants from China. In 1943 Miller Freeman, the long-time voice of anti-Japanese sentiment in the industry (as early as 1919 he had lobbied for the exclusion of Japanese from American fisheries and in the mid-1930s raved in the *Pacific Fisherman* about the encroachment of Japanese fishing vessels on Alaska waters and the salmon fisheries), called for the repeal of the Chinese Exclusion Act. He argued that "we should recognize the heroic accomplishments of the Chinese people as a member of the United Nations in the struggle against totalitarianism."[98] Chinese, according to Freeman, should be allowed to enter under the national-origins quotas set in the 1920s. Only several hundred would enter each year, but Freeman hoped these new immigrants might fill the gaps in the cannery labor market. Congress rescinded the Chinese exclusion laws in December 1943, but that action had little impact on the canned-salmon industry.[99]

The union and the canneries survived the war, but the postwar epoch differed greatly from the prewar one. Although still dominated by Filipinos, the union fell prey to renewed divisions among Filipinos as AFL-backed locals used red-baiting rhetoric to disable the CWFLU, a particularly effective tactic as the Cold War developed in the late 1940s and early 1950s.[100] Non-Filipinos in organized labor echoed the fear of communists and added strong jingoist language of their own. The steady decline in the industry itself further eroded the local's position. Government regulations against fish traps raised the price of salmon for the canners and placed their product out of reach of most consumers. Canned tuna became the cheap fish of the second half of the twentieth century, while salmon became a luxury item in the fresh fish markets. Better transportation and storage facilities for fresh fish also worked against the more expensive canning plants. The resource had dwindled like the great buffalo herds, a prophecy made by some nineteenth-century observers. This ultimately killed the industry. The salmon fisheries did not withstand the crippling effects of the construction of large hydroelectric dams on the Columbia River and the destruction of spawning grounds all along the Pacific Coast.[101]

With the loss of the resource and markets, the industry has slowly withered to the point that, as the twentieth century nears its close, canned salmon is a high-priced, selectively marketed product. On November 14, 1991, the National Marine Fisheries Service determined that "former" runs amounted to 11 million fish compared to 2.5 million that year and that only 2 percent of the fish were nonhatchery raised.[102] To protect salmon on the way to the spawning grounds, the Fisheries Service placed Sockeye salmon on the endangered species list. Bonneville Power Administration officials expect the listing to divert $70 million of water away from power generation to assure the fish safe passage. Those efforts, they argue, will increase power rates between 2 and 10 percent. The status of other kinds of salmon are also under consideration.[103] On April 11, 1992, the Pacific Fishery Management Council, after four days of hearings, limited the ocean catch of all salmon from Tilamook, Oregon, to the Canadian border to half the 1991 levels and banned ocean salmon fishing between a point ninety miles north of San Francisco Bay to Florence, Oregon.[104]

Long before those rulings, however, most of the canneries fell into the bays and rivers of the coast or were converted to tourist resorts. Those that remain are large automated plants, some of them seagoing, which are staffed with college students, resident Alaskans, and a few Filipinos. The postwar story of the industry and its workers is one of decline and is markedly different from its expansive prewar history.[105]

From the first moves toward inclusive unionization late in 1936 to 1942, Asian immigrants and Asian Americans contributed to the creation of a system of ethnic representation in the union that satisfied their personal and ethnic interests but still allowed for union control. The multiethnic alliance forged by workers and the union locals was strong enough to ward off competing labor organizations, company efforts at control of the labor market, and potentially crippling interethnic conflict. The brief, fragile alliance that workers built failed to weather the storms of market forces, national and international politics, and war. The alliance gradually disintegrated, first with the move of major Alaska canners from San Francisco to Seattle that effectively denied most Chinese entry into the cannery crews and then with the wartime internment of Japanese. In their absence, much of the "internationalist" vision of the prewar years faded as the cannery workers' union increasingly served the interests of the Filipino majority.

Conclusion

A brave man meeting an untimely adversity,
All day long, unable to eat or sleep.
Rushing about over ten thousand miles,
    deep in sorrow,
Every hour, every minute, mind and body
    toil in pain.
Heaven's will is extreme!
This big roc wants to spread its wings.
Yet scores are not evened up; the mind is not
    at ease.
Alas, I can't rest in peace, I just can't rest
    in peace.[1]

SO WROTE an anonymous poet in the 1915 anthology of Cantonese rhymes, *Songs of Gold Mountain* (*Jinshan ge ji*), of one Chinese immigrant's experience.[2] In rough, folksy Cantonese, the poet expresses many elements that are at the center of this book. I have argued that Asian immigrant and Asian American men and women met frequent, often "untimely adversity" and "toil[ed] in pain" in the United States. The laborers among them quite literally traversed "ten thousand miles" in their annual work-related migrations. Regarding such travails another writer for the same volume says: "If fate is indeed Heaven's will, what more can I say?"[3] Yet there is much more to be said. Aspirations for a better life and a sense that more could be had did exist among Asian immigrants and Asian Americans. So, too, does evidence that they took action to even the "scores." At times they responded as individuals, but more commonly they looked to collective action as a means to push back constraints placed on them by life in a largely hostile society and by labor in seasonal enterprises.

The boundaries Asian immigrants and Asian Americans faced, though ever-present, were not constant, as illustrated by their involvement in the canned-salmon industry. Chinese entered the industry early in its development. They found the work culture in flux as operations expanded from a single family-run shop to dozens of large industrial enterprises. Despite their relegation to a lower tier of jobs in the canneries, Chinese carved out a sphere of influence, participated in the establishment of a labor recruitment and management system, and eventually came to occupy a position of power relative to later entrants into the labor force. Instead of comparatively primitive social organizations, as Lloyd Fisher suggests they formed in the nineteenth-century harvest labor market,[4] they developed complex responses well suited to the particular characteristics of the industry at that time. In relations with contractors, Chinese workers attempted to exert an influence through kinship, friendship, and immigrant association ties, as well as through job related actions such as organizing work stoppages or absconding with advance wages.[5] Moreover, Chinese established a network of communities because their economic livelihood depended on an ability to move quickly from one worksite to another throughout the year.[6] For Chinese cannery hands, that network included not only the large Chinatowns in San Francisco, Portland, and Vancouver, British Columbia, but also smaller industrial towns and even factory villages. By the turn of the century, new technologies and new groups of workers in the industry prompted a host of new actions by Chinese. Through it all, Chinese constantly modified the work culture and, whenever possible, bent circumstances to their benefit.

In the first three decades of the twentieth century, the entrance of many other ethnic groups into the cannery labor force made relationships among workers more difficult than they had been in the largely Chinese crews of the nineteenth century. So, too, did the emergence of Japanese and then Filipino subcontractors and contractors, and tremendous industrial expansion. In the complex social milieu of the twentieth-century canneries, workers of Chinese, Japanese, and Filipino ancestry struggled with one another for control of the portion of the industry in which they worked. Like the Chinese before them, Japanese and Filipinos drew on family, friendship, and emigrant association ties, but in doing so they reinforced ethnic divisions in the workforce. Increasingly, demographic differences among the ethnic groups also set them apart from each other: Chinese workers were largely middle-aged bachelors; Filipinos, though mostly single men, too, were in their late teens and early twenties; Japanese often labored as families with men, women, and children involved. Factionalization of the workforce led to an intense racialism that workers only occasionally transcended.

By the mid-1930s, though, the Great Depression, government activism, labor organization, and the onset of scarcity in the salmon runs brought tremendous changes. Wild swings in the economy, federal involvement, and labor scarcity were no strangers to the American West.[7] The actions of Asian immigrants and Asian Americans, with the assistance of organized labor, to build an alliance that was a blend of ethnic and class associations, however, was something new. Labor organizers had to draw on the same preexisting patterns of work that had contributed to ethnic factionalism. Nonetheless, they were able to construct a functioning alliance based on ethnic pluralism. Workers continued to identify with a particular ethnic group, but found increasingly fewer rewards in focusing on ethnic concerns to the exclusion of their common class interests with other workers. That trend might have continued and an Asian American working class might have developed a strong association with European American workers,[8] had not World War II, the internment of Japanese Americans, the imperatives of a wartime economy, and changes in the canned-salmon industry torn apart the pluralism and left Filipinos struggling among themselves for power within the union. The seeming failure to maintain the link between ethnic and class associations was not the result of weaknesses in the system that workers and unionists developed but was caused by forces outside the workers' control.

From the time when Ah Shing stood along the processing line at George Hume's cannery on the Columbia River in 1870 until unionist Dyke Miyagawa left for the internment camps early in World War II, Asian immigrants and Asian Americans were not content to "rest in peace." Their actions were central in an industry that epitomized the complexities of the American West—heavy reliance on extractive enterprises, tremendous ethnic diversity, and rapid economic and social change. Asian immigrants and Asian Americans struggled to play a role in the creation of the industry's patterns of work and in the labor recruitment and management system. When the time came for the revision of that system, those ethnically diverse workers joined in a loose confederation that made them indispensable allies behind the push for a multiethnic union. Their struggle is an integral part of the history of the American West's industrial and social transformation at regional, national, and global levels.

APPENDIX

TABLE 1

OCCUPATIONS OF CHINESE MEN IN ASTORIA, ORE., 1870–1910

	1870	*1880*	*1900*	*1910*
CANNERY WORKERS				
Unspecified	—	1,624	325	81
Cook	—	14	1	1
Foreman	—	—	—	3
Contractor	—	1	6	6
Total	—	1,639	332	91
ENTREPRENEURS				
Barber	—	14	2	1
Clothier	—	—	—	1
Laundryman	—	14	6	4
Merchant/grocer	—	27	31	34
Pawnbroker	—	2	—	—
Restaurateur	—	2	1	6
Saloonkeeper	—	1	—	—
Tailor	—	1	4	—
Truck gardener	—	4	8	11
Total	—	65	52	57
PROFESSIONAL/SKILLED LABORERS				
Butcher	—	1	—	—
Carpenter	—	1	—	—
Physician	—	6	—	—
Schoolteacher	—	1	—	—
Tinsmith	—	1	—	—
Total	—	10	—	—

Continued on next page

Table 1—Continued

	1870	1880	1900	1910
COOKS				
Unspecified	7	9	20	3
Boardinghouse	—	—	3	—
Hotel	—	21	—	—
Private family	—	11	—	—
Restaurant	—	11	—	—
Total	7	52	23	3
SMALL BUSINESS EMPLOYEES				
Unspecified	—	1	—	—
Laundry	—	36	11	10
Saloon	—	—	—	1
Store (clerk)	—	9	—	2
Truck garden	—	—	19	6
Restaurant (waiter)	—	3	—	4
Total	—	49	30	23
UNSKILLED LABORERS				
Unspecified/common	—	257	123	7
Dishwasher	6	7	—	—
Domestic servant	—	13	—	—
Shoe factory worker	—	6	1	—
Total	6	283	124	7
GRAND TOTAL	13	2,098	561	181

Sources: U.S. Census Bureau, Manuscript Schedules of the Population Census, Clatsop County, Ore., 1870, 1880, 1900, and 1910.

TABLE 2
Occupations of Chinese Men in New Westminster, B.C., 1884

CANNERY WORKERS	390
ENTREPRENEURS	
Barber	15
Laundryman	20
Merchant/grocer	12
Truck gardener	9
Charcoal burner	18
Total	74
PROFESSIONAL/SKILLED LABORERS	
Carpenter	3
Physician	6
Schoolteacher	2
Total	11
COOKS AND DOMESTIC SERVANTS	50
STORE CLERKS	18
UNSKILLED LABORERS	
Ditch digger	156
Farm worker	400
Sawmill worker	190
Sewing machine operator	6
Wood chopper	82
Total	834
GRAND TOTAL	1,377

Source: Report of the Royal Commission on Chinese Immigration (Ottawa, 1885), 363.
Note: The report also lists 4 married women, 7 prostitutes, 2 girls, 90 boys, and 200 "new arrivals," in the total Chinese population figure of 1,680.

TABLE 3
OCCUPATIONS OF CHINESE MEN IN THE DALLES, ORE., 1880–1910

	1880	*1900*	*1910*
CANNERY WORKERS	—	15	31
ENTREPRENEURS			
Barber	1	1	—
Boardinghouse keeper	1	—	1
Laundryman	55	11	10
Merchant/grocer	2	4	4
Restaurateur	—	—	2
Truck gardener	1	10	1
Total	60	26	18
PHYSICIANS	2	—	—
COOKS	35	21	23
STORE CLERKS	9	2	—
UNSKILLED LABORERS			
Unspecified/common	—	31	1
Domestic servant	—	—	1
Wood chopper	4	7	—
Total	4	38	2
GRAND TOTAL	110	102	74

Sources: U.S. Census Bureau, Manuscript Schedules of the Population Census, Wasco County, Ore., 1880, 1900, and 1910.
Note: The census schedules also list, in 1880, 2 unemployed people and 4 women; in 1900, 5 unemployed people and 2 women; in 1910, 1 unemployed person and 1 woman.

200

TABLE 4
CHINESE AND JAPANESE SHOREWORKERS BY REGION, 1909

	Chinese		Japanese	
	N	%	N	%
ALASKA				
Western	1,069	42.7	1,432	57.3
Central	377	51.4	356	48.6
Southeast	546	61.1	348	38.9
PUGET SOUND	1,051	51.1	1,004	48.9
COLUMBIA RIVER	417	60.9	268	39.1
COASTAL OREGON AND WASHINGTON	213	71.2	86	28.8
TOTAL	3,673	51.2	3,494	48.8

Source: John N. Cobb, *Salmon Fisheries of the Pacific Coast,* Bureau of Fisheries Document 751 (Washington, D.C., 1911), 68, 75, 83, 93, 98, 115.

TABLE 5
UNION JOB CLASSIFICATIONS, 1937

A Classification	B Classification	C Classification
Butchers (hand and machine)	Fish bin workers	Patching table workers
	Slimers	Can clinchers
Automatic butchering machine operators	Conveyors	Truckers
	Salting machine workers	Double seamers
Can catchers	Filling machine workers	
Relief men	Janitors	
Retort men	Can conveyors	
	Can reformers	

Source: Classification of Cannery Workers in Bristol Bay Packing Company, 1937, Exhibits, in the Matter of the Alaska Packers Association, Alaska Salmon Canning Company, Red Salmon Canning Company and Alaska Cannery Workers Local 5, Box 1201, National Labor Relations Board, Record Group 25, Washington National Records Center.

TABLE 6
UNION JOB CLASSIFICATIONS, 1939

A Classification	B Classification
Fish pitchers and loaders	Cooling tray carriers
Elevator operators	Patching table workers
Sorters/graders	Can-forming machine attendants
Filling machine attendants	Vacuum, clincher, and salter machine
Can catchers/feeders	attendants
Box (fiber) stitchers	Can loft
Fish inspectors	Warehouse crews
Can testers	Boxing crews
Automatic butchering machine (Iron	General cannery workers
Chink) operators	
Slimers	
Gang-knife operators	
Retort and lye gangs	
Cooler loaders	

Source: "Agreement with United Cannery Agricultural Packing and Allied Workers of America," May 19, 1939, file 12, box 2, Cannery Workers and Farm Laborers Union Records, University of Washington, Seattle.

NOTES

Introduction

1. I use the term "American West" throughout this book, rather than the more specific label "U.S. West," because of the former's more common acceptance and because I discuss early activities in Canadian canneries.

2. Asian immigrants and Asian Americans did not necessarily think of the region as "West." See Patricia Nelson Limerick, "Disorientation and Reorientation: The American Landscape Discovered from the West," *Journal of American History* 79, no. 3 (1992): 1021–1049; Yasuo Okada, "The Japanese Image of the American West," *Western Historical Quarterly* 19, no. 2 (1988): 141–159.

3. Before the 1882 Chinese Exclusion Act, the cannery labor market encompassed British Columbia as well as U.S. states and territories. After the 1880s, exclusionary and restrictive immigration legislation in the United States and Canada made it increasingly difficult for Asian cannery workers to cross the border. The result was two separate cannery labor markets. I focus on U.S. canneries with only occasional references to those in Canada. For labor relations in British Columbia's canneries, see Patricia Marchak, Neil Guppy, and John McMullan, eds., *Uncommon Property: The Fishing and Fish Processing Industries in British Columbia* (Toronto, 1987); Alicja Muszynski, "The Creation and Organization of Cheap Wage Labor in the British Columbia Fishing Industry," Ph.D. dissertation, University of British Columbia, 1986, 105–111; and idem, "Class Formation and Class Consciousness: The Making of Shoreworkers in the B.C. Fishing Industry," *Studies in Political Economy*, Summer 1986, 98–113.

4. U.S. Bureau of the Census, Manuscript Schedules of the Population Census, 1870, 1880, Wahkiakum County, Washington; ibid., 1880, Pacific County, Washington; ibid., 1880, Clatsop and Columbia counties, Oregon.

5. David Starr Jordan and Charles H. Gilbert, "The Salmon Fishery and Canning Interests of the Pacific Coast," in *The Fisheries and Fishery Industries of the United States*, vol. 5, ed. George Brown Goode (Washington, D.C., 1887), 753; John N. Cobb, *Salmon Fisheries of the Pacific Coast*, Bureau of

Fisheries Document 751 (Washington, D.C., 1911), 68, 75, 80, 83, 90, 93, 98, 112, 115; and U.S. Bureau of Fisheries, *Alaska Fishery and Fur-Seal Industries* (Washington, D.C., 1907–1939), passim.

6. Edna Bonacich, "Asian Labor in the Development of California and Hawaii," in *Labor Immigration under Capitalism: Asian Workers in the United States before World War II*, ed. Lucie Cheng and Edna Bonacich (Berkeley and Los Angeles, 1984), 151.

7. June Mei, "Socioeconomic Origins of Emigration: Guangdong to California, 1850–1882," in Cheng and Bonacich, *Labor Immigration*, 196.

8. Sucheng Chan, *This Bittersweet Soil: The Chinese in California Agriculture* (Berkeley and Los Angeles, 1986), 68–69; and June Mei, "Socioeconomic Developments among the Chinese in San Francisco, 1848–1906," in Cheng and Bonacich, *Labor Immigration*, 374.

9. Chan, *This Bittersweet Soil*, 68–69; John W. Stephens, "A Quantitative History of Chinatown, San Francisco, 1870 and 1880," in *The Life, Influence and the Role of the Chinese in the United States, 1776–1960* (San Francisco, 1976), 71–88; and Mei, "Socioeconomic Developments," 370–378.

10. Homer E. Gregory and Kathleen Barnes, *North Pacific Fisheries with Special Reference to Alaska Salmon* (New York, 1939), 251.

11. Dorothy O. Johansen and Charles M. Gates, *Empire of the Columbia: A History of the Pacific Northwest* (New York, 1967), 405–411, 556–557; Joseph A. Craig and Robert L. Hacker, "History and Development of the Fisheries of the Columbia River," U.S. Department of the Interior, Bureau of Fisheries, *Bulletin* 32, 1940.

12. For a good, brief summary of the various Chinese exclusion acts, see Sucheng Chan, "European and Asian Immigration into the United States in Comparative Perspective, 1820s to 1920s," in *Immigration Reconsidered: History, Sociology, and Politics*, ed. Virginia Yans-McLaughlin (New York, 1990), 62.

13. Cobb, *Salmon Fisheries* (1911), 68, 75, 80, 83, 90, 93, 98, 112, 115.

14. Edna Bonacich, "Some Basic Facts: Patterns of Asian Immigration and Exclusion," in Cheng and Bonacich, *Labor Immigration*, 70–71.

15. U.S. Bureau of Fisheries, *Alaska Fishery and Fur-Seal Industries, 1920* (Washington, D.C., 1921), 54; idem, *Alaska Fishery and Fur-Seal Industries, 1930* (Washington, D.C., 1931), 48.

16. U.S. Bureau of Fisheries, *Alaska Fishery and Fur-Seal Industries, 1936* (Washington, D.C., 1937), 310.

17. James H. Cellars, Testimony, Transcript, Official Report of Proceedings before the National Labor Relations Board in the Matter of Columbia River Packers Association, Inc., and Columbia River Gillnet Fishermen's Union, etc., 27, Astoria, Ore., February 16, 1942, box 3134, Transcripts and Exhibits, 1935–1948, Administrative Division, Files and Dockets Section, National Labor Relations Board, Record Group 25, Washington National Records Center, Suitland, Md.; Evart Hendrickson, Testimony, ibid., 50–69; Clarence M. Brooks to George O. Pratt, February 17, 1942, Case R-3549,

ibid.; Crew Lists, Columbia River Packers Association Altoona and Ellsworth Plants, 1941, Exhibit 4, February 16, 1942, Cases XX-R-819 and XX-R-820, ibid.

18. On the organization of the Seattle local, see Jack Masson and Donald Guimary, "Asian Labor Contractors in the Alaskan Canned Salmon Industry, 1880–1937," *Labor History* 23, no. 3 (Summer 1981): 377–397; idem, "Pilipinos and Unionization of the Alaskan Canned Salmon Industry," *Amerasia* 8 (Fall/Winter 1981): 1–30; Gerald Gold, "The Development of Local Number 7 of the Food, Tobacco, Agricultural and Allied Workers of America-C.I.O.," Master's thesis, University of Washington, 1949, 109–156; Lauren W. Casaday, "Labor Unrest and the Labor Movement in the Salmon Industry in the Pacific Northwest," Ph.D. dissertation, University of California, Berkeley, 1938, 356–385, 718–719. On the San Francisco local, see Him Mark Lai, "A Historical Survey of the Chinese Left in American Society," in *Counterpoint: Perspectives on Asian America*, ed. Emma Gee et al. (Los Angeles, 1976), 63–80; Karl Yoneda, *Ganbatte: A Sixty-Year Struggle of a Kibei Worker* (Los Angeles, 1983), 85–90; Casaday, "Labor Unrest," 386–395. Very separate unionization movements took place in the Puget Sound and on the Columbia River. For a survey of those efforts, see Casaday, "Labor Unrest," 386–389, 589–594.

19. Fred Cordova, *Filipinos: Forgotten Asian Americans* (Dubuque, Iowa, 1983), 115–121; Gold, "Development of Local Number 7," 1–109.

20. For a few of the more recent general works that include discussions of Asians in the canneries, see Shih-Shan Henry Tsai, *The Chinese Experience in America* (Bloomington, Ind., 1986), 24; Yuji Ichioka, *Issei: The World of the First Generation Japanese Immigrants, 1885–1924* (New York, 1988), 72, 78–80; Cordova, *Filipinos*, 57–80; Ronald Takaki, *Strangers from a Different Shore: A History of Asian Americans* (Boston, 1989), 317–318. The industry itself has received much more attention. See Richard A. Cooley, *Politics and Conservation: The Decline of the Alaska Salmon* (New York, 1963), 26; Vernon Carstensen, "The Fisherman's Frontier on the Pacific Coast: The Rise of the Salmon Canning Industry," in *The Frontier Challenge: Responses to the Trans-Mississippi West*, ed. John G. Clark (Lawrence, Kans., 1971), 57–79; Gordon B. Dodds, *The Salmon King of Oregon: R. D. Hume and the Pacific Fisheries* (Chapel Hill, N.C., 1959); Gordon B. Dodds, ed., *A Pygmy Monopolist: The Life and Doings of R. D. Hume Written by Himself and Dedicated to His Neighbors* (Madison, 1961); Patricia Roppel, *Salmon from Kodiak: An History of the Salmon Fishery of Kodiak Island*, Alaska Historical Commission Studies in History 216 (Anchorage, 1986). Several authors have focused on technological change. See Patrick William O'Bannon, "Technological Change in the Pacific Coast Canned Salmon Industry: 1864–1924," Ph.D. dissertation, University of California, San Diego, 1983; idem, "Waves of Change: Mechanization in the Pacific Coast Canned-Salmon Industry, 1864–1914," *Technology and Culture* 28 (1987): 558–577; idem, "Technological Change in the Pacific Coast Canned Salmon Industry, 1900–1925: A Case Study," *Agricultural History* 56

(1982): 151–166; Margaret Willson and Jeffery MacDonald, "The Impact of the 'Iron Chink' on the Chinese Salmon Cannery Workers of Puget Sound," *Annals of the Chinese Society of the Pacific Northwest*, 1984, 79–89.

21. Robert A. Nash, "The 'China Gangs' in the Alaska Packers Association Canneries, 1892–1935," in *Life, Influence and the Role of the Chinese*, 257–283.

22. Masson and Guimary, "Asian Labor Contractors," 377–397; idem, "Pilipinos and Unionization," 1–30.

23. Lloyd Fisher, *The Harvest Labor Market in California Agriculture*, (Cambridge, Mass., 1953), 21; Chan, *This Bittersweet Soil*, 292.

24. Fisher, *Harvest Labor Market*, 21.

25. "The Contract Labor System in California Agriculture," Oakland, Calif., 1938, 1–200, file 3, "A Documentary History of Migratory Farm Labor in California," Federal Writers Project, Bancroft Library, University of California, Berkeley.

26. John Bodnar, Roger Simon, and Michael P. Weber, *Lives of Their Own: Blacks, Italians, and Poles in Pittsburgh, 1900–1960* (Urbana, Ill., 1982), 57, 83n.3, note the presence of labor agents but argue that workers relied more heavily on kinship ties than contracting to find work. On networks, see Charles Tilly, "Transplanted Networks," in Yans-McLaughlin, *Immigration Reconsidered*, 79–95.

27. *Issei* refers to first-generation Japanese immigrants, most of whom immigrated to the United States between the late 1890s and 1924.

28. *Nisei*, meaning second generation, refers to the children of Issei parents.

29. Masson and Guimary, "Pilipinos and Unionization," 1–30; Cordova, *Filipinos*, 57–80; Peter Bacho, "Alaskeros: A Documentary Exhibit on Pioneer Filipino Cannery Workers," (Seattle, n.d.), 1.

30. Ronald Takaki, *Pau Hana: Plantation Life and Labor in Hawaii, 1835–1920* (Honolulu, 1983); Edward D. Beechert, *Working in Hawaii: A Labor History* (Honolulu, 1985). Both works provide the best existing studies of interethnic relationships among Asians and Asian Americans at the workplace. Hawaii, with its nonwhite majority, was significantly different than the Pacific Northwest, however. On the islands, the large contingents of Japanese and Filipinos, in particular, provided a base on which to build ethnic solidarity. Laborers drew on that solidarity to organize early unions, but that strength also worked against class alignments for much longer in Hawaii than in the canned-salmon industry.

31. Masson and Guimary, "Pilipinos and Unionization," 25–30.

32. For recent reviews of that literature, see the various essays in Patricia Nelson Limerick, Clyde A. Milner II, and Charles E. Rankin, eds., *Trails: Toward a New Western History* (Lawrence, Kans., 1991); Richard W. Etulain, "Visions and Revisions: Recent Interpretations of the American West," in *Writing Western History: Essays on Major Historians*, ed. Richard W. Etulain (Albuquerque, 1991), 335–358; Gerald D. Nash, *Creating the West: Historical*

Interpretations, 1890–1990 (Albuquerque, 1991), 49–195. Richard White, *"It's Your Misfortune and None of My Own": A New History of the American West* (Norman, Okla., 1991), esp. 236–297, provides the best available synthesis of this approach for the analysis of the West.

33. For some of the best current works on immigration, see the essays in Yans-McLaughlin, *Immigration Reconsidered;* Rudolph J. Vecoli and Suzanne M. Sinke, eds., *A Century of European Migrations, 1830–1930* (Urbana, Ill., 1991); Peter Kivisto and Dag Blanck, eds., *American Immigrants and Their Generations: Studies and Commentaries on the Hansen Thesis after Fifty Years* (Urbana, Ill., 1990). John Bodnar, *The Transplanted: A History of Immigrants in Urban America* (Urbana, Ill., 1985), provides one of the best available syntheses.

34. White, *"It's Your Misfortune,"* 236–297. A debate exists on the continuity of the West's colonial, or peripheral, status in the twentieth century. For a general review of the debate, see Brian W. Dippie, "The Winning of the West Reconsidered," *Wilson Quarterly* 14, no. 3 (1990): 70–85; William G. Robbins, "The 'Plundered Province' Thesis and the Recent Historiography of the American West," *Pacific Historical Review* 55 (1986): 577–597. Gerald D. Nash, *The American West Transformed: The Impact of the Second World War* (Bloomington, Ind., 1985), holds that the post–World War II economic diversification and cultural and political independence achieved by Westerners broke the East's colonial hold on the region. Robert G. Athearn, *The Mythic West in the Twentieth Century* (Lawrence, Kans., 1986), 108–130, argues that the West's colonial status endured after World War II but was far more complex than before the war. Evidence from the canned-salmon industry, though, supports the thesis put forth by Patricia Nelson Limerick, *The Legacy of Conquest: The Unbroken Past of the American West* (New York, 1987), 122, that the loci of power were varied and that the European American culture of conquest, not colonialism, defined the West before and after the war. Nonetheless, even she implies that the West since World War II is different. Donald Worster, in *Under Western Skies: Nature and History in the American West* (New York, 1992), esp. 19–33, and idem, *Rivers of Empire: Water, Aridity, and the Growth of the American West* (New York, 1985), holds that the West emerged as a technocratic, resource-hoarding, power-wielding empire after the war. Regardless of their interpretations, most historians agree that the post–World War II West was markedly different from the West before the war.

35. Limerick, "Disorientation and Reorientation," advocates a more systematic analysis by future researchers on how Asian immigrants and Asian Americans viewed the landscape. Unfortunately, her call came too late for incorporation into this work.

36. White, *"It's Your Misfortune,"* 236–297; William Cronon, *Nature's Metropolis: Chicago and the Great West* (New York, 1991), 264–269; Limerick, *Legacy of Conquest,* 30; Worster, *Under Western Skies,* 19–33.

37. Howard Lamar, "From Bondage to Contract: Ethnic Labor in the American West," in *The Countryside in the Age of Capitalist Transformation:*

Essays in the Social History of Rural America, ed. Steven Hahn and Jonathan Prude (Chapel Hill, N.C., 1985), 293–324.

38. Ewa Morawska, "The Sociology and Historiography of Immigration," in Yans-McLaughlen, *Immigration Reconsidered*, 191. Cheng and Bonacich, *Labor Immigration*, delineate a larger system very well, but overstate the case and portray immigrants as mere cogs in some machine. Chan, "European and Asian Immigration," in Yans-McLaughlin, *Immigration Reconsidered*, 37–75, and Bodnar, *The Transplanted*, 57ff., give immigrants a place in the system and an ability to affect it, at least in their immediate surroundings, but focus on the sending countries. Alvin Y. So, *The South China Silk District: Local Historical Transformation and World-System Theory* (Albany, N.Y., 1986), illustrates the usefulness and limitations of the world-system theory.

39. On work cultures in cannery settings, see Patricia Zavella, *Women's Work and Chicano Families: Cannery Workers of the Santa Clara Valley* (New York, 1987), 99–129; Vicki L. Ruiz, *Cannery Women, Cannery Lives: Mexican Women, Unionization, and the California Food Processing Industry, 1930–1950* (Albuquerque, 1987), 21–39. For studies of other work cultures, see Paula J. Johnson, " 'Sloppy Work for Women': Shucking Oysters on the Patuxent," in *Working the Water: The Commercial Fisheries of Maryland's Patuxent River*, ed. Paula J. Johnson (Charlottesville, Va., 1988), 35–51; Barbara Melosh, *"The Physician's Hand": Work Culture and Conflict in American Nursing* (Philadelphia, 1982); Patricia A. Cooper, *Once a Cigar Maker: Men, Women, and Work Culture in American Cigar Factories, 1900–1919* (Urbana, Ill., 1987), 1–10, 218–246; Louise Lamphere, "Bringing the Family to Work: Women's Culture on the Shop Floor," *Feminist Studies* 11 (1985): 518–540; Susan Porter Benson, " 'The Customers Ain't God': The Work Culture of Department-Store Saleswomen, 1890–1940," in *Working-Class America: Essays on Labor, Community, and American Society*, ed. Michael H. Frisch and Daniel J. Walkowitz (Urbana, Ill., 1983), 185–211.

40. Worster, *Under Western Skies*, 27.

41. *Forest and Stream*, October 25, 1877, 233.

42. Craig and Hacker, "Fisheries of the Columbia River"; Arthur F. McEvoy, *The Fisherman's Problem: Ecology and Law in the California Fisheries, 1850–1980* (Cambridge, England, 1986).

43. Limerick, *Legacy of Conquest*, 27. For more detail on the racial and ethnic diversity of the West, see Richard White, "Race Relations in the American West," *American Quarterly* 38 (1986): 396–416. The South also had more diversity than most have recognized. On Asians in the South, for example, see Lucy M. Cohen, *Chinese in the Post–Civil War South: A People without a History* (Baton Rouge, 1984); James Loewen, *The Mississippi Chinese: Between Black and White* (Cambridge, Mass., 1971).

44. Limerick, *Legacy of Conquest*, 260.

45. Including the Survey of Race Relations Documents, 1924–1927, Hoover Institute for War and Peace, Stanford University; William Carlson Smith Documents, University of Oregon; Charles Kikuchi Papers, Special

Collections, University of California, Los Angeles; and Japanese-American Evacuation and Relocation Service Records, War Relocation Authority, Bancroft Library, University of California, Berkeley.

46. Demonstration Project for Asian Americans, Seattle; Filipino Project, Washington State Oral/Aural History Program, 1974–1977, Washington State Archives, Olympia. (The collections includes some, but not all, of the interviews done by the Demonstration Project for Asian Americans); Skagit County Oral History Project, Skagit County Historical Museum, LaConner, Wash.

47. Alexander Saxton, *The Indispensable Enemy: Labor and the Anti-Chinese Movement in California* (Berkeley and Los Angeles, 1971), very effectively discusses the centrality of anti-Asian sentiments in late nineteenth-century California. See Cohen, *Chinese in the Post-Civil War South*, and Chan, *This Bittersweet Soil*, for studies that demonstrate that Chinese were not merely coolies.

Chapter 1

1. U.S. Bureau of the Census, Manuscript Schedules of the Population Census, 1870, Wahkiakum County, Washington (hereafter cited as Population Census, 1870, Wahkiakum County). The most comprehensive descriptions of processing that also show technological developments are John N. Cobb, *Salmon Fisheries of the Pacific Coast*, Bureau of Fisheries Document 751 (Washington, D.C., 1911); idem, *Pacific Salmon Fisheries*, Bureau of Fisheries Document 839 (Washington, D.C., 1917); idem, *Pacific Salmon Fisheries*, Bureau of Fisheries Document 902 (Washington, D.C., 1921); idem, *Pacific Salmon Fisheries*, Bureau of Fisheries Document 1092 (Washington, D.C., 1930).

2. Economists argue that the factors of production form the basis of the market system, and most basic textbooks will have some discussion of them. For examples, see William P. Albrecht, Jr., *Microeconomic Principles*, 2nd ed. (Englewood Cliffs, N.J., 1983), 6–7; Edwin G. Dolan and David E. Lindsey, *Microeconomics*, 5th ed. (Chicago, 1988), 5.

3. *Pacific Fisherman Annual*, 1904, 19–20; Robert D. Hume Dictation, 1887, Bancroft Library, University of California, Berkeley; Edgar H. Schein, "The Role of the Founder in Creating Organizational Culture," *Organizational Dynamics* 12 (1983): 13–28.

4. *Pacific Fisherman Annual*, 1904, 19–20.

5. Richard White, *"It's Your Misfortune and None of My Own": A New History of the American West* (Norman, Okla., 1991), 242–244.

6. *West Shore*, June 1876, 1; *Pacific Fisherman Annual*, 1904, 19–21; Robert A. Nash, "The 'China Gangs' in the Alaska Packers Association Canneries, 1892–1935," in *The Life, Influence and the Role of the Chinese in the United States, 1776–1960* (San Francisco, 1976), 257–283; Jack Masson and Donald Guimary, "Asian Labor Contractors in the Alaskan Canned Salmon

Industry, 1880–1937," *Labor History* 22, no. 3 (1981): 377–397; Cobb, *Pacific Salmon Fisheries* (1917), 23, 29; "William Hume," *Columbia County History*, 1973, 51; Sister Mary de Sales McLellan, "William Hume, 1830–1902," *Oregon Historical Quarterly* 35 (1934): 269; Earl Chapin May, *The Canning Clan: A Pageant of Pioneering Americans* (New York, 1938), 107–108; Gordon B. Dodds, *The Salmon King of Oregon: R. D. Hume and the Pacific Fisheries* (Chapel Hill, N.C., 1959), 4–5.

7. Gunther Barth, *Bitter Strength: A History of the Chinese in the United States, 1850–1870* (Cambridge, Mass., 1964), is often cited and expresses such notions.

8. Hume Dictation; May, *Canning Clan*, 108; McLellan, "William Hume," 271; Gordon B. Dodds, ed., *A Pygmy Monopolist: The Life and Doings of R. D. Hume Written by Himself and Dedicated to His Neighbors* (Madison, 1961), 18, 23, 30, 32, 35, 85; *Pacific Fisherman Annual*, 1904, 19; Ralph W. Andrews and A. K. Larssen, *Fish and Ships* (Seattle, 1959), 50; "William Hume," *Columbia County History* 12 (1973): 51; Hugh W. McKervill, *The Salmon People: The Story of Canada's West Coast Fishing Industry* (Vancouver, 1967), 30.

9. Dodds, *Pygmy Monopolist*, 23, 32–33; *West Shore*, June 1876, 1; *Pacific Fisherman Annual*, 1904, 19–21.

10. *Pacific Fisherman Annual*, 1904, 19–21.

11. Ibid.; Hume Dictation; McKervill, *Salmon People*, 30; Dodds, *Pygmy Monopolist*, 31; Joseph A. Craig and Robert L. Hacker, "History and Development of the Fisheries of the Columbia River," U.S. Department of the Interior, Bureau of Fisheries, *Bulletin* 32 (1940): 150; Nash, "China Gangs," 260. A case of salmon consists of forty-eight one-pound cans or the equivalent in two-pound cans (often used in the nineteenth century), or in half-pound cans (used in the twentieth century).

12. Hume Dictation; Daniel B. Deloach, *The Salmon Canning Industry* (Corvallis, Ore., 1939), 12, 14; McLellan, "William Hume," 271; "William Hume," *Columbia County History*, 51; Craig and Hacker, "Fisheries of the Columbia," 151; Frances Fuller Victor, *All Over Oregon and Washington* (San Francisco, 1875), 60; Dodds, *Salmon King*, 6; Cobb, *Pacific Salmon Fisheries* (1921), 28; Nash, "China Gangs," 260.

13. Messrs. Platt and Newton to Hume and Company, June 20, 1871, Letters and Invoices, 1870–1871, box 10, Andrew Hapgood and Company Records, University of Oregon Manuscripts, Eugene; *Pacific Fisherman Yearbook*, 1920, 81; Dodds, *Pygmy Monopolist*, 24, 31.

14. *Hutching's California Magazine*, June 1860, 530; *Forest and Stream*, May 13, 1875, 217, and April 13, 1876, 147; Cobb, *Salmon Fisheries of the Pacific Coast* (1911), 14, 35; Deloach, *Salmon Canning*, 11; Nash, "China Gangs," 260.

15. Hume Dictation; Cobb, *Pacific Salmon Fisheries* (1921), 26; *Portland Oregonian*, September 8, 1881; Craig and Hacker, "Fisheries of the Columbia," 150; Keith D. Gerh, "The Bay View Cannery-Skamokawa Village Site,"

Northwest Anthropological Research Notes 9 (1975): 123. Some debate exists over the starting date for the first Columbia River cannery. From the evidence available, I have concluded that operations began in 1866. Others have cited 1867; see Vernon Carstensen, "The Fisherman's Frontier on the Pacific Coast: The Rise of the Salmon Canning Industry," in *The Frontier Challenge: Responses to the Trans-Mississippi West*, ed. John G. Clark (Lawrence, Kans., 1971), 74; Patrick William O'Bannon, "Technological Change in the Pacific Coast Canned Salmon Industry: 1864–1924," Ph.D. dissertation, University of California, San Diego, 1983, 30.

16. Hume Dictation; *Portland Oregonian*, September 8, 1881; Andrews and Larssen, *Fish and Ships*, 50; *Pacific Fisherman Annual*, 1904, 20; Dodds, *Pygmy Monopolist*, 22, 24, 28–29; McKervill, *Salmon People*, 30; Victor, *All Over Oregon and Washington*, 59; and "William Hume," *Columbia County History*, 53.

17. Dodds, *Pygmy Monopolist*, 36–37.

18. Population Census, 1870, Wahkiakum County.

19. Dodds, *Pygmy Monopolist*, 32–35, 38–39, 60; *Pacific Fisherman Annual*, 1904, 19; *Portland Oregonian*, September 8, 1881; Cobb, *Pacific Salmon Fisheries* (1921), 27; McLellan, "William Hume," 269; Carstensen, "Fisherman's Frontier," 66.

20. Dodds, *Pygmy Monopolist*, 32–35, 38–39; *Pacific Fisherman Annual*, 1904, 20; *Pacific Fisherman Yearbook*, 1920, 74; Hume Dictation.

21. McLellan, "William Hume," 275–276; "William Hume," *Columbia County History*, 51; *West Shore*, July 1876, 1.

22. Cobb, *Pacific Salmon Fisheries* (1917), 29.

23. Hume Dictation; J. W. Welch Dictation.

24. Glen Cunningham, "Oregon's First Salmon Canner, 'Captain' John West," *Oregon Historical Quarterly* 56 (1953): 241, 243–244; Hittell, *Commerce and Industries*, 382–383; Victor, *All Over Oregon and Washington*, 58; Hume Dictation; Population Census, 1870, Wahkiakum County; U.S. Bureau of the Census, Census of Manufactures, 1870, Wahkiakum County, Washington (hereafter cited as Census of Manufactures, 1870, Wahkiakum County); Dodds, *Pygmy Monopolist*, 32, 36; Census Office, *Ninth Census*, vol. 1, *The Statistics of the Population of the United States* (Washington, D.C., 1872), 241. The percentages for Wahkiakum should be taken as an indication, not a precise measure, of the people available for work in the county. The figures for the county exclude farm laborers because many were farmers' children. Chinese workers were not counted as residents and are not included. Neither are Native Americans, since there is no record of them working in the first canneries on the Columbia River. They did find employment in, and fish for, the earlier salmon salteries, but not the canneries. See Dodds, *Pygmy Monopolist*, 32.

25. Cunningham, "Oregon's First Salmon Canner," 243–244.

26. Dodds, *Pygmy Monopolist*, 31–32; Victor, *All Over Oregon and Washington*, 46, 57–58; Charles Nordoff, "The Columbia River and Puget Sound," *Harper's New Monthly Magazine*, February 1874, 339.

27. *Ninth Census*, vol. 1, *Population*, 242; Dodds, *Pygmy Monopolist*, 31–32; Nordoff, "Columbia River and Puget Sound," 339.

28. Alfred A. Cleveland, "Social and Economic History of Astoria," *Oregon Historical Quarterly* 4 (June 1903): 137.

29. Nordoff, "Columbia River and Puget Sound," 339.

30. Theodore Kirchhoff, *Oregon East, Oregon West: Travels and Memoirs*, ed. and trans. Frederic Trautmann (Portland, Ore., 1987), 109–110.

31. Paul G. Merriam, "The 'Other Portland': A Statistical Note on Foreign-Born, 1860–1910," *Oregon Historical Quarterly* 80 (1979): 258, 261–262, 266; McLellan, "William Hume," 272; *Portland Oregonian*, April 1, 1869, April 22, 1870; *Daily Astorian*, July 26, 1890.

32. Merriam, "Other Portland," 262–263; Population Census, 1870, Wahkiakum County. Forty-six Native Americans are not counted for Wahkiakum County because they are not included in the comparative figures from Portland. In Wahkiakum County, excluding Native Americans, 21.1 percent had only one foreign-born parent, 3.1 percent had two parents of foreign birth.

33. Population Census, 1870, Wahkiakum County.

34. Hittell, *Commerce and Industry*, 382; *West Shore*, July 1876, 1; May, *Canning Clan*, 107.

35. Internal labor markets refer to the job ladders or paths of upward or downward promotion in a particular firm. For a review of the concept, see Robert P. Althauser and Arne L. Kalleberg, "Firms, Occupations, and the Structure of Labor Markets: A Conceptual Analysis," in *Sociological Perspectives on Labor Markets*, ed. Ivar Berg (New York, 1981), 121–123.

36. Alejandro Portes and Robert L. Bach, *Latin Journey: Cuban and Mexican Immigrants in the United States* (Berkeley and Los Angeles, 1985), 11–14.

37. Ewa Morawska, "The Sociology and Historiography of Immigration," in *Immigration Reconsidered: History, Sociology, and Politics*, ed. Virginia Yans-McLaughlin (New York, 1990), 198; E. M. Beck, Patrick M. Horan, and Charles M. Tolbert, "Stratification in a Dual Economy: A Sectoral Model of Earnings Discrimination," *American Sociological Review* 43, no. 5 (1978): 706; David M. Gordon, Richard Edwards, and Michael Reich, *Segmented Work, Divided Workers: The Historical Transformation of Labor in the United States* (Cambridge, Mass., 1982); Edna Bonacich, "The Past, Present, and Future of Split Labor Market Theory," *Research in Race and Ethnic Relations* 1 (1979): 17–64.

38. Althauser and Kalleberg, "Labor Markets," 123; Morawska, "Sociology and Historiography of Immigration," 198–199.

39. Morawska, "Sociology and Historiography of Immigration," 200.

40. Edna Bonacich, "A Theory of Ethnic Antagonism: The Split Labor Market," *American Sociological Review* 37, no. 5 (1972): 547–559; Portes and Bach, *Latin Journey*, 15.

41. U.S. Bureau of the Census, Manuscript Schedules of the Population Census, 1860, Yolo County, Putah Township, California; *Pacific Fisherman*

Year Book, 1920, 71; Sucheng Chan, *This Bittersweet Soil: The Chinese in California Agriculture* (Berkeley and Los Angeles, 1986), 101.

42. Thomas W. Chinn, H. Mark Lai, and Philip P. Choy, eds., *Syllabus: A History of the Chinese in California* (San Francisco, 1969), 21; Melford S. Weiss, *Valley City: A Chinese Community in America* (Cambridge, Mass., 1974), 46–47; Dodds, *Pygmy Monopolist*, 23.

43. Several authors give different dates for the first hiring of Chinese by the Humes and Hapgood. John Collins, *Story of Canned Foods* (New York, 1924), 140, implies that Chinese worked in the Sacramento cannery crew, but none of the Hume and Hapgood documents reveal any more than one Chinese cook for the cannery workers on the Sacramento. Masson and Guimary, "Asian Labor Contractors," 383, hold that 1872 was the first year, but they incorrectly cite Dodds, *Salmon King*, 26–27. Dodds makes no mention of the specific date in which the Humes hired Chinese as cannery workers in that work. Dodds, *Pygmy Monopolist*, 23, mentions that the Humes hired a Chinese cook in their second season, 1865.

44. Census of Manufactures, 1870, Wahkiakum County; Population Census, 1870, Wahkiakum County.

45. Hugh Clark, *Portland's Chinese: The Early Years* (Portland, Ore., 1978), 7–8.

46. Ibid., 8.

47. Ibid.

48. Ibid.

49. P. Scott Corbett and Nancy Parker Corbett, "The Chinese in Oregon, c. 1870–1880," *Oregon Historical Quarterly* 68 (March 1977): 73.

50. Nelson Chia-Chi Ho, *Portland's Chinatown: The History of an Urban Ethnic District* (Portland, Ore., 1978), 7–10; Clark, *Portland's Chinese*, 9; Christopher Edson, *The Chinese in Eastern Oregon, 1860–1890* (San Francisco, 1976), 9, 32, 58; J. Scott Jones, "The Chinese Business Community in Portland, Oregon: 1863–1900" (1973), 4, Manuscripts Division, Oregon Historical Society, Portland.

51. Clark, *Portland's Chinese*, 10–11; Edson, *Chinese in Eastern Oregon*, 16.

52. Ho, *Portland's Chinatown*, 7; Census of Manufactures, 1870, Wahkiakum County.

53. *Columbia River Fishermen's Protective Union*, 14; Hume Dictation; Cunningham, "Oregon's First Salmon Canner," 244.

54. Census of Manufactures, 1870, Wahkiakum County; Cunningham, "Oregon's First Salmon Canner," 244.

55. Population Census, 1870, Wahkiakum County.

56. Ping Chiu, *Chinese Labor in California, 1850–1880: An Economic Study* (Madison, 1967), 128; Chinn et al., *Syllabus*, 43–58; John W. Stephens, "A Quantitative History of Chinatown, San Francisco, 1870 and 1880," in *Life, Influence and the Role of the Chinese*, 74; Chan, *This Bittersweet Soil*, 62, 64–66; Corbett and Corbett, "Chinese in Oregon," 73–85; Doug Chin and

Art Chin, *Uphill: The Settlement and Diffusion of the Chinese in Seattle* (Seattle, 1978), 3–8; Edson, *Chinese in Eastern Oregon*, 53–56.

57. Dodds, *Pygmy Monopolist*, 35–37.

58. Ibid., 32; Hume Dictation; Cobb, *Pacific Salmon Fisheries* (1917), 29; Hittell, *Commerce and Industries*, 382–383.

59. Sanford M. Jacoby, *Employing Bureaucracy: Managers and the Transformation of Work in American Industry, 1900–1945* (New York, 1985), 15–23.

60. Jack Chen, *The Chinese of America: From the Beginnings to the Present* (San Francisco, 1982), 74–75.

61. *Weekly Astorian*, February 13, 20, 1886, and February 13, 1894.

62. Morawska, "Sociology and Historiography of Immigration," 200.

63. Clark, *Portland's Chinese*, 10; Viola Neon Currier, "The Chinese Web in Oregon History," Master's thesis, University of Oregon, Eugene, 1928, 40–44; Ping Chiu, *Chinese Labor in California*, 128; Shih-Shan Henry Tsai, *The Chinese Experience in America* (Bloomington, Ind., 1986), 7–10; Chan, *This Bittersweet Soil*, 341–345; Tim Wright, " 'A Method of Evading Management'—Contract Labor in Chinese Mines before 1937," *Comparative Studies in Society and History* 23, no. 4 (1981): 656–678; idem, *Coal Mining in China's Economy and Society, 1895–1937* (Cambridge, England, 1984), 165–168; Lynda Norene Shaffer, "The Chinese Working Class: Comments on Two Articles," *Modern China* 9 (1983): 455–464; Hao Yen-ping, *The Compradore in Nineteenth Century China: Bridge between East and West* (Cambridge, Mass., 1970); Robert Y. Eng, "Institutional and Secondary Landlordism in the Pearl River Delta, 1600–1949," *Modern China* 12 (1986): 3–37. For a slightly different context, see Emily Honig, "The Contract Labor System and Women Workers: Pre-Liberation Cotton Mills of Shanghai," *Modern China* 9 (1983): 421–454.

64. Richard A. Kalish and Sam Yuen, "Americans of East Asian Ancestry: Aging and the Aged," *Gerentologist* 11 (1971): 40–41; Lucy Cha Yu, "Filial Piety, Generational Conflict, Acculturation and Status among Chinese Americans," Ph.D. dissertation, University of Michigan, 1981, 47; Raymond Lou, "The Chinese American Community of Los Angeles, 1870–1900: A Case of Resistance, Organization, and Participation," Ph.D. dissertation, University of California, Irvine, 1982, 58–59, 61; Davis Ying Ja, "The Chinese Aged in America: Housing Conditions and Their Effect on Health and Psychosomatic Symptoms," Ph.D. dissertation, University of Washington, 1981, 3, 7; Julia I Hsu Chen, *The Chinese Community in New York, 1920–1940* (San Francisco, 1974), 19, 21; Population Census, 1870, Wahkiakum County. Younger, less privileged men such as Ah Wook, Ah Lou, and Gee Fook probably took over from the non-Chinese, can-wiping "boys" of the earlier Hume operations. Ah Sing, Ching Lou, and another Chinese can maker possessed greater skills and more money, worked under different relations with the owners, and averaged several years older than the Chinese crew. How these three interacted with the Chinese crew cannot be determined.

65. Population Census, 1870, Wahkiakum County.

66. Tsai, *Chinese Experience in America*, 3, 12, 57; Sucheng Chan, *Asian Americans: An Interpretive History* (Boston, 1991), 54.

67. Population Census, 1870, Wahkiakum County.

68. Chin et al., *Syllabus*, 30–32; Ho, *Portland's Chinatown*, 7, 9.

69. Population Census, 1870, Wahkiakum County; Chan, *This Bittersweet Soil*, table 15, p. 154.

70. Corbett and Corbett, "Chinese in Oregon," 77; Edson, *Chinese in Eastern Oregon*, 61–62; Stephens, "Chinatown, San Francisco," 75–77; Population Census, 1870, Wahkiakum County.

71. Stephens, "Chinatown, San Francisco," 77; and Chan, *This Bittersweet Soil*, 2, 58–59, 341–358. Some, like Edson, *Chinese in Eastern Oregon*, believe that the increased age of Chinese immigrants indicated their "failure" to become rich quickly and to return to their home villages in glory. Quite the contrary, increased age and occupational mobility, though the latter was severely limited, might represent the success of the immigrant; see John Kuo Wei Tchen, "Editor's Introduction," in *The Chinese Laundryman: A Study of Social Isolation*, by Paul C. P. Siu (1953; New York, 1987), xxxi–xxxiii; Franklin Ng, "The Sojourner, Return Migration, and Immigration History," *Chinese America: History and Perspectives, 1987* (San Francisco, 1987): 53–71; Anthony B. Chan, "Orientalism and Image Making: The Sojourner in Canadian History," *Journal of Ethnic Studies* 9 (1981): 37–46; Woon Yuen-fong, "The Voluntary Sojourner among the Overseas Chinese: Myth or Reality?" *Public Affairs* 56 (1983–1984): 673–690.

72. Corbett and Corbett, "Chinese in Oregon," 77; Edson, *Chinese in Eastern Oregon*, 61–62.

Chapter 2

1. *Weekly Astorian*, May 14, 1874.

2. Scrapbook 51, 44–45, Oregon Historical Society, Portland, Ore.

3. Rudyard Kipling, *From Sea to Sea: Letters of Travel* (Garden City, N.Y., 1923), 33–34.

4. Ibid., 34–35.

5. For two definitions of work cultures in a canning industry, see Patricia Zavella, *Women's Work and Chicano Families: Cannery Workers of the Santa Clara Valley* (New York, 1987), 99–129; Vicki L. Ruiz, *Cannery Women, Cannery Lives: Mexican Women, Unionization, and the California Food Processing Industry, 1930–1950* (Albuquerque, 1987), 21–39.

6. For human capital arguments see Thomas Sowell, *Ethnic America: A History* (New York, 1981), 282–283; Jared J. Young, *Discrimination, Income, Human Capital Investments, and Asian-Americans* (San Francisco, 1977).

7. Lloyd Fisher, *The Harvest Labor Market in California Agriculture* (Cambridge, Mass., 1953), 21; Sucheng Chan, *This Bittersweet Soil: The Chinese in California Agriculture* (Berkeley and Los Angeles, 1986), 292.

8. *Weekly Astorian*, April 4, 1885; *Forest and Stream*, June 18, 1874, 290, and November 1875, 230; Livingston Stone, "The Salmon Fisheries of the Columbia River," U.S. Commission of Fish and Fisheries, Appendix III to the *Report of the Commissioner for 1875–1876* (Washington, D.C., 1878), 823; Raymond Lou, "The Chinese American Community of Los Angeles, 1870–1900: A Case of Resistance, Organization, and Participation," Ph.D. dissertation, University of California, Irvine, 1982, 24; Dorothy O. Johansen and Charles M. Gates, *Empire of the Columbia: A History of the Pacific Northwest* (New York, 1957), 352; Oscar Osburn Winther, *The Transportation Frontier: The Trans-Mississippi West, 1865–1890* (New York, 1964), 101; Peter J. Lewtey, *To the Columbia Gateway: The Oregon Railway and the Northern Pacific, 1879–1884* (Pullman, Wash., 1987), 11–12; Patrick William O'Bannon, "Technological Change in the Pacific Coast Canned Salmon Industry: 1864–1924," Ph.D. dissertation, University of California, San Diego, 1983, 42; Virginia Urrutia, "Kalama, Where Railroad and Water Meet," *Cowlitz Historical Quarterly* 27 (1985): 18–27.

9. *Forest and Stream*, June 18, 1874, 290.

10. *Weekly Astorian*, May 14, 1874, May 23, 1885; *Daily Astorian*, May 16, 1885, March 1, 1881; *Portland Oregonian*, September 8, 1881; Courtland L. Smith, *Salmon Fisheries of the Columbia* (Corvallis, Ore., 1979), 110.

11. *Washington Standard*, December 18 and January 3, 1876; *Weekly Astorian*, September 16, 23, October 7, 14, 21, 29, November 18, December 16, 1876, September 24, 1880, September 1, 22, 1888; *Daily Astorian*, November 7, 1879; *West Shore*, September 1888, 513; J. Orin Oliphant, "A Beef Canning Enterprise in Oregon," *Oregon Historical Quarterly* 34 (1933): 241–254.

12. O'Bannon, "Technological Change," 33–34, 78–83; Duncan Stacey, *Sockeye and Tinplate: Technological Change in the Fraser River Canning Industry, 1871–1912* (Victoria, British Columbia, 1982), 4–5.

13. *Tri-Weekly Astorian*, January 21, 1874; *Weekly Astorian*, May 1, 7, 14, 1874, May 22, 1875, January 3, 1876, March 14 and August 1, 1885, February 6, 27, 1886; *West Shore*, July 1876, 1, June 1877, 180, June 1883, 125–126, July 1887, 550–551; *San Francisco Journal of Commerce*, July 18, 1877; Stone, "Salmon Fisheries," 822; J. W. Collins, "Report on the Fisheries of the Pacific Coast of the United States," U.S. Commission of Fish and Fisheries, *Report of the Commissioner for 1888* (Washington, D.C., 1892), pt. 16, p. 207; William A. Wilcox, "Notes on the Fisheries of the Pacific Coast in 1895," U.S. Commissioner of Fish and Fisheries, *Report of the Commissioner for the Year Ending June 30, 1896* (Washington, D.C., 1898), pt. 22, p. 581; *Astoria Budget*, June 28, 1909, May 10, 1910, April 11, 1912.

14. U.S. Bureau of the Census, Manuscript Schedules of the Population Census, 1880 and 1900, Clatsop and Columbia counties, Oregon, Wahkiakum and Pacific counties, Washington.

15. *West Shore*, June 1877, 173; *Weekly Astorian*, March 23, 1878; Charles Koe, "Chinese Cannery Workers in Ilwaco," PAC 75–22dm, tran-

script of interview, October 7, 8, 1975, Washington State Oral/Aural History Program, 1974–1977, Washington State Archives, Olympia; John Cobb, *Pacific Salmon Fisheries*, Appendix I to the *Report of the United States Commissioner of Fisheries for 1921*, U.S. Bureau of Fisheries Document 902, 3rd ed. (Washington, D.C., 1921), 114; Lester E. Jones, *Bureau of Fisheries Report of Alaska Investigations in 1914* (Washington, D.C., 1915), 28–31; Kazuo Ito, *Issei: A History of Japanese Immigrants in North America*, trans. Shinchiro Nakamura and Jean S. Gerard (Seattle, 1973), 30; Elvin Wong, John Lum, and A. J. Lamie, interview by Chris Friday, February 3, 1988, Astoria, Ore.

16. Cobb, *Pacific Salmon Fisheries* (1921), 115; Anthony Netboy, *The Columbia River Salmon: Their Fight for Survival* (Seattle, 1980), 27; David Starr Jordan and Charles H. Gilbert, "The Salmon Fishing and Canning Interests of the Pacific Coast," in *The Fisheries and Fishing Industries of the United States*, ed. George Brown Goode (Washington, D.C., 1887), 5:747.

17. Cobb, *Pacific Salmon Fisheries* (1921), 116; Glenn R. Steiner, "Warren Cannery: Photographs and Text," *Puget Soundings*, Summer 1980, 10; Jordan and Gilbert, "Salmon Fishing and Canning Interests," 747; Joseph A. Craig and Robert L. Hacker, "History and Development of the Fisheries of the Columbia River," U.S. Department of the Interior, Bureau of Fisheries, *Bulletin* 32 (1940): 157; Koe interview.

18. *Pacific Fisherman Annual*, 1904, 21; Steiner, "Warren Cannery," 10–11; Jordan and Gilbert, "Salmon Fishing and Canning Interests," 747; *Weekly Astorian*, March 23, 1878; W. A. Carrothers, *The British Columbia Fisheries* (Toronto, 1941), 13; Washington State Bureau of Labor Statistics, "Special Report on the Salmon Canning Industry in the State of Washington and the Employment of Oriental Labor," *Tenth Biennial Report, 1915–1916* (Olympia, 1916), 115 (hereafter cited as WSBLS, "Special Report").

19. Steiner, "Warren Cannery," 11; Craig and Hacker, "Fisheries of the Columbia," 157; Carrothers, *British Columbia Fisheries*, 11; Julie B. Crandall, *The Story of Pacific Salmon* (Portland, Ore., 1946), 33.

20. *Weekly Astorian*, March 23, 1878; Steiner, "Warren Cannery," 11; Ito, *Issei*, 361; Robert A. Nash, "The 'China Gangs' in the Alaska Packers Association Canneries, 1892–1935," in *The Life, Influence and the Role of the Chinese in the United States, 1776–1960* (San Francisco, 1976), 278.

21. Ralph W. Andrews and A. K. Larssen, *Fish and Ships* (Seattle, 1959), 50.

22. Cobb, *Pacific Salmon Fisheries* (1921), 121; Columbia River Packers Association (hereafter cited as CRPA) to Ah Joe, February 4, 1904, Columbia River Packers Association Records, Astor Public Library, Astoria, Ore. (hereafter cited as CRPA-Astor); and CRPA to Ah Dogg, February 23, 1905, ibid.

23. *Reports of the Immigration Commission: Immigrants in Industry*, vol. 25, pt. 25, *Japanese and Other Immigrant Races in the Pacific Coast and Mountain States*, vol. 3, Senate Document 633 (Washington, D.C., 1911), 393 (hereafter cited as *Immigrants in Industry*); George Brown Goode, ed., *The Fisheries and Fishing Industries of the United States* (Washington, D.C., 1884), 1:41.

24. Chinese Workers Accounts, 1901, Seufert Brothers Cannery Records, Oregon Historical Society, Portland, Ore.

25. Ibid.; *Immigrants in Industry*, 393; Goode, *Fisheries and Fishing Industries*, 1:41; Leong Yip to CRPA, December 17, 1901, CRPA-Astor; Collins, "Fisheries of the Pacific Coast" (1892), 207; *Tri-Weekly Astorian*, January 21, 1874; *Weekly Astorian*, January 3, 1876, March 14, 1885, February 27, 1886; *Pacific Fisherman Yearbook*, 1953, 93.

26. Ito, *Issei*, 361.

27. *West Shore*, June 1883, 125–126; Koe interview; *Columbia River Fishermens' Protective Union* (Astoria, Ore., 1890), 1–30; Daniel DeLoach, *The Salmon Canning Industry* (Corvallis, Ore., 1939), 15.

28. *Pacific Fisherman*, February 1943, 19; Wong, Lum, and Lamie interview.

29. Wong, Lum, and Lamie interview.

30. Ibid.; Cathlamet Journals, February 1887 to March 1897, 8:233, Warren Packing Company Records, Oregon Historical Society, Portland; Chinese Workers Accounts, 1901, Seufert Brothers Cannery Records; *Immigrants in Industry*, 393–395; Julia Butler Hansen, *Cathlamet Pioneer: The Paintings of Maude Kimball Butler* (Tacoma, Wash., 1973), 29.

31. Wong, Lum, and Lamie interview; Frank Miyamoto, interview by Chris Friday, February 19, 1988, Seattle.

32. Ibid.; *Immigrants in Industry*, 392–393; Fu Zhufu, "The Economic History of China: Some Special Problems," *Modern China* 7 (1981): 23–24.

33. *Immigrants in Industry*, 393; Goode, *Fisheries and Fishing Industries*, 1:41; Chinese Workers Accounts, 1901, Seufert Brothers Cannery Records; Leong Yip to CRPA, December 17, 1901, CRPA-Astor.

34. Hugh M. Smith, "Notes on a Reconnaissance of the Fisheries of the Pacific Coast of the United States in 1894," *Bulletin of the United States Fish Commission* 14 (1895): 236.

35. Ito, *Issei*, 30; Koe interview; Wong, Lum, and Lamie interview; Miyamoto interview.

36. George Taki, interview by Chris Friday, January 10 and 11, 1989, Los Angeles; Collins, "Fisheries of the Pacific Coast" (1892), 207.

37. Koe interview; Evelyn A. Betto, Accident Report, September 23, 1940, envelope 7, box 1, Seufert Brothers Cannery Records; Julian Albera, Accident Report, September 28, 1940, ibid.; Stone, "Salmon Fisheries," 821; Emma H. Adams, "Salmon Canning in Oregon," *Bulletin of the United States Fish Commission* 5 (1885): 365; *Scientific American*, August 24, 1878, 122; *West Shore*, June 1883, 125–126.

38. *Astoria Budget*, October 4, 1893.

39. *Portland Oregonian*, August 1, 1881; Jefferson F. Moser, "The Salmon and Salmon Fisheries of Alaska: Report of the U.S. Fish Commission Steamer *Albatross* for the Year Ending June 30, 1898," U.S. Bureau of Fisheries, *Bulletin, 1898*, 1899, 110; Cobb, *Pacific Salmon Fisheries* (1921), 27.

40. Thomas Dublin, *Women at Work: The Transformation of Work and Community in Lowell, Massachusetts, 1826–1860* (New York, 1979), 65; Ruiz, *Cannery Women, Cannery Lives*, 28.

41. Francis Seufert, *Wheels of Fortune*, ed. Thomas Vaughan (Portland, Ore., 1980), 103.

42. Koe interview; Lester E. Jones, *Bureau of Fisheries Report of Alaska Investigations in 1914* (Washington, D.C., 1915), 28–31.

43. Steiner, "Warren Cannery," 10.

44. Koe interview; Wong, Lum, and Lamie interview; James Omura, interview by Chris Friday, March 25, 1988, Pullman, Wash.

45. Taki interview; Miyamoto interview; Koe interview; Craig and Hacker, "Salmon Fisheries of the Columbia," 157; Carrothers, *British Columbia Fisheries*, 11; Crandall, *Story of Pacific Salmon*, 33; Steiner, "Warren Cannery," 11. For more on the non-Chinese perspective of cannery operations, see the biographies of Montgomery Hawthorne, a former mechanic, foreman, and superintendent in salmon canneries. Martha Ferguson McKeown, *The Trail Led North: Mont Hawthorne's Story* (Portland, Ore., 1960); idem, *Alaska Silver: Another Mont Hawthorne Story* (New York, 1951).

46. CRPA to [Chan Ah] Dogg and Lam [On], November 19, 1913, CRPA-Astor; Omura interview.

47. *Chinese Nationalist Daily*, November 10, 1927; *Tai Ping Yang Rebao*, November 13, 1975; *Wei Min Bao*, May 1974; *Getting Together*, March 18–31, 1972, 7; Parker Po-fei Huang, *Cantonese Dictionary* (New Haven, 1970), 434; Lin Yutang, *Chinese-English Dictionary of Modern Usage* (Hong Kong, 1972), 1002; R. H. Mathews, *A Chinese-English Dictionary Compiled for the China Inland Mission* (Shanghai, 1931), 820; Koe interview.

48. *Cihai: The Encyclopaedic Dictionary* (Shanghai, 1979), 2:2227–2228. On the advice of a Cantonese speaker and because there is no standardized romanization of Cantonese, I have rendered the term as *sup*, rather than as *sap* as it appears in the above sources, to approximate more accurately the sound for non-Cantonese speakers.

49. Andrew F. Rolle, *The Immigrant Upraised: Italian Adventurers and Colonists in an Expanding America* (Norman, Okla., 1968), 90–93; John Bodnar, *The Transplanted: A History of Immigrants in Urban America* (Bloomington, Ind., 1987), 58.

50. Fisher, *Harvest Labor Market*, 21; Chan, *This Bittersweet Soil*, 292; Ping Chiu, *Chinese Labor in California, 1850–1880: An Economic Study* (Madison, 1967); Andrew Griego, ed., "Rebuilding the California Southern Railroad: The Personal Account of a Chinese Labor Contractor, 1884," *Journal of San Diego History* 25 (1980): 324–337; Paul Yee, "Sam Kee: A Chinese Business in Early Vancouver," in *Vancouver Past: Essays in Social History*, ed. Robert A. J. McDonald and Jean Barman (Vancouver, B.C., 1986), 86.

51. Alaska canneries, on which other scholars have concentrated, wholeheartedly adopted the piece-rate system very early and by 1900 so had most other canneries. The highly exploitative conditions of twentieth-century Alaskan canneries were not characteristic in the early years of Chinese labor on the Columbia River. On Alaska, see Lauren Wilde Casaday, "Labor Unrest and the Labor Movement in the Salmon Industry of the Pacific Coast," Ph.D.

dissertation, University of California, Berkeley, 1938; Jack Masson and Donald Guimary, "Asian Labor Contractors in the Alaskan Canned Salmon Industry, 1880–1937," *Labor History* 22, no. 3 (1981): 377–397; Nash, "China Gangs"; O'Bannon, "Technological Change."

52. *Tri-Weekly Astorian*, November 29, 1873; Hapgood and Company to Wing Sing and Company, June 11, 1890, Hapgood and Company Records, University of Oregon Manuscripts, Eugene.

53. Adams, "Salmon Canning in Oregon," 364.

54. Johansen and Gates, *Empire of the Columbia*, 352; Urrutia, "Kalama, Where Railroad and Water Meet," 18–27.

55. Goode, *Fisheries and Fishing Industries*, 1:41–42; Jordan and Gilbert, "Salmon Fishing and Canning Interests, " 747–748; Collins, "Fisheries of the Pacific Coast" (1892), 207; *Scientific American*, August 24, 1878, 122; *Weekly Astorian*, January 2, 1886; CRPA Records, passim, CRPA-Astor.

56. Collins, "Fisheries of the Pacific Coast" (1892), 207; *Weekly Astorian*, May 22, 1875; Charles Nordoff, "The Columbia River and Puget Sound," *Harper's New Monthly Magazine*, February 1874, 340–341.

57. Griego, "Chinese Labor Contractor"; Yee, "Sam Kee"; Patricia Cloud and David W. Galenson, "Chinese Immigration and Contract Labor in the Late Nineteenth Century," *Explorations in Economic History* 24 (1987): 22–42; Leigh Bristol-Kagan, "Chinese Migration to California, 1851–1882: Selected Industries of Work, the Chinese Institutions and the Legislative Exclusion of a Temporary Labor Force," Ph.D. dissertation, Harvard University, 1982; Charles Tilly, "Transplanted Networks," in *Immigration Reconsidered: History, Sociology, and Politics*, ed. Virginia Yans-McLaughlin (New York, 1990), 92.

58. *Weekly Astorian*, June 12, 1875.

59. *Portland Oregonian*, April 10, 1876.

60. *Daily Astorian*, May 4, 1876.

61. *Weekly Astorian*, June 15, 1878.

62. Ibid., March 23, 1878.

63. Jordan and Gilbert, "Salmon Fishing and Canning Interests," 748.

64. *Weekly Astorian*, March 23, 1878.

65. Adams, "Salmon Canning in Oregon," 364; Smith, *Salmon Fisheries of the Columbia*, 110; *Weekly Astorian*, February 6, May 29, 1886, February 18, 25, 1888; *Daily Astorian*, March 6, 1885. Sit Que ran one advertisement each week in the *Daily Astorian* during March 1885.

66. *Weekly Astorian*, May 14, 1874.

67. Adams, "Salmon Canning in Oregon," 364.

68. Shih-Shan Henry Tsai, *The Chinese Experience in America* (Bloomington, Ind., 1986), 67–72.

69. Ibid.; *Weekly Astorian*, March 15 and May 23, 1885, May 29, 1886, July 9, 1887; Robert Edward Wynne, "Reaction to the Chinese in the Pacific Northwest and British Columbia, 1850 to 1910," Ph.D. dissertation, University of Washington, 1964.

70. *Weekly Astorian*, March 14, May 23, 1885, May 29, 1886, July 9, 1887.

71. Benjamin Young to Lee Coey, July 8, 12, 14, 1887, Letterpress Book, 1886–1887, and February 25, 1887, Letterpress Book, 1884–1889, box 4, Benjamin Young Papers, University of Oregon Manuscripts, Eugene; Hapgood and Company to Wing Sing, May 16 and June 2, 1890, vol. 4, box 10, Hapgood and Company Records.

72. Contract with Seid Chuck, Indigenous Labor Contracts, 1898–1913, envelope 1, box 1, Seufert Brothers Cannery Records; Wong Get and Company to CRPA, January 11, 1900, CRPA-Astor; CRPA to A. B. Hammond, February 7, 1910, ibid.; Masson and Guimary, "Asian Labor Contractors," 379.

73. Hapgood and Company to Wing Sing and Company, May 17, 26, 1890, vol. 4, box 10, Hapgood and Company Records; Go Fun, Manager, Sun Yuen Company to CRPA, December 3, 13, 1900, CRPA-Astor; Leong Yip to CRPA, December 17, 21, 1901, August 21, 1901, ibid.

74. Young to Coey, February 25, 1887, Letterpress Book, 1884–1889, box 4, Young Papers.

75. Ibid., July 8, 12, 14, 1887, Letterpress Book, 1886–1887, box 4, Young Papers.

76. Ibid.

77. Hapgood and Company to Wing Sing, May 16 and June 2, 1890, vol. 4, box 10, Hapgood and Company Records.

78. Ibid., June 5, 1890.

79. Hapgood and Company to Thomas Duffy, June 5, 1890, ibid.

80. Lam On to CRPA, July 31 and September 11, 1902, October 17, 1904, May 27, 1905, April 30, 1907, July 4, 1908; WSBLS, "Special Report," 111–115; *Daily Astorian*, August 3, 1900; Steiner, "Warren Cannery," 9, 11; Koe interview.

81. E.J. Hobsbawm, *Worlds of Labour: Further Studies in the History of Labour* (London, 1984), 214–238; Robert Gray, *The Aristocracy of Labour in Nineteenth-Century Britain, c. 1850–1900* (London, 1981); Alejandro Portes and Robert L. Bach, *Latin Journey: Cuban and Mexican Immigrants in the United States* (Berkeley and Los Angeles, 1985), 16–20.

82. *Immigrants in Industry*, 397; *Weekly Astorian*, May 29, 1886, February 18, 25, 1888; Washington Fishermen's Association, *Washington: Salmon Fisheries on the Columbia River, 1882–1892* (Ilwaco, Wash., n.d.), 11, 13; Hapgood and Company to Wing Sing and Company, June 11, 1890, vol. 4, box 10, Hapgood and Company Records.

83. Hapgood and Company to Koons, Schwarz, and Company, June 13, 1890, vol. 4, box 10, Hapgood and Company Records; Cobb, *Pacific Salmon Fisheries* (1921), 121.

84. Hapgood and Company to Koons, Schwarz, and Company, June 13, 1890, vol. 4, box 10, Hapgood and Company Records.

85. Hapgood and Company to Wing Sing and Company, June 11, 1890, Hapgood and Company Records.

86. Wong Get to CRPA, November 24, 1899, CRPA-Astor.

87. Ibid., January 11, 1900.

88. Suill Duck, general manager Wing Sing, Long Kee and Company to CRPA, November 17, 1905, CRPA-Astor.

89. *Weekly Astorian*, March 30 and November 3, 1889; *Daily Astorian*, February 2, 1890, January 26, 1900; Nash, "China Gangs," 265; Masson and Guimary, "Asian Labor Contractors," 382.

90. Smith, *Salmon Fisheries of the Columbia*, 110.

91. *Weekly Astorian*, February 7, 1899, sec. 1, p. 4; Homer E. Gregory and Kathleen Barnes, *North Pacific Fisheries with Special References to Alaska Salmon* (San Francisco, 1939), 89–109; Ellen Greenberg, "Historical Note on the Alaska Packers Association and the Company Records," in *A Guide to the Alaska Packers Association Records, 1891–1970 in the Alaska Historical Library*, ed. Phyllis DeMuth and Michael Sullivan (Juneau, 1983), 2.

92. *Weekly Astorian*, February 7, 1899, sec. 1, p. 4.

93. CRPA to Lam On, May 25, 1909, CRPA-Astor; Lam On, Chan Ah Dogg, Chew Chew, and Chew Mock, correspondence with CRPA, ibid.; Lam On, Chan Ah Dogg, Chew Chew, Chew Mock, correspondence and records, Columbia River Packers Association Records, Oregon Historical Society, Portland.

94. *Daily Astorian*, January 26, 1900.

95. For example, see Seid Back correspondence, Fidalgo Island Packing Company Records, Anacortes Museum of History and Art, Anacortes, Wash.; Wong On correspondence, Macleay Estate Company Records, University of Oregon Manuscripts, Eugene; Lee Coey correspondence, Benjamin Young Papers.

96. *Daily Astorian*, March 6, 1885.

97. For a parallel development in California agriculture, see Chan, *This Bittersweet Soil*, 332–333.

Chapter 3

1. Samuel Elmore to A. B. Hammond, January 10, 1910, Columbia River Packers Association (hereafter cited as CRPA), Astor Public Library (hereafter cited as CRPA-Astor), Astoria, Ore.

2. Ibid.

3. CRPA to Hammond, January 20, 1910, CRPA-Astor.

4. National Canners Association, Pacific Fisheries Investigations, Fire Insurance Survey, Chignik Cannery, June 25, 1919, CRPA-Astor.

5. Otis W. Freeman, "Salmon Industry of the Pacific Coast," *Economic Geography*, April 1935, 117; Dianne Newell, "Dispersal and Concentration: The Slowly Changing Spatial Pattern of the British Columbia Salmon Canning Industry," *Journal of Historical Geography* 14, no. 1 (1988): 26.

6. Anthony B. Chan, "Chinese Bachelor Workers in Nineteenth-century Canada," *Ethnic and Racial Studies* 5, no. 4 (1982): 513–534; Lucie Cheng

and Edna Bonacich, eds., *Labor Immigration under Captialism: Asian Workers in the United States before World War II* (Berkeley and Los Angeles, 1984), 365–366.

7. *Weekly Astorian*, March 23, 1878.

8. Martha Ferguson McKeown, *Alaska Silver: Another Mont Hawthorne Story* (New York, 1951), 81.

9. Kazuo Ito, *Issei: A History of Japanese Immigrants in North America*, trans. Shinchiro Nakamura and Jean S. Gerard (Seattle, 1973), 362.

10. National Canners Association, Pacific Fisheries Investigations, Sanitary Survey of Salmon Canneries, Chignik Cannery, June 23, 1920, CRPA-Astor; idem., Fire Insurance Survey, Chignik Cannery, June 25, 1919, ibid.

11. John N. Cobb, *Pacific Salmon Fisheries*, U.S. Bureau of Fisheries, Document 1092 (Washington, D.C., 1930), 427; Lauren Wilde Casaday, "Labor Unrest and the Labor Movement in the Salmon Industry of the Pacific Coast," Ph.D. dissertation, University of California, Berkeley, 1938, 198–199; McKeown, *Alaska Silver*, 81; Anthony Netboy, *The Columbia River Salmon: Their Fight for Survival* (Seattle, 1980), 29.

12. Sanitary Survey of Salmon Canneries, Chignik Cannery, 1920, CRPA-Astor.

13. Ibid.

14. Ibid.

15. *Weekly Astorian*, March 23, 1878, and February 24, 1881; Elvin Wong, John Lum, and A. J. Lamie, interview by Chris Friday, February 3, 1988, Astoria, Ore.

16. Sanitary Survey of Salmon Canneries, Chignik Cannery, 1919, CRPA-Astor.

17. U.S. Bureau of the Census, Manuscript Schedules of the Population Census, Tenth Census, Columbia and Clatsop counties, Oregon, Wahkiakum and Pacific counties, Washington, 1880 (hereafter cited as Population Census, [place], [year]).

18. Population Census, Clatsop, Columbia, and Wasco counties, Ore., Wahkiakum and Pacific counties, Wash., and all districts of Alaska, 1900 and 1910; Charles Koe, "Chinese Cannery Workers in Ilwaco," PAC 75–22dm, transcript of interview, October 7 and 8, 1975, Washington State Oral/Aural History Program, 1974–1977, Washington State Archives, Olympia.

19. U.S. Census Bureau, Schedule No. 3, Census of Manufactures, Twelfth Census (1900), CRPA-Astor; CRPA to N.H. Weber, June 3, 1920, ibid.; and CRPA to Sara Wilburn, April 2, 1925, ibid.

20. Population Census, Clatsop, Columbia, and Wasco counties, Ore., Wahkiakum, Pacific, Skagit, and Whatcom counties, Wash., and Alaska, 1880, 1900, and 1910; *Astoria Budget*, September 28, 1911.

21. Robert H. Ruby and John A. Brown, *The Chinook Indians: Traders of the Lower Columbia* (Norman, Okla., 1976), 232–233, 237; John R. Swanton, *The Indians of North America* (Washington, D.C., 1952), 418–419, 458; Herbert C. Taylor, Jr., "Anthropological Investigations of the Chinook Indi-

ans," in *American Indian Ethnohistory: Oregon Indians*, ed. and comp. David Agee Horr (New York, 1974), 1:142; *Daily Astorian*, October 7, 1891; *Astoria Budget*, September 28, 1911; Francis Seufert, *Wheels of Fortune*, ed. Thomas Vaughan (Portland, Ore., 1980), 45.

22. Population Census, Alaska, 1900 and 1910.

23. McKeown, *Alaska Silver*, 141; Ivan Petroff, "Report of the Population, Industries and Resources of Alaska," in U.S. Census Office, *Tenth Census of the United States, 1880*, vol. 3, *Special Reports on Newspaper Periodicals, Alaska, Fur-Seal Islands, and Shipbuilding* (Washington, D.C., 1884).

24. The Population Census is probably most accurate before the 1882 Exclusion Act because Chinese immigrants had less incentive to mislead enumerators about their identities than after the act.

25. David Chuenyan Lai, *Chinatowns: Towns within Cities in Canada* (Vancouver, 1988), 15–19, 43–45, 47; Chinese Workers Accounts, 1901, Seufert Brothers Cannery Records, Oregon Historical Society, Portland, Ore.; Population Census, Clatsop and Columbia counties, Ore., Pacific and Wahkiakum counties, Wash., 1880, 1900, and 1910.

26. Robert F. Spencer and S. A. Barrett, "Notes on a Bachelor House in the South China Area," *American Anthropologist* 50 (1948): 463–478.

27. Ibid., 475, 471.

28. Population Census, Clatsop and Columbia counties, Ore., Pacific and Wahkiakum counties, Wash., 1880 and 1900.

29. *Weekly Astorian*, February 13 and 20, 1886, and February 13, 1894; Alejandro Portes and Robert L. Bach, *Latin Journey: Cuban and Mexican Immigrants in the United States* (Berkeley and Los Angeles, 1985), 13–20.

30. For a discussion of elderly bachelor workers, see Louis Chu, *Eat a Bowl of Tea* (Seattle, 1961).

31. Seid Chuck and Seufert Brothers Canning Company, Contract, 1908, January 4, 1908, Indigenous Labor Contracts, envelope 1, box 1, Seufert Brothers Cannery Records; and Seid Dye and Seufert Brothers Canning Company, 1913, December 1912, ibid.

32. Koe interview; Casaday, "Labor Unrest," 201; Yamato Ichihashi, *Japanese in the United States* (Stanford, Calif., 1932), 158; and May L. Dong, *No Speak English* (New York, 1962), 25.

33. Casaday, "Labor Unrest," 203; Robert A. Nash, "The 'China Gangs' in the Alaska Packers Association Canneries, 1892–1935," in *The Life, Influence and the Role of the Chinese in the United States, 1776–1960* (San Francisco, 1976), 257–283; Jack Masson and Donald Guimary, "Asian Labor Contractors in the Alaskan Canned Salmon Industry, 1880–1937," *Labor History* 22, no. 3 (1981): 377–397.

34. N. H. Webber to CRPA, September 10, 1902, CRPA-Astor.

35. Koe interview.

36. Ibid.; Wong, Lum, and Lamie interview.

37. Julia Butler Hansen, *Cathlamet Pioneer: The Paintings of Maude Kimball Butler* (Tacoma, Wash., 1973), 29–31; Elliot Coues, *The History of the*

Lewis and Clark Expedition by Meriwether Lewis and William Clark (New York, 1979), 3:824–825; Harriet L. Smith, *Wonderful Wapato, the Wild Potato: An Oregon Vignette* (Lake Oswego, Ore., 1982); G. A. Stuart, *Chinese Materia Medica: Vegetable Kingdom* (Shanghai, 1911), 389; Joseph Needham, Lu Gwei-Djen, and Huang Hsing-Tsung, *Science and Civilisation in China*, vol. 6, pt. 1, *Botany* (Cambridge, England, 1986), 344–346.

38. Koe interview.

39. Feelie Lee and Elaine Lou, "Traditions and Transitions," in *Linking Our Lives: Chinese American Women of Los Angeles* (Los Angeles, 1984), 61–62; Paul D. Buell, "Theory and Practice of Traditional Chinese Medicine," in *Chinese Medicine on the Golden Mountain: An Interpretive Guide*, ed. Henry G. Schwarz (Seattle, 1984), 35.

40. Casaday, "Labor Unrest," 79, 201, 240; Masson and Guimary, "Labor Contractors," 390–391.

41. Masson and Guimary, "Labor Contractors," 390–391.

42. Ibid.; Koe interview; David T. Courtwright, *Dark Paradise: Opiate Addiction in America before 1940* (Cambridge, Mass., 1987), 78–86.

43. Masson and Guimary, "Labor Contractors," 390–391.

44. Ibid.

45. George Taki, interview by Chris Friday, January 10 and 11, 1989, Los Angeles.

46. Casaday, "Labor Unrest," 240; Masson and Guimary, "Labor Contractors," 377.

47. *Weekly Astorian*, June 8, 1883; *Daily Astorian*, May 8, 1885, and July 3, 1900.

48. *Weekly Astorian*, June 3, 1881; *Daily Astorian*, July 3 and August 17, 1900.

49. *Tri-Weekly Astorian*, October 11 and 28, 1873; *West Shore*, October 1888, 531.

50. U.S. Dept. of the Interior, Census Office, *Ninth Census*, vol. 1, *The Statistics of the Population of the United States* (Washington, D.C., 1872), 241.

51. *Weekly Astorian*, August 14, 1875, and April 30, 1874.

52. Ibid., May 7 and 14, 1874, August 14, 1875, October 7, 1876, June 29, 1883, September 10, 1887; *Daily Astorian*, January 6 and 12, 1878, October 17, 1879, July 3 and 30, 1880, March 1, 1881, July 29, 1881, April 6, 1883; David Starr Jordan and Charles H. Gilbert, "The Salmon Fishing and Canning Interests of the Pacific Coast," in *The Fisheries and Fishing Industries of the United States*, ed. George Brown Goode (Washington, D.C., 1887), 5:745, 751; Emma H. Adams, "Salmon Canning in Oregon," U.S. Fish Commission, *Bulletin* 5 (1885): 363; Courtland L. Smith, *Salmon Fisheries of the Columbia* (Corvallis, Ore., 1979), 110; Hugh M. Smith, "Notes on a Reconnaissance of the Fisheries of the Pacific Coast of the United States in 1894," U.S. Fish Commission, *Bulletin* 14 (1895): 238–239; *Pacific Fisherman Yearbook*, 1937, 73; and *Pacific Fisherman Annual*, 1904, 72; 1905, 73; 1906, 60.

53. Population Census, Clatsop County, Ore., 1870 and 1880.

54. Ibid., 1880.
55. Ibid.
56. *Weekly Astorian*, May 23, 1879.
57. Portes and Bach, *Latin Journey*, 13–20.
58. Population Census, Clatsop County, Ore., 1880.
59. *Portland Oregonian*, September 8, 1881; *Weekly Astorian*, August 14, 1875, October 7, 1876, May 11, 1883, June 29, 1883, January 27, 1885, September 10, 1887; *Daily Astorian*, March 1, 1881.
60. Shih-shan Henry Tsai, *The Chinese Experience in America* (Bloomington, Ind., 1986), 67–71; Sucheng Chan, *Asian Americans: An Interpretive History* (Boston, 1991), 49–51, 53.
61. *West Shore*, March 1886, 71–72, 76–78, and October 1886, 291–298; Robert Edward Wynne, "Reaction to the Chinese in the Pacific Northwest and British Columbia, 1850 to 1910," Ph.D. dissertation, University of Washington, 1964; Leigh Bristol-Kagan, "Chinese Migration to California, 1851–1882: Selected Industries of Work, the Chinese Institutions and the Legislative Exclusion of a Temporary Labor Force," Ph.D. dissertation, Harvard University, 1982, chap. 5.
62. *Weekly Astorian*, February 13, 1886.
63. Ibid.
64. Ibid., June 27, 1885.
65. Ibid., September 10, 1887, March 3, 1888, January 11, 1884; *Daily Astorian*, March 27, 1890; *Portland Oregonian*, August 11, 1887; Richard Rathbun, "Fishery Investigation of the Columbia River Basin," U.S. Fish Commission, *Report, 1894*, 1896, 95–102.
66. Smith, *Salmon Fisheries of the Columbia*, 110; Population Census, Clatsop County, Ore., 1900.
67. Smith, *Salmon Fisheries of the Columbia*, 110; Population Census, Clatsop County, Ore., 1910.
68. Joseph A. Craig and Robert L. Hacker, "History and Development of the Fisheries of the Columbia River," U.S. Department of the Interior, Bureau of Fisheries, *Bulletin* 32 (1940): 152–153.
69. Wong, Lum, and Lamie interview.
70. *Weekly Astorian*, October 1, 1880, and January 15, 1887.
71. Ibid., Jan 15, 1887; *West Shore*, June 1883, 124.
72. *Weekly Astorian*, October 1, 1880, and January 15, 1887; *Astoria Budget*, January 17 and 18, and February 2, 1910.
73. Wong, Lum, and Lamie interview.
74. Population Census, Clatsop County, Ore., 1880; *Daily Astorian*, November 14, 1877, and January 8, 1880; *Weekly Astorian*, November 17, December 22, 1877, and October 17, 1879; Lucie Cheng Hirata, "Chinese Immigrant Women in Nineteenth-Century California," in *Women of America: A History*, ed. Carol Ruth Berkin and Mary Beth Norton (Boston, 1979), 223–244; Sucheng Chan, *This Bittersweet Soil: The Chinese in California Agriculture* (Berkeley and Los Angeles, 1986), 369, 387, 389–390.

75. Lucie Cheng Hirata, "Free, Indentured, Enslaved: Chinese Prostitutes in Nineteenth-Century America," *Signs* 5 (1979): 13–14; Judy Yung, *Chinese Women of America: A Pictorial History* (Seattle, 1986), 18–22; David Beesley, "From Chinese to Chinese American: Chinese Women and Families in a Sierra Nevada County," *California History* 67 (1988): 168–179, 206ff.

76. *Weekly Astorian*, October 17, 1879; *Daily Astorian*, April 19, 1888.

77. Peter Costovich, interview by Philip Sutton, KVAS Oral History Interview, tape 11, n.d., Astor Public Library, Astoria, Ore.

78. *Portland Oregonian*, September 8, 1881.

79. *Weekly Astorian*, November 17 and December 22, 1877, February 9, 1878.

80. Population Census, Clatsop County, Ore., 1880 and 1900.

81. Ibid., 1900.

82. Ibid.

83. Chan, *This Bittersweet Soil*, 385, notes similar trends among married women in California.

84. Population Census, Clatsop County, Ore., 1900; Chan, *This Bittersweet Soil*, 395; Hirata, "Chinese Immigrant Women," 232, 236–239.

85. Population Census, Clatsop County, Ore., 1910; *Daily Astorian*, November 12, 1891.

86. Population Census, Clatsop County, Ore., 1880, 1900, and 1910.

87. *Weekly Astorian*, June 3, 1881.

88. Ibid., October 9, 1880, and February 4, 1881.

89. *Daily Astorian*, August 17, 1900; *Astorian*, April 26, 1973, B8.

90. *Weekly Astorian*, July 29, 1881.

91. Ibid., April 6, 1883; Ronald Riddle, "The Cantonese Opera: A Chapter in Chinese-American History," in *The Life, Influence and Role of the Chinese*, 41, 44.

92. Costovich interview.

93. *Weekly Astorian*, June 16, 1888; Wong, Lum, and Lamie interview.

94. *Weekly Astorian*, August 14, 1886.

95. Ibid.; *Daily Astorian*, June 10, 1891.

96. *Weekly Astorian*, August 14, 1882, June 29, 1889, September 14 1889; *Daily Astorian*, June 10, 1891.

97. Him Mark Lai, "Historical Development of the Chinese Consolidated Benevolent Association/*Huiguan* System," *Chinese America: History and Perspectives, 1987* (San Francisco, 1987), 13–51; Eve Armentrout-Ma, "Urban Chinese at the Sinitic Frontier: Social Organizations in United States' Chinatowns, 1849–1898," *Modern Asian Studies* 18 (1983): 107–135; Ivan Light, "From Vice District to Tourist Attraction: The Moral Career of American Chinatowns, 1880–1940," *Pacific Historical Review* 43 (1974): 367–394; Stanford M. Lyman, "Conflict and the Web of Group Affiliation in San Francisco's Chinatown, 1850–1910," ibid., 473–499; Bristol-Kagan, "Chinese Migration to California," chap. 5.

98. *Weekly Astorian*, November 2 and December 1, 1888; *Daily Astorian*, October 7, 1883, December 6, 1888; *Astorian*, April 26, 1976, C30.

99. *Weekly Astorian*, December 1, 8, and 15, 1888; *Daily Astorian*, December 5 and 6, 1888.

100. Jordan and Gilbert, "Salmon Fishing and Canning Interests," 748.

101. Population Census, Clatsop County, Ore., 1880; *Astorian*, January 19, 1978, 4, and July 4, 1976, C30; Wong, Lum, and Lamie interview.

102. "Second Interview with Mr. Henry A. Monroe, Attorney," 1924, Survey of Race Relations Major Document 219–A, box 1, William Carlson Smith Documents, University of Oregon, Eugene; "Life History and Social Document of David Young," Seattle, 1924, Major Document 272, ibid.; "Life History and Social Document of Charlie Lui," Seattle, 1924, Major Document 178–A, ibid.; and "Interview with a Chinese Man," Seattle, 1924, Minor Document 279, ibid.

103. Population Census, Clatsop County, Ore., 1880; *Astorian*, January 19, 1978, 4, and July 4, 1976, C30; Wong, Lum, and Lamie interview.

104. Lyman, "Conflict and the Web of Group Affiliation," 473–499.

105. Light, "From Vice District to Tourist Attraction," 367–394.

106. *Daily Astorian*, March 30, 1917, February 13, April 19, and June 11, 1922.

107. *Astoria Budget*, October 4, 1893.

108. *Daily Astorian*, June 22, 1916.

109. *Astoria Budget*, January 29, 1917.

110. Ibid., March 31, 1904; Andrew F. Rolle, *California: A History*, 3rd ed. (Arlington Heights, Ill., 1978), 352; *Daily Astorian*, December 7 and 8, 1888, February 13, April 19, and June 11, 1922; *Astorian*, July 4, 1976, C30; Wong, Lum, and Lamie interview.

111. *Daily Astorian*, July 26, August 15, 17, and 19, and November 4, 1900.

112. *Astoria Budget*, August 22, 1940; Margaret Willson and Jeffery L. MacDonald, "International Chinese Business Directory of the World for the Year 1913," *Annals of the Chinese Historical Society of the Pacific Northwest* III (1985–1986): 79; L. Eve Armentrout Ma, *Revolutionaries, Monarchists, and Chinatowns: Chinese Politics in the Americas* (Honolulu, 1990), 40–51.

113. *Astoria Budget*, January 26, 1911; Melford Weiss, *Valley City: A Chinese Community in America* (Cambridge, Mass., 1974), 92–93; Lee and Lou, "Traditions and Transitions," 54–55.

114. *Weekly Astorian*, December 17, 1880.

115. Ibid., July 14, 1888.

116. *Daily Astorian*, March 7, 1890, and February 3, 1891.

117. *Astoria Budget*, January 26, 1911, and November 25, 1913; *Astorian*, July 4, 1976, C30; Wong, Lum, and Lamie interview.

118. George Brown Goode, ed., *The Fisheries and Fishing Industries of the United States* (Washington, D.C., 1887), 1:42.

119. Jordan and Gilbert, "Salmon Fishing and Canning Interests," 735–736.

120. *Weekly Astorian*, April 30, 1884; J. W. Collins, "Report on the Fisheries of the Pacific Coast of the United States," U.S. Commission of Fish and Fisheries, *Report, 1888*, 1892, pt. 16, p. 207.

121. Collins, "Report on the Fisheries of the Pacific Coast," 207.

122. *Columbia River Fishermens Protective Union* (Astoria, Ore., 1890), 1–28.

123. *West Shore*, June 1887, 173; *Portland Oregonian*, September 8, 1881.

124. *Washington Standard*, March 26, 1880; *Weekly Astorian*, March 14 and 28, 1885, and February 6, 1886.

125. CRPA to Eureka Cannery, March 17, 1903, CRPA-Astor; Benjamin Young to Fred Williams, June 3, 1887, Letterpress Book, 1886, box 4, Benjamin Young Papers, University of Oregon, Eugene.

126. George H. George to Rooster Rock Cannery, April 26, 1909, CRPA-Astor; Arthur C. Duncan to R. D. Hume, January 2, 21, and 23, 1896, Letterpress 1893–1896, vol. 84, R. D. Hume Papers, University of Oregon, Eugene.

127. *Weekly Astorian*, May 14, 1874; *Daily Astorian*, May 18, 1876.

128. *Daily Astorian*, May 14 and 16, 1878.

129. *West Shore*, June 1883, 125–126, June 1887, 173, and July 1887, 550–551.

130. *Astoria Budget*, July 28, 1893.

131. William A. Wilcox, "Notes on the Fisheries of the Pacific Coast in 1895," U.S. Fish Commisssion, *Report, 1896*, 1898, 587.

132. Population Census, Clatsop County, Ore., 1880, 1900, and 1910; Wong, Lum, and Lamie interview; *Daily Astorian*, June 15, 1890; *Astorian*, January 19, 1978, 4; Emma Woo Louie, "A New Perspective on Surnames among Chinese Americans," *Amerasia* 12, no. 2 (1985–1986): 8. Victor G. Nee and Brett de Bary Nee, *Longtime Californ': A Documentary Study of an American Chinatown* (New York, 1973), 64, note that the Wong, Chin, and Lee clans have been the most powerful in San Francisco.

133. *Weekly Astorian*, September 22, 1877; Population Census, Clatsop County, Ore., 1880; *Daily Astorian*, July 29 and 30, 1879, and January 8, 1880.

134. Sandy Lydon, *Chinese Gold: The Chinese in the Monterey Bay Region* (Capitola, Calif., 1985), 386–387.

135. Paul Yee, "Sam Kee: A Chinese Business in Early Vancouver," in *Vancouver Past: Essays in Social History*, ed. Robert A. J. McDonald and Jean Barman (Vancouver, B.C., 1986), 70–96; Population Census, Clatsop County, Ore., 1880, 1900, and 1910.

136. Population Census, Clatsop County, Ore., 1880, 1900, and 1910.

137. In CRPA correspondence, Chan Ah Dogg signed letters as Ah Dogg and company officials referred to him in that fashion or simply as Dogg. Because Chinese more consistently use their surnames in formal occasions, I refer to him as Chan.

138. *Astorian*, April 26, 1973, 8B; *Astoria Budget*, September 17, 1913, January 4, 1915, and June 23, 1916.

139. Lum, Wong, and Lamie interview; Washington State Bureau of Labor Statistics, "Special Report on the Salmon Canning Industry in the State of

Washington and the Employment of Oriental Labor," *Tenth Biennial Report, 1915–16* (Olympia, 1916), 111–112 (hereafter cited as WSBLS, "Special Report"); Chan, *This Bittersweet Soil,* 2.

140. "Interview with Mr. Farris," Seattle, Washington, 1924, Survey of Race Relations Major Document 190–A, box 1, Smith Documents.

141. *Astoria Herald,* February 22, 1902.

142. Records of Chinese Arriving Astoria, Oregon, from 1893 to 1903, Portland, Oregon, Chinese Exclusion Records, box 6, U.S. Customs Service, Record Group 36, Seattle Branch, National Archives and Records Administration (hereafter listed as Records of Chinese Arriving Astoria, RG 36, NARA, Seattle).

143. Ibid.

144. Population Census, Clatsop County, Ore., 1880.

145. In 1900 and again in 1910, officials conducted the census in April and May, rather than June, July, and August as had earlier been the case.

146. *Weekly Astorian,* October 22, 1876, June 29, 1883, and March 14, 1885; WSBLS, "Special Report," 111–112.

147. Population Census, Clatsop County, Ore., 1880, 1900, and 1910.

148. *Astoria Budget,* February 26, 1940, sec. 4, p. 6. The increase in number of self-designated merchants in the census was largely a result of changes in immigration legislation that permitted the entry of merchants, but not laborers. As a consequence, after exclusion many more Chinese tried to declare themselves merchants than before. See Chan, *Asian Americans,* 54–55.

149. Gregg Lee Carter, "Social Demography of the Chinese in Nevada: 1870–1880," *Nevada Historical Society Quarterly* 18 (1975): 24, notes a direct and proportional correlation between the size of the non-Chinese community and its Chinese satellite. Not all Chinese communities in the American West during the nineteenth century were entirely dependent on service occupations catering to non-Chinese. For the raw data with which to compare the Chinese businesses of Portland and Astoria, see Willson and MacDonald, "Business Directory for 1913," 79–81.

150. U.S. Census Office, *Report on the Population of the United States at the Eleventh Census, 1890* (Washington, D.C., 1893), pt. 1, p. 476.

151. U.S. Bureau of the Census, *Thirteenth Census of the United States, 1910,* vol. 3, *Population* (Washington, D.C., 1913), 522.

152. Ibid., 487.

153. Population Census, Clatsop County, Ore., 1880, 1900, and 1910.

154. Records of Chinese Arriving Astoria, RG 36, NARA, Seattle; Chan, *This Bittersweet Soil,* 346; Nash, "China Gangs," 266.

155. Wong, Lum, and Lamie interview; *Astoria Budget,* April 7, 1907, January 4 and 8, 1915, June 23, 1916; *Daily Astorian,* July 4, 1976, B8–B9.

156. *Report of the Royal Commission on Chinese Immigration* (Ottawa, Canada, 1885), 363–365; David Chuenyan Lai, *Chinatowns: Towns within Cities in Canada* (Vancouver, 1988), 49–50.

157. *Report of the Royal Commission on Chinese Immigration* (Ottawa, 1885), 363–365.

158. *Report of the Royal Commission on Chinese and Japanese Immigration* (Ottawa, 1902), 141–142.

159. Ibid.

160. Ibid.

161. Ibid., 294.

162. Ibid., 13, 16.

163. Seufert, *Wheels of Fortune*, 69–70; D. W. Meinig, *The Great Columiba Plain: A Historical Geography* (Seattle, 1968), 344–348, 456–457.

164. Population Census, Wasco County, Ore., 1880; P. Scott Corbett and Nancy Parker Corbett, "The Chinese in Oregon, c. 1870–1880," *Oregon Historical Quarterly* 68 (March 1977): 81.

165. U.S. Census Office, *Report on the Population of the United States at the Eleventh Census, 1890* (Washington, D.C., 1895), pt. 1, pp. 288, 512.

166. Population Census, Wasco County, Ore., 1900.

167. Population Census, Wasco County, Ore., 1880, 1900, and 1910; Christopher Edson, *The Chinese in Eastern Oregon, 1860–1890* (San Francisco, 1976), 9, 32, 58.

168. Willson and MacDonald, "Business Directory for 1913," 70–85.

169. Population Census, Wasco County, Ore., 1900 and 1910.

170. Seufert, *Wheels of Fortune*, 114.

171. Population Census, Wasco County, Ore., 1900 and 1910.

172. Seufert, *Wheels of Fortune*, 114.

173. Population Census, Pacific County, Wash., 1900; *Thirteenth Census . . . , 1910*, vol. 3, *Population*, 981, 995.

174. Population Census, Pacific County, Wash., 1910; *Thirteenth Census . . . , 1910*, vol. 3, *Population*, 981, 995; Koe interview.

175. Koe interview.

176. *Wahkiakum County Eagle*, 8th annual ed., May 1, 1980, 2.

177. Ibid.; Hansen, *Cathlamet Pioneer*, 28–31.

178. Population Census, Wahkiakum County, Wash., 1900.

179. *Thirteenth Census . . . , 1910*, vol. 3, *Population*, 981, 995.

180. Hansen, *Cathlamet Pioneer*, 28, 30.

181. Patricia Roppel, *Salmon from Kodiak: An History of the Salmon Fishery of Kodiak Island*, Alaska Historical Commission Studies in History 216 (Anchorage, 1986), 171–174, 176.

182. U.S. Census Office, *Report on the Population and Resources of Alaska at the Eleventh Census, 1890* (Washington, D.C., 1890), 218, 222; Nash, "China Gangs," 276; Roppel, *Salmon from Kodiak*, 145.

183. S .P. Beecher, "Diary of Alaska Trip, 1906," file 9, box 1, Alaska MSS Collection, Washington State Historical Society, Tacoma; Population Census, Alaska Territory, 1900 and 1910.

Chapter 4

1. Carl A. Sutter to H. Bell-Irving and Company, January 7, 1902, 1902–1904 Letterpress Book, Fidalgo Island Packing Company Records (hereafter cited as FIPC Records), Anacortes Museum of History and Art, Anacortes, Wash.

2. Ibid.

3. Ibid.

4. Crew List, 1902, 1902–1904 Letterpress Book, 252, FIPC Records.

5. Columbia River Packers Association (hereafter cited as CRPA) to Chew Chew, March 20, 1902, Columbia River Packers Association Records, Astor Public Library, Astoria, Ore. (hereafter cited as CRPA-Astor); Chew Mock to CRPA, February 2, 1906, ibid.; Jefferson F. Moser, "The Salmon and Salmon Fisheries of Alaska: Report of the Alaskan Salmon Investigations of the U.S. Fish Commission Steamer *Albatross* in 1900 and 1901," U.S. Bureau of Fisheries, Document 510, *Bulletin, 1901*, 1902, 185; *Seattle Times*, July 2, 1911.

6. Daniel B. Deloach, *The Salmon Canning Industry* (Corvallis, Ore., 1939), 17, 46; *Pacific Fisherman Annual*, 1906, 60.

7. E. J. Hobsbawm, *Worlds of Labour: Further Studies in the History of Labour* (London, 1984), 214–238; Robert Gray, *The Aristocracy of Labour in Nineteenth-Century Britain, c. 1850–1900* (London, 1981).

8. Patrick William O'Bannon, "Technological Change in the Pacific Coast Canned Salmon Industry: 1864–1924," Ph.D. dissertation, University of California, San Diego, 1983, 31; idem, "Waves of Change: Mechanization in the Pacific Coast Canned-Salmon Industry, 1864–1914," *Technology and Culture* 28, no. 3 (July 1987): 558–577.

9. O'Bannon, "Waves of Change," 558–577; Francis Seufert, *Wheels of Fortune*, ed. Thomas Vaughan (Portland, Ore., 1980), 71–74.

10. O'Bannon, "Technological Change," 55.

11. *Nanaimo (B.C.) Herald*, October 9, 1901; *San Francisco Chronicle*, October 14, 1901.

12. Contractor Wong On, for example, shifted workers between smaller coastal canneries, Columbia River plants, and Alaska operations. See his correspondence in the CRPA-Astor records, the CRPA records held at the Oregon Historical Society, Portland, and the Macleay Estate Company Papers, University of Oregon, Eugene.

13. John N. Cobb, *The Canning of Fishery Products* (Seattle, 1919), 71; O'Bannon, "Technological Change," 48–55.

14. *Bellingham Herald*, April 6, 1905; *Seattle Post-Intelligencer*, June 27, 1903; *Bellingham Reveille*, June 14, 1908; *Bellingham Sentinel*, April 4, 1913; Elvin Wong, John Lum, A. J. Lamie, interview by Chris Friday, February 3, 1988, Astoria, Ore.; *Reports of the Immigration Commission: Immigrants in Industry*, vol. 25, pt. 25, *Japanese and Other Immigrant Races in the Pacific Coast and Mountain States*, vol. 3, Senate Document 633 (Washington, D.C.,

1911), 393–394 (hereafter cited as *Immigrants in Industries*); Margaret Willson and Jeffery L. Macdonald, "The Impact of the 'Iron Chink' on the Chinese Salmon Cannery Workers of Puget Sound," *Annals of the Chinese Historical Society of the Pacific Northwest*, 1984, 79–89.

15. *Pacific Fisherman Annual*, 1904, 82.

16. Ibid., 1905, 91.

17. *Portland Telegram*, August 8, 1907.

18. William Barry to CRPA, June 8, 1902, CRPA-Astor; John Carlson to CRPA, July 25, 1904, ibid.; Moser, "Report of the *Albatross*, 1900 and 1901," 64, 191.

19. *Astorian*, April 29, 1900; John Carlson to CRPA, July 25, 1904, CRPA-Astor; CRPA to H. C. Fassett, October 1, 1904, ibid.

20. Rooster Rock Cannery to CRPA, February 21 and July 17, 1908.

21. *Pacific Fisherman Yearbook*, 1925, 98; 1927, 113; 1930, 27 and 90.

22. *San Francisco Call*, March 15, 1902; *San Francisco Chronicle*, March 19, 1902; *San Francisco Examiner*, April 16, 1901. The 1902 law extended Chinese exclusion, but a 1904 act made it permanent. For additional details, see Sucheng Chan, "The Exclusion of Chinese Women, 1870–1943," in *Entry Denied: Exclusion and the Chinese Community in America, 1882–1943*, ed. Sucheng Chan (Philadelphia, 1991), 109 and 142n.49.

23. *San Francisco Examiner*, April 16, 1901.

24. *San Francisco Call*, April 14, 1904.

25. *San Francisco Examiner*, April 16, 1901, and April 15, 1911.

26. *San Francisco Call*, June 27, 1903.

27. *San Francisco Chronicle*, March 13 and May 13, 1905; *San Francisco Examiner*, April 15, 1911, and April 10, 1916.

28. *Portland Oregonian*, September 2, 1905; Alicja Muszynski, "Major Processors to 1940 and Early Labour Force: Historical Notes," in *Uncommon Property: The Fishing and Fish Processing Industries in British Columbia*, ed. Patricia Marchak, Neil Guppy, and John McMullan (Toronto, 1987), 60–61.

29. *Portland Oregonian*, September 2, 1905.

30. *Anacortes Citizen*, August 21, 1914; Muszynski, "Major Processors," 60–61; Dianne Newell, "The Rationality of Mechanization in the Pacific Salmon-Canning Industry before the Second World War," *Business History Review* 62 (Winter 1988): 636.

31. Sit Que to CRPA, December 27, 1906, CRPA-Astor.

32. *San Francisco Chronicle*, May 13, 1905; Robert A. Nash, "The 'China Gangs' in the Alaska Packers Association Canneries, 1892–1935," in *The Life, Influence and the Role of the Chinese in the United States, 1776–1960* (San Francisco, 1976), 268–269; Lauren Wilde Casaday, "Labor Unrest and the Labor Movement in the Salmon Industry of the Pacific Coast," Ph.D. dissertation, University of California, Berkeley, 1938, 82.

33. *San Francisco Chronicle*, May 13, 1905.

34. Patricia Roppel, *Salmon from Kodiak: An History of the Salmon Fishery of Kodiak Island*, Alaska Historical Commission Studies in History 216 (Anchorage, 1986), 29, 170; Casaday, "Labor Unrest," 82.

35. Seufert, *Wheels of Fortune*, 108; Willard G. Jue and Silas G. Jue, "Goon Dip: Entrepreneur, Diplomat, and Community Leader," *Annals of the Chinese Historical Society of the Pacific Northwest*, 1984, 45–46.

36. Victoria Wyatt, "Alaskan Indian Wage Earners in the Nineteenth Century: Economic Choices and Ethnic Identity on Southeast Alaska's Frontier," *Pacific Northwest Quarterly* 78, nos. 1–2 (1987): 43–49.

37. Moser, "Report of the *Albatross*, 1900 and 1901," 320–321.

38. Ibid.

39. *San Francisco Call*, March 15, 1902, June 27, 1903, April 15, 1904; *San Francisco Chronicle*, March 19, 1902; *San Francisco Examiner*, April 16, 1901.

40. Moser, "Report of the *Albatross*, 1900 and 1901," 320–321.

41. Benjamin Young to Lee Coey, July 14, 1887, Letterpress 1886–1887, box 4, Benjamin Young Papers, University of Oregon, Eugene.

42. George Rounsefell to Carl Sutter, July 27 and 29, 1912, and June 20 and October 15, 1915, FIPC Records.

43. See Marchak, Guppy, and McMullan, eds., *Uncommon Property*, 171–290; Alicja Muszynski, "Class Formation and Class Consciousness: The Making of Shoreworkers in the B.C. Fishing Industry," *Studies in Political Economy*, Summer 1986, 98–113; idem, "The Creation and Organization of Cheap Wage Labor in the British Columbia Fishing Industry," Ph.D. dissertation, University of British Columbia, Vancouver, 1986; George North, *A Ripple, a Wave: The Story of Union Organization in the B.C. Fishing Industry*, ed. Harold Griffin (Vancouver, 1974), 11–16.

44. Hubert Howe Bancroft, *History of Alaska, 1730–1885* (Darien, Conn., 1970), 662; Moser, "Report of the *Albatross*, 1900 and 1901," 320–321; Clause-M. Naske and Herman E. Slotnik, *Alaska: A History of the 49th State*, 2nd ed. (Norman, Okla., 1987), 75.

45. Cutting Packing Company, "Alaska Fisheries," MSS, c. 1885, Bancroft Library, University of California, Berkeley; Bancroft, *Alaska*, 662; John N. Cobb, *Salmon Fisheries of the Pacific Coast*, U.S. Bureau of Fisheries Document 751 (Washington, D.C., 1911), 22; *Pacific Fisherman Annual*, 1904, 40; Tarelton H. Bean, "Resources and Fishing Grounds of Alaska," in *The Fisheries and Fishery Industries of the United States*, ed. George Brown Goode (Washington, D.C., 1887), 3:89; Jefferson F. Moser, "The Salmon and Salmon Fisheries of Alaska: Report of the U.S. Fish Commission Steamer *Albatross* for the Year Ending June 30, 1898," U.S. Bureau of Fisheries, *Bulletin, 1898*, 1899, 24–25, 50, 66, 109–112; Amy P. S. Stacey, "Journal of Alaska Trip, 1892," file 6, box 1, Alaska MSS Collection, Washington State Historical Society, Tacoma.

46. J. W. Collins, "Report on the Fisheries of the Pacific Coast of the United States," U.S. Commission of Fish and Fisheries, *Report of the Commissioner for 1888* (Washington, D.C., 1892), pt. 16, p. 173; William A. Wilcox, "Growth of the Fishery Industry in Alaska," U.S. Bureau of Fisheries, *Report, 1893*, 1895, 212.

47. John O. Snyder, "Salmon of the Klamath River," California Division of Fish and Game, *Fish Bulletin* (Sacramento), no. 34 (1931): 8; California Division of Fish and Game, "The Commercial Fish Catch of California for the Year 1947 with an Historical Review, 1916–1947," *Fish Bulletin* (Sacramento), no. 74 (1949): 39.

48. Alaska Packers Association, Alitak Cannery Logbook, 1920, Semiahmoo State Park, Whatcom County, Wash.

49. Ivan Petroff, "Report of the Population, Industries and Resources of Alaska," in U.S. Census Office, *Tenth Census of the United States, 1880*, vol. 3, *Special Reports on Newspaper Periodicals, Alaska, Fur-Seal Islands, and Shipbuilding* (Washington, D.C., 1884), 70–71.

50. Moser, "Report of the *Albatross*, 1900 and 1901," 187, 247; M. C. Holman, "Report of the U.S. Public School at Chignik, Alaska," August 31, 1922, CRPA-Astor; CRPA to A. B. Hammond, June 5, 1919, ibid.; Thomas Wootten to George Barker, September 17, 1921, ibid.; CRPA to John S. Osmund, June 22, 1921, November 6, 1922, and February 25, 1924, ibid..

51. *San Francisco Chronicle*, September 8 and 18, 1903; James W. VanStone, "Nushagak," *Alaska Journal* 3 (1972): 51–52; Roppel, *Salmon from Kodiak*, 172–177.

52. U.S. Department of Commerce, Bureau of Fisheries, "Statistics of Fishing Industry of Alaska," schedules for the CRPA Nushagak Cannery, 1919–1924, CRPA-Astor; and Office of Labor Commissioner, Territory of Alaska, "Schedules for Compiling Statistics of Trades and Industries," CRPA Nushagak Cannery, 1920–1925, ibid.

53. Daniel L. Boxberger, *To Fish in Common: The Ethnohistory of Lummi Indian Salmon Fishing* (Lincoln, Neb., 1989), 62–63, 81–87, 183–187.

54. *Pacific Fisherman*, August 1931, 37–40, and September 1931, 38–42.

55. Arthur L. Duncan to R.D. Hume, August 12, 1896, Letterpress vol. 86, R. D. Hume Papers, University of Oregon, Eugene; Gordon B. Dodds, *The Salmon King of Oregon: R. D. Hume and the Pacific Fisheries* (Chapel Hill, N.C., 1959), 26–30.

56. *Tacoma Ledger*, August 21, 1905.

57. *South Bend Pilot*, August 20, 1915.

58. *Hoquiam News*, July 22, 1911.

59. Collins, "Fisheries of the Pacific Coast, 1888–1889," 24, 159, 173, 176–177, 181, 185–186, 189–192, 194–198, 233, 239, 242, 260; Cobb, *Salmon Fisheries of the Pacific Coast* (1911), 75, 80, 90, 93, 98, 112.

60. John N. Cobb, *Pacific Salmon Fisheries*, Appendix I to the Report of the U.S. Commissioner of Fisheries for 1921, U.S. Bureau of Fisheries, Document 902 (Washington, D.C., 1921), 152–162.

61. Kazuo Ito, *Issei: A History of Japanese Immigrants in North America*, trans. Shinchiro Nakamura and Jean S. Gerard (Seattle, 1973), 353; Yuji Ichioka, *The Issei: The World of the First Generation Japanese Immigrants, 1885–1924* (New York, 1988), 3–4, 7–46; Alan Takeo Moriyama, *Imin-*

gaisha: Japanese Emigration Companies and Hawaii, 1894–1908 (Honolulu, 1985), 1–6; Donald T. Hata, Jr., *"Undesirables": Early Immigrants and the Anti-Japanese Movement in San Francisco, 1892–1893* (New York, 1979), 14–18, 43–61; Sucheng Chan, *Asian Americans: An Interpretive History* (Boston, 1991), 3–4.

62. Roger Daniels, *Asian America: Chinese and Japanese in the United States since 1850* (Seattle, 1988), 104, 110, 153.

63. Ibid., 115–116. Daniels gives only the figures for King County, Washington, and San Francisco County, California.

64. Alan Moriyama, "The Causes of Emigration: The Background of Japanese Emigration to Hawaii, 1885–1894," in *Labor Immigration under Capitalism: Asian Workers in the United States before World War II*, ed. Lucie Cheng and Edna Bonacich (Berkeley and Los Angeles, 1984), 250; Mikiso Hane, *Peasants, Rebels, and Outcastes: The Underside of Modern Japan* (New York, 1982), 17.

65. Moriyama, "Causes of Emigration," 252, 254–263; idem, *Imingaisha*, xvii.

66. Ito, *Issei*, 353; Collins, "Fisheries of the Pacific Coast, of the United States, 1888–1889," 268; F. L. Lord to H. Bell-Irving, January 13, 1896, Letterpress 1895–1899, FIPC Records; George A. Rounsefell and George B. Kelz, "The Salmon and Salmon Fisheries of Swiftsure Bank, Puget Sound and the Fraser River," U.S. Bureau of Fisheries, *Bulletin* 27 (Washington, D.C., 1938), 705–706.

67. Moser, "Report of the *Albatross*, 1900 and 1901," 262–264, and "Report of the *Albatross*, 1898," 321; U.S. Bureau of the Census, Manuscript Schedules of the Population Census, Alaska Territory, 1900 (hereafter cited as Population Census, [place], [year]).

68. Moser, "Report of the *Albatross*, 1900 and 1901," 262–264.

69. Population Census, Whatcom and Skagit counties, Wash., 1900.

70. Yuzo Murayama, "The Economic History of Japanese Immigration to the Pacific Northwest: 1890–1920," Ph.D. dissertation, University of Washington, 1982, 118–122; Calvin F. Schmid, *Social Trends in Seattle* (Seattle, 1944), 2, 131; Yamato Ichihashi, *Japanese in the United States* (Stanford, Calif., 1932), 101.

71. *San Francisco Examiner,* April 28, 1903; Roppel, *Salmon from Kodiak,* 29; *Honolulu Bulletin*, February 25, 1913; *Sacramento Union*, February 16, 1913; *San Francisco Call*, February 17, 1913.

72. *Seattle Times*, July 29, 1905.

73. Chew Chew to Samuel Elmore, January 4, 1902, CRPA-Astor; Chew Chew to CRPA, March 17 and 19, 1902, ibid.; CRPA to Chew Chew, March 20, 1902, ibid.

74. CRPA to N. H. Webber, July 31, 1902, CRPA-Astor.

75. CRPA to H. W. Kutchin, December 8, 1903, CRPA-Astor; John Carlson to CRPA, April 16, 1904, ibid.; Wootten to CRPA, July 7, 1904, ibid.; Ole Solomonsen to CRPA, July 9, 1904, ibid.; CRPA to Lam On, July

13, 1908, ibid.; Carl A. Sutter to Purser, *State of Washington* Str., November 1901, 1900–1902 Letterpress, FIPC Records; Notation on 1902 crew, 1902–1904 Letterpress, 252, ibid.; Notation on 1903 crew, 623, ibid.; Chinese Workers Accounts, 1901, Seufert Brothers Cannery Records, Oregon Historical Society, Portland; *San Francisco Chronicle*, December 25, 1906.

76. Carl A. Sutter to Hop Chong Lung Kee and Company, April 7, 1904, FIPC; Chinese Workers Accounts, 1901, Seufert Brothers Cannery Records; Washington State Bureau of Labor Statistics, "Special Report on the Salmon Canning Industry in the State of Washington and the Employment of Oriental Labor," *Tenth Biennial Report, 1915–1916* (Olympia, 1916), 107, 111 (hereafter cited as WSBLS, "Special Report").

77. CRPA to Chew Chew, July 31, 1902, CRPA-Astor; CRPA to Chew Mock, February 10 and 15, 1906, ibid.; and Chew Mock to CRPA, February 13, 1906, April 2 and 15, 1908, ibid.

78. William Barry to CRPA, July 1, 1902, CRPA-Astor.

79. CRPA to Lam On, May 25, 1909, CRPA-Astor.

80. *South Bend Pilot*, September 8, 1911.

81. Chinese Workers Accounts, 1901, Seufert Brothers Cannery Records; Frank Miyamoto, interview by Chris Friday, February 19, 1988, Seattle.

82. Oregon, Bureau of Labor Statistics and Factory Work, *Fifth Biennial Report, 1910–1912* (Salem, 1913), 83; idem, *Sixth Biennial Report, 1912–1914* (Salem, 1915), 64; idem, *Seventh Biennial Report, 1916–1918* (Salem, 1919), 71.

83. *Astoria Budget*, December 31, 1912.

84. *Immigrants in Industries*, 393–394, 406.

85. Wedderburn Trading Company to Macleay Estate Company, July 2, 1921, box 12, Macleay Estate Company Papers, University of Oregon, Eugene.

86. Cobb, *Salmon Fisheries of the Pacific Coast* (1911), 68, 75, 83, 93, 98.

87. Ibid., 68, 75, 83.

88. Frank Davey, *Report of the Japanese Situation in Oregon, August 1920* (Salem, 1920), 3–4; Wong, Lum, and Lamie interview; Nancy Bates and Charles Rogers, "Point Adams Packing Company (1920–1982)," *Cumtux* 7, no. 3 (1987): 8–13.

89. Davey, *Japanese Situation in Oregon*, 3–4.

90. Ibid.

91. Cobb, *Salmon Fisheries of the Pacific Coast* (1911), 93, 98.

92. Ibid., 115; U.S. Bureau of Fisheries, *Alaska Fishery and Fur-Seal Industries* (Washington, D.C., 1916–1919), passim.

93. Chinese Contract Account Sheet for FIPC cannery at Ketchikan, Alaska, October 22, 1915, FIPC Records.

94. Cobb, *Salmon Fisheries of the Pacific Coast* (1911), 83, 115; *Immigrants in Industries*, 391; *Pacific Fisherman*, April 1909, 12–13.

95. Schmid, *Social Trends in Seattle*, 131–137; S. Frank Miyamoto, *Social Solidarity among the Japanese in Seattle* (Seattle, 1984), 9–15; Keith Warriner,

"Regionalism, Dependence, and the B.C. Fisheries: Historical Development and Recent Trends," in Marchak, Guppy, and McMullan, *Uncommon Property*, 335.

96. Cobb, *Salmon Fisheries of the Pacific Coast* (1911), 75.

97. Ibid.

98. Ibid.

99. *Bellingham Herald*, August 8, 1905; *Seattle Post-Intelligencer*, August 8 and 9, 1905; *Vancouver World*, August 8, 1905.

100. *Portland Oregonian*, September 12, 1907; Paul Jacobs and Saul Landau, *To Serve the Devil*, vol. 2, *Colonials and Sojourners: A Documentary Analysis of America's Racial History and Why It Has Been Kept Hidden* (New York, 1971), 174–182; *Bellingham Herald*, July 21, 1915; *Seattle Post-Intelligencer*, July 22, 1915; WSBLS, "Special Report," 107–116.

101. *Bellingham American*, August 19, 1908; *Seattle Post-Intelligencer*, August 19, 1908; *Seattle Times*, December 3, 1913.

102. *San Francisco Bulletin*, July 29, 1915; *San Francisco Chronicle*, July 30, 1915; *Bellingham Herald*, July 2, 1915; *Seattle Post-Intelligencer*, August 25, 1915; WSBLS, "Special Report," 107–116.

103. Miyamoto, *Social Solidarity*, 16–22; James Omura, interview by Chris Friday, March 25, 1988, Pullman, Wash.

104. Miyamoto, *Social Solidarity*, 30–32; Harry H. L. Kitano and Roger Daniels, *Asian Americans: Emerging Minorities* (Englewood Cliffs, N.J., 1988), 58–59; *San Francisco Chronicle*, June 28, 1903; *Portland Telegram*, August 8, 1907; *Vancouver World*, August 11, 1906; *Pacific Fisherman Annual*, 1904, 82, and 1905, 91; *Pacific Fisherman Yearbook*, 1925, 98; 1927, 113; 1930, 27, 90; *Pacific Fisherman*, November 1922, 15.

105. U.S. Bureau of Fisheries, *Alaska Fishery and Fur-Seal Industries* (Washington, D.C., 1917–1930), passim.

106. Ibid.

107. *San Francisco Call*, September 21, 1918; *San Francisco Mefistofeles*, March 23 and 30, 1918; Shirley A. Baker, Warden, Bureau of Fisheries, "Investigation Regarding Treatment of Mexican Laborers by Alaska Fisheries Companies in 1917," n.d., file 4, Mexican Employment in Alaska Canneries, 1917–1931, box 2, U.S. Fish and Wildlife Service, Record Group 22, Historical Library, Alaska State Library, Juneau, Alaska.

108. California, Bureau of Labor Statistics, *Fifteenth Biennial Report, 1911–1912* (Sacramento, 1912), 51–61; idem, *Sixteenth Biennial Report, 1913–1914* (Sacramento, 1914), 17–18; idem, *Eighteenth Biennial Report, 1917–1918* (Sacramento, 1918), 32–38; idem, *Nineteenth Biennial Report, 1919–1920* (Sacramento, 1920), 38–41; Oregon, Bureau of Labor Statistics and Inspector of Factories and Workshops, *Eleventh Biennial Report and Industrial Directory, 1922–1924* (Salem, 1924), 11–13; idem, *Twelfth Biennial Report, 1924–1926* (Salem, 1926), 19; Washington, Bureau of Labor, *Eleventh Biennial Report, 1917–1918* (Olympia, 1918), 55–63; *Portland Telegram*, November 25, 1901; *San Francisco Chronicle*, November 26, 1901, October 24,

1907, April 25, 1923; *Seattle Times,* June 21, 1910; *San Francisco Examiner,* April 28, 1903; *Honolulu Bulletin,* February 25, 1913; *Sacramento Union,* February 16, 1913; *San Francisco Call,* February 17, 1913; *Phoenix Republican,* April 16 and 17, 1918; *San Francisco Daily News,* June 21, 1923; Roppel, *Salmon from Kodiak,* 29.

109. U.S. Bureau of Fisheries, *Alaska Fishery and Fur-Seal Industries* (Washington, D.C., 1929–1930), passim.

110. Ibid. (1930–1935).

111. Ibid. (1930–1939).

112. Ibid. (1917–1930).

113. Population Census, Territory of Alaska, 1910; Linda Pomerantz, "The Background of Korean Immigration," in Cheng and Bonacich, *Labor Immigration,* 305–306.

114. Population Census, Territory of Alaska, 1910.

Chapter 5

1. *San Francisco Call,* September 21, 1918; *San Francisco Mefistofeles,* March 23 and 30, 1918; Shirley A. Baker, Warden, Bureau of Fisheries, "Investigation Regarding Treatment of Mexican Laborers by Alaska Fisheries Companies in 1917," n.d., folder 4, Mexican Employment in Alaska Canneries, 1917–1931, box 2, U.S. Fish and Wildlife Service, Record Group 22, Historical Library, Alaska State Library, Juneau.

2. Evelyn Nakano Glenn, *Issei, Nisei, War Bride: Three Generations of Japanese American Women in Domestic Service* (Philadelphia, 1986), 22–23, 68; Roger Daniels, *Asian America: Chinese and Japanese in the United States since 1850* (Seattle, 1988), 16–17, 126–127.

3. Kazuo Ito, *Issei: A History of Japanese Immigrants in North America,* trans. Shinchiro Nakamura and Jean S. Gerard (Seattle, 1973), 353; Tsureyoshi Kikutake to Fidalgo Island Packing Company (hereafter cited as FIPC), September 21, 1914, Fidalgo Island Packing Company Records, Anacortes Museum of History and Art, Anacortes, Wash. (hereafter cited as FIPC Records).

4. *San Francisco Chronicle,* October 24, 1902; *Reports of the Immigration Commission: Immigrants in Industry,* vol. 25, pt. 25, *Japanese and Other Immigrant Races in the Pacific Coast and Mountain States,* vol. 3, Senate Document 633 (Washington, D.C., 1911), 392, 394, 406 (hereafter cited as *Immigrants in Industry*); California, Bureau of Labor Statistics, *Fifteenth Biennial Report, 1911–1912* (Sacramento, 1913), 51–52; Willard G. Jue and Silas G. Jue, "Goon Dip: Entrepreneur, Diplomat, and Community Leader," *Annals of the Chinese Historical Society of the Pacific Northwest,* 1984, 47.

5. H. Yamashito and M. Handa, Subcontractual Agreement with Chong Lock, June 9, 1905, courtesy of Steven G. Doi, Asian American Studies Program, San Jose State University, San Jose, Calif.

6. Ibid.; Japanese Metropolitan Contract and Employment Company, Subcontractual Agreement with Jim Sing, Jan. 25, 1905, courtesy of Steven G. Doi, Asian American Studies Program, San Jose State University, San Jose, Calif.

7. Japanese Labor Association to Columbia River Packers Association (hereafter cited as CRPA), March 10, 1905, Columbia River Packers Association Records, Astor Public Library, Astoria, Ore. (hereafter cited as CRPA-Astor); *San Francisco Chronicle*, July 25, 1905.

8. Hop Yick, Sing Kee and Co., Contract with the Union Fishermen's Cooperative Packing Company, Astoria, Ore., January 13, 1912, Columbia River Maritme Museum, Astoria, Ore.; *Immigrants in Industry*, 392, 394, 406; California, Bureau of Labor Statistics, *Fifteenth Biennial Report, 1911–1912*, 51–52; Yamashito and Handa, Subcontractual Agreement with Chong Long, June 9, 1905, courtesy of Steven Doi.

9. Ito, *Issei*, 364, 374; *San Francisco Chronicle*, April 15, 1910, and April 12, 1911; *San Francisco News*, April 14, 1910; *San Francisco Post*, April 14, 1910.

10. Ito, *Issei*, 371.

11. *Seattle Post-Intelligencer*, January 2, 1914.

12. *San Francisco Chronicle*, April 12, 1911.

13. Ito, *Issei*, 374.

14. *Anacortes American*, August 12, 1915.

15. Patricia Roppel, *Salmon from Kodiak: An History of the Salmon Fishery of Kodiak Island*, Alaska Historical Commission Studies in History 216 (Anchorage, 1986), 203; Ito, *Issei*, 374.

16. Ito, *Issei*, 371, 376, 377; Nakane Chie, *Japanese Society* (Berkeley and Los Angeles, 1970), 63–80; Mikiso Hane, *Peasants, Rebels, and Outcastes: The Underside of Modern Japan* (New York, 1982), 64–65; F. G. Notehelfer, "Between Tradition and Modernity: Labor and the Ashio Copper Mine," *Monumenta Nipponica* 39, no. 1 (1984): 13–14.

17. Ito, *Issei*, 377.

18. Ibid., 377–378.

19. *San Francisco Chronicle*, April 18, 1910; *San Francisco Call*, April 17, 1910; *San Francisco News*, April 14, 1910.

20. FIPC and J. T. Kikutake, Agreement, December 29, 1917, FIPC Records; California, Bureau of Labor Statistics, *Fifteenth Report, 1911–1912*, 52; John N. Cobb, *Pacific Salmon Fisheries*, Appendix XIII to the Report of the Commissioner of Fisheries for 1930, Bureau of Fisheries Document 1092 (Washington, D.C., 1930), 500; Chew Mock to CRPA, March 24, 1909, CRPA-Astor.

21. *San Francisco Chronicle*, October 1, 1908, and April 18, 1910; Ito, *Issei*, 376–377.

22. Wing Sing, Long Kee and Co., Japanese Foreman's Store Account with FIPC, Port Graham, Alaska, September 13, 1919, FIPC Records; California, Bureau of Labor Statistics, *Fifteenth Report, 1911–1912*, 52; *San Fran-*

cisco Examiner, March 8, 1914; *San Francisco Commercial News*, March 9, 1914; Ito, *Issei*, 374, 376–377.

23. S. Minami and Kikuzo Uyeminami to Fred Barker, October 12 and November 8, 1921, CRPA-Astor; Ito, *Issei*, 353–354.

24. FIPC Herendeen Bay Cannery 1917 Contract with J. T. Kikutake and Company, December 23, 1916, FIPC Records; ibid., 1918; FIPC Herendeen Bay Cannery 1919 Contract with F. K. Uyeminami, January 22, 1919, ibid.; FIPC Anacortes Cannery 1919 Contract with F. K. Uyeminami, March 21, 1919, ibid.; Washington State, Bureau of Labor Statistics, *Tenth Biennial Report, 1915–1916* (Olympia, 1916), 102; idem, "Special Report on the Salmon Canning Industry in the State of Washington and the Employment of Oriental Labor," *Tenth Biennial Report, 1915–1916* (Olympia, 1916), 111 (hereafter cited as WSBLS, "Special Report"); John N. Cobb, *Pacific Salmon Fisheries*, Appendix I to the Report of the U.S. Commissioner of Fisheries for 1921, Bureau of Fisheries Document 902, 3rd ed. (Washington, D.C., 1921), 154; Ito, *Issei*, 353–354.

25. Edith Robinson, interview by Barbara Heacock, Skagit County Oral History Preservation Project, March 8, 1978, RIII-165, 4–5, Skagit County History Society, LaConner, Wash.

26. CRPA to A. B. General Contractor, November 7, 1921, CRPA-Astor; Seid Gain Back to Arnold O. Johnson, June 14, 1930, FIPC Records.

27. K. Mori, section foreman, N. and M. Lumber Company, interview, Major Document 212, box 1, Survey of Race Relations Documents, William Carlson Smith Documents, University of Oregon, Eugene (hereafter cited as SRR, Smith Documents); Yuzo Murayama, "The Economic History of Japanese Immigration to the Pacific Northwest, 1890–1920," Ph.D. dissertation, University of Washington, 1982.

28. Mori interview, SRR, Smith Documents.

29. Ibid.

30. Daniels, *Asian America*, 133–135.

31. Ito, *Issei*, 356–357.

32. Charles Koe, "Chinese Cannery Workers in Ilwaco," PAC 75–22dm, transcript of interview, October 7 and 8, 1975, Washington State Oral/Aural History Program, 1974–1977, Washington State Archives, Olympia.

33. Ito, *Issei*, 356–357, 371, 373; Frank Miyamoto, interview by Chris Friday, February 19, 1988, Seattle, Wash.; James Omura, interview by Chris Friday, March 25, 1988, Pullman, Wash.

34. Ito, *Issei*, 371.

35. Omura interview; Ito, *Issei*, 359; *Seattle Post-Intelligencer*, June 27, 1903; Cobb, *Pacific Salmon Fisheries* (1930), 502.

36. John M. Liu, "Race, Ethnicity, and the Sugar Plantation System: Asian Labor in Hawaii, 1850 to 1900," in *Labor Immigration under Capitalism: Asian Workers in the United States before World War II*, ed. Lucie Cheng and Edna Bonacich (Berkeley and Los Angeles, 1984), 203.

37. Ito, *Issei*, 359; *Seattle Post-Intelligencer*, June 27, 1903; Cobb, *Pacific Salmon Fisheries* (1930), 502.

38. Robert I. Okazaki, interview by Joe Grant Masaoka, March 28, 1967, transcript 59, box 519, Japanese American Research Project (hereafter cited as JARP), Special Collections, University of California, Los Angeles; Ito, *Issei*, 355, 359–360, 364–365, 371.

39. Miyamoto interview; Omura interview; Ito, *Issei*, 355, 359–360, 361, 364–365, 371.

40. Jack Masson and Donald Guimary, "Asian Labor Contractors in the Alaskan Canned Salmon Industry, 1880–1937," *Labor History* 22, no. 3 (1981): 391.

41. CRPA to Dogg and Lam, August 2, 1921, CRPA-Astor; Choei Sakamoto, pseud. (Chutaro Shimamoto), Case History (hereafter cited as CH) 10, box 54, Charles Kikuchi Papers, Special Collections, UCLA. Many of the case histories conducted by Charles Kikuchi are duplicated in the Japanese Evacuation and Relocation Service, War Relocation Authority Records, held in the Bancroft Library, University of California, Berkeley (hereafter cited as JERS-WRA), but the Kikuchi papers contain much greater depth of information, keep the interviews intact as a whole (rather than in small segments arranged by topic as in the JERS-WRA materials), provide multiple drafts of the case histories, and in many cases reveal the names of his interviewees rather than just pseudonyms. I have used both here, but have found the Kikuchi papers more useful. I have provided pseudonyms and actual names of Kikuchi's interviewees where the information is available.

42. U.S. Bureau of the Census, Manuscript Schedules of the Population Census, Alaska Territory, 1910 (hereafter cited as Population Census, Alaska Territory, 1910).

43. Mori interview, SRR, Smith Documents; Takeo Frank Fujita, form 26, February 8, 1943, War Relocation Authority, "Occupational Inventory of Residents of War Relocation Authority Centers," E 2.445, JERS-WRA; "The Ishiwara Family," Document TL–10, Shibutani Case Histories, R 21.01A, ibid.; "The Morimoto Family," Document TL–21, Shibutani Case Histories, R 21.01D, ibid.

44. Jue and Jue, "Goon Dip," 54–46.

45. Otis W. Freeman, "Hop Industry of the Pacific Coast States," *Economic Geography* 12 (1936): 157–158; Paul H. Landis, "The Hop Industry: A Social and Economic Problem," *Economic Geography* 15 (1939): 91–92.

46. M. C. Holman, "Report of the U.S. Public School at Chignik Alaska . . . , August 31, 1922," CRPA-Astor.

47. The term used was *saibashi*; see Ito, *Issei*, 361. *San Francisco Bulletin*, September 11, 1907.

48. Okazaki interview, JARP.

49. Peter Ogata (pseud.), CH–38, box 48, Kikuchi Papers.

50. Ibid.; Ito, *Issei*, 370–372; Population Census, Alaska Territory, 1910.

51. Glenn, *Issei, Nisei, War Bride*, 31–32, 42–50, 196–200; Population Census, Alaska Territory, 1910; Sun Bin Yim, "The Social Structure of Ko-

rean Communities in California, 1903–1920," in Cheng and Bonacich, *Labor Immigration*, 515–518.

52. John Norris, *Strangers Entertained: A History of the Ethnic Groups of British Columbia* (Vancouver, 1971), 220; Daphne Marlatt, ed., *Steveston Recollected: A Japanese-Canadian History* (Vancouver, 1975), 9.

53. Patricia Marchak, "Organization of Divided Fishers," in *Uncommon Property: The Fishing and Fish Processing Industries in British Columbia*, ed. Patricia Marchak, Neil Guppy, and John McMullan (Toronto, 1987), 228; Alicja Muszynski, "The Organization of Women and Ethnic Minorities in a Resource Industry: A Case Study of the Unionization of Shoreworkers in the B.C. Fishing Industry, 1937–1949," *Journal of Canadian Studies* 19 (Spring 1984): 89–107.

54. Marchak, "Divided Fishers," 228.

55. Ibid., 228–229.

56. Ibid.; George North, *A Ripple, a Wave: The Story of Union Organization in the B.C. Fishing Industry*, ed. Harold Griffin (Vancouver, 1974), 7.

57. Marchak, "Divided Fishers," 229; North, *A Ripple, a Wave*, 11.

58. Charles H. Young and Helen R.Y. Reid, *The Japanese Canadians*, ed. H. A. Innis (Toronto, 1938), 45.

59. Marlatt, *Steveston Recollected*, 21.

60. Kanshi Stanley Yamashita, "Terminal Island: Ethnography of an Ethnic community: Its Dissolution and Reorganization to a Non-Spatial Community," Ph.D. dissertation, University of California, Irvine, 1985.

61. Marlatt, *Steveston Recollected*, 23.

62. Ibid.

63. Ibid.; Paula J. Johnson, "'Sloppy Work for Women': Shucking Oysters on the Patuxent," in *Working the Water: The Commercial Fisheries of Maryland's Patuxent River*, ed. Paula J. Johnson (Charlottesville, Va., 1988), 35–51.

64. Louise Lamphere, "Bringing the Family to Work: Women's Culture on the Shop Floor," *Feminist Studies* 11 (1985): 518–540; Patricia Zavella, *Women's Work and Chicano Families: Cannery Workers of the Santa Clara Valley* (Ithaca, N.Y., 1987); Vicki L. Ruiz, *Cannery Women, Cannery Lives: Mexican Women, Unionization, and the California Food Processing Industry, 1930–1950* (Albuquerque, 1987).

65. Marlatt, *Steveston Recollected*, 23.

66. Fred Barker to S. C. Turner, Elmore Cannery, Eureka Cannery, Ellsworth Cannery, Cold Storage Plant, March 15, 1919, CRPA-Astor; Glenn, *Issei, Nisei, War Bride*, 210–211; Takie Sugiyama Lebra, *Japanese Patterns of Behavior* (Honolulu, 1976), 141–142; Dianne Newell, "The Rationality of Mechanization in the Pacific Salmon-Canning Industry before the Second World War," *Business History Review* 62 (Winter 1988): 626–655.

67. Marlatt, *Steveston Recollected*, 23.

68. Ibid.

69. Dogg and Lam accounts, Elmore, Eagle Cliff, Ellsworth, and Eureka canneries, 1926, box 39, Columbia River Packers Association Record, Ore-

gon Historical Society, Portland (hereafter cited as Dogg and Lam accounts, 1926, CRPA-OHS). Antialien fishing laws and accustomed practices prevented the employment of many Japanese salmon fishermen in Oregon and Washington.

70. Dogg and Lam accounts, 1926, CRPA-OHS.

71. Elvin Wong, John Lum, A. J. Lamie, interview by Chris Friday, February 3, 1988, Astoria, Ore. For interviews of European American cannery working women, see the Skagit County Oral History Preservation Project, Skagit County Historical Society, Laconner, Wash.

72. Wong, Lum, and Lamie interview. Also see Zavella, *Women's Work and Chicano Families*, 112–120.

73. Timothy J. Lukes and Gary Y. Okihiro, *Japanese Legacy: Farming and Community Life in California's Santa Clara Valley* (Cupertino, Calif., 1985); S. Frank Miyamoto, *Social Solidarity among the Japanese in Seattle* (Seattle, 1984), xii.

74. "Interview with Mr. Hideo Robert Tashima," Seattle, 1924, reel 2, Survey of Race Relations Microfilm, Special Collections, University of California, Los Angeles; Omura interview; Miyamoto interview; George Taki, interview by Chris Friday, January 10 and 11, 1989, Los Angeles, Calif.; *Japanese American Courier*, April 7, 1928, April 26, July 12 and 19, August 16, 1930, and October 15, 1938; Jere Takahashi, "Japanese American Responses to Race Relations: The Formation of Nisei Perspectives," *Amerasia* 9, no. 1 (1982): 29–57; George Yani(gawa) (pseud.) [George Taki(gawa)], CH 17, box 47, Kikuchi Papers; Kikuchi, "Japanese American Youth," Kikuchi Papers. I draw the term "Boys of Summer" from a stinging criticism of Nisei schoolboys who did not take the work seriously from James Omura. Omura is no less critical of prounion Nisei who apparently excluded him from cannery work, an important source of income for him. Also see in the *Japanese American Courier* the series "Notes from Alaska," July 13, 20, and 27, and August 10, 17, and 24, 1935, and Bill Hosokawa, "Travelogue," June 27, July 4, 11, 18, and 25, August 1, 8, 22, and 29, and September 5, 1936, for additional information on Nisei perspectives on Alaska cannery work.

75. Frank Miyamoto interview; Anon., CH 63, carton 1, JERS-WRA, Bancroft Library; Kawasaki, CH 11, Kikuchi Papers.

76. *Japanese American Courier*, June 2, 1928, and January 11, 1930; Miyamoto interview; Shigeo Kawasaki (pseud.), CH 11, box 47, Kikuchi Papers; Yani(gawa) [Taki(gawa)], CH 17, ibid.; Okazaki interview, JARP.

77. Miyamoto interview; Omura interview; Yani(gawa) [Taki(gawa)], CH 17, Kikuchi Papers; Charles Kikuchi, "The Japanese American Youth in San Francisco: The Background, Characteristics and Problems" (n.p., 1941), box 46, Kikuchi Papers; Daniels, *Asian America*, 176. The overlapping of the contract system with family, friendship, and other networks reveals that the two were not mutually exclusive as implied in John Bodnar, Roger Simon, and Michael P. Weber, *Lives of Their Own: Blacks, Italians, and Poles in Pittsburgh, 1900–1960* (Urbana, Ill., 1982), 57, 83n.3.

78. *Japanese American Courier*, May 12, 1928; Takahashi, "Nisei Perspectives," 29–57.

79. Yani(gawa) [Taki(gawa)], CH 17, box 47, Kikuchi Papers.

80. Kawasaki, CH 11, Kikuchi Papers; Anon., Case History 63, carton 1, JERS-WRA.

81. Hiromasa Minami (pseud.) [Daiki Miyagawa], CH 21, box 47, Kikuchi Papers.

82. Albert Ikeda, CH 34, carton 1, JERS-WRA.

83. Sagi (pseud.) [George Akahoshi], CH 58, carton 1, JERS-WRA.

84. *UCAPAWA News*, July 1939, 4; Hyun-chan Kim and Cynthia Meija, comps. and eds., *The Filipinos in America, 1898–1974: A Chronology and Fact Book* (New York, 1976), 12; L. A. Crawford to J. H. Connors, April 24, 1935, Appendix VIII, in Casaday, "Labor Unrest"; Yani(gawa) [Taki(gawa)], CH–17, Kikuchi Papers.

85. Casaday, "Labor Unrest," 82.

86. Shigeo Kawasaki (pseud.), CH 11, box 47, Kikuchi Papers; Omura interview; Daisho D. (Dyke) Miyagawa, interview by Chris Friday, September 10, 1987, and August 18, 1988, Los Angeles, Calif.; Miyamoto interview.

87. Miyagawa interviews; Taki interview; Daisho ("Dyke") Miyagawa to ("Big") Bill Hosokawa, February 25, 1968, v.f. 611, University of Washington Libraries Manuscript Collection, Seattle; Takahashi, "Nisei Perspectives," 29–57.

Chapter 6

1. Ponce Torres interview, June 24, 1975, 3, and August 25, 1975, 1, Demonstration Project for Asian Americans, Seattle (hereafter cited as DPAA). The DPAA conducted all the Filipino interviews for the Washington State Oral/Aural History Program, 1974–1977, Washington State Archives, Olympia (hereafter cited as WSOAHP) and has continued to interview Filipinos about their experiences. Not all of the original DPAA interviews are in the WSOAHP collection.

2. Ibid., June 24, 1975, 14, and August 25, 1975, 5–6.

3. Ibid., August 25, 1975, 8.

4. Ron Takaki, *Strangers from a Different Shore: A History of Asian Americans* (Boston, 1989), 152–154, 321–323, notes that competition with other ethnic groups coupled with the late arrival of Filipinos and the failure of any opportunities in the United States to materialize pushed Filipinos toward ethnic-based unionism. Jack K. Masson and Donald L. Guimary, "Filipinos and Unionization of the Alaskan Canned-Salmon Industry," *Amerasia* 8, no. 1 (1981): 26, focus on unmet expectations, while Edward D. Beechert, *Working in Hawaii: A Labor History* (Honolulu, 1985), 199–232, argues that ethnic competition and relatively late arrival in Hawaii pointed Filipinos toward unionization, but he adds that it was strengthened by U.S. government

involvement in labor relations in the Philippines, New Deal intervention in Hawaii, and the competition between the organizations associated with the American Federation of Labor and those tied to what became the Congress of Industrial Organizations.

5. Fred Cordova, *Filipinos: Forgotten Americans* (Dubuque, Iowa, 1983), 14–17.

6. Ibid., 14; Barbara M. Posadas and Roland L. Guyotte, "Unintentional Immigrants: Chicago's Filipino Foreign Students Become Settlers, 1900–1941," *Journal of American Ethnic History* 9, no. 2 (1990): 26.

7. Sucheng Chan, *Asian Americans: An Interpretive History* (Boston, 1991), 55–56.

8. California, Department of Industrial Relations, *Facts about Filipino Immigration into California* (San Francisco, 1930), 11–13, 23–24 (hereafter cited as CDIR, *Filipino Immigration*).

9. Cordova, *Filipinos*, 17–18.

10. Ramon M. Tancioco, interviewed by Larry Skoog, December 28, 1970, Oregon Historical Society (hereafter cited as OHS), Portland; Ponce M. Torres interview, FIL-KNG 75-14tc, 5, WSOAHP; Mensalvas interview, FIL-KNG 75-1ck, ibid., 9.

11. CDIR, *Filipino Immigration*, 11–13, 23–24; and Miriam Sharma, "The Philippines: A Case of Migration to Hawaii, 1906 to 1946," in *Labor Immigration under Capitalism: Asian Workers in the United States before World War II*, ed. Lucie Cheng and Edna Bonacich (Berkeley and Los Angeles, 1984), 337–358.

12. CDIR, *Filipino Immigration*, 21; Bruno Lasker, *Filipino Immigration to Continental United States and Hawaii* (Chicago, 1931), 53, 356.

13. Lauren W. Casaday, "Labor Unrest and the Labor Movement in the Salmon Industry of the Pacific Northwest," Ph.D. dissertation, University of California, Berkeley, 1938, 82; U.S. Bureau of Fisheries, *Alaska Fishery and Fur-Seal Industries, 1921* (Washington, D.C., 1921), 37.

14. *Juneau Gateway*, June 29, 1925; Cordova, *Filipinos*, 61; Peter Bacho, "Alaskeros: A Documentary Exhibit on Pioneer Filipino Cannery Workers," Seattle, n.d., 1.

15. U.S. Bureau of Fisheries, *Alaska Fishery and Fur-Seal Industries, 1928* (Washington, D.C., 1928), 273.

16. Eddie F. Acena interview, Accession Number FIL-KNG 75-18bf, WSOAHP, 2–3; Torres interview, FIL-KNG 75-14tc, ibid., 5. Also see Rudy C. Romero interview, FIL-KNG 75-4tc, ibid., 3–4; Anacleto Corpuz interview, FIL-KNG 75-16tc, ibid., 5; Ben Rinonos interview, FIL-KNG 75-3tc, ibid., 3, 6; Mensalvas interview, ibid., 9; Tancioco interview, OHS; Lasker, *Filipino Immigration*, 5–6, 31, 87–89, 376–382, 392; idem, "In the Alaska Fish Canneries," *Mid-Pacific* 14, no. 2 (1932): 337–338; Sue Ellen Liljeblad, "The Filipinos and the Alaska Salmon Industry," *Alaska in Perspective* 1, no. 2 (1978): 1–2.

17. Toribio M. Martin, Sr., interview, FIL-KNG 76-44dc, WSOAHP, 12.

18. Manuel Buaken, *I Have Lived with the American People* (Caldwell, Idaho, 1948), 193–205, 212–214; Lasker, *Filipino Immigration*, 41–76; "Grays Harbor Commercial Company, Cosmopolis, Wash.," Major Document 201, box 1, Survey of Race Relations Documents, William Carlson Smith Documents (hereafter cited as SRR, Smith Documents), University of Oregon, Eugene; Virgil S. Dunyungan and Cornelio B. Mislang to Pedro Guevara and Camillio Osias, n.d., file 3, box 8, Cannery Workers and Farm Laborers Union, Local 7 Records, University of Washington, Seattle (hereafter cited as CWFLU Records); Honorato R. Rapada interview, FIL-KNG 75-11tc, WSOAHP, 10; Trinidad A. Rojo interview, FIL-KNG 75-17ck, ibid., 9, 14; and Tancioco interview, OHS.

19. Toribio P. Madayag interview, FIL-KNG, 75-22tc, WSOAHP, 10.

20. John Castillo interview, FIL-KNG 75-15jr, WSOAHP, 3; Rinonos interview, ibid., 19; Antonio Rodrigo interview, FIL-KNG 76-53dc, ibid., 13; Romero interview, ibid., 5; Sylvestre A. Tangalan interview, FIL-KNG 75-28ck, ibid., 5–6.

21. Zacarias M. Manangan interview, FIL-KNG 75-30ck, WSOAHP, 20; Castillo interview, ibid., 11–12.

22. Ibid.

23. Frank Miyamoto, interview by Chris Friday, February 19, 1988, Seattle.

24. Fidalgo Island Packing Company (hereafter cited as FIPC) to Seid G. Back, February 5, 1931, Fidalgo Island Packing Company Records, Anacortes Museum of History and Art, Anacortes, Wash. (hereafter cited as FIPC Records); Seid G. Back to FIPC, March 4, 1931, ibid.

25. Acena interview, WSOAHP, 11, 13, and 15.

26. Torres interview, WSOAHP, 5, 7–8; Romero and Gloria Alin interview, FIL-KNG 76-46dc, ibid., 1; Castillo interview, ibid., 14; Felix A. Narte interview, FIL-KNG 75-8tc, ibid., 9.

27. Casaday, "Labor Unrest," 164–190; and George Chu, "Chinatowns in the Delta: The Chinese in the Sacramento-San Joaquin Delta, 1870–1960," *California Historical Quarterly* 49, no. 1 (1970), 21–37.

28. Bibliana Castillano interview, FIL-KNG 75-19fc, WSOAHP, 14–19, 23.

29. John P. Mendoza, FIL-KNG 76-42dc, WSOAHP, 18.

30. Teodolo A. Ranjo interview, FIL-KNG 76-41cm, WSOAHP, 47.

31. Ibid.; Tancioco interview, OHS.

32. Lee P. Root to FIPC, October 17, 1931, FIPC Records; emphasis added.

33. Ibid.

34. Mariano E. Dumo to Carl A. Sutter, January 18, 1932, FIPC Records.

35. Sutter to Dumo, January 19, 1932, FIPC Records; and FIPC to William B. Magee, January 20, 1933, ibid.

36. FIPC to Archie Sheils, Jan. 16, 1932, FIPC Records.

37. Tangalan interview, WSOAHP, 10.

38. Narte interview, WSOAHP, 8; Seid G. Back to FIPC, April 30, May 31, June 14, 1930, May 26, 1931, May 20, 1933, FIPC Records; K. Mori, section foreman, N. and M. Lumber Company, interview, Major Document 212, box 1, SRR, Smith Documents; Oscar Evangelista and Susan Evangelista, "Continuity and Change among the Second-Generation Filipino-Americans in Seattle, Washington," *Philippine Historical Association Historical Bulletin* 26, no. 1 (1982): 173.

39. Alin interview, WSOAHP, 10.

40. Ibid.

41. Torres interview, WSOAHP, 6–8.

42. Acena interview, WSOAHP, 3.

43. Mike Castillano interview, FIL-KNG 75-23jr, WSOAHP, 8.

44. Martin interview, WSOAHP, 16; Liljeblad, "Filipinos and the Alaska Salmon Industry," 3.

45. Castillo interview, WSOAHP, 14.

46. Narte interview, WSOAHP, 9; National Canners Association, "Sanitary Survey of Salmon Canneries," Columbia River Packers Association (hereafter cited as CRPA), Chignik, Alaska, Cannery, August 12, 1919, Columbia River Packers Association, Astor Public Library, Astoria, Ore. (hereafter cited as CRPA-Astor); Territory of Alaska, Office of the Labor Commissioner, "Schedules for Compiling Statistics of Trades and Industries, 1919," CRPA, Chignik, Alaska, Cannery, 1919, ibid.

47. Romero interview, WSOAHP, 6; Narte interview, ibid., 10.

48. Acena interview, WSOAHP, 13; Alin interview, ibid., 12; "Interview with Mr. Daniel Begonia," Combined Asian American Resource Project, Asian American Oral History Composite, San Francisco, Calif., 1977, Bancroft Library, University of California, Berkeley; Cordova, *Filipinos*, 63.

49. Cordova, *Filipinos*, 69; Executive Board Meeting, February 23, 1940, file 11, box 1, CWFLU Records.

50. Miyamoto interview; James Omura, interview by Chris Friday, March 25, 1988, Pullman, Wash.

51. Rinonos interview, WSOAHP, 23; Jose Acena interview, ibid., 17; Martin interview, ibid., 7.

52. Alin interview, WSOAHP, 1, 4.

53. Del Fierro interview, WSOAHP, 4–5.

54. Martin interview, WSOAHP, 7; Jose Acena interview, ibid., 15.

55. *UCAPAWA News*, July 1939, 4; Hyun-chan Kim and Cynthia Meija, comps. and eds., *The Filipinos in America, 1898–1974: A Chronology and Fact Book* (New York, 1976), 12.

56. Torres interview, WSOAHP, 5; Mensalvas interview, ibid., 3; Madayag interview, ibid., 10.

57. Dunyungan and Mislang to Pedro and Osias, n.d., file 3, box 8, CWFLU Records.

58. Tancioco interview, OHS.

59. Torres interview, WSOAHP, 10.

60. The estimate is rough because of the lack of quantifiable data. The computations are based on Cordova, *Filipinos*, 123–130, and CDIR, *Filipino Immigration*, 17.

61. Torres interview, WSOAHP, 6–7; Kim and Meija, *Filipinos in America*, 13.

62. *Agricultural Worker*, December 20, 1933, February 20, 1934, and April 10, 1934; Kim and Meija, *Filipinos in America*, 13–15; Labor Research Association, *Labor Fact Book II* (New York, 1934), 163–164; Patricia Zavella, *Women's Work and Chicano Families: Cannery Workers of the Santa Clara Valley* (Ithaca, N.Y., 1987), 41–42; Vicki L. Ruiz, *Cannery Women, Cannery Lives: Mexican Women, Unionization, and the California Food Processing Industry, 1930–1950* (Albuquerque, 1987), 49–51.

63. Kim and Meija, *Filipinos in America*, 13–15.

64. Torres interview, WSOAHP, 9–10.

65. Ibid.

66. Bacho, "Alaskeros," 1.

67. Torres interview, WSOAHP, 12; Castillo interview, ibid., 16; Minutes, Special Meeting of the Filipino Labor Union, June, 10, 1933, file 1, box 1, CWFLU Records; Cannery Workers and Farm Laborers Union, *Annual Bulletin* 1, no. 1 (1936), 2; Trinidad Rojo, "Highlights in the History of the CWFLU," n.d. (1940?), CWFLU 7, UCAPAWA File, Institute of Industrial Relations Library, University of California, Berkeley; Gerald Gold, "The Development of Local Number 7 of the Food, Tobacco, Agricultural and Allied Workers of America–C.I.O.," Master's thesis, University of Washington, Seattle, 1949, 41–42; Evangelista and Evangelista, "Continuity and Change," 166.

68. On CAWIU activities and influences, see Cletus E. Daniel, *Bitter Harvest: A History of California Farmworkers, 1870–1941* (Ithaca, N.Y., 1981), 133–144; Bruce Nelson, *Workers on the Waterfront: Seamen, Longshoremen, and Unionism in the 1930s* (Urbana, Ill., 1988), 109.

69. Revised Constitution, CWFLU, AFL 18257, June 19, 1933, file 1, box 7, CWFLU Records.

70. Ranjo interview, WSOAHP, 24, 30–32, 34, 38, 42; Dionicio J. Cristobal interview, FIL-KNG 76-43cma, ibid., 14; Mensalvas interview, ibid., 25; Emiliano A. Francisco interview, FIL-KNG 75-20ck, ibid., 13–14; Lorenzo U. Pimentel interview, FIL-KNG 75-34cm, ibid., 8; Angel Pilar, and Pedro Quintero interview, FIL-KNG 76-48dc, ibid., 2; Rojo interview, ibid., 44; Cordova, *Filipinos*, 180.

71. Tangalan interview, WSOAHP, 17–18.

72. Rojo interview, WSOAHP, 44.

73. Mensalvas interview, WSOAHP, 25.

74. Revised Constitution, CWFLU, AFL 18257, June 19, 1933, file 1, box 7, CWFLU Records.

75. Ibid.

76. Torres interview, WSOAHP, 12.

77. Goon Dip and Company, Contract with F. Tongas for 1933, October 24, 1933, folder 16, box 1208, Canned-Salmon Code No. 429, Approved Code Industry File, National Recovery Administration, Record Group 9, National Archives and Records Administration, Washington, D.C. (hereafter cited as NRA, RG 9).

78. Ponce Torres interview, October 7, 1975, DPAA.

79. Mass Meeting, December 17, 1933, file 1, box 1, CWFLU Records.

80. CWFLU to Pio de Cano, January 24, 1934, file 12, box 7, CWFLU Records.

81. Ibid.; Meeting, March 28, May 20, and April 1, 1934, file 1, box 1, ibid.; Minutes, Contractors and Foremen Roundtable Conference, March 24, 1934, file 4, box 9, ibid.; Torres interview, August 25, 7–8, DPAA.

82. Virgil Dunyungan and Cornelio Mislang, "Code for the Fish Canning Industry," October 16, 1933, file 16, box 1209, NRA RG 9.

83. Dunyungan Testimony in "National Industrial Recovery Administration Hearing on Code of Fair Practices and Competition Presented by the Canned Salmon Industry," San Francisco, Calif., February 27, 1934, 2:342–372, University Research Library, University of California, Los Angeles (hereafter cited as "NRA Hearing").

84. Arai Testimony, "NRA Hearing," 382.

85. De Cano Testimony, "NRA Hearing," 390.

86. Minutes, Meeting, January 6, 1935, file 1, box 1, CWFLU Records.

87. Rojo, "Highlights"; Daisho D. ("Dyke") Miyagawa, interviews by Chris Friday, September 10, 1987 and August 18, 1988, Los Angeles, Calif.; George Taki, interview by Chris Friday, January 10 and 11, 1989, Los Angeles, California; James R. Green, *The World of the Worker: Labor in Twentieth-Century America* (New York, 1980), 162, 164.

88. Dunyungan and Mislang, "Code for the Fish Canning Industry"; Masson and Guimary, "Pilipinos and Unionization," 26; Rojo, "Highlights," Institute of Industrial Relations, University of California, Berkeley; Ayamo Testimony, "NRA Hearings," passim; Torres interview, August 25, 1975, 20–22, DPAA; F. C. Manuel, et al. to Mr. [?] Peters, CWFLU 18257 (n.d.), file 13, box 7, CWFLU Records; Margaret Mary Rae (Dunyungan) Mislang, "Who Murdered Virgil S. Dunyungan, Aurelio A. Simon and Placidio Patron?" file 15, box 9, ibid.; Margaret Dunyungan Mislang interview, FILKNG 75-12ck, WSOAHP, 8–10; August Buschman to All Salmon Canners, April 6, 1936, Exhibit 1a, Case XIX-R-700, Alaska Salmon Industry et al., National Labor Relations Board Records, Record Group 25, Washington National Records Center (hereafter cited as NRLB, RG 25); Gold, "Development of Local Number 7," 64–92.

89. Gary M. Fink, *Biographical Dictionary of American Labor* (New York, 1984), 105, 126–127, 133, 364–365; Miyagawa interviews.

90. S. M. Estepa to NRA Labor Advisory Board, January 2, and February 5, 1935, file 16, box 1209, NRA, RG 9.

91. Buschman to All Salmon Canners, April 6, 1936, Exhibit 1a, Case XIX-R-700, NLRB, RG 25; Bacho, "Alaskeros," 1.

92. John R. Arnold to R. J. McFall, April 21, 1934, file 22 box 1210, NRA, RG 9; and John R. Arnold, "[Report on] The Salmon Canning Industry," April 20, 1934, 32, Research Planning Division, ibid.

93. "Canned Salmon Code Approved," NRA Release, 5101, May 16, 1934, folder 8, box 1207, NRA, RG 9; Elvin Wong, John Lum, and A. J. Lamie, interview by Chris Friday, February 3, 1988, Astoria, Ore.; Patricia Roppel, *Salmon from Kodiak: An History of the Salmon Fishery of Kodiak Island*, Alaska Historical Commission Studies in History 216 (Anchorage, 1986), 220; Gold, "Development of Local Number 7," 35.

94. Carl Sutter to H. Bell-Irving and Company, November 21, 1933, FIPC Records; FIPC to H. Bell-Irving and Company, June 7, 1935, ibid.

95. Arnold to McFall, April 23, 1934, folder 8, box 1206, NRA, RG 9; James E. Bradford to John Swope, October 5, 1934, file 16, box 1209, ibid.; Tancioco interview, OHS; Roppel, *Salmon from Kodiak*, 220.

96. "Canned Salmon Code Approved," NRA Release 5101, May 16, 1934, folder 8, box 1207, NRA, RG 9; Buschman, et al., Labor Committee of Canned Salmon Industry to All Members of the Canned Salmon Industry, May 1, 1935, file 16, box 1208, ibid.

97. Seid Sing to Carl A. Sutter, February 21, 1934, FIPC Records.

98. Vance Sutter to FIPC, July 14, 1934, FIPC Records.

99. National Canners Association to All Canners, May 31, 1935, FIPC Records.

100. FIPC to H. Bell-Irving and Company, June 7, 1935, FIPC Records; A. I. Ellsworth to All Members of the Canned Salmon Industry, June 2, 1934, ibid.

101. General Correspondence, 1934, file 22, box 7, passim, CWFLU Records; CWFLU, *Annual Bulletin* 1, no. 1 (1936): 4–5, 13.

102. FIPC to CWFLU, October 17, 1936, FIPC Records.

103. Meeting, February 5, 1935, file 1, box 1, CWFLU Records.

104. Special Meeting, December 24, and February 12, 1935, file 1, box 1, CWFLU Records

105. Executive Council Meeting, Janauary 5 and 6, 1935, file 1, box 1, CWFLU Records.

106. Meeting, February 17, 1935, file 1, box 1, CWFLU Records.

107. Meeting, March 30, 1937, file 4, box 1, CWFLU Records.

108. Harry H. L. Kitano and Roger Daniels, *Asian Americans: Emerging Minorities* (Englewood Cliffs, N.J., 1988), 82–83; Gail M. Nomura, "Washingtons' Asian/Pacific American Communities," in *Peoples of Washington: Perspectives on Cultural Diversity*, ed. Sid White and S. E. Solberg (Pullman, Wash., 1989), 145–146.

109. Special Meeting, September 5, 1934, and May 4 and 5, 1935, file 1, box 1, CWFLU Records; Gold, "Development of Local Number 7," 47–48.

110. Masson and Guimary, "Pilipinos and Unionization," highlight this point very well, but for them Dunyungan's death brought about an inevitable

push toward unionization. Their study indicates the need to consider the pivotal role played by Japanese and Chinese in the unionization efforts, which are laid out in subsequent chapters of this study.

111. Margaret Mislang, "Who Murdered Virgil S. Dunyungan," File 15, Box 9, CWFLU Records; Trinidad Rojo, "Selective Service and Labor Supply for the Alaska Salmon Industry," 11, Trinidad Rojo Papers, ibid.; Joint Board Meeting, December 5, 1936, file 10, box 7, ibid.; Margaret Mislang interview, WSOAHP, 8–10; Torres interview, ibid., 40–44; Ranjo interview, ibid., 46; Tangalan interview, ibid., 14; Del Fierro interview, ibid., 17; Castillo interview, ibid., 4; Rodrigo interview, ibid., 49; Torres interview, August 25, 1975, 12–16, DPAA; Gold, "Development of Number 7," 52–54; Masson and Guimary, "Pilipinos and Unionization," 18.

112. Castillo interview, WSOAHP, 14, 48.

113. Joint Board Meeting, December 5, 1936, file 10, box 7, CWFLU Records.

114. Mislang, "Who Murdered Virgil Dunyungan"; Mislang interview, WSOAHP, 8–10.

115. Torres interview, WSOAHP, 42.

116. Joint Board Meeting, December 5, 1936, file 10, box 7, CWFLU Records.

117. Ibid.; Torres interview, WSOAHP, 42; Torres interview, August 25, 1975, 12–14, DPAA.

118. Ranjo interview, WSOAHP, 46.

119. Castillo interview, WSOAHP, 49.

120. Ibid., 4; Rojo, "Selective Service and Labor Supply," 11. Also see Tangalan interview, WSOAHP, 14; Del Fierro interview, ibid., 17.

Chapter 7

1. Ron Takaki, *Strangers from a Different Shore: A History of Asian Americans* (Boston, 1989), 152–154; John Modell and Edna Bonacich, *The Economic Basis of Ethnic Solidarity: Small Business in the Japanese American Community* (Berkeley and Los Angeles, 1980), 74–75; John Modell, "Class or Ethnic Solidarity: The Japanese American Company Union," *Pacific Historical Review* 38, no. 2 (1969): 193–206, note the strength of ethnicity as a basis for labor organization, while Edward D. Beechert, *Working in Hawaii: A Labor History* (Honolulu, 1985), 326–329, demonstrates how broader class concerns did not override ethnic affiliations until after World War II. Yen Le Espiritu, *Asian American Panethnicity: Bridging Institutions and Identities* (Philadelphia, 1992), 24, argues that a Pan-Asian American identity not specifically linked to class concerns emerged only after the social movements of the 1960s in the United States.

2. For details on those labor struggles, see Bruce Nelson, *Workers on the Waterfront: Seamen, Longshoremen, and Unionism in the 1930s* (Urbana, Ill.,

1988); Viki L. Ruiz, *Cannery Women, Cannery Lives: Mexican Women, Union-ization, and the California Food Processing Industry, 1930–1950* (Albuquerque, 1987), 41–85; Glenna Matthews, "The Fruit Workers of the Santa Clara Valley: Alternative Paths to Union Organization during the 1930s," *Pacific Historical Review* 54, no. 1 (1985): 51–70.

3. "Confidential Report on Employment, Hours, and Earnings in Salmon Canning Industry," n.d., file 16, box 1209, National Labor Relations Board, Record Group 25, Washington National Records Center, Suitland, Maryland (hereafter cited as NLRB, RG 25).

4. *Pacific Fisherman*, July 1909, 15, July 1912, 16; *San Francisco Call*, November 17, 1904, September 21, 1918; *San Francisco Examiner*, October 15, 1904; *Seattle Times*, May 27, 1914; and California, Dept. of Industrial Relations, "Facts about Filipino Immigration into California," *Special Bulletin* no. 3 (San Francisco, 1930), 48–55.

5. E. P. Marsh to H. L. Kerwin, August 18, 1920, file 165–261, Federal Mediation and Conciliation Board, Record Group 280, Washington National Records Center, Suitland Maryland (hereafter cited as FMCB, RG 280); *San Francisco Call*, January 26, 1913; *San Francisco Bulletin*, September 23, 1918; *San Francisco News*, October 9, 1922, and October 5, 1933; *San Francisco Examiner*, September 12 and 19, 1933; Gerald Gold, "The Development of Local Number 7 of the Food, Tobacco, Agricultural and Allied Workers of America-C.I.O.," Master's thesis, University of Washington, 1949, 17–22; Lauren Wilde Casaday, "Labor Unrest and the Labor Movement in the Salmon Industry of the Pacific Coast," Ph.D. dissertation, University of California, Berkeley, 1937, 156–158; Max Stern Papers, passim, Bancroft Library, University of California, Berkeley.

6. *San Francisco Post*, January 25, 1913; *San Francisco Chronicle*, *Call*, and *Examiner*, January 26, 1913; Marsh to Kerwin, August 18, 1920, file 165–261, FMCB, RG 280.

7. *San Francisco Examiner* and *Bulletin*, September 23, 1918.

8. *San Francisco News*, October 9, 1922; and Stern Papers, passim.

9. *San Francisco Call*, August 29, 1933.

10. *San Francisco News*, October 5, 1933.

11. Ibid., March 16, 1934.

12. *San Francisco Examiner*, October 19, 1934.

13. *San Francisco News*, March 16, 1934.

14. Karl Yoneda, *Ganbatte: A Sixty-Year Struggle of a Kibei Worker* (Los Angeles, 1983), 85; Casaday, "Labor Unrest," 286; Charles P. Larrow, *Harry Bridges: The Rise and Fall of Radical Labor in the United States*, 2nd ed. rev. (Westport, Conn., 1972), 15–16; Cletus E. Daniel, *Bitter Harvest: A History of California Farmworkers, 1870–1941* (Ithaca, N.Y., 1981), 275.

15. Larrow, *Harry Bridges*, 15–16; Daniel, *Bitter Harvest*, 275.

16. Willie Fong, interview by Him Mark Lai, July 31, 1971, courtesy Him Mark Lai, Asian American Studies Program, University of California, Berkeley; Him Mark Lai, "Summary of Information on Chinese Workers Mu-

tual Aid Association, September 25 and October 2, 1977, ibid.; Yoneda, *Ganbatte*, 86; Casaday, "Labor Unrest," 286.

17. Report of the National Labor Relations Board Proceedings, April 25, 1938, p. 48, Transcripts and Exhibits Dockets Section, 1935–1938, box 1201, NLRB, RG 25; F. G. Macasaet et al. to Frances L. Perkins, March 8, 1938, file 195–388, FMCB, RG 280; Yoneda, *Ganbatte*, 85–86.

18. Yoneda, *Ganbatte*, 85–87.

19. Ruiz, *Cannery Women, Cannery Lives*, 42, 100; Nelson, *Workers on the Waterfront*, 179, 186.

20. Macasaet to Perkins, March 8, 1938, file 195–388, FMCB, RG 280; E. Coleman to A. Simon, August 10, 1936, file 9, box 7, Cannery Workers and Farm Laborers Union, Local 7 Records, Manuscripts Division, University of Washington Library, Seattle, Wash. (hereafter cited as CWFLU Records); Yoneda, *Ganbatte*, 85ff.; Robert Okazaki interview, Tape 59, Box 519, Japanese American Research Project, Special Collections, University of California, Los Angeles (hereafter cited as JARP); Him Mark Lai, "A Historical Survey of the Chinese Left in American Society," in *Counterpoint: Perspectives on Asian America*, ed. Emma Gee et al. (Los Angeles, 1976), 63–80; Yuji Ichioka, "A Buried Past: Early Issei Socialists and the Japanese Community," *Amerasia* 1, no. 2 (1971): 1–25; Jere Takahashi, "Japanese American Responses to Race Relations: The Formation of Nisei Perspectives," *Amerasia*, 9, no. 1 (1982): 29–57.

21. Lai, "Chinese Left," 63–80; Willard G. Jue and Silas G. Jue, "Goon Dip: Entrepreneur, Diplomat, and Community Leader," *Annals of the Chinese Historical Society of the Pacific Northwest*, 1984, 47; *Chung Sai Yat Po*, April 14, 1900, April 17, 1901, April 3 and 23, 1902, March 13, 1903; *Mun Hey* (*Chinese Nationalist Daily*), April 13, 1928; Liu Beiji, *Meiguo huaqiao shi* (Taibei, R.O.C., 1981), 319. I am indebted to Him Mark Lai for his assistance in locating Chinese-language sources. For a sense of the younger American-born Chinese feelings about the depression era see the articles in the monthly publication, *Chinese Digest*; for Nisei see the *Japanese American Courier*.

22. *Chinese Digest*, November 15, 22, 1935, January 10, February 21, October 16, and November 27, 1936; San Francisco School of Social Studies, "Living Conditions in Chinatown" (n.p., 1930), 4, 7–9, Race Relations, China, box 144, Ray Lyman Wilbur Papers, Hoover Institution of War and Peace, Stanford University, Stanford, Calif.; Calvin F. Schmid, *Social Trends in Seattle* (Seattle, 1944), 131–132, 141, 142.

23. L. E. Kline, "History: Code of Fair Competition for the Canned Salmon Industry," 57, Approved Code Histories, box 7633, National Recovery Administration, Record Group 9, National Archives and Records Administration, Washington, D.C. (hereafter cited as NRA, RG 9).

24. Coleman to Simon, August 10, 1938, file 9, box 7, CWFLU Records; and CWFLU, *Bulletin*, July 1936.

25. Casaday, "Labor Unrest," 394–395; CWFLU, *Bulletin*, July 1936, 1–7; Yoneda, *Ganbatte*, 85–90.

26. Lai, "History of the Left," 63–80.

27. Ibid.; Willie Fong interview by H. M. Lai, July 31, 1971, courtesy of Him Mark Lai; summary of Tet Yee, Happy Lim, Bill Fong, and [Hu Hou] interviews by H. M. Lai, September 25 and October 2, 1977, ibid.; Karl Yoneda, "Notes on [the] History of Chinese and Japanese Labor in the U.S.A.," April 10, 1966, 10, file 6, box 152, JARP.

28. Lai, "History of the Left," 63–80.

29. Sam Young to Whom It May Concern, December 22, 1941, courtesy of Him Mark Lai.

30. Yoneda, *Ganbatte*, 88–89; idem, "Chinese and Japanese Labor," 10.

31. Yoneda, *Ganbatte*, 88–89; NLRB Release R-822, May 11, 1938, file 199–1629, FMCB, RG 280.

32. NLRB Release R-822, May 11, 1938, file 199–1629, FMCB, RG 280; Macasaet to Perkins, March 8, 1938, file 195–388, ibid.; Report of NLRB Proceedings, April 25, 1938, p. 175, Transcripts and Exhibits, Dockets Section 891–892, 1935–1938, box 1201, NLRB, RG 25. The Filipino Independent Union also may have been known as the Filipino Cannery Workers, Inc.

33. Macasaet to Perkins, March 8, 1938, file 195–388, FMCB, RG 280.

34. Lee P. Root to Fidalgo Island Packing Company, October 17, 1931, Fidalgo Island Packing Company Records, Anacortes Museum of History and Art, Anacortes, Wash.

35. Mun Ching to Executive Officers AFL 21161, CIO 5, and Filipino Independent Union, May 8, 1938, file 199–1629, FMCB, RG 280.

36. Yoneda, *Ganbatte*, 88. On the tensions between the San Francisco and Seattle locals, see CWFLU, *Bulletin*, July 1936.

37. Jue and Jue, "Goon Dip," 48; Seid Back, Jr., Biography, Oregon State File, Special Collections, University of Washington, Seattle, Wash.

38. Jack K. Masson and Donald L. Guimary, "Pilipinos and Unionization of the Canned Salmon Industry," *Amerasia* 8, no. 2 (1981): 17–24; Casaday, "Labor Unrest," 377–378.

39. Strategy Committee Meeting, April 28, 1938, file 7, box 1, CWFLU Records.

40. "Important [Notice] to Cannery Workers," n.d., file 2, box 9, CWFLU Records.

41. Yoneda, *Ganbatte*, 80, 85–86, 134–144, 203; Takahashi "Formation of Nisei Perspectives," 29–57.

42. *Seattle Times*, August 14, 1963; and *Japanese American Courier*, February 4, 1928, November 7, 1931.

43. *Seattle Times*, October 1, 1961, August 14, 1963; *Japanese American Courier*, January 21, 1928, April 13, May 19, 1928, September 27, 1930, and January 25, 1941.

44. Albert W. Palmer, *Orientals in American Life* (1939; reprt. San Francisco, 1972), 66.

45. *Japanese American Courier*, April 7, 1928, July 7, 1934; Frank Miyamoto, interview by Chris Friday, February 19, 1988, Seattle; Ewa Morawska

"The Sociology and Historiography of Immigration," in *Immigration Reconsidered: History, Sociology, and Politics*, ed. Virginia Yans-McLaughlin (New York, 1990), 189–190, and 212–216.

46. *Japanese American Courier*, February 28 and April 7, 1928.

47. Ibid., March 31 and April 7, 1928, March 2, 1929, June 2 and August 4, 1934, January 25, 1936, January 25, 1941; *Nichibei*, November 9, 1934; Yoneda, *Ganbatte*, 80.

48. *Japanese American Courier*, February 23, 1935.

49. Ibid.; Hiroshi ("Monks") Shimabara to Conrad Espe, May 22, 1937, file 7, box 14, CWFLU Records.

50. Okazaki interview, JARP; Daisho D. ("Dyke") Miyagawa, interviews by Chris Friday, September 10, 1987 and August 18, 1988, Los Angeles, Calif.; Membership Meeting, November 9 and 16, 1936, file 3, box 1, CWFLU; *Japanese American Courier*, November 28, 1931.

51. Membership Meeting, April 13, 1937, file 4, box 1, CWFLU Records; *Great Northern Daily News*, February 19, 1938; Okazaki interview, JARP.

52. George Taki, interview by Chris Friday, January 10 and 11, 1989, Los Angeles, Calif.; Membership Meeting, June 25, file 4, box 1, CWFLU Records.

53. Miyagawa interviews; Miyamoto interview; Membership Meeting, February 8, file 4, box 1, CWFLU Records; Membership Meeting, August 19, 1937, file 5, ibid.; Membership Meeting, November 4, 1937, and February 20, 1938, file 9, box 2, ibid.

54. Andress B. Bigornia to Ernesto Managawang, February 19, 1937, file 6, box 7, CWFLU Records.

55. Membership Meeting, February 8, file 4, box 1, CWFLU Records.

56. Miyagawa interviews; Taki interview; Dyke ("Daisho") Miyagawa to ("Big") Bill Hosokawa, February 25, 1968, v.f. 611, Manuscripts Division, University of Washington Library, Seattle; *Japanese American Courier*, July 21, 1934, April 24, February 27, 1937, April 15, 1939; *New World Sun*, March 25, 1937, file 9, box 7, CWFLU Records; Membership Meeting, February 14, file 4, box 1, ibid.; and George Woolf to Clarence T. Arai, February 12, 1937, file 9, box 7, ibid.

57. James Omura, interview by Chris Friday, March 25, 1988, Pullman, Wash.

58. Membership Meeting, February 14, April (n.d.), and May 4, 1937, file 4, box 1, CWFLU Records.

59. Shimabara to Espe, May 22, 1937, file 7, box 14, CWFLU Records.

60. Membership Meeting, February 23, 1937, file 6, box 1, CWFLU Records; J. W. Engstrom to William Green, March 3, 1937, file 6, box 1, ibid.

61. Conrad Espe, Open Letter to Membership of CWFLU, August 19, 1937, file 5, box 1, CWFLU Records.

62. Casaday, "Labor Unrest," 715, 720; Miyagawa interview; and John Castillo interview, FIL-KNG 75-15jr, Washington State Oral/Aural History

Program, 1974–1977, 18, Washington State Archives, Olympia, Wash. (hereafter cited as WSOAHP).

63. Special Membership Meeting, September 11, 1937, file 5, box 1, CWFLU Records.

64. Emergency Committee Meeting, September 13, 1937, CWFLU Records; Felipe G. Dumalo interview, FIL-KNG 75-35cm, 52, WSOAHP; and Ponce Torres interview, October 7, 1975, 15, Demonstration Project for Asian Americans, Seattle, Wash.

65. Emergency Committee Meeting, September 13, 1937, file 5, box 1, CWFLU Records; Special Membership Meeting, August 31, 1937, file 6, box 1, ibid.

66. Open Letter by Filipino Workers to the Executive Board, CWFLU 18257, August 10, file 7, box 16, CWFLU Records.

67. Special Membership Meeting, August 31, file 5, box 1, CWFLU Records.

68. Emergency Committee Meeting, September 13, 1937, file 5, box, 1, CWFLU Records.

69. Ibid.; Dumalo interview, WSOAHP, 56.

70. Emergency Committee Meeting, September 13, 1937, file 5, box 1, CWFLU Records.

71. Membership Meeting, October 1, 1937, file 5, box 1, CWFLU Records.

72. E. P. Marsh to J. P. Steelman, March 31, 1938, file 199–1410, FMCB, RG 280.

73. Ibid.

74. Membership Meeting, October 1, 1937, file 5, box 1, CWFLU Records.

75. Emergency Committee and Executive Board Meeting, October 25, 1937, file 2, box 1, CWFLU Records; Taki interview.

76. Membership Meeting, March 13, 1938, file 10, box 2, CWFLU Records; Miyagawa interviews.

77. Membership Meeting, March 13, 1938, file 10, box 2, CWFLU Records.

78. Yuji Ichioka, "Japanese Immigrant Nationalism: The Issei and the Sino-Japanese War, 1937–1941," *California History* 69, no. 3 (1990): 260–275, 310–311, argues that Issei nationalism was much more intense than among the Nisei. Ichioka's insights on Issei nationalism reveal the need for a rethinking of Nisei positions before the end of World War II.

79. *Japanese American Courier*, December 12, 1931, January 20 and July 7, 1934.

80. Ibid., January 25, 1941. Consistent with his Americanism, but marking an abandonment of his earlier cultural nationalism, Arai led the way in cooperation with internment authorities. Ironically, Karl Yoneda also assisted in the internment program. Yoneda had been an outspoken critic of Japanese aggression in Asia and had endorsed the boycotts. Both men came to be tar-

gets of criticism for their cooperation within the camps, particularly Arai, who had been supportive of Japanese nationalism. His about-face made him appear as a traitor to Japanese nationalists. Frank Miyamoto, "Seattle JACL," 10, file T6.24, Japanese Evacuation and Relocation Service, War Relocation Authority, Bancroft Library; Yoneda, *Ganbatte* 80, 85, 134–144; *Seattle Times*, October 1, 1961, August 14, 1963; Miyamoto interview; Omura interview; Miyagawa interviews.

81. Membership Meeting, April 10, 1938, file 10, box 2, CWFLU Records.

82. Mass Meeting, March 27, 1938, file 15, box 6, CWFLU Records.

83. Ibid.

84. Executive Board Meeting, January 15, 1938, file 7, box 1, CWFLU Records; Miyagawa interviews.

85. Executive Board Meeting, January 15, 1938, file 7, box 1, CWFLU Records.

86. Robert Gates to Art I. Ellsworth, I. R. Cabatit and L. A. Bellosillo, April 14, 1938, Exhibit 8, Alaska Salmon Industry et al., Case XIX-R-700, NLRB, RG 25.

87. Marsh to Steelman, March 31 and May 11, 1938, Case 199-1410, FMCB, RG 280.

88. Membership Meeting, April 7, 1937, file 4, box 1, CWFLU Records; "Attention Japanese Cannery Workers," [English and Japanese] n.d., file 2, box 9, ibid.

89. Executive Board Meeting, December 7, 1937, file 7, box 1, CWFLU Records.

90. Ibid.

91. Rally Meeting, May 2, 1938, file 7, box 1, CWFLU Records.

92. Ibid.; Taki interview; Miyagawa interviews.

93. Membership Meeting, March 13, 1938, file 10, box 2, CWFLU Records; Special Membership Meeting, May 3, 1938, ibid.; Executive Board Meeting, December 7, 1938, file 7, box 1, ibid.; Strategy Committee Meeting, April 28 and May 6, 1938, file 7, box 1, ibid..

94. Membership Meeting, May 19, 1938, file 10, box 2, CWFLU Records.

95. Ibid.; Membership Meeting, March 13, 1938, file 10, box 2, CWFLU Records.

96. Membership Meeting, May 19, 1938, file 10, box 2, CWFLU Records.

97. Woolf to Dunyungan, November 7, 1935, file 9, box 7, CWFLU Records; Ramon M. Tancioco interview by Larry Skoog, December 28, 1970, Oregon Historical Society, Portland, Ore.

98. Strategy Committee Meeting, April 28, 1937, file 7, box 1, CWFLU Records.

99. Ibid.; Membership Meeting, April 7 and May 21, 1937, file 1, box 4, CWFLU Records; Executive Board Meeting, Dec. 5, 1938, file 8, box 1, ibid.

100. Mass Meeting, March 27, 1938, file 14, box 6, CWFLU Records.

101. Election Results, Exhibit 11A, Alaska Salmon Industry et al., Case XIX-R-700, NLRB, RG 25; Marsh to Steelman, May 24, 1938, file 199-1410, FMCB, RG 280.

102. Joseph C. Cheeny to J. R. Steelman, May 7, 1938, file 199-1410, FMCB, RG 280.

103. Marsh to Steelman, May 24, 1938, file 199–140, FMCB, RG 280.

104. Ibid.

105. Ibid.

106. *Pacific Fisherman*, September 1931, 39, 42.

107. Membership Meetings, July 1, 1938, file 10, box 2, CWFLU Records; Executive Committee Meeting, July 1, 1938, file 8, box 1, ibid.

108. Membership Meetings, May 19, 1938, file 10, box 2, CWFLU Records; Executive Board Meeting, May 10, 1938, file 7, box 1, ibid.; *Japanese American Courier*, May 21, 1938.

Chapter 8

1. U.S. Bureau of Fisheries, *Alaska Fishery and Fur-Seal Industries, 1939* (Washington, D.C., 1939), 128; Election Results, Exhibit 11A, Alaska Salmon Industry et al., Case XIX-R-700, National Labor Relations Board, Record Group 25, Washington National Records Center, Washington, D.C. (hereafter cited as NLRB, RG 25). European Americans and Native Alaskans from the small communities of Alaska made up the resident crews that fell outside the jurisdiction of the Asian-led locals. Alaskan residents sought union representation through separate locals, sometimes in competition with the crews represented by the local in San Francisco and Seattle. A discussion of their activities is beyond the scope of this study. For more information, see Cannery Workers and Farm Laborers Union, United Cannery, Agricultural, Packinghouse, and Allied Workers of America (UCAPAWA), Congress of Industrial Organizations, Local 7 Records, Library Manuscripts Division, University of Washington, Seattle, Wash. (hereafter cited as CWFLU Records).

2. Executive Board Meeting, May 21, 1940, file 13, box 1, CWFLU Records; Daisho D. ("Dyke") Miyagawa, interviews by Chris Friday, September 10, 1987, and August 18, 1988, Los Angeles, Calif.

3. Executive Board Meeting, May 21, 1940, file 13, box 1, CWFLU Records.

4. Executive Board Meeting, March 1, 1940, file 11, box 1, CWFLU Records.

5. Miyagawa interviews; George Taki, interview by Chris Friday, January 10 and 11, 1989, Los Angeles, Calif.; Frank Miyamoto, interview by Chris Friday, February 19, 1988, Seattle, Wash.

6. E. P. Marsh to J. R. Steelman, May 24, 1938, file 199-1410, Federal Mediation and Conciliation Board Records, Record Group 280, Washington

National Records Center, Washington, D.C. (hereafter cited as FMCB, RG 280); Membership Meeting, May 10, 1938, file 7, box 7, CWFLU Records; Executive Board Meeting, Local 5, March 19, 1941, file 2, box 6, ibid.; Membership Meeting, May 19, 1938, file 10, box 2, ibid.; Executive Board Meeting, May 10, 1938, file 7, box 1, ibid.; Executive Board Meeting, April 30, 1939, file 9, box 1, ibid.; *Seattle Post-Intellegencer*, March 29, 1938; *Pacific Fisherman*, November 1940, 56.

7. *Japanese American Courier*, June 17, 1939; Membership Meeting, May 3, 1939, file 11, box 2, CWFLU Records.

8. Hiromasa Minami (pseud.) [Daiki Miyagawa], Case History 21, box 47, Charles Kikuchi Papers, Special Collections, University of California, Los Angeles, Calif.

9. Negotiating Committee, April 29, 1939, file 9, box 1, CWFLU Records; Membership Meeting, February 14, 1937, file 4, box 1, ibid.

10. "Agreement with United Cannery Agricultural Packing and Allied Workers of America," May 19, 1939, file 12, box 2, CWFLU Records; *UCA-PAWA News*, July 1939; *Great Northern Daily News*, May 27, 1939.

11. Joint Executive Board Meeting Local 7 and Local 226 UCAPAWA-CIO, May 23, 1939, file 9, box 1, CWFLU; Membership Meeting, April 14, 1940, file 1, box 3, ibid.

12. Miyagawa interviews; Taki interview; Willard G. Jue and Silas G. Jue, "Goon Dip: Entrepreneur, Diplomat, and Community Leader," *Annals of the Chinese Historical Society of the Pacific Northwest*, 1984, 48.

13. Hiroshi ("Monks") Shimabara to Conrad Espe, May 22, 1937, file 14, box 7, CWFLU Records; Petition signed by twenty-one Filipino members of Local 7, 1937, file 7, box 9, ibid.; Special Executive Council Meeting, July 2, 1941, file 3, box 2, ibid.; *Japanese American Courier*, June 19, 1939.

14. Leo M. Serquinia to Executive Board Members 18257, July 4, 1937, file 16, box 7, CWFLU Records.

15. Executive Board Meeting, May 10, 1938, file 7, box 1, CWFLU Records; Executive Board Meeting, April 12, 1940, file 12, box 1, ibid.

16. Marsh to Steelman, May 24, 1938, file 199-1410, FMCB, RG 280.

17. Executive Board Meeting, May 21, 1939, file 9, box 1, CWFLU Records.

18. Executive Board Meeting, April 13, 1940, file 12, box 1, CWFLU Records.

19. Special Executive Council Meetings, July 2 and 14, 1941, file 3, box 2, CWFLU Records.

20. H. G. Davis to Frances Perkins, March 11, 1940, file 196-1849, FMCB, RG 280; *Seattle Post-Intellegencer*, March 29, 1938; *UCAPAWA News*, April 1940; *Great Northern Daily News*, May 27, 1939; U.S. Bureau of Fisheries, *Alaska Fishery and Fur-Seal Industries, 1939* (Washington, D.C., 1939), 128; "Research by Rojo—Statistics," Trinidad Rojo Writings, file 5, box 6, CWFLU Records.

21. John McKean to CWFLU, Local 18257, July 7 and 17, and August 3, 1937, file 5, box 7, CWFLU Records.

22. Membership Meeting, April 1937, file 4, box 1, CWFLU Records; Membership Meeting, Local 5, February 19, 1939, file 3, box 6, ibid.

23. Executive Board Meeting, April 15, 1939, file 9, box 1, CWFLU Records; Executive Council Meeting, June 11, 1941, file 3, box 2, ibid.; Executive Board Meeting, Local 5, San Francisco, January 8, 1942, file 10, box 6, ibid.; George Minato to George [Taki?], May 18, 1937, file 14, box 7, ibid.; "Agreement," May 19, 1939, file 12, box 2, ibid.; Executive Board Meeting, May 21, 1940, file 13, box 1, ibid.

24. Executive Council Meeting, June 11, 1941, file 3, box 2, CWFLU Records.

25. Executive Board Meeting, Local 5, San Francisco, January 8, 1942, file 10, box 6, CWFLU Records.

26. Ibid.

27. Ibid.

28. Ibid.

29. George Minato to George [Taki?], May 18, 1937, file 14, box 7, CWFLU Records.

30. Executive Board Meeting, January 8 [n.d.], file 10, box 6, CWFLU Records; "Agreement," May 19, 1939, file 12, box 2, ibid.

31. Executive Board Meeting, January 8 [n.d.], file 10, box 6, CWFLU Records; Executive Board Meeting, May 21, 1940, file 13, box 1, ibid.

32. "Agreement," May 19, 1939, file 12, box 2, CWFLU Records.

33. Trinidad Rojo, "Gains in CIO Local 7, Report to Chicago Convention of UCAPAWA," n.d., 11, Trinidad Rojo Writings, CWFLU Records.

34. "Agreement," May 19, 1939, file 12, box 2, CWFLU Records.

35. "Canned Salmon Code Approved," National Recovery Administration (hereafter cited as NRA) Release 5101, May 16, 1934, file 8, box 1207, Approved Code Industry File, Code 429, Canned Salmon, Record Group 9, National Archives and Records Administration, Washington, D.C. (hereafter cited as NRA, RG 9).

36. "Confidential: Cost of Production, 1929, Canned Salmon," Statistics, file 23, box 1210, NRA, RG 9; *UCAPAWA News,* July 1939.

37. Steve Glumaz to CWFLU 7, April 12, 1942, file 4, box 6, CWFLU Records.

38. Membership Meeting, April 13, 1937, file 4, box 1, CWFLU Records.

39. Ibid.

40. Executive Board Meeting, September 15, 1939, file 10, box 1, CWFLU Records; "Agreement," May 19, 1939, file 12, box 2, ibid.; "Wages, 1940 and 1941," Executive Council Meeting, May 1941, file 2, box 2, ibid.

41. "Agreement," May 19, 1939, file 13, box 2, CWFLU Records; Classification of Cannery Workers in Bristol Bay Packing Company, 1937, Exhibits, In the Matter of the Alaska Packers Association, Alaska Salmon Canning Company, Red Salmon Canning Company and Alaska Cannery Workers Local 5, box 1201, NLRB, RG 25.

42. "Wages, 1940 and 1941," Executive Council Meeting, May 1941, file 2, box 2, CWFLU Records; "1934 Pack Cost—NRA Scale," file 12, box 8, ibid.; John Castillo interview, Accession Number FIL-KNG 75-15jr, Washington State Oral/Aural History Program, 1974–1977, Washington State Archives, Olympia (hereafter cited as WSOAHP).

43. Membership Meeting, Alaska Cannery Workers Union Local 5, UCAPAWA-CIO, March 18, 1941, file 4, box 6, CWFLU Records.

44. Membership Meeting, February 14, 1937, file 4, box 1, CWFLU Records.

45. "Code of Fair Practices and Competition Presented by the Canned Salmon Industry," National Recovery Administration Hearing Transcript, February 26–27, 1934, San Francisco, Calif., University Research Library, University of California, Los Angeles; "Agreement," May 19, 1939, file 12, box 2, CWFLU Records; Delegates Report, n.d., file 6, box 8, ibid.; Castillo interview, WSOAHP, 19.

46. Karl Yoneda, *Ganbatte: The Sixty-year Struggle of a Kibei Worker* (Los Angeles, 1987), 89.

47. "Agreement," May 19, 1939, file 12, box 2, CWFLU Records; Delegates Report, [n.d.]., file 6, box 8, ibid.; Castillo interview, WSOAHP, 19; CWFLU, *Bulletin*, July 1936.

48. Petition to Executive Board, August 10, 1937, file 16, box 7, CWFLU Records.

49. Executive Board Meeting, September 13, 1938, file 8, box 1, CWFLU Records.

50. Executive Board Meeting, June 14, 1940, file 14, box 1, CWFLU Records; Executive Board Meeting, May 21, 1939, file 9, box 1, ibid.

51. Executive Board Meeting, May 6, 1939, file 9, box 1, CWFLU Records.

52. Executive Board Meeting, May 21, 1939, file 9, box 1, CWFLU Records; Membership Meeting, Local 226, April 30, 1939, file 6, box 6, ibid.; Executive Board Meetings, March 23 and 30, 1940, file 11, box 1, ibid.; Davis to Perkins, March 11, 1940, file 196-1849, FMCB, RG 280; "Memoranda, Seafood Workers Union," [n.d.], Victorio Velasco Papers, file 10, box 12a, Library Manuscripts Division, University of Washington, Seattle, Wash.

53. "Agreement," May 19, 1939, file 12, box 2, CWFLU Records.

54. Membership Meeting, Alaska Cannery Workers' Union, UCAPAWACIO Local 5, San Francisco, Calif., February 19, 1939, file 3, box 6, CWFLU Records; Executive Board Meeting, May 21, 1941, file 13, box 1, ibid.; "Rules Governing Duties and Relationships Between Foreman and Delegates," April 4, 1940, file 12, box 1, ibid.; Membership Meeting, February 29, 1939, file 12, box 2, CWFLU Records; Emergency Executive Board Meeting, June 20, 1939, file 10, box 1, ibid.

55. Executive Board Meeting, May 21, 1941, file 13, box 1, CWFLU Records.

56. "Rules Governing . . . Foremen and Delegates," April 4, 1940, file 12, box 1, CWFLU Records.

57. Lists—Delegates, 1937, file 11, box 9, CWFLU Records; Joint Meeting of the Negotiating, Dispatching, Foremen, and Messhouse Committees and the Executive Board, April 22, 1939, file 9, ibid.; Executive Board Meeting, May 21, 1940, file 13, ibid.; Castillo interview, WSOAHP, 15.

58. Lists—Delegates, 1937, file 11, box 9, CWFLU Records.

59. Ponce Torres interview, January 24, 1975, 5, Demonstration Project for Asian Americans (hereafter cited as DPAA), Seattle.

60. "Rules Governing . . . Foremen and Delegates," April 4, 1940, file 12, box 1, CWFLU Records; Miyagawa interviews.

61. "Rules Governing . . . Foremen and Delegates," April 4, 1940, file 12, box 1, CWFLU Records.

62. Joint Meeting of the Negotiating, Dispatching, Foremen, and Messhouse Committees, and the Executive Board, April 22, 1939, file 9, box 1, CWFLU Records.

63. Yoneda, *Ganbatte*, 85–90.

64. Ronald Lautaret, *Alaskan Historical Documents since 1867* (Jefferson, N.C., 1989), 98; Claus-M. Naske, "Alaska's Long and Sometimes Painful Relationship with the Lower Forty-Eight," in *The Changing Pacific Northwest: Interpreting Its Past*, ed. David H. Stratton and George A. Frykman (Pullman, Wash., 1980), 63.

65. Ibid.; Special Executive Council Meeting, November 12, 1941, file 3, box 2, CWFLU Records; Membership Meeting, August 24, 1943, file 5, box 6, ibid.

66. Membership Meetings, May 4, 1941, and May 17, 1942, file 4, box 6, CWFLU Records.

67. "Research by Rojo—Statistics," Trinidad Rojo Writings, CWFLU Records.

68. Membership Meeting, August 24, 1943, file 5, box 6, CWFLU Records; *UCAPAWA News*, August 1 and 15, 1943; Elvin Wong, John Lum, and A. J. Lamie, interview by Chris Friday, February 3, 1988, Astoria, Ore.; Cannery Workers, International Longshore Workers Union, Cannery Workers Local 37, *Yearbook*, 1952, 34–44.

69. Cannery Workers, *Yearbook* (1952), 34–44.

70. Executive Board Meeting, May 22, 1940, file 13, box 1, CWFLU Records; *Japanese American Courier*, June 24, 1939.

71. Executive Board Meeting, March 15, 1940, file 11, box 1, CWFLU Records.

72. Ibid.; Executive Board Meeting, April 15, 1939, file 9, box 1, CWFLU Records; Taul Watanabe, interview by Richard Berner, April 23, 1969, Seattle, Wash., University of Washington Manuscripts Collection, Seattle.

73. Membership Meeting, December 12, 1941, file 5, box 3, CWFLU Records.

74. Dick Kanaga to Executive Council and Membership, CWFLU Local 7, December 10, 1941, CWFLU Records.

75. Executive Council Meeting, April 6, 1942, file 4, box 2, CWFLU Records; Special Executive Council Meeting, July 2, 1941, file 3, ibid.; *UCAPAWA News*, December 22, 1941.

76. *Japanese American Courier*, March 13, 1942.

77. The silence in the union record is unnerving and frustrating. One can only speculate on why the void exists. See boxes 2 and 3, passim, CWFLU Records.

78. Executive Council Meeting, June 9, 1942, file 4, box 2, CWFLU Records.

79. *UCAPAWA News*, August 15, 1942, and April 1, 1943.

80. Cannery Workers, *Yearbook* (1952), 34–44.

81. Felix A. Narte interview, FIL-KNG 75-8tc, WSOAHP, 22–23.

82. Trinidad Rojo, "Selective Service and Labor Supply for the Alaska Salmon Industry" [n.d.], 8, Trinidad Rojo Writings, CWFLU Records; "Research by Rojo—Statistics" [n.d.], ibid.; Steve Glumaz to CWFLU 7, April 12, 1942, file 4, box 6, ibid.; Prudencio P. Mori, "An Evaluation of Manerto Ventura's Labor Record" [n.d.], file 6, box 12a, Victorio Velasco Papers, Library Manuscripts Division, University of Washington, Seattle.

83. *UCAPAWA News*, July 1, 1942, and August 15, 1943.

84. Mori, "Evaluation of Manerto Ventura's Labor Record," file 6, box 12a, Velasco Papers.

85. Teodolo A. Ranjo interview, FIL-KNG 76-41cm, WSOAHP, 50.

86. Executive Council Meeting, March 16 and 20, 1942, file 4, box, 2, CWFLU Records.

87. Executive Council Meetings, June 22 and 26, 1942, file 4, box 2, CWFLU Records; Executive Council Meeting, June 21, 1943, file 6, box 2, ibid.; Ranjo interview, WSOAHP, 47.

88. Gail Nomura, "Within the Law: The Establishment of Filipino Leasing Rights on the Yakima Indian Reservation," *Amerasia* 13, no. 1 (1986–1987): 99–117.

89. *Pacific Fisherman*, July 1942, 14; *UCAPAWA News*, July 1, 1942; Ben Rinonos interview, FIL-KNG 75-3tc, WSOAHP; Executive Council Meetings, June 22 and 26, 1942, file 4, box 2, CWFLU Records; *Japanese American Courier*, April 12, 1942.

90. *Pacific Fisherman*, April 1942, 21, and January 1946, 52.

91. *UCAPAWA News*, August 15, 1943; Torres interview, June 24, 1975, 4, DPAA.

92. Membership Meeting, December 12, 1941, file 5, box 3, CWFLU Records; Executive Council Meeting, January 23, 1942, file 4, box 2, ibid.; Membership Meeting, January 24, 1942, file 6, box 3, ibid.

93. *UCAPAWA News*, December 15, 1942.

94. Trinidad A. Rojo interview, FIL-KNG 75-17ck, WSOAHP, 22, 29; *UCAPAWA News*, September 1, 1944.

95. *Pacific Fisherman*, September 1943.

96. Ibid., February 1943, 18.

97. For good examples of European American women in the canned-salmon labor market, see the interviews in the Skagit County Oral History Preservation Project, 1977–1978, Skagit County History Society, LaConner, Wash.

98. *Pacific Fisherman*, November 1943, 29.

99. Harry H. L. Kitano and Roger Daniels, *Asian Americans: Emerging Minorities* (Englewood Cliffs, N.J., 1988), 36–42.

100. Gerald Gold, "The Development of Local Number 7 of the Food, Tobacco, Agricultural and Allied Workers of America–C.I.O.," Master's thesis, University of Washington, 1949, 109–156; Velasco Papers, passim.

101. *Pacific Fisherman*, May 1941, 14; *Pacific Fisherman Yearbook*, 1946, 119; Joseph A. Craig and Robert L. Hacker, "History and Development of the Fisheries of the Columbia River," U.S. Department of the Interior, Bureau of Fisheries, *Bulletin* 32 (Washington, D.C., 1940); Homer E. Gregory and Kathleen Barnes, *North Pacific Fisheries with Special References to Alaska Salmon* (San Francisco, 1939); Anthony Netboy, *The Columbia River Salmon: Their Fight for Survival* (Seattle, 1980). For a nineteenth-century comparison of salmon and buffalo, see *Forest and Stream*, October 25, 1877, 233.

102. *Washington Post*, November 15, 1992, A1, A26; *New York Times*, November 15, 1992, D19; and *Wall Street Journal*, November 15, 1992, B10A.

103. Ibid.

104. *New York Times*, April 12, 1992, 26.

105. *UCAPAWA News*, January 15, 1944; *Pacific Fisherman*, January 1946, 51; Membership Meeting, Portland Branch of CIO Local 7, April 15, 1948, file 8, box 6, CWFLU Records; Ponce M. Torres interview, FIL-KNG 75-14tc, WSOAHP, 46; Cannery Workers, *Yearbook* (1952), 5–11, 30; Gold, "The Development of Local Number 7," 109–156. The Alaska Packers Association cannery at Semiahmoo, near Blaine, Washington, was converted in the 1980s into a luxury marina and resort complex.

Conclusion

1. Marlon K. Hom, *Songs of Gold Mountain: Cantonese Rhymes from San Francisco Chinatown* (Berkeley and Los Angeles, 1987), 107. Hom notes: "'Big roc,' [is] an allusion from [the Chinese classical poet] *Zhuang zi* [c. 369–286 B.C., and] commonly refers to a person who is about to seek out a great future." Burton Watson, trans., *The Complete Works of Chuang Tzu* (New York, 1968), 29–31, indicates that it was also a call for individuals to think beyond the mundane, individual, and personal and aspire to actions that positively affect the broader society.

2. Hom, *Songs of Gold Mountain*, 53–54.

3. Ibid., 94.

4. Lloyd Fisher, *The Harvest Labor Market* (Cambridge, Mass., 1953).

5. John Bodnar, Roger Simon, and Michael P. Weber, *Lives of Their Own: Blacks, Italians, and Poles in Pittsburgh, 1900–1960* (Urbana, Ill., 1982), 57, 83 n.3; Gunther Peck, "Padrones and Protest: 'Old' Radicals and 'New' Immigrants in Bingham, Utah, 1905–1912," *Western Historical Quarterly* 24, no. 2 (May 1993): 157–178. Bodnar, Simon, and Weber argue that family connections proved more important than contractors in providing jobs. Peck, though his focus is on the movement away from labor contracting to unionization, demonstrates that padrones were central in bringing industrial laborers to the American West. His study illustrates that as contractors began to recruit outside their own ethnic circles, any mutual relationships with workers broke down quickly. Both perspectives can be seen in the formation and then transformation of the contract system in the canned-salmon industry.

6. A focus on "rural" Asian American communities is a relatively recent development. See Sucheng Chan, *This Bittersweet Soil: Chinese in California Agriculture* (Berkeley and Los Angeles, 1986); Gary Y. Okihiro, "Fallow Field: The Rural Dimension of Asian American Studies," in *Frontiers of Asian American Studies: Writing, Research, and Commentary,* ed. Gail M. Nomura et al. (Pullman, Wash., 1989), 6–13; Gail M. Nomura, "Interpreting the Historical Evidence," in *Frontiers of Asian American Studies,* 2.

7. Federal involvement and the swings in the economy are well covered in Patricia Nelson Limerick, *Legacy of Conquest: The Unbroken Past of the American West* (New York, 1987).

8. Susan Model, "Work and Family: Blacks and Immigrants from South and East Europe," in *Immigration Reconsidered: History, Sociology, and Politics,* ed. Virginia Yans-McLaughlin (New York, 1990), 130–159, notes the importance of family networks and organized labor in assisting the upward mobility of European immigrants, while racial discrimination prevented a similar move for African Americans. Bodnar, Simon, and Weber, *Lives of Their Own,* 57–58, find a similar situation. Peck, "Padrones and Protest," forcefully demonstrates that ethnicity and class were "highly mutable social constructs" and were consistently redefined in the labor conflicts of Utah's mines. Oliver Zunz, *The Changing Face of Inequality: Urbanization, Industrial Development, and Immigrants in Detroit, 1880–1920* (Chicago, 1982), describes how industrialization in Detroit remade and nearly obviated many ethnic distinctions. By 1920, he notes, "neighborhoods had become as much working class as ethnic" (p. 400). Taken as a whole these works, and this study on Asians and Asian Americans, illustrate that ethnic and class identities are constructed and reconstructed, not constants.

Index